marybeth@colecommunications.com

DES**i**GN
FOR MEDIA

THE LONGMAN PRACTICAL JOURNALISM SERIES

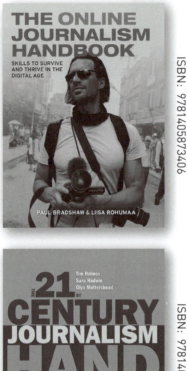

ISBN: 9781405873406

ISBN: 9781408245217

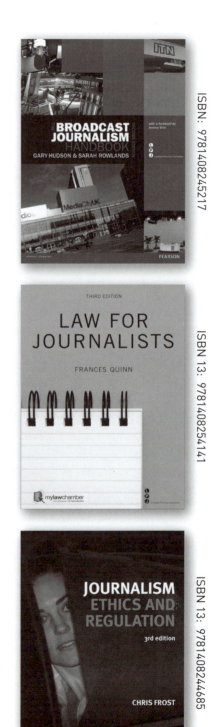

ISBN: 9781405846325

ISBN 13: 9781408254141

ISBN 13: 9781408244685

Longman Practical Journalism

For further information or to order these
books, please visit:

www.pearsoned.co.uk/mediajournalism

DES**I**GN
FOR MEDIA

A handbook for students and professionals in journalism, PR and advertising

Di Hand & Steve Middleditch

Harlow, England • London • New York • Boston • San Francisco • Toronto • Sydney
Auckland • Singapore • Hong Kong • Tokyo • Seoul • Taipei • New Delhi
Cape Town • São Paulo • Mexico City • Madrid • Amsterdam • Munich • Paris • Milan

Pearson Education Limited
Edinburgh Gate
Harlow
Essex CM20 2JE
England

and Associated Companies throughout the world

Visit us on the World Wide Web at:
www.pearsoned.com/uk

First published 2013

ISBN: 978-1-4058-7366-6

British Library Cataloguing-in-Publication Data
A catalogue record for this book is available from the British Library

Library of Congress Cataloging-in-Publication Data
A catalog record for this book is available from the Library of Congress

10 9 8 7 6 5 4 3 2 1
17 16 15 14 13

Typeset in 9.25/12.5pt Photina by 30
Printed and bound in Malaysia, CTP-PJB

CONTENTS

INTRODUCTION

'Like an iceberg, 90 per cent of visual communication is hidden beneath the surface. And just like an iceberg, it is the invisible 90 per cent that provides the raw power of visual communication'.

Jonathan Baldwin and Lucienne Roberts

We are all designers

Whenever we start to write on a page or select a heading style in Word we make design decisions. Everyone is aware of design – we use it to choose colours, shapes and patterns when we decide what to wear and how to decorate our homes, and we know that every choice we make identifies us and communicates something about ourselves to others. For a media title, the visual qualities that make it stand out from the crowd are the design decisions about layout, the use of colour and typefaces that can say as much about a newspaper, magazine or website as the words and information they contain.

The *Design for Media* book and accompanying website are an essential guide on how to utilise and develop the innate design skills that everyone possesses and apply them to a career in a dynamic and fast-moving media industry that is often at the forefront of technological innovations. Media companies offer excellent career opportunities, a lively working atmosphere and the opportunity of being involved in the design and production of print, online and multimedia titles. The book and website will provide you with a comprehensive, fully illustrated introduction to the role of design in the industry, and together they form a professional and study resource for media students and those already employed in the industry whose job involves page presentation and production for online and print.

Multitasking, multi-skills, multimedia

Design for Media provides a wide-ranging introduction to design and production for print and online media. The book, together with the accompanying website, covers key information and practical skills for people who have not been trained as designers, but who need some page handling and production knowledge. The ability to handle design is now an intrinsic element of many media jobs, and skills that were once the sole province of the design specialist are now part of the day-to-day work of journalists, advertising executives and those in marketing and PR. As the media industry changes to accommodate new technological and social developments, these tasks can include being able to create page layouts for print, online and mobile devices, using type effectively, knowing how to commission, select and prepare still and moving imagery as well as working with sound and multimedia.

If you are considering a career in the media today, you can expect to become involved with many of the production processes that create communication brands. And those already employed in the industry will be only too aware of the need to broaden and update their knowledge and skills in order to remain effective in their work and competitive in the employment marketplace.

Design for Media covers the influence and development of media design and technology, and the use of design from developing a new media brand to the technology that underpins print and online titles. The colourful *How to work with* pages include detailed advice with clear step-by-step illustrations on page creation, type, pictures and colour. The companion website provides practical support materials available for downloading including information sheets, sample page templates and typography and colour guides. *Design for Media* includes an extensive glossary of media and design key terms, with contact details of websites that show examples of good design practice, as well as those of leading designers and key industry organisations.

Digital page make-up allows those working on titles to develop complex design ideas efficiently and economically.

From the morning paper to 24/7 news

Design for Media provides a brief history and review of the media industry and traces the growth of popular media from the start of the twentieth century to now, with a discussion on the continuing effects of the digital revolution. The first three chapters describe how media design has become increasingly important as people have become far more visually literate, and titles now have to fight for attention in an oversaturated market that has been splintered by media proliferation.

The subjects covered include how the structure of the industry has evolved, how it funds itself, typical jobs, the role of design and production, and the inter-action between these areas. The final chapter in this section looks at design in practice – the way in which design is employed in the media – and the effect of convergence on what a media brand is and how and where it reaches its audience. The change in the relationship between the media and their audience and the questions provoked by the spread of the Social Web are also examined.

Working on media design and production

Design for Media supplies practical advice, examples and diagrams on how to work with the techniques of design, and covers how to prepare platform-specific material for production technology. The *Design for Media* website provides you with further information on media design and production that can be combined with the down-loadable support materials to help you develop a wide range of skills. These include guidance on how to lay out pages and work in different styles, a range of colour palettes, typographic guides that provide examples of complementary typefaces and practical picture handling instructions. It also provides you with feedback on the questions and action points that are featured in each chapter, links to media and designers' websites and a glossary of standard industry terms.

Chapters 4 to 10 and the colour *How to work with* pages contain design examples and visual guides that will help you develop your layout and production skills. Used in conjunction with the downloadable support

The immediacy of web pages and mobile media requires a mix of design skills, the ability to handle still and moving images and sound, together with an understanding of the underlying technologies.

material available from the *Design for Media* website, the *How to work with* pages provide you with a resource that will enable you to create successful print and online pages.

Chapter 4 gives an overview of the business application of design, in particular what tasks you might be expected to undertake should you become involved in the planning and launch of a new print title or website.

Chapter 5 provides an introduction to the principles of applied design and page layout, and how ideas can be presented visually.

Chapters 6, 7 and 8 works in conjunction with the full colour *How to work with type, pictures* and *colour* pages and the companion website to introduce the basic building blocks of design – typography, imagery and colour – that you need to understand to work successfully in print and online.

Chapter 9 shows you how the techniques and skills learned in the previous chapters are employed to produce pages on a day-to-day basis.

Chapter 10 covers media production to help you gain some knowledge of the technologies and systems underlying page production.*

In creating the *Design for Media* resource for students and media professionals, we have set out to demonstrate how you can develop cross-platform design skills, and the advice given will help those working on page creation to develop the ability to use type, imagery and colour to convey nuances of meaning. The aim is to help anyone faced with working on page presentation and production to be able to handle design with confidence.

* The information in Chapter 10 reflects the practices and production systems current at the time of writing, and some of these are likely to change.

ACKNOWLEDGEMENTS

ABC: www.abc.org.uk

Alain Carpentier: acarpentier@groupemedia.ca

Alessi: www.alessi.com/en

APA: www.apa.co.uk

Aztek, Inc.: www.aztek.com

Before & After magazine: www.bamagazine.com

BP: www.bp.com

Charles James Fox

ComScore: www.comscore.com

Dyson: www.dyson.co.uk

eBay: www.ebay.co.uk

Epson Corporation: www.epson.co.uk

Evening Standard Ltd: www.thisislondon.co.uk

Facebook: www.facebook.com

Gary Hayes: www.personalizemedia.com

Google: www.google.co.uk

Hewlett-Packard Company: www.hp.com

Icon magazine: www.iconeye.com

IPC: www.ipcmedia.com

Jakob Nielsen: www.nngroup.com

Jamie Oliver: www.jamieoliver.com

Kevin February: www.meiklejohn.co.uk

Komori Corporation: www.komori.com

Kristian Bjornhard: www.flickr.com/photos/
bjornmeansbear

Levi Strauss: www.levistrauss.com

Martin Cloake: www.martincloake.com

McKinsey: www.mckinsey.com

Microsoft: www.microsoft.com

National Office of Statistics: www.statistics.gov.uk

Nielsen Media Research: www.nielsenmedia.co.uk

Nigel Tanburn

Nigel Young/Norman Forster + Partners:
www.fosterandpartners.com

Ofcom: www.ofcom.org.uk

Paul Glennon: www.paulglennon.co.uk

RAJAR: www.rajar.co.uk

Romolu Oliveira: romulusremo@hotmail.com

Samsung: www.samsung.com/uk

Sean Power

Technorati: www.technorati.com

Tom Taylor/Newspaper Club: http://tomtaylor.co.uk

Twitter: www.twitter.com

Unilever plc: www.unilever.co.uk

WC3: www.w3.org

Xeikon: www.xeikon.com

PUBLISHER'S ACKNOWLEDGEMENTS

We are grateful to the following for permission to reproduce copyright material:

Cartoons
Cartoons on page 205 reproduced with permission from Kevin February.

Figures
Figure on page 4, cover of *Woman's Weekly*, IPC Media Limited, © IPC+Syndication; Figure on page 6, cover of *Rugby World*, IPC Media Limited, © IPC+Syndication; Figure on page 7, cover of *Wallpaper**, March 2004, IPC Media Limited, © IPC+Syndication; Figure on page 10, from Volkswagen 'Think Small' advertisement, used with permission of Volkswagen Group of America, Inc; Figure on page 11 from OfCom research, fieldwork carried out by Saville Rossiter-Base in April to May 2009, copyright Ofcom; Figure on page 19, *Icon Magazine* front cover images, the Africa Issues cover design by Emma Chui (art editor); illustration by Chaz Maviyane-Davis, with permission from Media 10 Ltd; Figure on page 19, BP logos from 1922–1957, 1989–2000, 2000–, with permission from BP plc; Figure on page 30, front covers from *The Guardian*, Copyright Guardian News & Media Ltd; Figure on page 32 from Office for National Statistics, contains public sector information licensed under the Open Government Licence (OGL) v1.0.http://www.nationalarchives.gov.uk/doc/open-government-licence/open-government; Figure on page 78 from www.paulglennon.co.uk, with permission from Paul Glennon; Figure on page 81, spread from *Jamie Magazine*, reproduced with permission; Figure on page 119, spread from *ALN House Style Guide*, with permission from London College of Communication; Figure on page 204 from iGIZMO, http://issue.igizmo.co.uk/1I49d61974494c1012.cde/page/4?detectflash=false, with permission from Dennis Publishing; Figure on page 247 from *Color Workflows for Adobe Creative Suite 3, A Self-Help Guide showing a CMYK Commercial Print Workflow*, p. 5, © 2011 Adobe Systems Incorporated. All rights reserved. Adobe, Illustrator, InDesign and Photoshop is/are either [a] registered trademark[s] or a trademark[s] of Adobe Systems Incorporated in the United States and/or other countries; Figures on pages 255, 259 from The Color Wheel Company; Figure on page 256 from Global Colour Research; Figures on page 287 from *Émigré* magazine, designed by and reprinted with permission from Rudy VanderLans; Figure on page 328, HP Indigo 7000 Digital Press, courtesy of HP; Figure on page 331 from data provided by NetApplications.com at http://www.netmarketshare.com.

Screenshots
Screenshot on page 24 from Hairdressers Journal Interactive, http://www.hji.co.uk/Home, screen grab courtesy of www.hji.co.uk; Screenshot on page 35 from http://www.tescomagazine.com, with permission from Tesco Stores Limited; Screenshot on page 35 from New Scientist homepage, http://www.newscientist.com/, © New Scientist; Screenshots on pages 35, 81 from www.jamieoliver.com, reproduced with permission; Screenshot on page 38 from Hotel Rate Key, http://www.microsoft.com/presspass/presskits/bing/imageGallery.aspx#channel_contentListTop, screenshot used with permission from Microsoft Corporation; Screenshots on page 38 iPhone App, for more information on work by Romulo Oliviera please visit his website at www.romulosolivier.com; Screenshot on page 38 from Martin Cloake Online, www.martincloake.com; Screenshot on page 55 from eBay homepage, www.ebay.co.uk. These materials have been reproduced with the permission of eBay Inc. © 2011 EBAY INC. ALL RIGHTS RESERVED; Screenshot on page 55 from Design for Media Facebook group, Facebook is a Trademark of Facebook Inc; Screenshot on page 58 from Gary Hayes' Social Media Counts, www.personalizemedia.com/garys-social-media-count; Screenshot on page 81 from Before & After magazine 'Design below the line', http://www.bamagazine.com, with permission from Before & After magazine/bamagazine.com; Screenshots on pages 106, 107 with permission from London College of Communications; Screenshot on page 119 from Pearson Knowledge Base, kb.pearsoned.com, Pearson Education Ltd; Screenshots on pages 172, 173, 174, 175, 178, 220, 221, 222, 223, 224, 225, 226, 227, 313 Adobe product screenshots reprinted with permission from Adobe Systems Incorporated; Screenshot on page 178 Apple Font Book screenshot, reproduced with permission from Apple Inc; Screenshot on page 178 Apple screenshot frame, reproduced with permission from Apple Inc; Screenshot on page 178 from www.type.co.uk, with permission from Fontworks UK Limited, Creative Publishing Solutions; Screenshot on page 180 from Typetester, with permission from Creative Nights, http://creativenights.com; Screenshot on page 180 from http://csstypeset.com, reproduced with permission from CSS Typeset; Screenshot on page 180 from www.typechart.com, with permission from Panduka Senaka; Screenshot on page 200 still from Dove Evolution advertisement, reproduced with kind permission of Unilever PLC and group companies; Screenshot on page 201 from Guardian Points of View video, reproduced with permission from Guardian News & Media Ltd; Screenshot on page 257 from myPANTONE website, with permission from X-Rite Europe GmbH; Screenshot on page 259 from Petr Stanicek; Screenshot on page 313 Adobe Acrobat InDesign screenshot frame, Adobe product screenshot reprinted with permission from Adobe Systems Incorporated; Screenshot on page 313 from Arts London News banner, London College of Communications; Screenshot on page 313 from QuarkXPress, www.quark.com; Screenshot on page 337 from www.guardian.co.uk, Guardian News & Media Ltd; Screenshots on page 338 from CNN.com, CNN © 2011 Cable News Network. Turner Broadcasting System, Inc. All Rights Reserved.

Publisher's acknowledgements

Tables
Table on page 92 from Jakob Nielsen and Marie Tahler, reproduced with permission.

Text
Box on page 94 from Jakob Nielsen and Marie Tahler, reproduced with permission.

The Financial Times
Figure on page 288 *Financial Times* front page, © Financial Times, 11 July 2011.

Photographs
(Key: b-bottom; c-centre; l-left; r-right; t-top) **13** Village Underground. **19** photo Nigel Young/Foster + Partners. **23** ©Carlos Cazalis / Corbis. **47** picture by Kristian Bjornard, reused under Creative Commons License Deed Attribution-ShareAlike 3.0 Unported, http://creativecommons.org/licenses/by-sa/3.0/deed.en. **51** Epson Perfection V330 Photo scanner, Epson Europe B.V. **144** © 2010 Amazon.com, Inc. or its affiliates. **190** © 2010 Amazon.com, Inc. or its affiliates. **196** photo and copyright Nigel Tanburn; **197** Migrant Mother (1936) by Dorothea Lange, Library of Congress, Prints & Photographs Division, FSA/OWI Collection, LC-USF34-9058-C. **203** © Telegraph Media Group Limited 2009 / Geoff Pugh. **231** Sean Power. **242** Pantone Spectrometer, PANTONE Colors displayed here may not match PANTONE-identified standards. Consult current PANTONE Color Publications for accurate color. PANTONE® and other Pantone trademarks are the property of, and are used with the written permission of, PANTONE LLC. © Pantone LLC, 2011. All rights reserved. **246** X-Rite Europe GmbH. **247** X-Rite Europe GmbH. **256** X-Rite Europe GmbH. **256** Pantone Hotel, PANTONE Colors displayed here may not match PANTONE-identified standards. Consult current PANTONE Color Publications for accurate color. PANTONE® and other Pantone trademarks are the property of, and are used with the written permission of, PANTONE LLC. © Pantone LLC, 2011. All rights reserved. **280** Sam Todd: (tr). **282** Jumping cheese, this file has been released into public domain by its author: (tr). KillerChihuahua licensed under Creative Commons Attribution-Share Alike 3.0 unported licence: (tl). US Air Force, as a work of US federal government the image is in the public domain: (bl) (br). **292** Charles Fox. **293** Charles Fox. **301** Alain Carpentier. **325** with permission from Komori UK Ltd: (tr). **325** with permission from Tom Taylor: (br).

In some instances we have been unable to trace the owners of copyright material, and we would appreciate any information that would enable us to do so.

1 THE EVOLUTION OF PUBLISHING MEDIA

This chapter discusses:

- Media proliferation
- The twentieth-century press barons
- Design in the golden age
- The influence of magazine design on newspapers
- Directing design
- The evolution of modern magazine design
- Media diversification
- Advertising and revenue generation
- Media transitions
- Creative directors and digital media agencies
- Media groups

This chapter will provide you with an introduction to the development of the modern media industry. It describes the influence of the press and the role of individual newspaper proprietors during the twentieth century and how design has become a key element in the success of media products. It examines the symbiotic relationship between editorial and advertising, as well as the key developments in technology that have led to the current trend for multimedia, convergent titles. Background knowledge of how the media industry has been consolidated into large groups and organisations that produce and distribute multi-platform media will help you understand the media areas and work practices you may encounter during your career.

'The new electronic interdependence recreates the world in the image of a global village.'
Marshall McLuhan, author and philosopher

'Design, in its broadest sense, is the enabler of the digital era – it's a process that creates order out of chaos, that renders technology usable to business. Design means being good, not just looking good.'

Clement Mok, designer and digital pioneer

The media industry

From Gutenberg in the fifteenth century to websites in the twenty-first century, the key to successful media has been the union between technology, communication, education and visual presentation. Most modern media have their origins in the nineteenth century, when the combination of wealth generated by industrialisation, coupled with the introduction of compulsory education, created a mass market for newspapers and magazines. The journey from the era of print to the digital age has taken over two centuries, through years that have seen, and are still seeing, great historical upheavals and many profound social changes. The period has also included great scientific advances and the development of technologies that were once regarded as radical and groundbreaking, only to be supplanted by further innovations. Print, cinema, radio and television all, at one time, commanded the mass audience that has now switched to the Internet.

Design has always been at the centre of media development, and when it is combined with financial acumen, clever technology and the right moment in history, the visual style of a title can come to embody an era – and make a fortune for its producer. This has come from taking an approach to design that does not just regard it as making things look nice, but as a fundamental aspect of how the media industry unites technology and functionality with art and literature. All design must function in the context for which it has been created, and it is known that well-designed titles present content in the best possible manner to attract readers, viewers, visitors and advertisers. Understanding how the publishing industry has evolved will help you to gain an insight into the structure of the industry and the application of media design.

Media proliferation

Britain, from the seventeenth to the twentieth century, built one of the largest and richest empires the world has ever seen, controlling, at its height, almost a quarter of the globe and a quarter of the world's

The key developments in mechanical printing 1790–1950

1790–1838	1840–1879	1880–1949
1798 **Lithography** Invented by Alois Senefelder	1847 **Rotary drum printing** Invented by Richard Hoe	1881 **Trichromatic halftone process** Invented by Frederick Ives
1804 **Iron printing press** Invented by Earl Stanhope	1853 **Negative/positive photography** Invented by William Fox Talbot	1886 **Linotype typesetting machine** Invented by Ottmar Mergenthaler
1810 **Foundrinier papermaking machine** Invented by Nicolas Robert	1860 **Commercial line block process** Invented by Paul Pretsch	1886 **Point measurement system** Based on a unit of 1/72in (0.3527mm)
1810 **Steam-driven printing press** Invented by Friedrich Koenig	1860 **First rotary offset litho machine** Invented by William Bullock and John Walters	1886 **Halftone engraving process** Developed by Frederick Ives
1835 **The rotary web press** Invented by Rowland Hill	1860 **Colour separation** Developed by James Clerk Maxwell	1887 **Monotype typesetting machine** Invented by Tolbert Lanston
1837 **Chromolithography** Invented by Engelmann and Lasteyrie	1861 **First colour photograph** Taken by James Clerk Maxwell	1890 **Rotary lithographic press** Developed by Hippolyte Marinoni
1837 **First photographic image** Taken by Joseph Niepce	1879 **Lithographic mechanical tints** Invented by Benjamin Day	1904 **Three-cylinder litho offset press** Developed by Ira Rubel
1837 **First electric printing press** Invented by Thomas Davenport		1948 **Colour flatbed scanner** Invented by Hardy and Wurzburg
1839 **First photographic printing process** Invented by Louis Daguerre		1949 **Type photosetting** Developed by Rene Higonnet and Louis Moyroud

The Village Underground in East London is a cutting edge space that acts as a focus for writers, designers and other artists and performers. The recycled London Underground carriages above the cultural centre provide a creative studio space.

the media company to publish on an ongoing basis. The *Guardian*'s website, originally designed by Neville Brody's company Research Studios, has since been redesigned and update by the *Guardian*'s in-house web team with extra digital products, such as mobile news links, that have been added as technology and media usage changes. The magazine publisher, H. Bauer, employed the Ralph and Co. Agency to undertake the website development for *FHM* and *HeatWorld*. In 2005, Poke, the digital media arm of Mother, a leading advertising agency, was responsible for major redesigns of BBC Worldwide Publishing's websites for the *Radio Times*, *Top Gear* and *Gardener's World*. Mother, like many contemporary ad agencies, describes itself as creative innovators. Digital media agencies are now combining digital technologies with real world experiences such as events and street installations, to provide a rich media service.

Media groups

The twentieth century saw the development of large conglomerates that owned newspapers, magazines and radio and TV stations. This trend has continued over recent years and most of the major media platforms are controlled by global organisations. Some of these groups are sub-companies of larger media groups: for example, the Hearst Corporation owns NatMags, and IPC, which had its origins in Lord Northcliffe's Amalgated Press group, is now part of the Time Warner empire. A number of international companies such as Hachette Filipacchi, a French magazine group, and the German publisher Gruner and Jahr (now part of NatMags) have moved into the British market. Media groups now have products that cross over platforms and industries, and some titles are **printed under licence** in a number of countries and different languages. Hachette Filipacchi's *Psychologies*, a magazine that began in France, is now produced in several countries by locally based publishers; the magazine uses shared, translated content as well as editorial and advertising tailored for a national audience.

The major international media groups operate in TV, film, print, radio and on the Internet, and also own secondary trading activities such as exhibitions and trade fairs and companies involved in music, travel, retail and book publishing. The owners of media groups are able to take advantage of adapting content for use in a number of titles and are able to utilise in-house expertise for development projects. They also cross-sell their products to adverting clients, for example by offering ad spaces in print and online in conjunction with associated exhibition stands and market research information. Their wide range of business interests adds credibility to their products, which attracts higher revenues from advertisers and increases the depth and coverage of editorial content, which also creates interest for the audience. Although these large conglomerates dominate most of the industry, there are still a number of smaller, independent publishers, many of which cover specialist interest and business subjects, and individuals prepared to start up their own media enterprise and launch new products on to the market.

The Village Underground has created a relaxed working environment that encourages a free flow of ideas.

13

'The world has changed, and it's up to newspapers to adapt to that.'

Rupert Murdoch in an interview for *Media Revolution*, BBC2, February 2009

Media moguls

Rupert Murdoch has been one of the most influential of the twenty-first century's media proprietors, with a media empire that covers print, radio, TV and the Internet. He and his family run many of the major news and entertainment outlets in a number of countries throughout the world, and he had tremendous political power and influence. He was one of the earliest adopters of digital technology and he has kept his News International Corporation moving with the times by buying online media businesses and building new printing plants.

The media industry has always attracted entrepreneurs, and current media owners include Richard Desmond, owner of the Daily Express Group, who originally made his money from soft pornography titles. The Telegraph Media Group is owned by the Barclay Brothers, who made their billions through media, retail and property. Sir Anthony O'Reilly, one of the richest men in Ireland, owns the Independent News and Media Group. The Guardian Media Group has never had an owner–proprietor. However the Scott Trust, originally a charitable foundation set up to ensure editorial independence, has now become a commercial company.

The huge power of newspapers, and the money that could be made, attracted some very dubious individuals. Most notorious of all Britain's twentieth-century newspaper proprietors was Robert Maxwell, owner of the *Daily Mirror* in the 1970s–1980s, who was infamously emotionally volatile and abusive to his staff. He died at sea in mysterious circumstance and was then found to have 'asset stripped' the company's staff pension fund. In 2007, Conrad Black, a former owner of the *Daily Telegraph*, was convicted of defrauding the media companies he controlled. However, these men are the exceptions, and many owners of media groups allow their companies to operate independently and prefer to remain in the background.

UK media groups

- Condé Nast: *Vogue*, *GQ*, *Glamour*, *Tatler* and *World of Interiors* with associated websites
- Dennis Publishing: *Computer Shopper*, *Viz*, *PC Pro*, *Bizarre*, *igizmo*, *imotor*, *Monkey Mag*, *Men's Fitness*, etc., with associated websites
- H. Bauer: *Grazia*, *Closer*, *Bella*, *Take a Break*, *TV Choice*, *Zoo*, *Empire*, *FHM*, *Arena*, etc., with associated websites. Radio: Kiss, Magic and a number of local radio stations
- Hachette Filipacchi (Lagardère Active): *Elle*, *Elle Decoration*, *Red*, *Sugar*, *Psychologies*, *Inside Soap*, etc., with associated websites
- IPC Media (Time Warner Inc.): *Woman*, *Marie Claire*, *Ideal Home*, *Nuts*, *Yachting*, *Practical Boat Builder*, etc., with associated websites
- NatMag – National Magazine Company (Hearst Corporation): *Cosmopolitan*, *Company*, *She*, *Esquire*, *Reveal*, *Best*, etc., with associated websites. Websites: netdoctor and handbag.com
- News International (UK): *Times*, *Sunday Times*, *Sun*, *News of the World*, *Sky* magazine with associated websites
- Northern and Shell Media Publications: *Daily* and *Sunday Express*, *Daily Star*, *OK!* and *New!* magazines, regional newspapers with associated websites
- The Daily Mail and General Trust plc: *Daily Mail*, *The Mail on Sunday*, *Metro*, *London Lite* and *Loot* plus local and regional publications with associated websites
- The Guardian Media Group: *Guardian* and *Observer*, regional and local papers, *Autotrader*, TV and radio stations with associated websites
- The Independent Media Group: *Independent* and *Independent on Sunday* with associated websites
- The Telegraph Media Group Ltd: *Daily Telegraph* and *Sunday Telegraph* with associated websites
- Thomson Corporation: Thomson Reuters plus website
- Trinity Mirror: The *Daily* and *Sunday Mirror*, *People* and *Daily Record*, regional newspapers and magazines with associated websites

The ownership of media groups and the titles they publish change frequently as mergers and demergers occur, and new titles are launched while others close. For more information visit *mediauk.com*, a website that lists British media groups and publishers, and for current industry news go to *http://magforum.wordpress.com* or *www.guardian.co.uk/media*.

Summary: The evolution of publishing media

Print was the most influential media for most of the twentieth century, as the majority of people obtained news and much of their entertainment from publications. This meant that newspaper proprietors and magazine publishers could wield enormous political and social influence. Cinema and radio were also hugely popular in the middle years of the century, but in the 1950s–1960s TV took over as the most influential media and remained the dominant platform up to the 2000s, when the Internet took over. Advertising has been the main source of revenue for all media since the nineteenth century. In the twenty-first century, consolidated advertising agencies run integrated media campaigns that exploit technology and other interactive opportunities, to extend their marketing activities outside the range of standard media. Large multinational media groups that operate in print, TV and online radio, as well as staging events, exhibitions and trade fairs, dominate the current media industry.

- The key to successful media has been the union between technology, communication and visual presentation.

- In the twentieth century, newspapers were the main source of information on national and international affairs and had considerable power to influence public opinion.

- Very rich tycoons who understood the power of the press ran the early twentieth-century media industry in Britain and the USA.

- The twentieth century was the most successful period in the history of the newspaper industry.

- The introduction of desktop publishing (dtp) and photo imaging software in the late 1980s made it possible for newspapers to include more design features.

- Modernism and the art deco style inspired twentieth-century newspaper and magazine design with type and images placed on an underlying geometric page grid.

- Punk and deconstruction magazine design tried to interpret the feel of the content, rather that just presenting words and pictures.

- Advances in digital printing technology, coupled with the Internet, made it possible to launch specialist niche titles that have marketing and publishing profiles aimed at demographic and special interest groups.

- The nineteenth century saw the establishment of the commercial relationship between editorial and advertising.

- Early twentieth-century advertising agencies began to offer a full range of services to their clients.

- The modern era in advertising began in 1950s' North America after the end of the Second World War.

- The later decades of the twentieth century saw the consolidation of the main advertising agencies into larger groups.

- Media website development is often handled by web agencies with multi-skilled teams that can provide design and technological solutions.

- Large conglomerates that publish newspapers dominate twenty-first-century media and magazines, control radio and TV stations and offer online products.

Activities and development

The questions and action points for this chapter are intended to provide you with guidance on areas that you can research and investigate to help you build your knowledge of the media industry. Visit the *Design for Media* website for more fact and action sheets, sample templates, type schemes and colour palettes at **www.pearsoned.com/hand**.

Questions

Question 1
Study a newspaper that has a compact (tabloid), Berliner or broadsheet format.

(a) Investigate whether the newspaper has changed its original paper size and, if so, discuss why this decision may have been taken.

(b) How does the current paper size and the design style of the publication relate to the title's editorial values and political stance?

Question 2
Select two magazine titles published in print and online that cover the same subject, namely business, health, lifestyle, sports. Look at the advertisements and note whether the subject of the products and services being promoted is matched in the editorial content. Describe the reasons why the advertiser might have chosen to place their advertisement in one particular title but not another.

Question 3
How do producers of popular TV and radio programmes with a mass audience employ print and online media to promote their shows?

Question 4
Look at a well-known brand's current advertising campaign. How many different media does it run in, and what content and design features link the various elements of the campaign?

Action points

Action point 1
The press barons and the newspaper industry of the 1930s are satirised by Evelyn Waugh in his book *Scoop*. Waugh had worked for the *Daily Mail* as a foreign correspondent. His monstrous newspaper proprietor of the 'Daily Beast' is called Lord Copper, and is generally thought to be an amalgamation of Northcliffe and Beaverbrook.

Read or watch *Scoop* and examine other sources from the period. Consider the influence of the press barons and international news reporting on public opinion in the 1930s.

Scoop by Evelyn Waugh, 1938, Penguin Modern Classics
Scoop, 1987 film directed by Gavin Millar, available on DVD

Action point 2
Examine the influence and use of geometric modernist grids in current print, online and digital magazines.

Action point 3
Review a number of leading brands' websites and note how many seek to involve their customers in the sort of promotional campaigns and activities that have traditionally been handled by advertising agencies (e.g. NikeiD, PepsiMax, Persil.com).

2 TWENTY-FIRST CENTURY MEDIA: DESIGN IN PRACTICE

This chapter discusses:

- Content presentation and production
- Media branding and identity
- Design in practice
- The role of advertising
- Business development and strategy
- Employment structures
- The role of design
- Contract publishing
- Convergence and the Web
- Technology, change and the media
- A paperless future?
- Media by other means

This chapter describes how design and technology are employed in the media industry with a breakdown of the occupations, specialist skills and knowledge involved in producing media products for the Web and print. The information will provide you with a guide to the business sectors that make up the industry and explain what you need to know about the current state and possible future development of the media in order to plan your career.

'This is a time of fundamental change.'
Rupert Murdoch, News International Group

*'It's art if it can't be explained.
It's fashion if no one asks for an explanation.
It's design if it doesn't need explanation.'*

Wouter Stokkel, designer

The role of media design

The two main methods of presenting text-based content to the public rely heavily on design. Printed publications and websites need to have a clearly defined visual structure that can communicate complex sets of information and relay the cultural status and political stance of a title or its publisher to attract the corresponding audience. Web and print publication designers have to consider a media company's commercial and editorial requirements in order to create a distinctive identity that can become a marketable brand. They are also responsible for developing a visual treatment that will ensure the content appeals to the chosen audience of consumers and advertisers.

Design marries media objectives to the technology that will be used to produce the finished product. The process can involve knowledge of the hardware and software employed within the media industry in order to achieve the desired outcome, as well as establishing working systems for how the technology will be used. The look of a media product should result from the analysis of market research and knowledge of current Internet and print production practices combined with graphic and information design skills.

Those involved with the media design process need to keep track of the latest software, IT devices and Internet trends, as well as have some knowledge of the history of design and current design styles. Contemporary websites, magazines and newspapers use existing design conventions together with innovative ideas to exchange or provide information, influence opinion, provoke emotions and direct intentions. No

What is design?

Design, as opposed to art, is defined as a process that produces a functional object, working system or structure. The word design comes from a Middle English word, *designen*, that meant to mark out, and the current usage has also been influenced by the French words *dessin*, the art of drawing, and *dessiner*, to lay out or delineate. The modern interpretation of design includes developing the visual concept behind an object or structure and working towards an intended outcome that involves an industrial or technological process. A designer will gather as much information as possible on the specific goal to be achieved and then ask questions so that they can create solutions to any problems or issues that occur. Their aim is to develop an answer that is efficient, economic and emotionally appealing.

one designs in a vacuum, and while media designs may be intended primarily to inform, entertain and amuse a target audience, it is a truism that the typography, imagery and layout of publications cannot help but reflect the wider social, political and economic environment. The look of a media product should be matched to its brand objectives and the production technologies used – not just styled to conform to the latest ideas. Good design can solve the problems involved in communicating clearly by presenting content in a relevant, engaging and accessible manner.

Design solutions

Design is more than a method of devising objects; it can also be used to resolve complex social problems and create systems for living. Design can influence us and the way in which we regard the world. It can be employed to uphold ideals and beliefs as well as to solve communication issues and maintain social values. Design contributes to and reflects contemporary taste, and the techniques and materials available at any one time will affect what is designed and how it is produced.

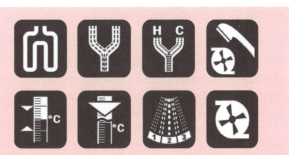

Logos for Mira showers

Source: Icon Magazine, www.iconeye.com

Icon magazine: cover design by Emma Chui (Art Editor); illustration by Chaz Maviyane-Davis.

Design gives order and clarity to complex information structures

Levi's online retailing at levi.com.

Design creates distinctiveness and sets the identity of a publication

Source: Nigel Young/Foster + Partners

30 St Mary's Axe, London, Swiss Re headquarters

1922–1957, 1989–2000, 2000–

Source: BP plc

Design can evolve to reflect current trends and values

Design communicates and amplifies the meaning of the content

Alessi kettle with a bird-shaped whistle

Design puts information into a format appropriate to the target audience

Design can inspire action and promote beliefs and values

Dyson ball barrow

Design creates the desire for products and services

Media branding and identity

In the past, serious newspaper editors sneered and journalists groaned when the layout of pages was handed over to designers, as they believed a news publication survived on its content alone. However, increased competition due to the proliferation of titles in print publishing, the rapid expansion of online media and a shift in advertising revenues from print to the Web have forced those in news reporting to accept that design has an important role in the communication of news and the financial success of a brand. Magazines, on the other hand, have employed design as a major marketing tool since the 1920s. Current print and web titles recognise the need for a strong brand image, as well as good content, to make their product stand out from the vast amount of options available to media consumers. The design process for a media product involves working within a **brand identity** called the **house design style** when applied to the visual style of newspapers, magazines and websites. The brand identity describes a set of values that allow a target audience to recognise the profile of a title, while the house design style establishes visual consistency that reassures print readers and website visitors and helps them find their way through the content.

A new idea for a media product may be designed to fit within a brand family. Elements of a house design style, such as logos, colours and typefaces, can be used for related cross-media material, such as websites, advertisements on both platforms and printed marketing items such as mail-outs, giveaways and leaflets that may be used for promotional campaigns. An audience will generally accept other branded items that follow the ethos of the original concept as they carry the associated values of the core product. Most people trust the information given by the publications or websites they

> '*I think design covers so much more than the aesthetic. Design is fundamentally more. Design is usability. It is Information Architecture. It is Accessibility. This is all design.*'

Mark Boulton, design consultant

Concept values

BRAND VALUES

|

Reputation – Associations – Culture
Accessibility – Ethics – Innovation

|

PRODUCT

Design values

Logo/name   Product design

|

Typefaces – Colours – Image
Multimedia – Technology

The value of a brand lies in both its design and intrinsic qualities.

identify with and use it as a guide for making decisions, for example whether or not to go to see a film or eat at a restaurant. They will also trust other products offered by the title, such as clothing, food, drink and holidays, which opens up the possibility for media companies to make money from other business areas (secondary trading).

The main aims of media design are to establish a visual structure and content form that will convey editorial information, bring in advertising and provide a consistent look for secondary trading items and areas, such as travel brochures and exhibition staging. The look of a media product has to make an immediate impact, and a design must elicit the audience response required by the media company and its advertising clients. A successful design will achieve this by making the website or publication visually attractive and by tailoring that attraction to appeal to readers or visitors that have synergy with the editorial and advertisers' content. Top magazines such as *Vogue* and *GQ* have a look that is both individual and stylistically linked to the world of fashion. This rule applies to niche publications as well. The Campaign for Real Ale's *Beer* magazine has won several awards for its well-targeted and appropriate design.

Media designs are generally ephemeral, and the look of printed material and websites is frequently updated to comply with the latest cultural trends and fashionable graphic design styles. The media industry tends to apply the rule 'evolution not revolution'. Whenever a title is designed or relaunched, the brand must remain identifiable and will often retain elements of the previous style to maintain continuity and acceptance by the existing audience. Often, when a title is losing readers and advertising revenue, a media company will try changing its look. But if the content is weak or the product no longer relevant to the market, simply making tired content more presentable will not prevent eventual closure.

Design in practice

The presentation of content for magazines, websites, newspapers, marketing, company brochures, etc. is subject to rules that ensure a set design style is maintained. These are usually set out in a design guide or on help pages that provide examples and explain how to style each page or section, with detailed instructions on picture preparation techniques and how the typefaces are to be used. The advice given should cover most of the situations you may come across when producing pages for a print or online title on a day-to-day basis.

Designs for print are set up in **desktop publishing** software and stored as **templates** that contain the house design style for the sections and pages, the typographic styling and any graphic items that appear on each page, such as the issue date and page number. These are used as the basis for each issue's **page layouts**. Web pages are normally created using a computer program called a **content management system**, software that is specifically written for a media company's online products or an individual website. The content management system (CMS) will take into account the company's working practices and provides an interface through which content can be added to or removed from the website. Some design or IT publications may use web design programs to create new

pages, but doing so requires specialist skills and would take more time than a news media website has available when uploading breaking stories.

The production process starts with planning the content for an issue or update, and then gathering suitable material, which can involve obtaining pictures and copy on specific subjects by commissioning photographers, film-makers and writers, sourcing copy and visual material from other media organisations and buying images from picture agencies and libraries. Once all the written and pictorial content has been assembled, the imagery and text need to be assessed and technically prepared for the required media. Once all the items are ready, they are assembled, following house style, on a page. **Page make-up** involves putting the text into the correct type style, making sure it is free from errors and fits in the space available, and combining the copy with images and other graphic items. The material often goes through several stages as it is edited and adjusted to make sure it looks good.

If you are doing a job that involves page creation, you will need to be able to work with a house design style to prepare media-specific content. You may also need a wider understanding of production technologies, depending on the way in which the company works. Some larger media organisations handle production in-house or use specialist web and print publishing design companies. There are also freelance designers and layout subeditors who can be booked directly or through media personnel agencies (see page 29).

The role of advertising

Large multinational groups own a good deal of the media industry, but there are also small to medium-sized companies and independent publishers of very specialist titles. The media industry has a number of trading areas such as national and regional newspapers, consumer and business-to-business magazines and local publications with print titles, websites and other related commercial ventures (see page 22). All these sectors are dependent upon advertising revenue raised by selling **advertising space** and other marketing activities. The cost of an advertisement is calculated from the readership and circulation of a print publication, the duration of the advertisement – how often

Cross-media communications

Media/device	Product	Publication type
Print	Newspapers Magazines Newsletters	National/regional/local news Consumer/business/special interest B2B, not-for-profit, small to medium, local
Internet	Websites Multimedia Blogs Podcast E- and webzines Tweets Enewsletters Search engines	Media, retail, entertainment, info, social networking, sports and gaming Interactive, video, audio Info, media, personal comment, social networking Info, entertainment Media, retail, entertainment, info Social networking, media, entertainment, info B2B, not-for-profit, small to medium, local General, specialist and aggregators
Mobile phone	Websites, apps	Info, media, retail, entertainment, social networking, sports and gaming
iPad/tablet	Websites, apps	Info, media, retail, entertainment, social networking, sports and gaming

and how long it will appear, and website page views or **click-throughs** – and the title's ranking in its market sector. High-end magazines and websites that appeal to a sophisticated and wealthy target audience may charge their advertisers many thousands of pounds for an advert, especially one in a prime position such as the home page or inside front cover.

Media companies usually have a range of business interests, such as radio and TV stations, and also generate income through tie-ins with films, live performance events, music and books. The cover price of a newspaper or magazine is used to fund some of the operating and production costs, but the charge does not reflect the true cost of producing a print publication – the actual amount would make a title so expensive no one would buy it.

Most websites generate income through advertising, sponsored links and secondary trading. While there are subscription-only websites, the majority give free access to all their information and hope that sufficient visitors will respond to their clients' advertisements, and provide them with enough click-throughs to persuade advertisers it would be worthwhile placing their business with the site.

In the good years, there are plenty of advertisers ready to buy space in newspapers and magazines, providing media companies with good incomes, and titles can have generous budgets that allow them to increase

the pagination or number of pages and produce more content. This adds value for the media customer, with the result that the circulation and readership of printed titles increase. But the reliance on advertising makes the media industry particularly vulnerable to the typical boom/bust cycle of free market capitalism. When the economy suffers a downturn, advertising cuts its

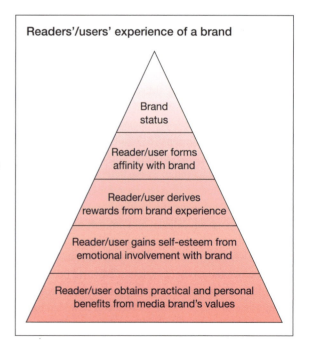

Readers'/users' experience of a brand

Brand status

Reader/user forms affinity with brand

Reader/user derives rewards from brand experience

Reader/user gains self-esteem from emotional involvement with brand

Reader/user obtains practical and personal benefits from media brand's values

Al Jazeera's Doha headquarters media hub combines technology with digital news gathering.

promotional budgets, which are normally set a year or more in advance. As a result, the industry tends to see a later decline and then a trailing recovery in income later than other sectors. Any fall in **advertising revenue** can lead to companies having to cut costs by reducing the size of issues and, coupled with the fact that printed publications are seen as an unnecessary expense by many people, this can cause a fall in readership that further discourages advertisers. The boom/bust cycle affects the Web as well, because when the global economy contracts, all advertising revenues reduce.

The media tend to be in a constant state of flux, no matter what the wider economy is doing, because, as well as financial factors, the digital environment also drives change. When there is plenty of money to be spent, media companies are willing to try new ideas and launch different types of products. The 2000s saw several major titles rebuild or refit their headquarters so that all their media products across the various platforms – print, online, audio and visual – could be produced together. This trend towards media convergence saw multimedia content become standard on most websites and a greater emphasis on the connections between print and online titles.

The great dilemma for media companies is how to protect and increase their revenue in the constantly changing media environment. Traditional publishing methods of earning money are becoming less profitable, and there is an urgent search going on to find

new sources of revenue. Production costs for print and online have to be covered and companies want to make a profit. The practice of selling space still brings in revenue: in fact, up to 2009, printed publications were earning more than websites, even though readership of some titles has been dropping. But, as advertisers use the **Audit Bureau of Circulation's** official figures **(ABC or ABCe ratings)** for a title's circulation and/or **unique users (UUs)** as a guide for where to place their advertisements, the huge rise in website visitors set against the slow decline in readership of print titles appears to show a continuing trend. The move from print advertising to online has hit the print publishing industry very hard, while figures show a comparative increase in web-generated income.

The Web offers a broad range of advertising and marketing opportunities for media websites, but also allows for direct interaction with consumers without the need for advertisers to rely on a title's ability to deliver a specific audience. Print has not been able to compete with the Internet's ability to include interactive competitions, games, social networking, customer services and support, discussion groups and viral campaigns, such as NikeID that allows customers to design their own Nike products, or Coca-Cola's lifestyle site, CokeZone. Traditional publishing houses have been slow to engage with these developments and recognise that there has been a fundamental change in media consumers' behaviour and attitude.

Business development and strategies

Media companies are trying to find ways to add value for visitors to their website and generate income by other means than the standard **pop-up**, **banner** and **skyscraper** ads (see page 70). Websites have become business and entertainment centres, with some running their own retail stores and service operations, while others work in partnership with specialist companies. Magazine websites often have sponsored links that connect to other related companies in mutual agreements aimed at promoting both businesses. As a result of competition and economic pressures, there have been a number of mergers and major restructuring within the media industry.

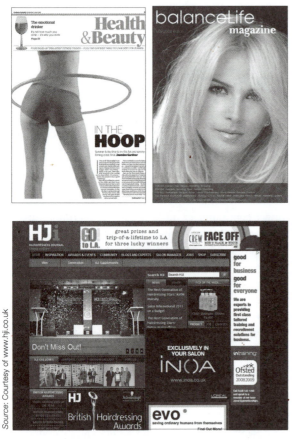

Print and web publications need a strong design concept if they are to withstand competition from other media.

Over recent years, a range of publishing concepts have been introduced, including **Freemiums** – high-quality magazines with no cover price, such as men's glossy magazines *Shortlist* and *Profile*. Media companies work with industries such as retail, automotive and travel on free customer magazines that encourage existing clients to remain loyal to the brand. Titles such as the *Metro* international series of city newspapers, which are distributed free, have proved successful. These publications highlight a change in how audiences consume media, throughout the media audience.

People no longer expect to pay for general information; why should they, if they can get similar material for free from a variety of media sources? British publishers have also struggled with the notion that they now have a global audience. Most of their websites still only feature local advertising when the technology exists that could be used to replace British ads with those from the visitor's country. This makes the site more relevant to global audiences, and offers the media a greater potential international income.

Media companies may also have to change their traditional business model that relies on a number of people working together in large editorial and production teams. Web pundits have been saying for some time that the way to make money from the Internet is to de-staff media titles, and it is possible to run a website with far fewer people than a print publication traditionally required, although modern work practices and technology have led to a reduction in the level of staffing on many print titles.

There are instances of editorial content being shared between British and international titles, and examples of subediting being handled in centralised departments or overseas. Modern communication systems have enabled publishers to move away from expensive city centre offices, and some have already downsized their operation and moved to smaller out-of-town business parks. The introduction of computerised presses and print management systems that automate the work involved in printing has also reduced the number of people needed to handle the process (see page 73).

The possibilities held out by digital communication technology are enticing. World events are now

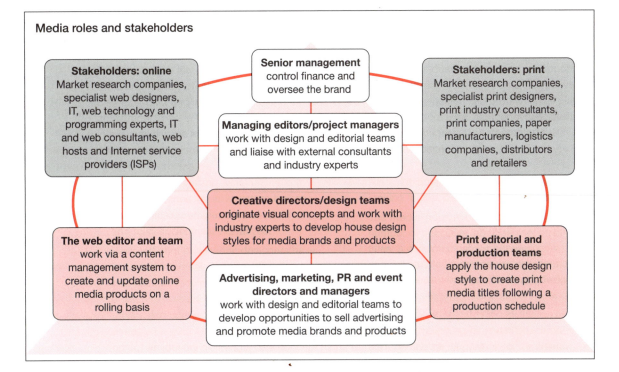

Media roles and stakeholders

Stakeholders: online
Market research companies, specialist web designers, IT, web technology and programming experts, IT and web consultants, web hosts and Internet service providers (ISPs)

Senior management
control finance and oversee the brand

Stakeholders: print
Market research companies, specialist print designers, print industry consultants, print companies, paper manufacturers, logistics companies, distributors and retailers

Managing editors/project managers
work with design and editorial teams and liaise with external consultants and industry experts

Creative directors/design teams
originate visual concepts and work with industry experts to develop house design styles for media brands and products

The web editor and team
work via a content management system to create and update online media products on a rolling basis

Print editorial and production teams
apply the house design style to create print media titles following a production schedule

Advertising, marketing, PR and event directors and managers
work with design and editorial teams to develop opportunities to sell advertising and promote media brands and products

reported person to person as they happen, and people create their own content and share it for free. The Web was originally conceived of as a free entity, and there has always be a dichotomy between those who want to use it to make money and the average user who expects open access to the entire Web. Web 2.0 brought in the possibility of more interactivity and social connectivity, and with the other developing trends, it increased the pressures on corporate media groups that rely on charging for content.

Employment structures: who does what

Anyone considering a media career has to be able to multi-task. Employers are increasingly looking for people who can work across platforms and are familiar with the production criteria for each title or product. However, there are still specialist roles and, on larger titles, a division of labour between print and online. To some degree, this is simply practical – one person

can only do so much, and some of the software used to generate multimedia content requires a separate set of skills from writing copy or preparing photographs. Some companies have kept traditional work practices rather than risk changing the entire production process. But as the technology advances, there will be an increasing amount of media convergence and unification of work areas and jobs.

The media industry has a number of design job titles and functions that can vary from company to company, and which may be applied to different roles. Some companies have a **creative or design director**, the senior manager in charge of the design staff working on the company's media product branding. They oversee the look of all the publications and websites, as well as the creative direction of the visual content. Other major titles have a large design team led by an **art director** who may be more involved with individual titles, developing concepts for the visual treatment of features, choosing locations, models, props, clothing and directing photo shoots.

The title of **art editor** may mean someone who does the same job as an art director, or who has a solely office based job with responsibility for the day-to-day editorial production. The role involves gathering in the text-based and visual content and seeing that it is prepared for the page make-up process. The art editor is in charge of how this material is used to produce the pages in the title's design style, and of making sure the production deadlines are met. An art editor may work alone or, for a title with a great many pages, manage a team consisting of assistant art editors and/or designers who will make up the pages in the relevant production software. There are publications that use the title senior designer, which basically means the same as art editor.

The **chief sub** manages a team of **subeditors**. The chief sub is responsible for maintaining the standard of the editorial copy. A subeditor's role depends on the nature of the publication, but generally entails checking and preparing copy. It can also include page make-up or correcting the page layouts. This means that subeditors work very closely with the design and production teams.

Some smaller publications have an editor who handles both design and production, or for a company with a larger number of titles and websites, there can be a **production manager or editor**. This job deals with the more technical side of the process, managing the page flow through editorial production, the final published output in print or on the Web. Production managers may set up the scheduling and handle all online or print material for a company, such as client advertising, in-house promotions and catalogues, as well as liaising with IT departments, web management companies, **Internet service providers (ISPs)**, printing companies and distributors. Companies with a large number of publications and websites may have a **production director**

in overall charge who negotiates budgets with printing companies, paper merchants and web service providers.

Web production can be either handled within a media organisation or subcontracted to an IT/communications company, a web design agency or web management company. A typical in-house web team can consist of a **web editor**, **web designer** and/or a **web production manager**, supported by an IT team or manager. The day-to-day updating of a news media site is more likely to be done by **production journalists** using a content management system that has a fixed page design, while a computer magazine's web pages may well be created by specialist web designers in Dreamweaver or Flash, so they can be altered to show the title's grasp of current technological trends.

A picture editor or researcher is responsible for sourcing and commissioning the visual material for a company or publication. Their job can be to source images to order, following instructions from editors, and can also include processing the pictures for the publishing media. They may be in charge of ordering still pictures and video from **image banks** and also be responsible for administering backup software to build up a picture archive. The position of web/digital imaging editor can be a separate post, or the picture editor may also source multimedia content.

Large media companies will have an advertising sales director and/or manager and there may also be a separate digital advertising sales manager or team. Advertisements are normally supplied by advertising agencies or clients as digital files or as pdfs for print and JPEGs or gifs for online. Advertisers are often sold a particular position and time slot for their ads to appear. The advertising department or team works with the editorial and production teams to keep them informed about what ads are coming in and when they need to

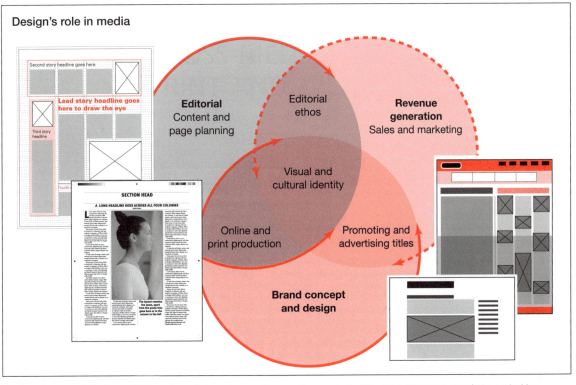

Design's role in media

Editorial
Content and
page planning

Editorial
ethos

Revenue
generation
Sales and marketing

Visual and
cultural identity

Online and
print production

Promoting and
advertising titles

Brand concept
and design

Design plays a role in the activities of most departments in a media company. The brand image not only is carried by the individual titles and across media, but also affects the choice of editorial material as subjects need to be considered in terms of how they might be visualised in the house design style. Design is important for advertising and promotional activities as the brand must remain clearly identifiable no matter where, when, how or what form the product's marketing takes. All departments should work closely together to ensure that the brand image remains consistent and attractive to the reader or users.

be published, and to collate all the supplied ad material for inclusion with the other content that makes up a print publication or website.

Some media companies also have **brand or marketing managers** who are in charge of promoting their titles. There can be event managers who run exhibitions and trade fairs, and subscription managers whose job it is to come up with special offers and giveaways to encourage people to subscribe to the title on a regular basis and gain access to premium online material. Producing promotional material is sometimes part of an in-house design team's work, or larger projects can be commissioned from design groups or agencies that specialise in **media collateral**. Conferences, exhibitions and promotions/events can be organised by divisions or managers within a media company, or by external specialist companies.

TIP Try to get to know all the people and teams you will be working with. It is important to know who does what, and how you can perform your tasks and activities in a way that will help the smooth running of your own and others' departments. Maintaining good relationships with colleagues is the key to avoiding any conflicts between editorial and advertising, design and production, that might lead to unnecessary production problems.

The specialist's role in media design

Media companies employ specialists who have art, design and software skills that fall outside the range of expertise of the in-house staff. As well as print and web designers and page production experts, there are other art contributors, who are normally freelancers who would be asked to produce content such as Photoshop illustrations or video reports for a specific feature or web page. Traditional painted or drawn illustrations are still used by some publications and can be commissioned from illustrators who specialise in particular topics.

Photography can be commissioned from independent photographers, or images can be sourced from **photo agencies** and **stock image** banks such as Getty Images, Corbis, Magnum and Thomson Reuters. These companies commission or buy a range of photographs, videos and other visual media on top news stories and frequently use subjects from film-makers, photographers and illustrators. They sell the licence to use the image, not the images themselves. Image banks offer a cost-effective way of obtaining high-quality photographs and illustrations.

The images bought from a stock image bank can be altered to suit the title's editorial purpose, and commissioned photography may be amended, with the photographer's consent. Some media companies employ Photoshop experts as **retouching** or **photo-manipulation** of digital images has become the norm, certainly for fashion shoots, celebrity pictures and ads. More controversially, the practice has begun to be used for news media that have traditionally resisted **photo-editing** pictures of an actual event or person.

Free image sharing websites, sometimes called **microstock sites**, offer an alternative source of professional and amateur photographs and illustrations on similar subjects to paid-for image sites, although the quality can vary, and the copyright laws covering the material may be restrictive.

Media specialisms include children's and general illustrations, Photoshop airbrushing and photography which has several subcategories such as fashion, food and travel.

Media specialists

- Freelance publication and website designers handle the design development of a new title from concept through to production

- Typographers and type designers create typefaces for new print publications or the redesign of an existing one

- Animators and effects designers create websites and effects for animated websites and graphics

- 2D and 3D digital artworkers specialise in graphics for maps, charts or diagrams for print and online

- Photoshop specialists work on the adjustment, photomanipulation and retouching of digital imagery

- Freelance illustrators tend to specialise in one area such as fashion or lifestyle

- Illustrators' agents represent illustrators and digital artworkers

- Caricaturists and cartoonists can be commissioned to produce topical images of high-profile people and events or may write their own comic strip

- Photographers usually specialise in one area such as news, features, sports or portraits

- Photographers' agents represent photographers
  www.photographersdirectory.org
  www.photoagentslondon.co.uk

- Photo agencies and image banks provide photography, video and film footage
  www.rexfeatures.com
  www.magnumphotos.com
  www.ap.org
  www.reuters.com

- Paparazzi are news photographers who specialise in celebrity pictures

- Freelance subeditors and page production professionals can be used by online and print titles to supplement permanent staff

- Production companies organise complex projects that require location scouts, photo/film shoot managers, film directors, photographic, film and lighting crew, stylists, hairdressers, make artists, catering, etc.

- Media lawyers and accountants cover the legal and financial aspect of the industry

- Multimedia website content specialists include sound recordists and editors, film and video editors and 3D digital modellers

- Web testers are specialists in usability who advise web designers and producers and carry out sample testing with a target audience

- Market research companies carry out research on new media products and track customer preferences for existing offerings

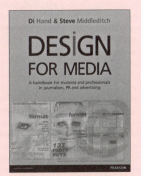

Case study: the *Guardian*

The *Guardian* was the first newspaper in Britain to instigate a design-led approach and has always prided itself on being at the forefront of publication design. In 1988, David Hillman, a partner at the leading British design group Pentagram, redesigned the newspaper with a distinctive logo (masthead) that mixed serif and sans serif typefaces (see pages 156, 157). The new design gave the paper's visual appearance equal weighting to its journalistic content. This caused uproar among the more conservative Fleet Street journalists and editors, but won the paper many design awards. The newspaper was redesigned and switched to the Berliner size in 2005, in response to the challenge set by the editorially similar *Independent*'s success and increased circulation following its relaunch in compact format. The *Guardian*'s creative director, Mark Porter, and editor Alan Rusbridger collaborated to create an updated, Internet-era look for the title, with new typefaces designed for the newspaper by Christian Schwartz and Paul Barnes. The Guardian Egyptian typeface has also been used for the signage in the *Guardian*'s new building in London.

www.studiodavidhillman.com/home

www.researchstudios.com/neville-brody

www.estersonassociates.co.uk

www.markporter.com

www.christianschwartz.com/bio.shtml

www.moderntypography.com

David Hillman's radical new approach to the *Guardian* had a significant influence on UK newspaper design.

The 2005 design fully exploited the opportunities presented by affordable colour printing, resulting in a greater integration of design and editorial.

'The world is moving from mass media to 'my media'.'

Daniel L. Rosensweig, Yahoo! Inc., 2004

Convergence and the Web: The Internet revolution

The Internet revolution has brought about a sea change in the relationship between media companies and their audience. The World Wide Web has transformed how and where people look for information and entertainment. The generation who have grown up in the information age no longer expect to sit passively reading a static page or staring at a scheduled TV programme. They do not think in terms of 'print or online', but move from platform to platform to use whatever media and devices will allow them to investigate, originate, organise, contribute and share whatever they are interested in, whenever and wherever they are, often all at the same time.

The question for the media industry is how to adapt and survive in this 'brave new world'. Some trends are already clear: the growth in use of online news and the introduction of digital TV have been major factors in the decline of readership of printed newspapers and viewers for terrestrial TV channels. Government and advertising industry figures indicated that many UK households had already moved to digital TV before the scheduled switchover in April 2012. However, the viewing figures of the main channels were already in decline as the key 16–34-year old audience showed a preference for on-demand and streaming services that could be accessed through a range of digital devices.

Some media companies have tried solutions such as tying the launch of a band's new album to an existing publication, in the hope of boosting the sales of both products. In 2008 the *Mail on Sunday* linked up first with Prince, and then with the band McFly, to give away their latest albums as free CDs inside the paper. The McFly offer saw an increase in the paper's circulation for that day of 20,000 copies to approximately 2.5 million, rather less than for the Prince album that saw an increase of 60,000. The apparent success of the *Mail*'s offer started a trend

for news-papers to give away first-release music; however, figures for March 2009 from the media industry title *UK Press Gazette* showed that none of the newspapers' promotions, free gifts and offers made a significant difference to the evidence of an overall continuing drop in readership. The *Mail on Sunday*'s month-by-month sales continued to decline, if only by 0.2 per cent, and during the same period the *Daily Express* saw a 2.86 per cent month-on-month loss of readers, despite 20 special offers and free gifts.

A fundamental change

The problem for the media industry is that these changes represent an ongoing shift in consumer behaviour, rather than a sudden, great upheaval with everyone using the Web in preference to print or TV. It is said that it takes 50 years for a new technology to become fully established (the Redwine–Riddle maturation model, see the illustration below), and this appears to hold true for the history of the modern computer. The first machines were developed in the 1940s

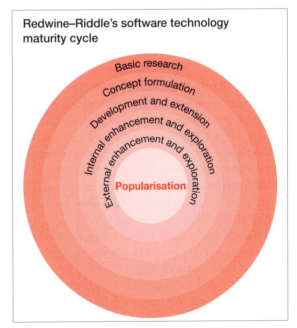

Redwine–Riddle's software technology maturity cycle

Basic research
Concept formulation
Development and extension
Internal enhancement and exploration
External enhancement and exploration
Popularisation

The Redwine–Riddle model identifies the cycle of research, development and adoption of new technologies.

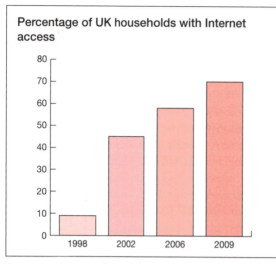

Percentage of UK households with Internet access

Government figures showed that most people accessed the Internet from home, and that, while more were using laptops, encouraged by the increase in the number of Wi-Fi hotspots, only a third of those who owned Internet phones used them to browse the Web. iPhones were still mostly used for chatting or texting, and their web facility was mainly being used for sending photos or videos; 50 per cent of iPhone users did not employ any of the other Internet functions.

Overall, the number of people using the Internet to buy goods and services showed an increase from 44 to 55 per cent in two years, with most taking advantage of travel, accommodation, lottery and betting websites.

Source: Office for National Statistics, August 2009

during and after the war, and computing for wider commercial use only began to come in with the 'baby boomer' entrepreneurs of the 1970s–1980s. It has taken until the 2000s for digital technology to become embedded in our daily lives. The benefits of this gradual drift are that it has provided some space for all commercial enterprises, and organisations such as public broadcasters to try to reposition themselves and adapt to the digital revolution.

Consumer behaviour is undergoing constant adjustments as one technology or device replaces another. The twenty-first century has seen 35mm stills cameras that use film become almost obsolete for everyday use. Even digital cameras as a separate entity are becoming less common, other than for professional photographers, as more people simply use their camera phones, since many can now take high-quality images. **PDAs**, tablets and Smart phones, coupled with Bluetooth and Wi-Fi

hotspots, give people media mobility – access to information from multiple locations – and this phenomenon is increasing as new devices, such as pocket video cameras, are being produced with direct Internet connectivity.

The major media companies have set up digital publishing arms, such as Ceros (NatMags), and most publishers have **digital magazines**, such as Dennis Publishing's *iGizmo* and *iMotor*. The twenty-first century has seen the launch of several innovations such as Refresh Mobile's mobizine, a system for publishing magazines on mobile phones that offered access to a range of titles. The service has become Mippin, one of the functions on the Apple iPhone. Other publications are sending out breaking news via email, offer customers text services and tweets. Most titles interact with their audience using social media websites.

All the main web browsers and other news services run **news aggregators** – specialised **search engines** which list all the news stories on one subject from the various news media around the world, with mobile phone versions and Twitter links available. Hubdub is a news prediction website that combines one of the Internet's great successes, online betting, with the news by allowing people to wager on the outcome of a news story, in the same way as they would on a sports event.

Internet take-up in the UK

Government figures* showed that, between 2004 and 2009, more than 1 million homes a year had joined the Internet society. In 2009, 18.3 million UK households had an Internet connection, and 90 per cent of those households used **broadband**. Together with public access, business and educational use, this translated into 76 per cent of the UK adult population regularly using the Internet. A breakdown of the figures revealed that men used the Internet slightly more than women – 75 per cent compared with 66 per cent. As one might expect, the retirement generation (over 65s) were the least likely to be web users, with 70 per cent that had never used the Internet, while nearly one-half of the 8 to 17 age group regularly used social networking websites. The research discovered that only 44 per cent of people aged 15 and over had read a national daily newspaper during the previous 12 months, compared with 72 per cent in 1978.

*National Statistics Omnibus Survey, 2009

Cross-media approach

The use of multimedia has led to a **platform agnostic** approach: that is, situating the story in the media best suited to the content, and planning the content to fit the production process, rather than writing for print or online and then adapting the same material. The shift in attitude has seen an enormous growth in video reports, the inclusion of user-generated content and discussion of current events via blogs and tweets. This multimedia, more inclusive approach has attracted a new generation of visitors who rely on the established organisations and titles to verify the news, even when the information can be gained from hundreds of independent sources. Magazine websites linked to print versions and Internet-only titles have also expanded the range of media and services they offer, as they have become aware of the need to build an online community around their brand, with magazines as diverse as *Elle* and *Car* maintaining discussion forums.

It is probably true that very few people ever read a newspaper or magazine from cover to cover, unless they are in a situation where no other activity is possible, such as on an aeroplane or in a waiting room. But it does seem that modern media encourage a 'butterfly' approach to gathering information, with the consumer moving freely and quickly between platforms and devices. The problem for media companies is to accommodate this constant flittering.

Contract publishing

A number of companies in other business sectors, such as retailers, car manufacturers and airlines, commission titles from **contract publisher's**, media companies that manage the design, production, advertising and marketing of the brand's promotional magazines and websites. This is a significant part of the media industry and, in 2009, there were 40–50 major contract publishing companies in Britain. The 2011 list of top British magazines, listed by circulation, was led by eight **customer magazines**, with nearly a third of the top 100 being customer titles.

Customer magazines' defining characteristic is that they are produced for a client, but the frequency of publication, number of issues, revenue sources and

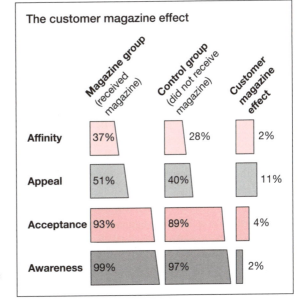

The customer magazine effect

	Magazine group (received magazine)	Control group (did not receive magazine)	Customer magazine effect
Affinity	37%	28%	2%
Appeal	51%	40%	11%
Acceptance	93%	89%	4%
Awareness	99%	97%	2%

Brands have a measurably stronger appeal and affinity among those who are exposed to a customer magazine. The analysis shows that the group which did receive the magazine felt the brand offered something more than its competitors and was therefore a more attractive proposition.

Source: Based on APA (Association of Publishing Agencies) www.apa.co.uk

Top 20 UK magazines, July to December 2011*

Ranking	Title	Total circulation
1	**Tesco Magazine**	**2,018,375**
2	**Asda Magazine**	**1,949,451**
3	**The National Trust Magazine**	**1,948,384**
4	TV Choice	1,304,382
5	What's on TV	1,253,697
6	**Tesco Real Food**	**1,220,503**
7	**Morrisons Magazine**	**1,150,937**
8	Radio Times	925,373
9	Take a Break	791,001
10	Saga Magazine	631,530
11	**Birds (RSPB)**	**608,851**
12	Pet People (Petplan Insurance)	531,387
13	Shortlist	526,359
14	New!	510,758
15	**John Lewis Edition**	**484,991**
16	Closer	467,048
17	Glamour	466,327
18	**ASOS.com**	**456,450**
19	Good Housekeeping	448,129
20	Stylist	429,034

*Customer titles are indicated in **bold**.

Source: Based on ABC

distribution methods vary. Contract publishing titles are often given away free in stores or can be sent out to regular customers by post without subscription, and they make up a significant proportion of the most widely read magazines. The practice of issuing printed publications without a cover price works for media and other companies, as advertisers can precisely target their audience. While the publishers and their clients may lose out on the income from a cover price, they gamble on the fact that a large-circulation free title will bring extra advertising revenue to cover any shortfall.

The variety of products being published in this area undoubtedly contributes to the sector's success, as does the connection to well-known figures, organisations and businesses. Many companies use celebrities to endorse their products or services, and personality-based promotional tie-ins are a significant feature of contract media products. These include editorial websites that offer company news, features and advice on how to use the product or service, and some also offer opportunities to take part in an online community. Supermarkets, in particular, tend to market themselves through their support for charity and local social initiatives and will use both their print and online media to try to encourage people to communicate and act through the brand.

As well as the online titles, there are a range of customer-directed print items. These can be glossy magazines, for example *The National Trust* and *BMW* magazines, or have fewer pages and a more mainstream look, such as the NatWest Bank's free magazine, the lifestyle title *Sense*, available to be picked up in a branch as well as mailed to existing customers.

Many high street stores and supermarkets place their magazines by the tills for shoppers to pick up and use the information gained from loyalty or store cards to target customers, often sending the magazine to them free of charge to encourage them to return. Such database information is important to contract publishers and their clients as many titles are mailed to their customers. Transport sector companies, such as airlines and railways, also commission publications that are given away free to passengers, although some

airlines have announced they will no longer follow this practice. The companies have stated that their decision was due to environmental concerns, as the extra weight of carrying a magazine for every passenger caused unnecessary fuel consumption.

The fact that the titles can be very tightly focused on a particular audience, and delivered in a way that directs them to those people, also helps to ensure they have a strong uptake among the intended readership. The BBC Customer Publishing Division produces a significant amount of revenue for the corporation. It handles short-run, prestigious magazines for English Heritage, among others, as well as free Christmas gift guides for retail companies with print runs in the millions.

Zone is a large contract publisher with a number of customer titles, including Jamie Oliver's magazine that is sold through newsagents and supermarkets. The lastminute.com 2008 summer magazine Zone produced to tie in with an advertising campaign was distributed to over a million people through Superdrug stores and as inserts in other publications. Another major player, River Publishing, runs *Weightwatchers Magazine*, which is sold through standard retail outlets and has a circulation of over 800,000. It also publishes Harrods' magazine, which is mailed out to 70,000 subscribers.

Inter-media links

A 2007 marketing survey by PPA and BMRB found that magazines and TV had a powerful role in driving people online. Of those questioned 50 per cent said they had gone online in response to a TV ad, 45 per cent had been motivated by a magazine and just over 30 per cent by newspaper advertising, with radio contributing another 17 per cent. Overall, 70 per cent of the respondents had visited a website as a result of seeing an offline sales message. Another finding was that, of the people who also regularly used the Internet, 58 per cent had made a purchase online as a result of seeing or hearing a TV, radio or print advertisement.

Jamie Oliver uses his website not only for his commercial interests but also to promote his personal philosophy and food reform campaigns.

Tesco Magazine website expands the role of a supermarket with editorial content that helps to build a sense of community among their customers.

New Scientist's website publishes daily news and uses multimedia to provide an enhanced resource and archive material for their readers.

The move to online

The trend towards multimedia suits some topics better than others, and it fits particularly well with those titles that cater for niche audiences. Music titles have seen their readers switch to online in parallel with the increase in music downloading and use of online music sites. One of the country's leading titles, *NME*, has seen its print readership decline, but its unique users (visitors who had clicked on a site or ad) figures had soared, mainly because a website can offer music fans so much more than just reading an article, as they can listen to music, watch videos of their favourite artistes, buy tickets and band merchandise or join a club.

At the start of the twenty-first century, the 'lads' mags' were a publishing success story, but most of them experienced a decline in print sales during the following years. However, the online lads' mag, *Monkey*, has seen an increase in its visitor numbers. It is very much a niche product and has always been innovative; it was one of the first websites to offer **mobile TV**. In February 2009, it had 283,541 unique users (UUs), more than the readership of its rivals *Nuts* and *Zoo* combined. The same year saw rival title *Maxim* moving to online only in Britain. The magazine had, at one time, been extremely successful in print, and the brand had been sold to several other countries, where it continued to be printed. One reason for *Maxim*'s decision might have been that the British lads' mag market had become overcrowded, as all the major media companies had launched products for the 18–30 young male readership, an audience of heavy media consumers that attracts lucrative

advertising. Another cause may have been that this audience is stereotypically gadget oriented and likely to be accustomed to new technology and devices.

However, reading printed publications has not yet died out. Newspapers seem to be losing out to real-time 'as it happens' reporting, media 'mashups' between devices and web services, such as including Google Maps to show the location of online news stories, and using software that can instantly analyse web survey data to highlight cultural or political trends. However, many people of all ages still like the tactility and portability of paper-based titles. Some US newspapers have moved their main reporting online, but run a subscription-only printed issue. It is likely that printed titles will continue to be issued for the foreseeable future, although there may be shifts in how they are funded and distributed.

Media consumers are continuing to purchase printed publications as well as use websites, whatever economic conditions apply at any one time. The media, when reporting on themselves, are sometimes overly dramatic and can tend to exaggerate the importance of progress in new areas, while too loudly bewailing their losses in bad times. The industry figures published since 2000 do show a decline in readership of most printed publications, in particular newspapers have shown a considerable drop in readership of their printed issues, but at the same time they have experienced a massive increase in online users. The Sun had 3.5 million readers in 2001 but numbers had dropped to 2.6 million by 2012. By contrast, newspaper websites have seen an exponential increase in visitors. In March 2012, the Sun's website was reported as having 24 million global

Preferred source of news by age group: 2006 and 2009

% age group	Television		Websites		Daily newspapers		Radio		Magazine		Sunday newspapers	
16–24	85	88	72	44	64	53	44	52	36	37	26	27
25–34	87	90	76	56	61	51	51	58	30	29	32	29
35–44	90	91	67	41	63	52	56	61	22	16	38	34
45–54	95	92	60	51	59	58	52	66	15	15	38	37
55–64	91	92	53	47	65	65	59	65	10	12	45	46

Key: █ = 2009 █ = 2006

Source: Based on McKinsey media and entertainment news surveys, 2006 and 2009

UUs. Similarly, the Daily Telegraph has seen a decline in print issue sales from 975,000 in 2001 to 576,378 in 2012, while its website visitor numbers for March 2012 were 46 million global UUs. Looked at this way, newspapers as a brand are far from failing organisations. In fact, the professionalism of UK journalism has vastly increased their worldwide audience.

A paperless future?

It has long been said that print will last because paper products are convenient to carry around and hand on to others – the success of free newspapers and magazines including many customer titles seems to support this. However, as relatively cheap, portable, web-linked devices with an easy-to-read screen become available and affordable, why should people continue to read old news, or carry yet another object around? David Carson, in an interview in 2003, wryly observed that his book, *The End of Print*, which was first published in 1995, was even then in its fifth edition. But as the Internet generation replace those that were raised on books and magazines, will print actually survive?

New ideas are being developed all the time and, in order not to be left behind, some news organisations have created communities of web developers working on **application program interfaces** (APIs) that look for ways to combine media and web technology. International news agencies such as Thomson Reuters offer support to developmental projects, and the BBC runs BBC Backstage, a platform that allows developers to discuss their concepts and helps to produce and publicise their ideas. The telegraph.com runs Telegraph Labs and has instigated an annual prize for the best idea. The first prize in 2008 was awarded to an API that combined *Telegraph* news stories with YouTube videos and Google Maps. The *Guardian* launched its Open Platform in 2009. It acts as a data resource archive and has an API that allows people to develop their own applications using *Guardian* content. In the USA, the *New York Times* is a leader in this field and also developed the 'data universe', an open resource for journalists to store and share information such as reviews, events listing and facts on public figures.

All the new developments and devices on the market at the time of writing, such as touchscreen camera phones with mini projectors that beam the screen image on to a wall, HD monitors that adjust their own colour balance and large-screen ereaders sold with direct trading links to booksellers or publishing companies, are intended to make technology more intuitive and simpler to use. The 2009 Apple iPhone advertising campaign emphasised its huge range of functions and how they apply to everyday life, such as apps that could find a local taxi, automatic calendar/contacts that sent someone an electronic note of an appointment, visual voicemail and video conferencing as well imaging and video.

On the Internet, Google had developed from a search engine into an online lifestyle platform, with a vast number of users worldwide, and is looking set to become the twenty-first century's Microsoft. Google uses an Internet model known as **cloud computing**. This concept is based on people using the Web as the infrastructure to access services and carry out functions, instead of buying their own costly programs. Google specialises in developing online products and systems that cover much of what a person might wish to do on the Web.

Technological futures

Companies are looking for opportunities to use new technologies and industrial processes to enhance and develop the media experience. There is talk of fabrics that could be 'Internet-ready', allowing connectivity through clothing, and futurologists foresee a connected digital world where all products 'talk' to each other and to us through BioIT – technology based on neurons rather than silicon chips. Our homes may be bio-synchronised and react to our moods or body heat to adjust wall colour using heat-sensitive paint, and will lower or raise the ambient temperature to keep us comfortable, and may be able to create a virtual environment or physical sensation triggered by a video or sound – some of the technology to do this already exists.

The Internet is promoted as being more environmentally friendly than printed publications. 'Save the environment' competitiveness is called green upmanship, and green marketing strategies are a driving force for change across the media and related industries. At present, IT devices are manufactured using heavy metals that are non-biodegradable and poisonous, and computers can be very energy-hungry. Research into future science and manufacturing is looking at ways to improve energy efficiency and lessen the environmental impact of the devices and technologies.

'If it works, it's obsolete.'

Marshall McLuhan, philosopher and writer

Technology round-up

- Fabrics have been developed that incorporate fine strands of metal that can generate electricity and could be used to power iPods, smart phones, etc.

- There are spectacles that contain cameras to record video page content.

- BioIT could be used to create a search engine for media consumers which selects editorial content, music and video to match their mood.

- Augmented reality is now being used to create real-time miniblogs for mobile phones, TV programmes, exhibitions, ads and children's iBooks with 3D animated pictures that project from the page.

- Multimedia entertainment systems on airlines offer on-demand movies, multi-player games, iPod, iPad and iPhone connections, and access to mobile media devices.

- Sky broadcast the first 3D TV programme in April 2009 and launched Sky 3D in 2010.

- Autostereoscopic 3D TV displays that can be viewed without special glasses are in development.

- Software has been created that can render classic movies into 3D.

- Web-compatible TVs, DVD and Blu-ray players have been launched by several major manufacturers that offer social networking, photo share, mobile phone connectivity with access to a range of web apps.

- Several Internet companies, such as Facebook, offer open source developer software that enables users to create their own apps.

- A new generation of 'sense and share' web apps for enhanced devices and utilities are in development. These will use the Internet in an interactive way, making contact to suggest actions or purchases based on your known preferences linked to your current location. For example, informing you where you can buy a particular item or find a local restaurant.

Source: Microsoft

Source: Romulo Oliveira

Source: Romulo Oliveira

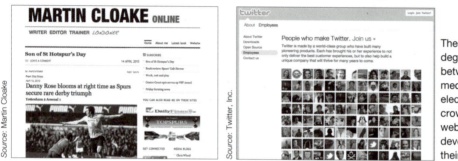

Source: Martin Cloake

Source: Twitter, Inc.

There is an increasing degree of convergence between the traditional media, communication and electronics industries and crowdsourced, open platform websites with many people developing and disseminating their own forms of media.

Microblogging and crowdsourcing

Microblogging is a smaller scale form of multimedia communication that can use the Web, text and instant messaging, email, video and audio to send very brief – 150 words or less – messages between the members of a user group. It is a marriage between the commentary of blogs and the real-time exchanges of texting. Twitter dominates this area, but does have some rivals around the globe as it is an English language service. Twittering became so popular that the *Guardian*'s April Fool's Day prank in 2009 was to announce that the paper was to be the first to issue its entire output as tweets. This was a sarcastic response to the growth in Twitter-based news searches and reporting, as the information on Twitter is basically personal comment. Twitter had become the fastest place to get first-hand information on what might be happening worldwide, but what was required was a system of verification, as the Internet is notoriously a playground for hoaxers. Yahoo's solution was to develop a Twitter-based news feed called TweetNews, which compared Yahoo's news results with the latest stories on Twitter.

The success of the medium has also led to Twitter search engines that displayed results based on real-time activity – termed the 'pulse' of the Web. The new form of search looks at **crowdsourcing** news from the 'Twitterverse' and lists the most recent entries first with contact details for the contributors. There are several Twitter aggregators, and Twitter search engines are interactive, allowing people to pick up a tweet and join in. Many websites, as well as 'celebs', media pundits and others, now offer Twitter links. In 2008, *Wired* magazine declared that the blog had had its day, as it has been overtaken by Facebook, Flickr and tweeting.

Ereaders tablets and smart phones

Ereaders are digital devices with the capacity to store content and an integral screen with a book-like display. Launched in 2007, the Amazon Kindle was one of the first ereaders to become commercially successful. It weighs much the same as a paperback but has the advantage of access to hundreds of titles. With the increase in commercially produced **epublications**, ereaders are likely to become more popular, especially among those who are more used to reading from a screen than on paper. In 2009, the Hearst Corporation announced its intention to introduce a large A4 or A3 ereader for use with its products.

Apple's iPad, a hand-held tablet computer, was launched in 2010. It combined the large screen of an ereader with all the facilities of Apple's successful iPhone. At the time of writing, the prediction was that the device might herald a boom and that sales of media tablets – aimed at those who read publications online – could total 57 million by 2015.

The argument about print portability may also not withstand developments in mobile technology, such as mini projectors that can beam a 127cm screen image on to a nearby plain wall or surface. The new generation of Internet phones have much larger, touch-activated screens, and Steve Jobs, the late founder of Apple, claimed that, while only 16 per cent of those who own a small-screen mobile with Internet connectivity use their phones to go online, 98 per cent of Apple iPhone users regularly access the Web.

Electronics companies such as Samsung are now producing mini projectors for mobile phones as well as phones with in-built projectors that enable the user to display an enlarged phone screen image.

Mobiles are seen as a very important area for future connectivity. During 2009, the first mobile film festival, MoFilms, was launched, and TV and video websites had already started producing **mobisodes** of popular programmes and films. Video-on-demand services have been introduced by most phone companies, and Sky+ remote recording is available on smartphones.

The mobile phone camera opens up other possibilities, such as the use of **2D quick response (QR) barcodes** that can be scanned from newspaper and magazines for instant access to a website. Another suggestion is that broadband video will begin to replace written information. People do prefer to talk face to face, and spoken instructions are often easier to follow, if not remember. HD pocket video cameras (PVCs) that can upload video directly to the Web are growing in popularity in parallel to video sharing sites. YouTube's advertising data for 2009 showed that its US site was receiving more than 50 videos per minute.

Some futurologists have stated that the days of mass marketing are over, and that **ultra niching** will take its place, with personalised marketing delivered to an individual's phone or tablet. Advertising market analysts now talk of **triple play campaigns** – print, online and mobile – as a given, with increasing evidence of **media creep** – online influencing print, mobile use spreading into films and TV, and user-generated content pushing through into the mainstream.

Augmented reality is beginning to take off, with applications available that combine text and pictures on a mobile phone to create **real-time placestream-ing** – a stream of content originating from a specific place that can be next door or on the other side of the world. The results can be posted on the **Live Web** through links to Twitterlocal and other livestreamed websites. Placestreaming can be used for news media websites as part of a local information service to record what is going on in a given area, and to provide livestreamed updates for real-time discussions on events, people and entertainment.

'There are four relevant media models: One-to-Many; Many-to-One; One-to-One; Many-to-Many. Of these, the One-to-Many or Broadcast model is the only one going down. The hot space now is Many-to-Many, the community of friends that is MySpace or Facebook. This need to express yourself is the defining experience for our future customers who are photo and blog driven.'

Nandan Nilekani, CEO, Infosys, 2006

Large screens display news content at London's Liverpool Street Station

Sharing the media

Media companies already have a role as mediators and are relied on as sources of well-regulated, accurate information. Such news and similar filtering services are expected to become more important, as most people appreciate that using an established company or organisation's website removes the necessity of sorting through the masses of online information. Magazines and other websites connected to older media forms already attract a global audience that knows they will provide familiar content, but the titles have to adapt to a new role as web community leaders.

The American Founding Father, Benjamin Franklin, who was a newspaper editor and printer, said only two things were certain, death and taxes, but change is also an undeniable constant. Newspapers have been authoritative sources for news and magazines have entertained or promoted trade for over 250 years. These print publications, as well as radio and TV stations, have made fortunes for press magnates, commercial broadcasters and ad agencies. But now the media, advertising and marketing industries must adapt to the Internet age.

The switch from an entrenched culture of informing people to one of sharing the responsibility of content generation with 'amateurs' is something that alarms many journalists. The breakdown of the concept of paying for news and other content is equally worrying for those trying to finance large companies with many employees. The question is not so much whether we will see the end of print, but whether traditional forms of media can survive at all.

The future is, perforce, an unknown quantity and there have been some spectacularly inaccurate predications over the years. An American banker refused engineering visionary Henry Ford's backing on the grounds that automobiles were just a passing fad. Lord Kelvin, the physicist who developed the Kelvin temperature scale, thought that flying machines heavier than air were a physical impossibility, and the 1970s president of DEC, an electronics firm that produced minicomputers, refused to take his company into the personal computing market as he could not see why anybody would want one.

Those who instigated the Industrial Revolution could not have envisaged the enormous technological and social changes that have taken place over the last 200 years. It is possible that the twenty-first century will see just as radical a shift in how we live and work. What this will mean for what we currently understand to be the media is open to the vagaries of what is to come politically, environmentally and socially, and only limited by the scope of human inventiveness.

Summary Design, technology and the future of the media

Design plays an integral part in publishing, advertising and related industries. It is used to support the brand identity of titles, create clarity of communication and attract media consumers. Creative directors, print and web designers and those involved in day-to-day design and production all play an important part in the creation of media products, and there is also a large number of specialists in areas as diverse as fashion styling, 3D computer animation and paparazzi photography that contribute to the look and mood of both print publications and websites.

- Print publications and websites need to have a clearly defined visual structure that can communicate complex sets of information and relay social meta-narratives.

- Web and print publication designers have to consider a media company's commercial and editorial requirements in order to create a distinctive visual identity that can become a marketable brand, and the design process for a media product can involve contributing to a corporate identity or fitting a new concept to a pre-existing brand family.

- The main aims of media design are to establish a visual structure and content form that will convey editorial information, bring in advertising and provide a consistent look for secondary trading materials, as well as offer entertainment and/or promote businesses and services.

- The media industry has a number of sectors such as national and regional newspapers, consumer and business-to-business magazines, and local publications with print titles, websites and connected operations.

- Media companies usually have subsidiary and partner business interests, such as radio and TV stations, and also generate income through tie-ins with films, live performance events, music and books.

- Anyone considering a media career in the second decade of the twenty-first century has to be able to multi-task as employers are looking for people who can work in all media.

- The media industry currently still has a number of specialist job titles and, on larger titles, a division of labour between print and online. Media companies also employ specialists who have particular art, design and software skills which fall outside the range of ability expected from in-house staff.

- Contract publishing firms design, produce and market the magazines for non-media companies, such as supermarkets, car manufacturers and airlines, and some publishers.

- The World Wide Web has transformed how and where people look for information and entertainment.

- The major media companies have set up digital publishing arms.

- The use of multimedia has led to a 'platform agnostic' approach – situating the story in the medium best suited to the content.

- The trend towards multimedia fits particularly well with those titles that cater for niche audiences.

- Newspapers have shown a considerable drop in readership over the last 10 years, but at the same time they have experienced a massive increase in online users.

- Media companies are looking for ideas on how to adapt their products to the Internet age.

Activities and development

Addressing the questions and action points below will enable you to assess the strengths of a range of current media and devices, and consider how design can help to communicate information, entertain and support interactions with an audience. You should examine how print and online titles balance the demands of technology against the need to provide attractive design and pertinent content. Visit the *Design for Media* website for more fact and action sheets, sample templates, type schemes and colour palettes at **www.pearsoned.com/hand**.

Questions

Question 1
Study a printed local paper and its website. Does the web offering undertake all the functions of the paper-based product? How might the loss of printed local and regional newspapers affect local politics and communities?

Question 2
Select one breaking news story and compare how it is covered in a number of media such as news websites, RSS (Really Simple Syndication) feeds, blogs, tweets, videos, podcasts, etc. What are the main similarities of presentation, and what adjustments have been made for the individual media?

Question 3
What future opportunities and threats might the convergence of news media create for journalists and others working on newspapers, news websites and news apps.

Question 4
What current and future technologies – including those not obviously related to publishing, advertising or marketing – might be integrated into media delivery?

Action points

Action point 1
Build a resource bookmark folder of websites whose design and structure you feel are particularly effective, and also collect printed magazine and newspaper pages that you consider to be well designed and laid out, and keep them in a ring binder for reference.

Action point 2
You are going to launch a new online fashion/lifestyle magazine based around exceptional-quality still and moving images from top photographers and film-makers. List the skills, for example what software your team would need to be able to use, the number of staff, freelance contributors and other resources you may require.

Action point 3
Select three electrical appliances in your home and consider how connection to a media product might enhance the usability and usefulness of each device.

3 CROSS-MEDIA PRODUCTION: PRINT AND WEB PUBLISHING

This chapter discusses:

- The digital revolution
- From paper to screen
- Computer design: the graphical interface
- Digital type
- Pre-digital page make-up – layout
- The introduction of desktop publishing
- Portable document formats
- Digital image processing
- A fundamental change in practice
- The digital learning curve
- The political implications of digital technology
- The birth of the Web
- Online media
- Web software
- Media trends

This chapter explains the developments in technology and computing that sparked the digital media revolution and instigated the terminology and work practices you will encounter today. It examines the continuing impact these changes have had on the media and how they have led to a shift in both the social standing and structure of the publishing and related industries. The information will help you understand why particular makes of computer and programs became standard for both for print and web production, and how the media industry has evolved and embraced new communication technologies.

'Never before in history has innovation offered the promise of so much to so many in so short a time.'
Bill Gates

'Whatever the device you use for getting your information out, it should be the same information.'

Tim Berners-Lee, World Wide Web founder

The digital revolution

When you come to work with print and online media, many of the processes you will encounter have evolved from pre-digital mechanical methods of production that were adapted for use with digital technology. Contemporary digital production has a direct relationship to previous technologies, and their influence still underlies the latest computers and software developments. Studying the background to current technology and how digital media work practices have developed will help you to gain the knowledge and skills you will need in your media career.

The first catalyst that started a fundamental change in the way the media worked was the microcomputing revolution of the 1970s. The introduction of the desktop computer has affected not only how media production is handled, but also how many people work on a title. Many of the areas that were formerly the responsibility of a skilled technician are now part of the day-to-day work any media employee may be expected to do. Those working in print and online production need to know the processes involved and how digital technology is used to prepare material for the media. Having said that, any digital device is no more than 'a means to an end' – a tool to be used to communicate. The technology is not important in itself; it is merely what you use to get your message to an audience.

The computerisation of the media started with the digitisation of the printing process and the introduction of desktop publishing. The devices and programs developed for print set the parameters for how media production hardware and software worked. The Apple Macintosh computer and Aldus PageMaker program were key to the development of a new way of producing titles that replaced the previous production processes. The second major wave of innovation was initiated in 1991, when Tim Berners-Lee developed the World Wide Web as a method of sharing simple word-based documents. The web design programs and browsers that were developed to make this new medium accessible were, to a large extent, based on the software designed for print publishing, and use many of the same terms and work practices.

Today's digital technology has made it necessary to work with a variety of media, as you may need to create, source or prepare material for cross-platform use. While there are still specialists in various areas, media convergence has made it increasingly important to have an understanding of underlying technological concepts and processes that will help you achieve a range of skills.

From paper to screen

Many of the work practices you will encounter have evolved from long-established methods that were used successfully in the pre-digital era. These have been adapted for use with digital technology; for example, cut and paste once literally referred to using a knife or scissors to cut out images and columns of type and pasting them on to a paper page template. The template would

1950	1960s	1970s		1980s	
Magnetic tape for computer storage	ARPAnet	Apple founded	Icon-based operating systems	Apple Lisa	Digital video
Mainframe computers	BASIC computer language	CD	Microcomputer	Apple PostScript laserwriter	Imaging and graphics softw
	Minicomputers	Digital audio	Microprocessors	BBC Micro	Inkjet printers
	Mouse	email	Microsoft founded	Computer typesetting	Laptop
	Satellites	Floppy disks	WYSIWYG software	Desktop publishing software	Microsoft MS-DOS
		Laser printer		Desktop scanners	Mobile phones
					Professional digital camera
					World Wide Web

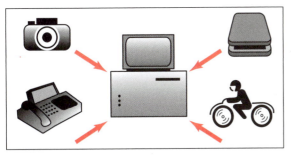

The visual information for early desktop publishing systems had to be digitised using a scanner. A media and printing company had to exchange all the material for page layouts by telephone, fax or motorbike messenger.

have been taped to a flat surface called a pasteboard that was used as a holding area for copy and pictures. This is why the white screen around a digital page that is used for the same purpose is called the pasteboard.

The computer industry targeted the media sector as the traditional production systems used were subject to restrictive work practices, and the process was expensive and time consuming. Digital technology offered the opportunity to streamline the process and reduce the cost and time involved in producing books, magazines, newspapers and other media. A huge raft of platforms, devices, operating systems, computer programs and digital typefaces were developed and launched in a relatively short space of time. However, the early desktop computers had far less memory processing capacity than modern machines. This limited the amount of work that could be on them at any one time, and the software could only handle simple page layouts and black and white pictures.

There was a large number of companies that began to offer new programs and devices, such as photo-editing software and digital scanners. These all worked

Online and print production computer programs, 1986–2010

Print publishing
FrameMaker, InDesign, InCopy, Office Publisher, PageMaker, QuarkXPress, QuarkCopyDesk, Ventura, PagePlus, Print Artist

Vector graphics
CorelDRAW, Expression Design, Fireworks, Flash, Illustrator, FreeHand, OpenOffice.org Draw, Microsoft Visio, Intaglio

Photo-editing and management
Aperture, Bridge, Jasc Paint Shop Pro, Photo Plus, Photoshop, Picasa, Zoner Photo Studio

Proofing and press ready
Acrobat Distiller, Acrobat Professional, Imposer

Text editing
SimpleText, TextEdit, NotePad

Web design
Amaya, Dreamweaver, GoLive, Firebug, Expressions Web, Panic Coda, Web developer (Firefox extension)

Blogging
WordPress, Moveable Type, TypePad, Blogsmith, Gawker

3D and animation
Maya, 3D Max, After Effects, Director, Sketchup Pro, Anim8or

Video and audio
Audacity, Audition, Final Cut Pro, Premiere Pro, Motion, Propaganda

This list covers the main computer programs used by the media industry. There are many others that may also be used and some larger companies have software developed for them.

1990s		2000s		
Apple QuickTime movies	MP3 players	Apple iPods/iPads	Online TV	Tablet computers
Broadband	Online magazines	Apple OSX	Livestreaming video and audio	Touchscreen
Browser software	Online newspapers	Blogging	Media players	Tweeting
Commercial and retail websites	Web design software	Bluetooth	Microblogging	USB drives
Dialup modem	Web file transfer	Broadcast 3D	Multimedia publishing	User-generated content
DVDs	Windows movie player	Camera phones	PDAs	Video hosting websites
HTML		Camera videos	Peer to peer sharing	Wi-Fi
		Cloud computing	Search engines	Wireless mouse
		Internet HD TV	Second Life virtual society	
		Smart phones	Social networking websites	

using their own software and were often incompatible with each other and the various computers and operating systems. The media industry soon found out that there had to be a degree of consistency in the computer technology chosen. The industry also discovered that it needed a system of agreed digital working practices, with everyone using compatible software, or production became well nigh impossible.

The introduction of new technology changed the way people worked. Production teams which were used to creating layouts drawn on paper templates, using photographic prints and hand-drawn illustrations, now had to grasp the idea of typefaces, images and pages existing as computer files. Companies also had to develop a way of organising material for managing these files, and the now familiar computer system of folders containing subfolders and files was developed to control storage and production work flow. They also needed to understand that the programs were developed to do particular tasks, and that these programs produced separate files for text, pictures and pages. The various makes of software did different things in different ways and, as with computer hardware, some file types would work together while others did not. The computer industry had to address this problem, and Adobe's invention of portable document format files that combine different file types into one file went a long way towards resolving the issue.

The icon-based operating system

One of the first personal computers was the Apple Lisa (1983), designed by Steve Jobs and Steve Wozniak. The Lisa's interface differed from other small-scale commercial computers at that time, as it was the first to use an **operating system** that employed a graphical interface – a white screen with a top panel of drop-down menus and icon-indicated files. Apple went on to use the graphical, icon-based operating system on the more powerful Macintosh range of computers.

Computer design: the graphical interface

Apple's visual, icon-based screen approach meant the user did not have to enter the complex keyboarded instructions needed by other systems such as Microsoft DOS. This held a strong appeal for artists and designers, as well as graphic and imaging software developers, and the Mac quickly became the creatives' computer of choice. The Apple operating system was intuitive and therefore easy to learn and use. The software was written using the terminology that designers and journalists were accustomed to: typesizes followed the traditional points system and the page shown on the

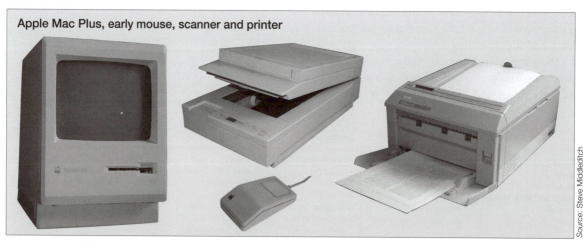

Apple Mac Plus, early mouse, scanner and printer

Source: Steve Middleditch

Three major breakthroughs combined to make desktop publishing a commercial success: small, powerful microcomputers with a user-friendly interface, laser printers that could produce accurate representations of the finished page or design and computer programs that were straightforward to learn. Other important developments included desktop scanners that could produce print-quality images, external media such as floppy disks, the larger capacity optical disks and external hard drives.

screen retained the use of grids, margins, columns and gutters (see Chapter 7). The early programs created for use on the Mac replicated established manual processes and allowed **typesetting** to be done by non-experts. The Mac's good image quality and technical flexibility made it a good platform on which to create design and edit images. The software made it possible for anyone to work with imagery, as pictures could be moved freely around the page on-screen.

Many of the programs in use today were orginally developed for the Apple Mac. For example, Photoshop was written on an Apple Macintosh Plus by Thomas Knoll and his brother, John, who was working for *Star Wars* producer George Lucas's company, Industrial Light and Magic. The program was licensed by Adobe and released for use on the Mac only in 1990, but was soon made available for the PC in response to market demand. Photoshop is now one of those products that are so ubiquitous their names are used as verbs, with 'to photoshop' being used to mean to **photomanipulate** (alter) an image.

Digital type

Digtal typesetting replaced the heavy industrial process of cast metal developed in the nineteenth century. Computer-based type represented a complete shift from the concept of **movable type** – using individual metal letters – that had remained much the same for

Letterpress typesetting used individual metal letters set in reverse, separated by blanks and by horizontal strips of lead that were placed in a locking tray called a forme.

Source: Kristian Bjonard, licenced under Creative Commons Attribution-ShareAlike 3.0 Unported

500 years. Computer typesetting started in the 1970s with a system called imagesetting that projected lines of type on to photographic paper. The results were not particularly accurate compared with cast metal type, but the process was quick and cheap. The type software created for desktop computers produced fonts that could match the quality of cast metal type, and the new programs such as PageMaker produced good-quality typesetting. However, the dot matrix printers used with early desktop computers were not able to print out type with smooth edges. The key development that made digital typesetting viable was PostScript (1984),

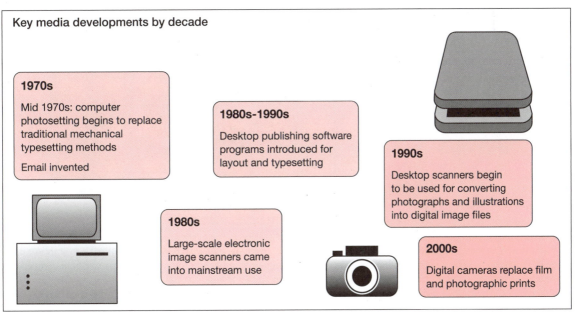

Key media developments by decade

1970s

Mid 1970s: computer photosetting begins to replace traditional mechanical typesetting methods

Email invented

1980s-1990s

Desktop publishing software programs introduced for layout and typesetting

1990s

Desktop scanners begin to be used for converting photographs and illustrations into digital image files

1980s

Large-scale electronic image scanners came into mainstream use

2000s

Digital cameras replace film and photographic prints

a computer language for desktop printers that enabled digital typefaces to look like traditional printers' metal-based typesetting. PostScript could be printed out as WYSIWYG – What You See Is What You Get – and it was a major factor in making computer production viable for the media industry.

The publishing, design and advertising industries were quick to realise that desktop computers and the new production programs could achieve a commercially usable result. The technology allowed media companies to purchase a wide range of licensed fonts from type manufacturers, which spared them the expense of professional typesetting. This was another impetus to adopt digital production, and the result was the swift demise of an entire sector of the production industry, as in-house desktop computers replaced typesetting companies.

The range of digital typefaces was quite limited to begin with, compared with the variety of traditional cast metal **fonts**, but once type designers and manufacturers realised the potential of computerised type design, hundreds and then thousands of digital

typefaces in software formats such as PostScript, TrueType and Bitmap began to be produced. Each individual computer had to have all the same make of typefaces installed, and, initially, typeface software was platform specific. This caused problems, as fonts produced for Macs would not work on PCs, or vice versa. In 2000, a new form of type software called OpenType was introduced that could be used on both Macs and PCs. Much of the media industry has now mostly moved from PostScript to OpenType following Apple's switch to Intel (Mactel) processing in 2005.

OpenType has resolved many of the problems associated with incompatible type software; however, typefaces are produced by a number of companies which produce their own software versions of classic typeface designs. Although these fonts may be called by the same name, for example Helvetica, there can be subtle differences that affect how they appear on a page. Operating systems and web browsers generate another set of type problems, as they display fonts in different ways. This led to the adoption of a set of 'safe' typefaces that are recommended for use on the Web.

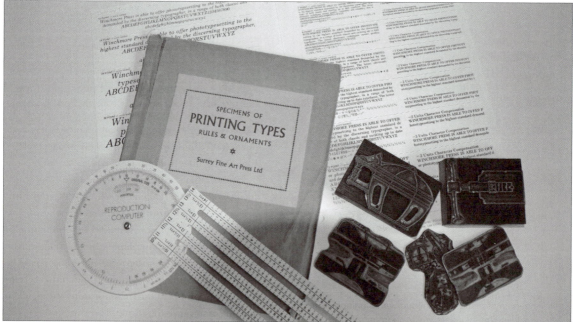

Source: Steve Middleditch

Graphic designers and layout artists would undertake a series of precise calculations to work out the area to be taken up by the type and images on a page. In order to do this, they would use type specimen books that contained examples of the range of typefaces held by a printing company, type depth scales that showed how many lines of type would fit vertically down a page, and image reproduction 'computer' wheels that were used to calculate the percentage enlargement or reduction of a photograph or graphic, which would then be etched on to a metal plate called a line or half tone black.

Pre-digital page make-up – layout

The digital page production process evolved from layout artists drawing page designs by hand with written instruction for typesetters. The typesetting company followed the layout and input the copy and turned it into type. They handled the photomechanical production that transformed hand-drawn page layouts into **press-ready artwork (mechanicals)** that were supplied to the printers. The typesetters would follow a publisher's layout that consisted of a page plan with hand-written **mark-up** instructions. The page plans would include the specification for the typeface to be used, its size and style, and the position of all the type, colour and pictures on the page. The type setting company would run the type as galley proofs, and process and size the photographs and other graphic elements to prepare them for print. Once the proofs were approved, the typesetters would cut out the galleys and pictures and paste them on a **grid** sheet (template). A large rostrum camera was used to photograph the press-ready artwork and the resulting film was contact printed on to paper as a **proof.**

Pre-digital copy flow

Using traditional methods, copy would first be subedited on paper for spelling, grammar, accuracy and sense, and to make sure it followed the house style for journalism before being supplied to the typesetter (see page 276). The typesetters would run galley proofs to be checked by their **proofreader** who would write in **proof correction marks** to show any type amendments. The galley proofs were then sent back to the publishing company to be used for page make-up. The layouts would be subjected to further checks, and the copy cut if there was any **overmatter** – text that did not fit on the page.

The whole process was very elaborate and time consuming, and often required several sets of revisions that had to be sent by messenger between the typesetters and the publishers. Every page went through this process, occasionally several times before it was **passed for press**. Page production was finally speeded up in the 1980s by the adoption of fax machines to transmit black and white proofs between typesetters and publishers. However, faxed proofs were notoriously hard to read and difficult to work with. Digital technology enabled media companies to replace many of these stages and keep production in-house.

The introduction of desktop publishing systems

The digital page make-up software written for the Mac and PC, such as PageMaker and QuarkXPress, made it possible for one person to create documents in which all the graphic material for a page could be assembled and prepared for print. QuarkXPress, which was launched in 1987, was adopted as the industry standard program for print publications. The program merged a range of layout functions with typesetting and the pre-press printing process. Both Aldus's PageMaker and Quark allowed designers far greater control when working with typography and images, which made it possible for them to produce a variety of design solutions on their own computer.

Paul Brainerd, the founder of Aldus, the company that had developed PageMaker, was the first to use the term desktop publishing (dtp) to describe the new method of digital production. Dtp software allowed people to make up pages quickly and easily at their desks. The programs were customisable and allowed titles to be set up in different sizes, and for type to be entered and manipulated. Digital image files could be

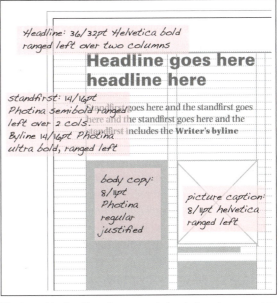

The layout instructions for every element of each page were marked up on a sheet of paper.

placed in picture boxes and sized to fit. Those providing the content could now work closely with the team or person preparing the title, or create the page themselves. The introduction of dtp meant that most of the text and layout could now be handled in-house and the digital content saved on a disk to be sent to the printing company by messenger or post. But it was still necessary for the printer and media company to exchange paper proofs. Despite some teething problems, the production process became considerably faster as digital technology was widely adopted.

Adobe InDesign and Quark are still the most commonly used page make-up programs for print, and essentially they work in the same way as the original dtp software. Additions to the programs include facilities for collaboration that let several people work on separate sections of a layout at the same time. The software now also has more graphic drawing and image editing controls. All media production software has gone through several generations of updates that have refined how it works, and today, due to the Internet and email, the programs are fully integrated into a print production work flow. Dtp files can now follow a path that runs directly from the editorial team to pre-press production and on to the printing company.

Portable document formats

The fast rate of change and uncoordinated adoption of digital technology led to a number of production problems. The large number of hardware and software developers all employed their own file formats when producing their machines and programs. As a result, digital production systems had to be able to handle all the different files needed to set up a title. Each page file had to be linked to type software, image and graphic files, all of which had to be kept together in a folder that was burnt onto a disk to be sent to the printing company. It only needed one missing or corrupted file to prevent a design from working and render the page unprintable.

In 1993, Adobe developed the portable document format (pdf), which resolved many of the problems caused by incompatibility and multiple program files. A pdf embeds all the separate files that make up a

digital design into one document that can be viewed on any platform. The pdf software programs, Acrobat Professional, Reader and Distiller, represented a major breakthough, as previously a digital layout could only be viewed in its source program and required the installation of the relevant typeface software. Acrobat Reader enabled people without the dtp software to view the page on-screen and to print the page without the specific fonts installed. Another innovation was that the pdf files took up little memory space and were suitable for transfer by high-speed phone lines.

Pdfs revolutionised the print production work flow, as now only a single file needed to be sent to the printer. Pdf files were a more secure method of sending pages than dtp files, as they were less vulnerable to either deliberate or accidental change after they had been passed for press (see Chapter 10, page 315). High-resolution pdfs are suitable for making printing film or plate. This made it practical for a media company to prepare all its own pre-press process work. The result was that the production process houses that had formerly handled the media companies' pre-press work were no longer needed.

Soft proofs and epublishing

Media companies seized on the commercial opportunities of the new format and began to use pdfs to distribute digital 'soft' proofs, which helped to speed up the production process. They also began to publish emagazines and enewsletters – pdf versions of their printed titles – and to launch new digital titles that were distributed via email or the Internet. This was the first step towards screen-based publishing.

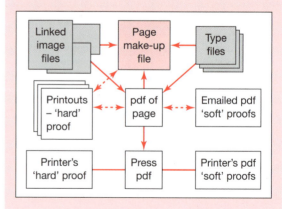

Digital image processing

Up to the late twentieth century, imagery had been prepared by process houses using a photochemical process that employed red, green, blue and gold (RGB) filters to separate each image into a set of black and white negatives (see page 247). This was another time-consuming and costly industrial process that involved hazardous chemicals and large-scale equipment. The first digital **drum scanner** was invented in 1957. Early drum scanners were large, extremely expensive machines that converted printed pictures or film negatives. The scanner used technology based on lasers to divide the image into four colour separations and could produce very good results when used by a skilled scanning operator (see *How to work with colour*, page 247). The cost of drum scanners and the technical complexity of scanning, sizing and cropping high-quality photographic imagery for print meant that picture production had to be handled by professional process houses.

An important element in the development of digital media production was put in place by Ray Kurweil, a scientist, author and futurist, who invented the first **flatbed scanner** (1975). The advantage of Kurweil's flatbed scanner was that it could be made at a small, desktop size, and it was soon in commercial production. The first desktop scanners were expensive, but large media companies invested in the equipment. In-house scanners brought another part of the production process under their control as the scanners could be used with imaging software to process pictures and graphics. Adobe Photoshop had become the imaging software of choice for the media industry, and some scanner manufacturers began to ship their products with the program already installed. Media companies began to expect their designers, production team and writers to be able to work with a computer, printer and scanner, and trained their staff to use dtp, imaging and production software.

The full digital integration of the production process came with the development of digital cameras that allowed images to be transferred straight to a computer. Digital cameras have largely replaced scanning images, and film-based cameras are now only used by specialist or art photographers. The ease with which pixel images can be uploaded/downloaded from the

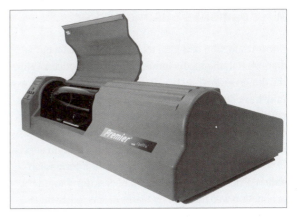

Publications and advertising agencies that require accurate colour and detail use drum scanners to capture extremely high-resolution digital imagery.

Source: Epson Europe B.V.

Publishing companies often use flatbed scanners to allow them to undertake more of the page production process in-house.

Internet has led to many pictures being sourced from online image banks and photo sharing websites. The evolution of digital technology since the mid twentieth century has led to the range of hardware and software that is used in-house by media companies to publish in print and online. It also means that those working on titles are now expected to carry the full responsibility of digital production, whereas, in the past, publishing was a cooperative effort that involved a number of specialist companies.

A fundamental change in practice

The introduction of digital technology caused a paradigm shift in the media industry's work practices. While the dtp programs, such as PageMaker and QuarkXPress, may have developed from older technologies and industry practices, media companies found they had to adopt different ways of working to accommodate the new production hardware and software. One of the main effects of the digital production process was **de-intermediarisation**. Prior to the introduction of desktop computers, production was handled by teams of specialists that included writers, editors, layout artists, photographers, illustrators, typesetters and printing companies that worked across several locations to produce magazines, newspapers and books. Digital production meant that these tasks were now done by a smaller number of people, based at only a few sites.

Digitisation fundamentally changed how the media worked. Prior to the introduction of computers, the industry had developed a solid tradition of disciplines and working practices that resulted from the industrial processes underlying print production. The way in which people worked was also tightly controlled by the rules on working conditions and hours enforced by the print, broadcast and journalism unions. While these working methods had occasionally been affected by changes in technology, those working in the industry in the mid twentieth century would have had a degree of control and certainty about the way they did their job, and might have expected to continue using much the same skills and techniques throughout their career.

For newspapers and magazines, the printing press set a pattern that regulated the lives not only of the typesetter and printers directly involved in the technical production process, but also of the journalists, production editors, layout artists, ad agencies and other contributors. The press schedules, which were strict and inflexible, worked backwards from the time and date the publication had to **go to bed** – be on the printing press. Work revolved around a fixed timetable that meant people knew what they should be doing, and when to do it by.

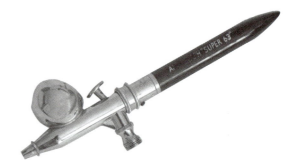

Pre-digital airbrushes used compressed air to create a fine ink spray that produced very subtle transitions of tone and colour.

Digital airbrushes have opacity and flow settings that can create a wide range of spray effects.

New tools, new roles

Many pre-digital specialists' roles were affected by the introduction of computer technology and programs. For example, the professional photographic retouchers who were employed to alter photographic images would have worked with mechanical airbrushes, paintbrushes and dyes. Today's digital image manipulators use Photoshop's Airbrush and Brush tools with image correction filters to edit pictures pixel by pixel. Adobe Illustrator and other graphic programs have taken the place of the print finished artworkers who specialised in translating rough sketches for diagrams and charts into highly finished pen and ink camera-ready artwork. The programs are also used by illustrators, many of whom no longer paint or draw by hand. The technology makes it possible for anyone to produce high-quality photographs and graphics and has led to a new culture of image creation.

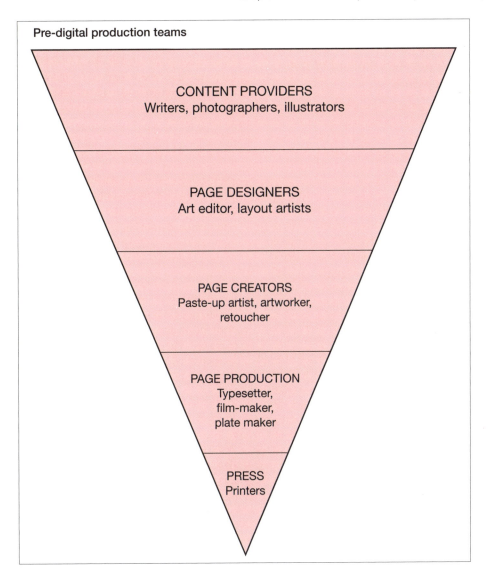

Pre-digital production teams

CONTENT PROVIDERS
Writers, photographers, illustrators

PAGE DESIGNERS
Art editor, layout artists

PAGE CREATORS
Paste-up artist, artworker,
retoucher

PAGE PRODUCTION
Typesetter,
film-maker,
plate maker

PRESS
Printers

The digital learning curve

A popular dictum of the 1980s was that dtp 'placed the means of production in the hands of the designer'. This was undoubtedly true, but involved what was called, half seriously, 'a steep learning curve'. The skills that a designer or page layout artist had previously required – type cast-off techniques, drawing with a pencil or Rotring (a fine ink cartridge pen) and pasting up finished artwork/mechanicals (artwork ready for the camera) – were no longer needed. The new publishing and imaging programs allowed pages to be built on-screen to a finished level.

Journalists, designers and people working on production had to learn a new set of skills, starting with discovering how to use a mouse. Looking at a page on-screen and typing with a computer keyboard was a completely different experience from working directly on a sheet of paper. The new digital production systems required an understanding of the virtual space in which people now worked, and they needed to know how to organise digital files and folders and be able to cooperate in a virtual environment using a centralised computer system called a server – an entirely new concept.

'I'm a catalyst for change. You can't be an outsider and be successful over 30 years without leaving a certain amount of scar tissue around the place.'

Rupert Murdoch, proprietor, News International

The political implications of digital technology

By the 1970s–1980s, the trade union movement was strongly entrenched in the printing industry. The print unions ran a 'closed shop' – all printers, plate makers and typesetters had to join a union in order to get a job, and unionised printers were reluctant to handle work from non-union sources. This gave unions such as the National Graphical Association (NGA) and the Society of Lithographic Artists, Designers & Process Workers (SLADE) considerable influence over the media industry. Probably apocryphal tales were told of printers' 'Spanish practices' (a corruption of established practices). It was alleged that jobs were handed down through families and that there were companies that employed two people for some jobs to allow one always to be free to attend union chapel meetings. What is certain is that, in the aggressive political atmosphere of the Thatcher era (1979–1990), there was considerable resentment between the media companies' management and the journalism and print unions that were seeking to protect their members' jobs, some of which would be threatened by computerisation. The media companies wanted to introduce new technology and practices; the unions wanted extra money for their members who would have to retrain to use the new systems and change their ways of working.

In the 1980s, there was a growing realisation that change was inevitable if the media industry was to survive. Many companies negotiated 'new technology' agreements with the unions; however, some media industry figures sought ways to circumvent the unions and speed up the introduction of digital technology. These included Eddie Shah, who published *Today*, the first digitally produced newspaper in Britain, and Rupert Murdoch, both of whom introduced new computerised systems without an agreement with the unions. In 1986, Rupert Murdoch moved *The Times*,

Sunday Times, *Sun* and *News of the World* newspapers literally overnight to a new location in London's dock-lands, simultaneously sacking 5,000 employees. This led to, at times, the violent and prolonged clash with the unions known as the 'Battle of Wapping', which became the most notorious of several disputes over the introduction of digital publishing. The situation continued for 13 months, and the final outcome was seen as a defeat for the print unions as it greatly diminished their power over the newspaper industry.

The unions' reduced influence resulted in many changes. For example, the job of page layout and type-setting moved from being the sole province of print unions to being carried out by members of the National Union of Journalists (NUJ), and then became the work of non-union designers and computer operators. The end of the unions as a significant political force, and the liberalisation of their enforced working practices, freed the media companies and the pace of digitisation increased. There was a drop in the number of people needed to work on a title and the conditions they worked under changed beyond recognition. However, the rise of digital media has created new opportunities for careers in the industry.

'Rupert Murdoch's justification for the sudden move to Wapping and the brutal sacking of 5,000 of his workers was the claim that this would give back to journalists their editorial freedom and the right to be creative and independent. Whilst there were some initial benefits from the computerised access to front end single key-stroking for the input of copy, over the passage of time journalism has become a factory process. The real benefit and freedom of the Murdoch-led changes has been the capacity of proprietors to make more profit and indulge in price wars with each other and create anti-competitive mergers. This is what has led to today's crisis in the media. Editors in particular have lost their independence and are now seen as business managers for the accountants and the current proprietors who, in the main, are only interested in maximising profit and destroying competition.

Today's journalists have seen their profession degraded with a production system that controls them rather than facilitates the news that good journalism demands.'

Barry Fitzpatrick, head of publishing, National Union of Journalists

The birth of the Web

The World Wide Web has grown exponentially since Tim Berners-Lee, who worked at CERN in Switzerland, launched it as a free worldwide service in 1991. Berners-Lee had a radical vision for his invention; he wanted it to be free and available to all. The first **software browser**, MOSAIC, developed by Marc Andreesen in 1993, was also free and its creators were dedicated to open source – sharing the technology behind a web invention. However, the media industry, along with many others, were more interested in this new method of communication for its revenue-generating possibilities. The development of commercial WYSIWYG picture-based web browsers, such as Netscape and Internet Explorer, created the opportunity for web publishing. However, at first, the main print-based publishing companies were dismissive of the new media, and it was mostly entrepreneurial and creative individuals who began to exploit its potential.

The Web's global reach made it the obvious place to publish, and throughout the 1990s a large number of online titles were launched. The challenge for these websites was the same as for print – how to make money. From the beginning, there has been a clash between the libertarian origins of the Web and those seeking to exploit it commercially. Media companies found that most users expected free access to a website's content and that online advertising needed a different approach in order to attract attention. A number of the early online media titles failed because some companies, used to the rhythms of print publishing, struggled with the speed of the online world. They were slow to adjust to the concept that content and advertising had to be constantly updated. The Internet boom of the 1990s saw many companies investing heavily and rushing to set up on the Web. A large number of these ill-thought-through ideas that had no real market potential collapsed spectacularly in 2001, in a giant 'dot.com crash'. The 'bricks and mortar' companies bought up the best of the online ventures and went on to use their expertise to establish an effective Internet presence.

(a)

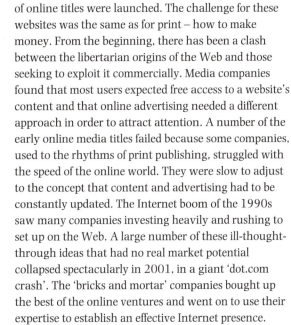

(b)

(c)

Source: eBay Inc.

Source: Facebook Inc.

(a) eBay, founded in 1995 as AuctionWeb, is a pioneering Internet company and one of the notable survivors from the first wave of commercial web ventures.

(b) Google was launched in 1998 and has expanded from providing a simple search engine to supplying a comprehensive cloud-computing-based resource.

(c) The social networking site Facebook was founded in 2004, and by 2011 had grown to include 75 million active users worldwide.

The most successful websites have achieved a global influence and become embedded in how people consume media and communicate socially. These companies have expanded their commercial model, enabling advertisers and marketers to interact with a vast audience.

Online media

Media companies had begun developing an online presence in the 1990s, but it was only at the start of the twenty-first century that they really began to grasp the fluid and communicative nature of the Internet and many stopped leveraging existing print material. It became obvious that publishing on the Web was significantly different from print. Media companies that had been used to issuing information at fixed intervals struggled to find a working model that could cope with continuous updating and with presenting information in a non-linear, interactive manner.

The real move towards online media began once fast Internet connections became widely available. The digital publications that have survived from the early days of the Web are those that keyed into the new digital world, such as *wired.com*, which still provides information on the latest science and technology, software and gadgets. *Salon.com* was one of the first online titles to realise the potential of linking news media and cultural interests to interactive discussion, and it has become the model for many current media websites and blogs.

The major differences between web and printed content was, and still is, the connectivity between web pages that made online navigation fluid and multidirectional, and the enormous advantages offered by moving images and sound. As interest in web publishing grew, software developers started to produce web programs that could be used to create websites and pages without the need to employ specialist computer programmers. Many of the new websites followed the conventions of printed titles, and it took the best part of a decade before video and audio became fully integrated.

Web software

A number of web authoring and management programs have been developed over the years to handle animation, multimedia graphics, sound and video editing. In 1996, a US company, Macromedia, launched Flash, a web animation package, and Dreamweaver, a web design program. These were WYSIWYG programs that allowed non-specialists to create web pages and prepare

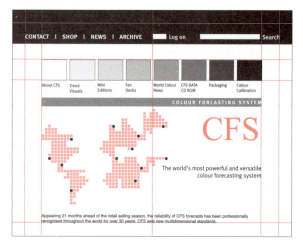

Traditional media companies were quick to establish an online presence. The design of their websites relied heavily on existing content and they were slow to introduce specific Web content, especially interactive elements, and many early online titles and enterprises failed to attract an audience or make money.

content for websites. The user did not have to be able to write computer code – although it was still necessary to know coding basics to sort out bugs. Dreamweaver was intended for designing websites, but media companies soon found that they required a more efficient program to update content on a day-to-day basis.

Media companies also discovered that websites could be expensive to run and maintain, and began to look for ways to standardise page production. Many had chosen not to develop or design their own websites, but commissioned them from outside specialist web companies that better understood the technology.

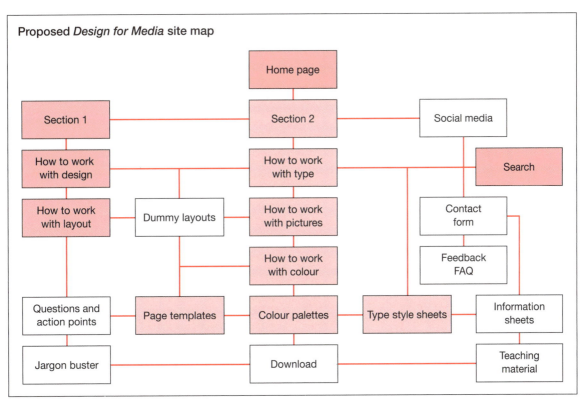

Proposed *Design for Media* site map

It is essential to draw up a site map before the website build begins that will allow people easily to access the content.

These web experts charged considerable fees for their services, which included web hosting businesses, IT maintainance and programming. The media companies wanted a way of producing pages that retained the structure of their website once it was launched, but they also needed an in-house system that would allow the page content to be altered quickly and economically. Several entrepreneurial web companies saw an opportunity to market programs, customised for each website, called **content management systems** (CMSs). These are individual software solutions that enable writers, editors and in-house web production teams to upload content into pre-set page templates.

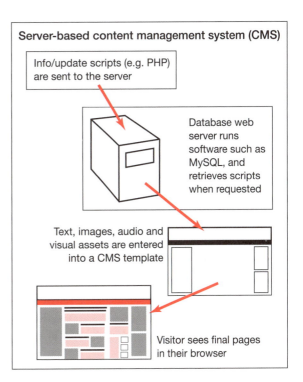

Server-based content management system (CMS)

Info/update scripts (e.g. PHP) are sent to the server

Database web server runs software such as MySQL, and retrieves scripts when requested

Text, images, audio and visual assets are entered into a CMS template

Visitor sees final pages in their browser

Media trends

Early websites consisted of little more than text and a couple of pictures, with a simple navigation system. Today, such a basic-looking site would not attract an audience, no matter how worthy the content. There is conclusive evidence from monitoring services, such as the government's National Statistics Office and Ofcom, that shows that the generation who have grown up with the Web expect different things from online media compared with their parents and grandparents. They are known to find static ink on paper dull and the 'refresh rate' unbelievably slow. Digital natives are used to communicating through social media, and interactivity has become the established norm.

The introduction of faster broadband connections has had an enormous impact on web media. By 2009, the major newspaper websites in Britain were receiving more hits in a day than their print co-editions sold in a week, and some US papers had taken the decision to drop their print issue altogether. Modern newspapers are now run from multimedia digital newsrooms with rolling deadlines throughout the day. Major stories run through from a ticker display to RSS feeds for breaking news, and are then issued as detailed reports or covered in longer features in web and printed media.

The advertising and marketing industry is also moving away from traditional methods of reaching an audience towards running online-based **viral advertising** campaigns – the first truly digital methods of marketing and selling. The success of viral advertising and the phenonemon of cultural events spread by social networking software have convinced advertisers of the power and reach of the Web. The tipping point was 2009, when online and cross-media advertising campaigns first generated more revenue than any other media.

There are wider changes in social attitude and behaviour that have been brought about by technological advances. Print, TV, film and radio are now described as traditional media, and while these platforms still have an audience of millions, they are increasingly being used to complement rather than compete against online media. The established broadcast and publishing companies are developing long-term strategies that will enable them to converge their print, broadcast and online titles.

The Social Web 2000–2010

- **YouTube**: 1 billion videos watched each day, with aproximately 20 hours of video uploaded per minute
- **Facebook**: 600,000 people join each day; 700 million photographs and 4 million videos are uploaded each month
- **Twitter**: 80 million new users gained in a year and 50 million tweets sent each day
- **Second Life**: £170,000 worth of virtual goods handled per day and 1250 text messages generated per second
- **Flickr**: 73 million visitors and 700 million photographs uploaded each month
- **Google**: 2 billion searches each day of IT URLs
- **Wikipedia**: 684 million visitors each year, 10 million articles in 260 languages
- **Mobile social networks**: had 92.5 million subscribers to the main companies in 2008; this figure is predicted to rise to 800 million by 2013
- **SMS**: over 2.3 trillion messages handled by the major networks during the year
- **Social network trading**: £3.6 billion spent on virtual goods in 2008–2009
- **Blogs**: 33 million blogs since 2002 have been indexed by Technorati, the organisation that monitors the blogosphere; blogs are read by 77 per cent of active Internet users and there are on average 900,000 blog posts each day, written in 81 languages

Sources: Gary Hayes' social media count, Technorati, Comscore

Source: Gary Hayes

Visit *www.personalizemedia.com/garys-social-media-count/* to see the count in action.

Video content

Media companies are increasing the amount of content they provide as moving imagery, and if you work on a website you will be expected to be able to upload videos and embed links to video hosting sites. Video has become central to most people's online experience and website users have come to expect a high level of interactive and video content. Research has found that people place more trust in websites that feature a range of contemporary media, and can consider those that do not keep up with the latest Internet trends to be less successful or untrustworthy. This makes it very important that generating and updating video content are considered as vital and that you have the skills needed to handle moving images.

> **TIP** A video's HTML (Hypertext Markup Language) coding or URL can be copied and pasted into a web page; however, CMS and web design software may require the video's URL or HTML coding to be inserted via an assets management menu or window.

> **Warning** It is important to check the copyright status of a video before grabbing it from a video hosting site.

'Regardless of who your audience is, chances are at least some of them are on Facebook or Linkedin or on another social media site.'

Jennifer Snyder, senior inbound marketing specialist, HubSpot

The influence of social media

The most important change brought about by communications technology is the huge increase in the use of social media. By 2010, visiting social networks and blogs was the fourth most popular Internet activity and had overtaken email as the most frequently used form of online interpersonal communication. All the social networks have shown an expotential leap in numbers of users. Facebook gained over 400 million worldwide users in the six years since its launch, with over 100 million joining in 2009 alone. The social media commentator, Gary Hayes, has set up a social media count on his blog that monitors the Social Web and gives a second-by-second update of how many new blog posts are being made, the number of people joining Facebook, videos being watched on YouTube, money spent online, etc. In Britain, a survey found that a third of all adults were active on a social site at least once a week and a quarter regularly published a blog and uploaded audio/visual

Most heavily used web brands in the UK 2008–9

Rank	Brand	Total UK minutes (millions) April 2009	Total UK minutes (millions) April 2008
1	Facebook	6,160	2,385
2	MSN/Windows	4,463	3,369
3	Google	2,560	1,610
4	eBay	1,978	1,672
5	Yahoo!	1,719	1,133
6	AOL Media Network	1,462	1,060
7	BBC	1,129	759
8	YouTube	898	648
9	Microsoft	733	660
10	Apple	719	554

Source: Based on Nielsen Media

Communication and entertainment websites accounted for the most UK time spent online, with the amount of UK time spent on Facebook increasing by 3.8 billion minutes – from 2.4 to 6.2 billion.

content. Overall, nearly 60 per cent of the population had set up a profile and 70 per cent read blogs, tweets and watched User-Generated Content (UGC) video.

The publishing, broadcast and advertising industries have found ways to work with social media and to exploit its interpersonal connectivity and immediacy by including links to Facebook, Twitter and Digg, and encouraging their writers, contributors and visitors to run blogs and twitter feeds. Advertisers and marketeers are also increasingly exploiting social media. In Britain, No Smoking Day, a national charity, has developed a Facebook application, WeQuit, to help people stop smoking, and Volkswagen ran a competition to find a 'people's reviewer' that began with YouTube video auditions, with contestants encouraged to build up a following on Twitter, Facebook and Flickr in support of their entry.

The challenge for media companies is to provide users with better or different media than they can create for themselves. There is likely to be an ongoing shift in the boundaries between formal and personal media, and as someone working in the communications industry you should be prepared for technological change and able to adapt your skills to work with 'the next big thing'.

UK men's magazine websites, average unique users each month, 2009

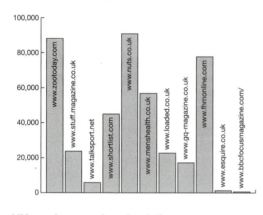

UK women's magazine websites, average unique users each month, 2009

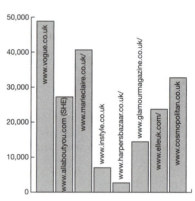

UK men's magazine circulation year-on-year comparisons, January–June 2008 to January–June 2009

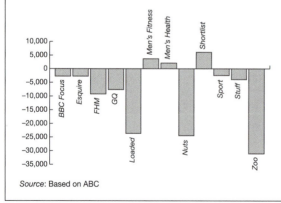

Source: Based on ABC

UK women's magazine circulation year-on-year comparisons, January–June 2008 to January–June 2009

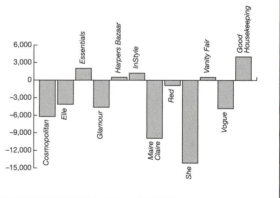

The graphs show the number of individual visitors – referred to as unique users (UUs) – per month to a publication's website, with the circulation figures for the equivalent print issue compared year on year (YOY) over a given period, for example January to June.

Summary The development of desktop and web publishing

The introduction of desktop publishing led to a paradigm shift in working practices for the media and related industries, but the transition from the previous technology and working systems was not always smooth, as there were a number of social, political and technical issues that had to be accommodated or overcome. The changes in the media caused by the introduction of new hardware and software have continued over the last three decades and show no sign of decreasing. Those working in the media have to be ready to learn new skills and adapt to the impact of the latest technological innovation or Internet trend.

- The pioneers of digital technology created personal computers and other office or home-based devices such as scanners and printers that put the means of production into the hands of designers, publishers and advertisers.

- The pre-digital print production process involved a large number of people in specialist businesses as well as those employed by the media company. The introduction of desktop publishing reduced the number of people needed as the new computer programs allowed one person to set type, create or edit images and lay out pages on a single computer.

- The early picture-based Apple Mac became, and remains, the computer of choice of designers, artists and film-makers and is used throughout the creative and media industries because the first PCs lacked a graphical interface.

- Software companies have continued to develop design, imaging and digital type programs for both print and online. Adobe's portable document format (pdf) files led to a major change in the digital production process as the software can embed all the information from any other program used to create a document into one single file.

- The development of image-based web browsers made using the Internet viable for media products, and many companies began to exploit the potential of the platform by setting up web titles.

- The demand for websites with the same design criteria as print titles led to more advanced web design programs being developed.

- Use of the Web has grown rapidly since the introduction and general takeup of broadband, and the Internet has now replaced print as the dominant media and advertising platform.

- Social media have grown exponentially with social networking and user-generated content becoming integral to media websites.

- All media are now becoming convergent, and journalists, designers and others working in related industries need to know how to handle cross-media production.

Activities and development

The questions below relate to the subjects covered in this chapter and will help you develop your knowledge of the media industry. The action points are intended to provide you with investigative projects that will aid your understanding of media products. You should carry out active research and take notes before preparing your answers. Visit the *Design for Media* website for more fact and action sheets, sample templates, type schemes and colour palettes at **www.pearsoned.com/hand**.

Questions

Question 1
Name 10 of the key technological developments that have led to modern digital publishing.

Question 2
What pre-digital technologies and practices did a typesetter use to produce pages for print before the introduction of desktop publishing?

Question 3
How has the introduction of the Web changed how, where and when the media publish news and current affairs?

Question 4
Explain how the development of the Social Web and introduction of mobile Internet devices and software apps changed the way in which media companies interact with their audience.

Action points

Action point 1
Consider where you obtain news information from: compare the depth of coverage of a major news story between the website and print version of one title. Which carries most information and which gives you the most immediate impression of events?

Action point 2
Carry out an online search to obtain audited data on the print edition circulation and website visiting rates of a national newspaper. Do the figures indicate a clear audience preference for either medium?

This information can be obtained from articles on ABC (ABCe) rates that are regularly carried by the Media Guardian and the UK Press Gazette, amongst others.

Action point 3
Choose a feature from an online or digital magazine and note how the items listed below have been employed. Compare the contents with an article on the same subject from a printed magazine. Look particularly at the presentation including the use of imagery, the writing style for headlines and introductions, and the overall amount of copy.

   Logo/masthead

   Headlines

   Placement and sizing of images

   Text placement

   Length of copy

   How content has been highlighted or emphasised

   Captions and picture credits

   Navigation, menus, buttons and hyperlinks

   Video, music and podcasts

Answers to questions

paste-up, marked up proofs by hand, early computer typesetters.

Typesetting machine, type galleys, photomechanical prints of photographs, graphics and illustrations, paper layouts for

Question 2

software, desktop publishing software, imaging software, digital type, PostScript printers, desktop printers.

(PC, keyboard, mouse, GUI operating systems, icon-based software, desktop scanners, computer typesetting, WYSIWYG

Question 1

4 PRE-PLANNING A PUBLICATION AND WEBSITE

This chapter discusses:

- How to launch a new title
- Marketing research – perceived values
- Funding, distribution, promotion and advertising
- Revenues and budgets
- The role of advertising
- Developing new media products
- Planning designs for print
- Launching a new print product
- Setting up a website
- Website design
- Usability testing
- Going live
- E-zines and newsletters

This chapter examines how print and online media products are devised and taken through the early stages of market research and concept development. It also describes the planning stage and actions required to initiate a new publication. It covers who you might expect to work with on creating new titles and explains the design and technical criteria that have to be considered when setting up dummy versions and prototypes, and the stages involved in preparing a product launch.

'Design is not just what it looks like and feels like. Design is how it works.'

Steve Jobs, joint founder, Apple Inc.

'Design is almost unique in reconciling realities and the zeitgeist of cultural behaviour in a way that connects finance, manufacturing, marketing, brands and strategy.'

Sir Christopher Frayling, writer, broadcaster and critic

Launching a new title

The media industry is one of the most competitive businesses in the world and many new print publications, websites and other digital titles are launched on to the market each year. The sector seeks to identify new trends that may present the commercial opportunity to launch titles that will attract readers or visitors and generate advertising revenue. In order to develop titles, media companies undertake research into potential markets and business areas. They will react to changes in consumer behaviour, such as the increase in downloading and growing interest in environmental concerns. Social trends and cultural interests have traditionally been supported by media titles; for example, gardening titles now present growing vegetables as a green lifestyle activity. The business sector also presents opportunities to launch new business-to-business (B2B) titles that cover a wide range of areas such as management, manufacturing, marketing and services. The large media groups are constantly looking for ways to increase their revenues but will only launch titles that they predict can produce a GPP (Gross Publishing Profit – the money left after all overheads have been deducted). Major companies often prefer to launch into an established market, while more entrepreneurial individuals and smaller companies are prepared to start up ventures that reflect personal interests and ambitions. The large media groups keep an eye on the non-mainstream titles and, once they have become successful, will often purchase the magazine or website. However, large organisations can find it hard to maintain the editorial ethos of an alternative

lifestyle title, and even new titles that may have run for some time may fail and close as fashions and interests change and technology advances.

This chapter describes the processes involved in developing a concept from the planning stage through to introducing the product to its audience. Most media companies look to those working for them to initiate new ideas to support established titles and to suggest ideas for possible launches. If you work in the media as part of an editorial and production team, you may be expected to become involved with handling the development of a new print or online product. Alternatively, you may intend to create your own specialist title on a topic of personal expertise or interest and decide to set up the title yourself. This chapter explains why media ventures need to be based on a strong editorial and commercial concept that can become the basis for the design brief. It also looks at the key stages involved in developing a successful visual treatment for the relevant technology, production criteria and intended commercial outcome.

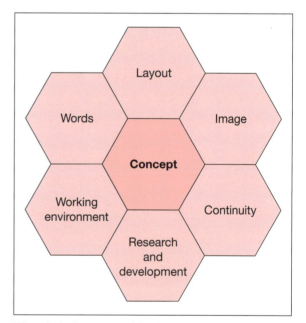

When designing a new publication concept you need to ensure that a number of key areas are taken into consideration; most importantly, the look, budget and resources and the production environment.

Pre-planning a title

A newspaper, magazine or website is as much a commodity as a tin of baked beans, but it is also a social concept and a conveyor of thought. It is the design of a title that gives it a unique identity and enables it to communicate its particular editorial ethos. The materiality of a print publication and the connectivity of a website have to present an unequivocal message to the reader or visitor. The design process will require practical decisions to be taken, such as on the content, organisation and information structure. However, every action has to be linked to a reader's or visitor's perception and expectations of the title. As the format for a title is developed, every page must convey the values and authority of the media company, as well as offer an enjoyable experience for the audience and provide advertisers with the business advantage they expect. The challenge for those planning a title is to create a cultural entity that will fulfil the required ideological, practical and financial criteria, as well as work across media and in different locations.

There is a number of decisions that have to be made before starting on the design and technical development of a title. The nature and range of the contents is key, in particular the main subject area and topics to be covered, and whether these can generate enough advertising revenue and sufficient editorial material to make the title sustainable. It is also vital to have determined which media it is to be published in – print, online or both – and the frequency – how often it will be issued or updated. Any project needs to start by establishing the parameters of the media product, such as what the focus is – information, entertainment, instruction or commerce? The cultural message – what will give this title a unique identity? The intended impact on the reader or visitor – is it meant to trigger an emotional response, provoke action, influence behaviour or change ideas?

All new titles are expected to have cross-media links, and any new media concept should feature multimedia content or develop spin-offs and take advantage of related promotional opportunities. It is now very rare to find a magazine or newspaper that does not have both a print and online version, and many use audio and video as well as have their own

Globalisation and international editions

In today's media industry, it is common to find titles that are produced internationally, for example *Psychologies*, a magazine that started in France and is now produced in several European countries. The advantage for media companies producing multi-country issues is that they can spread their production costs, by adapting the same content and supplementing it with material produced by a small local editorial and advertising team.

Many leading women's titles are published in a number of different languages and countries. In this case, it is the brand name that crosses borders rather than the content, which is normally regionally specific as cultural interests and fashion taste vary. *Cosmopolitan* magazine has 58 international print editions with readers in more than 100 countries and is published under licence in 34 languages. The brand also exists as Cosmo websites, *Cosmo Girl* magazine, Cosmo Radio and three Cosmo TV stations. Other magazine brands with a global presence include *Grazia*, first launched in Italy, which is published under licence in 11 countries, and French titles *Elle*, which has 39 international print editions and websites in over 20 countries worldwide, and *Marie Claire*, which is issued in 29 countries.

online TV channel and mobile device delivery. The rapid pace of change in technology means that any plan needs to be flexible enough to adapt, as readers and visitors are increasingly able to access media products through a range of devices.

The Internet and digital printing techniques have made it much cheaper and easier to produce specialist interest publications, which has enabled titles to make a profit in a shorter amount of time. This has led some media companies and entrepreneurs to take the approach of looking for a gap in the market and launching a publication that may only run for a year or two, rather than looking for an idea that will still be in existence in many years' time. Digital printing also means that high-quality magazines can be produced for very small personal interest groups, and this has fuelled the growth in customer magazines. Media companies and others may now factor in a degree of redundancy and this would affect how a title's design and production processes are planned.

Initial market research: establishing a USP

Media companies use market research to identify a market and to create a profile of their target readers and/or visitors. The media companies' marketing departments or specialist companies, such as Mori and Gallup, may be responsible for carrying out the research. Potential readers' and visitors' interests and opinions are garnered using interviews and questionnaires designed to test the market, and to determine what the audience might want from a media product. The data gathered will be analysed and used to decide whether the basic idea is feasible. If the concept goes ahead into development, the readers' and visitors' profiles and market analysis become the criteria used to decide how to align the title's design and editorial content to its audience. The design and concept will be tested using focus groups made up of the target audience and presented to other stakeholders such as industry figures, subject specialists and advertising agencies.

The market and target audience's expectations play a large part in determining both the content and design style of print publications and websites. That the content of any title is dictated by its political, social or cultural subject is an incontrovertible fact. But while this is a major consideration when establishing a publication or website's structure and layout, there are other factors that influence both the choice of editorial and advertising material and how it is to be used, such as how long the reader is expected to use the product and whether they may keep it for reference or as a collector's item, or throw it away. The ephemeral nature and inherent disposability of a print publication have to be taken into consideration when content is chosen and have a considerable influence on how and in what media a title is presented.

A media company looking to develop a new venture will need to look at rival titles both in print and online, to see what other publications or websites there are on the same or similar topics. A title will need a unique selling proposition (USP) if it is to succeed in the crowded media market. While it can be a strength for a new publication to be similar to an existing title, it needs to be sufficiently different to encourage advertisers to support it and the public to buy it. New consumer

Media usage

- Free papers: rapid read, high pass-on rate, instant disposability

- Daily newspapers: quick to read and extract information – disposed of almost immediately

- Saturday and Sunday newspapers: leisurely read, may be kept for reference and for content such as TV listings, and longer features may be read during the week

- Weekly news/gossip magazines: quick, topical read – immediate use, may be kept for a short time to glance through or revisit unread articles

- Freemiums: middle- to high-quality magazines without a cover price, read at leisure, kept to read over a short period or passed on

- Monthly magazines: read at leisure, kept to read over a number of occasions during the month, may be saved, collected for future reference or passed on

- News and business websites: used as the source of continually updated information; may be visited at least once a day or very regularly, bookmarked or visited for specific information through a search engine, subscriptions to RSS feeds and news alerts or business information, and linked to aggregation websites

- Entertainment, communication and social websites: used daily or very regularly for pictorial, TV and video content, downloads, gaming, betting, competitions, social interaction and communication via blogs and tweets

- Email news, information alerts and SMS message updates: immediate information on the move – timing set to recipients' preference

- Print newsletters: information quick to extract, may be disposed of or kept for future contact/information reference or passed on to colleague

- E-newsletters: information delivered to recipient's desktop to read at their convenience; may be downloaded and archived

- Corporate brochures: leisurely read of information; may be kept for reference or passed on to a colleague, or disposed of if lacking perceived content value

print titles need to gain the support of the media distribution and retail industries; companies such as WH Smith and the major supermarkets have to be convinced that a new publication is marketable before they will offer retail shelf space. Specialist or business magazines and websites that rely on subscriptions may need the support of the relevant professional association and major sector players to establish their title with the intended audience.

Perceived values

The perceived value of a title is of enormous importance, and design is fundamental in assuring that the targeted reader or visitor is able to recognise the brand and react to its particular market qualities. The professional level of presentation and technological excellence of media companies' products imply that the content is authoritative and reliable, and high production values attract and reassure an audience. The organisation behind these products should underpin their performance and maintain the standards that separate them from the myriad personal webzines, blogs and vanity publishing projects.

Most magazines produced by media companies have a positive perceived value as they are usually printed on good-quality paper, often with a gloss finish. The paper quality affects how a print publication looks and feels, and the more substantial a title feels, the more value a reader will assign to its content. The Internet is not immune to perceived values; the average user of a youth-oriented website expects plenty of interactivity and social connectivity and will award a higher perceived value to a site with exciting graphics and dynamic content. A reader or user has a huge number of competing websites to choose from and is more likely to return to those they perceived as having a positive value.

An online news site may cover a major story in video, audio and written form to increase the news value and try to offer a better service than its media rivals. The continuing belief in mainstream news gathering services can be attributed not only to high reporting standards, but also to good design, imaginative and dynamic content and use of the

latest innovations. All these factors add to the authority of the written content and make the websites of organisations such as CNN or the BBC appear more trustworthy in comparison with any private individual's blog or website.

Many consumers still trust 'bricks and mortar' media companies and organisations and will take into account the reputation of their existing printed newspapers, magazines or TV stations when judging the authority and trustworthiness of unfamiliar digital media. A well-known offline brand with established values is generally perceived to be more trustworthy and likely to provide a good service, as it is assumed it will have transferred its traditional attributes and standards to the Web.

Key editorial and advertising values

Editorial integrity

Credibility of information/opinion
Awareness of cultural trends
Quality of written editorial content
Exclusive content
Authoritative contributors
Industry recognition

Commercial authority

Ownership and market standing of title
Relevance to audience
Promotion and marketing of title
Reliability of services
Range/quantity of advertising

Brand extension

Awards and prizes given
Exhibitions and events staged
Spin-offs and cross-media tie-ins
Games and competitions

Brand image

Visual originality
Creative excellence
Technological innovation
Appropriateness of design
Attractiveness of design
Variety and application of multimedia
Interest of visual content

Production quality

Standard of execution
Technical excellence
Website usability
Download speed
Printing and paper quality
Reliability and frequency

Corporate social responsibility

Charity activity and support
Social connectivity/community
Environmental and green profile

Funding, distribution, promotion, advertising

The amount of money a media product can raise directly affects the funding available for the design, content and production of a title. A business plan will normally be devised that forecasts how much revenue can be raised and this is used to allocate funds to each area of a publication, for example salaries, office space, production expenses and marketing and design development. Advertising, traditionally, has provided the greatest source of funds for media companies (see pages 10 and 21). However, a significant proportion of a title's revenue may be derived from sponsorship, exhibitions, product endorsements and events. The design for a title with links to other funding activities should be planned to include features that attract stakeholders from those areas.

The budget assigned to a media product has to include the cost of distribution. As most printed publications are distributed by road and rail, this means considering the effects of the weight and size of a magazine or newspaper on postal and transportation costs. Titles must also fit the average retail shelf or trolley space. The specifications for a new print title need to achieve a balance between the optimum weight of paper and ideal size for a title and the distribution costs.

Although a website does not have a material presence, there are distribution costs associated with web publishing. For example, if a website contains a great deal of data, such as streaming TV/video, it will require a large number of servers and a high bandwidth, which will add to running costs (see page 336). A new website needs to plan for these costs by anticipating the number of visitors, how many may visit at the same time and how much data they may download.

The media industry spends a considerable amount promoting and advertising its own products. This may be done by the title, the media company's central marketing department or an outside marketing company. Media groups may choose to promote a new title using their existing products, or for a major launch may run an integrated advertising campaign through other media companies. The promotion and advertising of a new title fixes not only the launch issue date and when a website goes live, but also when the design development has to be completed.

Sources of revenue

Ad words
Award ceremonies
B2B links
Blog advertising
Books, associated
   publications
Classified advertising
Clubs, social organisations
Competitions,
   crosswords, quizzes
Conferences
Cover price
Cross-media links
Database information
Display advertising
Downloads
Events, co-productions
Exhibitions, shows and
   trade fairs
Games and gaming
Holiday companies
Music downloads, DVDs
   and CDs
Offers and promotions
Online gambling
Online premium (paid-for)
   content
Organised travel and
   excursions
Partner companies
Print paid for content
   (advertorials)
Reciprocal deals
Retail and retail
   partnerships
RSS feeds
Search engine and
   aggregators listings
Seminars, talks and
   lectures
Sponsorship
Smart phone apps
Staging concerts,
   performance arts and
   festivals
Subscriptions print
Ticket sales
Travel agencies
Virtual football and other
   interactive sports
   games
Website advertising
Web sponsored links

Revenues, budgets and costs

Most media titles can only exist if they make a profit, and any expenditure on a new title has to fall within projected revenues. Before a print publication or website is developed, the media company will decide on a **page budget** – how much is to be spent on generating the editorial content for each page. This is based on the requirements of the page and balanced against the content of other pages. For example, an editor's or journalist's opinion page or blog is normally text led with no more than a single portrait picture, and would therefore be assigned a lower budget than the main feature or news pages. Other pages may include pictures commissioned or sourced from specialist image libraries, global news services or freelance photographers, which adds to the cost and means the page has to be assigned a higher budget.

The budget for a new title will be allocated page by page and you need to ensure that design and production costs are maintained. However, it is possible to reduce the cost of one page to increase spending on another as long as the overall budget is controlled. Fashion pages can be the most costly to design and produce, as the budget has to include hiring models, stylists, make-up artists, hairdressers and the photographer or videographer and their studio and assistants. If you know that you have to include pages that are expensive to produce, you will often need to balance their cost against the design of less complex pages.

Most titles have three main sources of income: cover price or subscriptions, advertising and secondary trading (see the box on page 68). Anyone initiating a new media product has to consider whether the idea will be saleable to companies as a good place to reach their customers and whether the target audience will be prepared to pay the cover price or subscription on a regular basis. The amount of advertising the media company expects to sell and the revenue it can generate will determine how many editorial pages the title will support.

Designers need to know all the financial implications before they begin to plan a publication, so they can make sure their ideas reflect what will be affordable once the title is in production. A publication not only needs to stay within its budget, but must also look good and reflect its particular market. For example, there is no point in trying to launch a new 'glossy' magazine on a limited budget as the title needs to convey an upmarket flavour. This is likely to require an investment in high-quality paper and printing as well as the development of a website that can support multimedia and handle a large volume of page hits. The audience for top-level titles are known to relate their perceived status to high production values and are unlikely to respect a less well-printed product on paper that looks cheap, or a poor website design.

Advertising space

Almost all publications and websites carry advertising that is sold to generate revenue. This is referred to as advertising space – blocks or panels of differing sizes and shapes. Advertising has two basic categories: display ads

Web advertising revenue

Advertising on a website is costed by per thousand ad views – each click on a web page containing advertisements equals revenue measured in terms of ad views. This is different from page hits, which is a term for a single visit to a website or page, or request for a file on that page, that is used to determine a website's number of unique users (UUs). An ad view or impression is related to an individual ad, and as there may be several ads on one page, a site may register more ad views per minute than page hits. The website's server can log the ad views and store a record, and software is available that can keep track of the number of ad views and user clicks.

and classified ads. Display ads are sold in page units and normally contain a creative visual element. Classified ads are generally smaller in scale, more factual and aimed at conveying basic details.

Advertisers see certain positions in a title as being of a higher value, and the design for a title needs to include as many prime positions as possible, without overwhelming the other content. The ads that generate the most income include the inside front and back covers in print and the main home page banner and skyscraper adverts for websites. Advertisers will pay more to have their ad appear next to a related story or in a particular section (special positions). If an ad has not been booked to appear in a special position, the media company will match the ad to one of the available spaces and make sure that it works with the other content.

Web advertising features animation, dynamic imagery, sound and video. In addition, web publications use interactive competitions and games, as well as other non-traditional methods of advertising that involve sharing film clips, music downloads and social networking. Sponsored links to other sites are another way of making money, and most websites also feature Google adwords that place it in the right list on a Google search page. Ads should be positioned where they will not annoy people; if they are dropped into a feature page they can break the eye flow and disturb the reader's or visitor's concentration. Pop-ups have a bad reputation and are best avoided, unless they are clearly benign.

Planning advertising positions

When planning a title it is essential to notify advertisers of the benefits, availability and technical specification of the advertising positions prior to completing the dummy issue or prototype website. This allows a media company's advertising department to pre-sell space and test the potential advertising market. They will plan a schedule that lists either how many print issues there will be each year or how long website ads can be booked for and the number of times they may appear. The advertising department will plan the number and size of ad spaces to be sold, where they may appear and what they will cost. The advertising requirements are combined with the editorial objectives to compile a brief for the designer to let them know what ad positions must be included. This could be that the front page of a section will always have an ad position on the page, or that the lead feature in a magazine will offer **facing matter** positions – an ad on an adjacent page related to the subject of an article.

Advertising spaces for web and print editions are sold at given prices related to dimension and frequency – how long and how often an ad is to appear. Advertisers will compare media and ad positions and select those that will reach the relevant target audience. They will also consider the cost of the ad set against the number of readers or visitors that the title claims to reach, which will enable them to decide on the title that will provide the most economic **cost per viewing** for their ad.

The cost of advertising space and technical requirements are published in a **rate card** which media companies make available on their website. The rate card will contain the prices, sizes and when ads have to be supplied by (copy deadline). The rate card will normally also have a list of regular and special features that identify the topics to be covered. It is important to make potential advertisers and advertising agencies that run accounts for larger companies aware of your new title and its relevance to their market.

The good, the bad and the ugly

The look of the ads is an integral part of the overall design feel of a title. The design dummy or prototype can be used to set the quality and style of the ads the

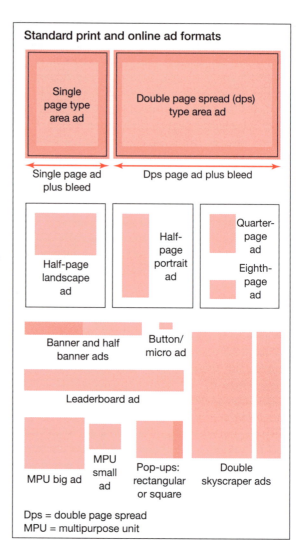

Standard print and online ad formats

Single page type area ad

Double page spread (dps) type area ad

Single page ad plus bleed

Dps page ad plus bleed

Half-page landscape ad

Half-page portrait ad

Quarter-page ad

Eighth-page ad

Banner and half banner ads

Button/ micro ad

Leaderboard ad

MPU big ad

MPU small ad

Pop-ups: rectangular or square

Double skyscraper ads

Dps = double page spread
MPU = multipurpose unit

title would like to feature. A title should give clear guidelines for the visual standard an ad needs to achieve so that advertisers can ensure they supply material that meets the standards for the title. There are few areas that cause more tension between the editorial and advertising departments than the quality and design of ads. Large companies normally use advertising agencies to produce ads for titles to a very high standard. However, titles may encounter problems dealing with clients that supply ads they have produced themselves as these may be poorly designed and technically incorrect.

Some magazines sell page space as **advertorials** – sponsored articles that are produced by the media company on behalf of an advertiser. If the title is to feature client pages, there should be strict rules on how the content can be presented. These should ban the advertiser from mimicking the magazine or website's look by intentionally designing an ad that could be mistaken for an editorial. Media companies generally disapprove of ads made to look like editorials, as this can make it look as though the title is endorsing the product rather than just advertising it. A style should be set up for advertorials that clearly differentiates the client pages from the editorial.

The nature of the ads that the title may be asked to carry should also be considered at the planning stage as featuring the wrong kind of ad can adversely affect how readers, visitors, other advertisers and the media industry view the title. Ethical issues and matters of taste can be contentious areas; for example, whether to allow nudity in ads or feature alcoholic drinks that have adverse social implications, even though they may raise revenue. There have been complaints from parents and medical experts over fashion images of very skinny models – sometimes made more exaggeratedly thin by Photoshop retouching – that, it is claimed, may encourage anorexia nervosa in teenagers. A policy on what may or may not be accepted by the title should be included in the launch information.

Solving the bad ads versus revenue problem

That badly designed or unattractive ads bring in revenue for a publication or website is a hard argument to counter, and ads, no matter how poor, should not necessarily be rejected outright. Media companies should have a process in place to deal with any really serious problem with the look or content of an ad. This may include asking the advertising department to request a new advert, or to suggest an alternative treatment for the ad to the client. Some media companies have large design departments and it can be part of their role to revamp or redesign unattractive or unsuccessful ads, or to offer advice on how they may be improved. Refusing to run an ad on any but ethical grounds should be the final resort.

Conforming with advertising standards

A media company must remain within the law and has to ensure its employees and advertisers comply with all relevant legislation. All titles need to comply with any legal requirements and industry guidelines that cover advertising or place restrictions on what a title may include. Legal restrictions include bans on advertising tobacco and some pharmaceutical products, and there are industry agreements on what is or is not acceptable when it comes to advertising aimed at children or a younger audience. **The Advertising Standards Authority (ASA)** advises on and polices the advertising industry's code of conduct for the media in Britain. It operates in agreement with other international organisations such as EASA (the European Advertising Standards Alliance) to review complaints about ads.

Advertising specifications

The technical criteria for a title's advertisements will be developed at the planning stage. A title will need separate specifications for print and online ads that are matched to the technology of the different media. This could be to control the quality of imagery for either platform, or to set parameters for video file sizes and the length of time they may run. You may also need to keep the audience profile in mind. If you know that the website users are unlikely to have the latest versions of the programs, or may be unwilling to update their computers to browser versions that can view the ads, you should issue technical requirements that ensure the ads are compatible with older software. Some advertising designers and agencies like to impress their clients by using the latest technology and software. However, if you carry ads that are not easily accessible, or are slow to download, your audience will blame you for any frustration and annoyance, not the advertiser.

TIP Animated ads should have an **animation time limit** that defines the number of repeats an ad can perform during a set length of time (seconds).

Editorial–advertising balance

The **editorial–advertising ratio or balance** is an aspect of the overall design of a publication or website. While funding is important, usability of the title has to be the primary consideration. A title where the editorial is dominated by ads may reduce the apparent value to the reader and visitor as there can appear to be less editorial content, and a large number of pages of advertising throughout the magazine may disrupt the editorial content flow. Research has shown that most readers or visitors prefer titles with no less than 60–70 per cent of editorial content. But this may be a case of media companies giving people what they are used to, rather than an absolute truth. *Wallpaper**, a high-end interiors magazine, has had great success because it carries a very large number of advertising pages of products and services. These are closely linked to the editorial content and are seen as providing extra value to its particular readership.

Careful planning at the web design stage can ensure that advertising positions are placed for maximum income generation without imposing on, or distracting from, other content. You should establish a visual balance between editorial and advertising that reflects the nature of the title. One way of achieving this for websites is to include a review of how well a focus group of potential visitors react to the positioning of ads during market research testing. Sites need varying types of content to provide **stickiness** – hold on to the user – without becoming too busy. It is important to ensure the visual effect is not diluted and the message lost by having too many, overactive ads that disrupt the users' concentration and disturb their online experience.

TIP Make sure you obtain a selection of existing advertisements from potential advertisers before the dummy or prototype is designed. This will help avoid any clashes between the advertising and the editorial design.

Editorial–advertising coordination

Event: London Fashion Week (held in February and September)

- Monthly fashion magazines: news and features
- Print advertising pre-sold and supplied in February for the March issue and September for the November issue
- Website advertising: prebooked and supplied one to two weeks prior to event

Product: men's and women's perfume

- Monthly/weekly/daily general publications: product reviews and features
- Print advertising presold and supplied by October for November/December issues to tie in with peak Christmas sales
- Website advertising: prebooked and supplied for November/December updates

Topics: politics – budget, elections

- Monthly/weekly/daily general publications: news and features
- Print advertising presold and supplied one month in advance of event date
- Website advertising: prebooked and supplied for closest timed updates to events

Topic: food – barbeques

- Monthly/weekly/daily women's and food publications: product reviews and features
- Print advertising presold and supplied by June for July issue, keeping September issue for back-to-school features and advertising
- Website advertising: prebooked and supplied for June/July updates

Content pre-planning

Media products justify their existence by providing fresh information on topical issues, and titles maintain the interest of their readers and visitors by varying the subjects they cover. The subjects for a title are often planned on a yearly basis, so the editorial, advertising and marketing departments are able to fulfil readers' and visitors' expectation of a constant throughput of new information. Content pre-planning enables all those involved to coordinate their activities. A well-thought-through plan makes it possible to move ahead with commissioning and sourcing content, and for the media company to produce successful titles within its budget and to deadline.

'Before deciding what makes a good design, it is well worth considering why we spend the time, effort and expense required to produce good design.'

Professor Chris Frost, head of journalism,
Liverpool John Moores University

New media project management

When a media company develops a new product, the company will carry out an assessment of what the project may involve and then decide whether the company's employees have the expertise and capacity to undertake the work. If the company feels that the title requires more skills and knowledge than can be sourced in-house, it may take the decision to contract the work out to specialist digital media agencies and designers. Launching a media product can involve many different people in a number of specialist areas and it is useful to have one individual who is responsible for overseeing the editorial, design and technical development. For major launches, it may be necessary to recruit staff in advance of publication to handle the product's development. This may include appointing an editor as well as marketing and production teams.

Media design and communication issues can be complex to resolve, and it is important that everybody

The development brief

The development brief should be a guide to how the project is to be managed and define the tasks and responsibilities of all those involved. It is important that the brief is clearly written in straightforward terms and contains all the information and major decisions relevant to the task of creating a new title, such as:

- the corporate objectives
- the philosophy of the publication
- editorial aims
- intended readership and/or unique users
- desired market position
- background information on the marketplace and any possible rivals
- revenue targets
- development budget
- technological requirements or prerequisites
- potential advertisers or sponsors
- approvals/launch period

involved in the development of a new publication or website is clear about the aims and intended outcome of the project. The main points of information that everyone needs to know are compiled in a **development brief** (see box). This is intended to give all those involved a clear understanding of the project and is given to everyone who will be working on the title, both the in-house team and any media specialists, to ensure they fully understand what they are being asked to achieve and the timescale involved.

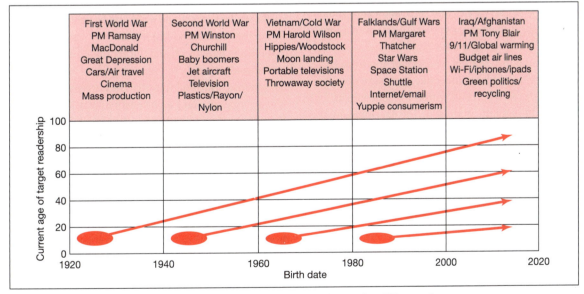

Each generation's values and preferences are influenced by their background and life experience.

Creative development

As soon as the product has a clear plan and a brief has been prepared, it can go into final development. A new title should aim for a unique look but also needs a visual approach that adheres to the basic principles of information design. Titles that will be published in more than one medium should be designed so they can be transferred across the different technologies without losing their identity. They must be visually cohesive, with each page of the design tailored to suit the production techniques, market area and target audience. And the designs have to allow for some flexibility so that the content will look different from the previous issue or update, but also needs sufficient structure in order that brand recognition is maintained.

To ensure that the creative development fulfils the correct objectives, a **design brief** is normally written to set the parameters for a new design. The media company will provide the designer or digital media group with key criteria that will enable them to create a brand identity that will achieve the objectives set out in the development brief. This is to ensure that the design places the title in its intended target market and that the contents are visualised in a style which will elicit the right response from the right people. The design brief will set out the structure of the title, the budget (and how it is to be spent) and a timescale and schedule for each stage. New project development often involves working in untried areas, and some allowance should be made for the necessary process of design revisions and technical development.

Although the creative process can appear to be artistic rather than business-like, to ensure that you achieve the correct result within the schedule, it needs to be carefully managed. The development of a media product design follows a number of stages. The designer or digital media group will often present visual research for the title as **mood boards** – collages of images, type, colour samples and graphic styles that portray a possible design treatment. The mood boards are a good way of checking that the initial

Download Action sheet: CHAPTER4_concept/ storyboards at **www.pearsoned.com/hand**

Stakeholders and strategic partners

A publication or web design has to focus on the reader or visitor. However, they also need to consider the 'internal audience' – the media company and its stakeholders, for example financial investors, advertising clients, web and printing companies. The media company and stakeholders will need to be convinced that the design answers their requirements.

ideas fulfil the brief before any detailed design work is undertaken. The mood boards should show the general inspiration behind the concept: the graphic and pictorial styles, possible colour schemes and typefaces. Once the design concept has been chosen, the mood boards become the basis for producing detailed **storyboards** – a plan for the content of each page of a print publication or website. These are then developed into finished design solutions and used to produce a dummy issue and/or prototype website (see page 78). Following this process should ensure that the finished design solution meets all the criteria you have set.

The name

An early key decision in the process is the title's name, as the logo or **masthead** becomes the main identifier of the brand. The right name can convey the concept of a media product in a single word and be central to visualising the whole look. *Vogue* is a clever choice of word that reflects its subject, and the connotation of stylishness appeals strongly to the readership of an upmarket fashion magazine and website. The current masthead conveys elegance and sophistication by using a condensed, ultrafine serif typeface. Titles such as *OK*, *Now*, *Closer* and *Heat* are bright, quick and upbeat words that suggest exuberance and immediacy. These gossip magazines tend to have mastheads that use soft, rounded type, sometimes in italics as the slope of the letters suggests forward movement and emphasis. The typeface used for the masthead may convey far more than just the name; it can also suggest the title's values and the reader's or visitor's aspirations. *Men's Health* is a name that is direct and honest about its intentions, and the masthead/logo is set in a curvi-linear serif typeface. The letters have been tightly spaced and slightly condensed to bring them closer together in a graphic unit that gives the impression of masculine strength and solidity.

The name for a site needs to be chosen with care to be individual and memorable, but needs to avoid the pitfalls associated with domain names and Internet searching. A good website name will contain a key word that contributes to its search engine ranking. A check should be made by carrying out a trial search to make sure the name could not be confused with that of another title. Certain words should be avoided as they can throw up undesirable connections – unless that is being used as a marketing tool. If the website is being created for an existing print title, company or product, the brand name can be used or adapted to benefit from the time and investment in its reputation. However, if the brand requires refreshing or repositioning, a more contemporary title may be devised.

Names and brand identity

The name of a title should give the intended reader or visitor a clear indication of its market position and content and match their perception of the status and subject of the magazine, newspaper or website. The name can include them in a community: *Heat* magazine's website is called heatworld, while another magazine in the women's sector, *Chat*, also publishes the print titles *Chat Passion* and *Chat Futures*. There are some instances where a similar name indicates very different publications: for example, the *Morning Star* is a British communist newspaper, while the *Daily Star* is a mass market tabloid.

Website hostname and domain names

Your website's name should be as easy to use as possible. The hostname – the website's address (URL) – ideally should not be more than 20–25 characters long to fit the average search panel, and those 20–25 letters should include the title's main identifying words. The **Internet Corporation for Assigning Names and Numbers (ICANN)** regulates website names, and a new site's name must be registered with a domain name registrar who issues permission to use the name for a set period of time. It is important to remember to renew your registration to prevent the name being assigned to someone else. Websites may use **domain names** that end with any word the company or organisation wishes, so a website could be called titlename.fashion or .sport.

Subtle changes in the choice of typeface and type colour for a cover or home page design can alter the mood of a masthead or logo and change the reader or user's perception of a title.

A number of alternative covers will be designed for a new consumer magazine to ensure it has the greatest possible impact on and appeal for the target audience.

Design development

The mood and storyboards help to establish the basis of all the design decisions about the title's look and informational structure. These include how the content is to be organised and positioned and the visual presentation style. The design structure of a title, and how the contents will be treated, should reflect the relative importance of each subject area, and the visual treatment will be developed using a working title and sample contents. Design is a developmental process and changes are often made to the nature and order of the title as the project progresses. The design process should encourage experimentation as the development stages can generate further ideas that add value to the title. The design style may be reconsidered several times before a final dummy issue or prototype website is produced.

It is common practice to begin by producing a selection of designs for the pages to be compared against each other, before one or two are chosen for further development. Most designers start by producing two or three ideas for the cover or home page, and a number of content pages for discussion, and these initial designs may go through several sets of changes before the final treatment is decided upon. The first major decision, both for online and print, is the dimensions and page structure of the title, although this is not always purely a design choice as there are also economic, technological and other factors (see page 65).

When planning a title, you need to set a budget. This is based on the time and cost of producing each type of page. Most online and print titles employ an underlying grid that provides a spatial framework for the design and that allows the page to be put together quickly and efficiently. The designer may work up more than one style of grid for the page templates and try out several structural formats to see how the proposed contents might best be positioned. The designer will also test a number of key page designs using different typefaces and possible alternative colour schemes on varying styles of grid.

You will need to provide the designer with examples of the type of content that the title will feature. You may have a budget that allows you to generate new material, or you may be able to use the media

The quick brown fox jumps over the lazy dog. The quick brown fox jumps over the lazy dog. The quick brown fox jumps over the lazy dog. The quick brown fox jumps over the lazy dog. The quick brown fox jumps over the lazy dog.

The quick brown fox jumps over the lazy dog. The quick brown fox jumps over the lazy dog. The quick brown fox jumps over the lazy dog. The quick brown fox jumps over the lazy dog. The quick brown fox jumps over the lazy dog.

The quick brown fox jumps over the lazy dog. The quick brown fox jumps over the lazy dog. The quick brown fox jumps over the lazy dog. The quick brown fox jumps over the lazy dog.

The quick brown fox jumps over the lazy dog. The quick brown fox jumps over the lazy dog. The quick brown fox jumps over the lazy dog. The quick brown fox jumps over the lazy dog.

The quick brown fox jumps over the lazy dog. The quick brown fox jumps over the lazy dog. The quick brown fox jumps over the lazy dog. The quick brown fox jumps over the lazy dog. The quick brown fox jumps over the lazy dog. The quick brown fox jumps over the lazy dog. The quick brown fox jumps over the lazy dog. The quick brown fox jumps over the lazy dog. The quick brown fox jumps over the lazy dog. The quick brown fox jumps over the lazy dog. The quick brown fox jumps over the lazy dog. The quick brown fox jumps over the lazy dog. The quick brown fox jumps over the lazy dog. The quick brown fox jumps over the lazy dog.The quick brown fox jumps over the lazy dog.

The quick brown fox jumps over the lazy dog. The quick brown fox jumps over the lazy dog. The quick brown fox jumps over the lazy dog. The quick brown fox jumps over the lazy dog. The quick brown fox jumps over the lazy dog. The quick brown fox jumps over the lazy dog. The quick brown fox jumps over the lazy dog. The quick brown fox jumps over the lazy dog. The quick brown fox jumps over the lazy dog. The quick brown fox jumps over the lazy dog. The quick brown fox jumps over the lazy dog.The quick brown fox jumps over the lazy dog.

The quick brown fox jumps over the lazy dog.The quick brown fox jumps over the lazy dog.The quick brown fox jumps over the lazy dog.The quick brown fox jumps over the lazy dog.The quick brown fox jumps over the lazy dog.The quick brown fox jumps over the lazy dog.The quick brown fox jumps over the lazy dog.The quick brown fox jumps over the lazy dog.The quick brown fox jumps over the lazy dog.The quick brown fox jumps over the lazy dog.The quick brown fox jumps over the lazy dog.The quick brown fox jumps over the lazy dog.The quick brown fox jumps over the lazy dog.

The phrase 'The quick brown fox jumps over the lazy dog' contains every character in the alphabet and is useful for setting sample copy as it contains all the letterforms that make up a typeface.

company's archive if it contains copy and pictures suitable for the project. If you do not provide content, the designer will work with imagery from general sources such as other similar titles, stock picture libraries and the Internet. Some people prefer to use dummy headlines and **printer's Greek** for the body copy (despite its name, printer's Greek is actually mock Latin). The advantage of using dummy headlines and text is that they focus attention on the design and prevent those assessing the page from becoming distracted by the copy.

The group or person directing the project should be presented with a series of page visuals, worked up to look more or less like the published result. Some will be rejected, while others will be worked on further until everyone is satisfied that the design style is correct, and a look for all the pages has been agreed. The next step is to design the title using the relevant software for the media. At this stage, the design has to be prepared in absolute detail, page by page, and you also need to make sure that each page complies with the technical requirements. This may mean you should ask the designer to prepare a number of variations of each approved page design. This is to ensure that the page format works and will be easy to assemble when the title is published on a regular basis. The discussion and amendment process should continue until you are

happy with the look of the final design and are sure it will be practical to produce. The last step is to set up a dummy issue or test website using real copy and pictures that is subjected to further market research.

Many people need to see a representative dummy or prototype before they can give a clear opinion on whether they would read a print title or visit a website. Another round of market research will be carried out in order to get a final set of views on the design and content. This involves printing a dummy issue and/or creating a functioning test website for discussion and to test usability. Market research will be able to provide you with more accurate feedback if the articles and photographs are realistic. The dummy or test site should be as close to the finished product as possible, but even at this late stage things will be changed if the findings suggest any negative reactions or reader/user resistance.

> **TIP** A Word file called 'Lorem ipsum' is available from the Internet for use as dummy text.

Many print designers start by preparing rough sketches of pages before preparing the finished dummy as this helps them decide on the position of the fixed page furniture and where the content might fall.

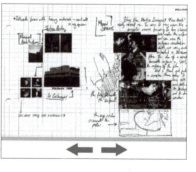

Professional website designers begin with detailed site plans that include the informational relationship between the pages and how they will be linked, and will decide beforehand upon the position of the menus, tabs and buttons as well as what content will go where.

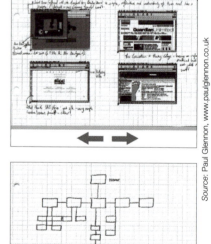

Design consistency

Presenting a consistent design to readers and visitors helps them to use the title as well as establish their relationship to the brand. This can be managed by using typefaces and colours in a similar manner throughout the sections and pages (see page 154). Having fixed page grids and typographic styles may seem restrictive and to offer a limited number of solutions. However, having pre-set page formats can be convenient where a production schedule is tight and there has to be a rapid turnaround of pages, such as a newspaper or news website. Other titles, such as monthly magazines, may need layouts with more life and energy and this can be achieved by taking a flexible approach. There are certain types of publication where the design rules are treated as more of a guide than a set of unbreakable laws. Even for more formal titles, you may consider allowing an occasional break in the structure, as this can change the dynamic and give an extra twist to excite interest. However, the design rules should never be completely abandoned as they form part of the branding and maintain visual cohesion (see page 162).

House design style

Once the dummy or prototype has been agreed and the design has been finalised, the completed, tested design is used as the basis for a house design style guide – a document or online help page(s) that describe the overall design ethos. These will specify, in very precise detail, how every section and page is to be set up.

Print and web design and production software allows for the creation of individual page templates that contain the house style design and are used for day-to-day production. You will need to arrange for a set of page production templates to be created for the title. These may be provided by the print or web designer, or the specialist digital media company that is producing the content management system (CMS) – the software that handles the website's editorial process. You may also need to ensure that a web designer, IT department or web management company is available to handle any complex changes to the structure

A house design style has to be applied consistently; however, the presentation of content should be varied following the overall style ethos, as in these examples which show three layout treatments using the same pictures and copy.

or page layout. The designer or originating company should supply a house style guide or online help pages containing the work practice guide for the production team. The guide or help pages also need to include the design parameters for those working on the editorial content, such as how many words fit in a headline or other content area.

> **TIP** Some magazines allow typefaces to be chosen that are linked to the mood or subject matter. However, the typography of a title should be used in a consistent manner. The vast majority of print publications have very precise rules about what style of type is used.

'The initial step in thinking about how a publication becomes a reality is to focus on what the subject matter of the message may be.'

Timothy Samara, educator and author

New print media

The market for printed publications is still very active, despite changes in reading and viewing habits during the first decade of the twenty-first century (see Chapter 2, page 31). The 24/7 news media have created a challenge for newspapers that have experienced a considerable decline in sales, but while magazines appear to be more resilient to these changes, they too have seen a reduction in readership as a large number of people move to using digital media. Advertising revenues have also dropped as companies switch their spending to online in preference to print. At the same time, the costs of paper and transportation have risen, making it more difficult for media companies to make a profit from print titles. Nonetheless, the right print product can still win critical acclaim and be a financial success. A print title that has something innovative or

topical to offer should be able to establish itself in the sector. In recent years, new launches that have done very well are those that exploited celebrity connections, while others have succeeded by identifying and targeting niche markets.

Any new title must have a strong USP to establish itself in its sector. This is especially important for a launch into the overcrowded print market where there may already be several other titles on similar subjects. Over the last few years there has been a huge number of new print titles as media companies have taken advantage of new technological developments in software and printing to launch magazines more quickly and with less initial investment. A consequence has been that, as soon as a publisher comes up with a successful format, several others will produce similar titles, and the effect of this has been to fragment the potential readership in a particular market. The increased competition has also reduced the profitability of many publications.

Media companies may not appear to be greatly concerned by this while the economy is doing well, as long as they are able to sell enough advertising to run large issues. But ultimately, too many identical print publications are bad for the media industry. One example of saturation in a print market is the lads' mags, such as *Loaded*, *FHM* and *GQ*, that were very popular during much of the 2000s. However, when the economy weakened, these titles struggled as they were all chasing the same advertiser's budgets, and there simply was not enough revenue to support a large number of lads' magazines. Their downfall was also partially caused by a market overcrowded with titles producing repetitive, formulaic content. This led to the readership losing interest in buying the magazines, and readers were also defecting to the Web where similar content could be accessed for free.

A successful print title can only stand out if its potential market has been well researched, the product development well targeted and it features innovative content that will attract and retain an ongoing readership. Quite often, a media company will wait until it becomes clear whether a new idea for a print title has worked before publishing its own version. The title that becomes a market leader does not necessarily need to be the first to launch, but it does have to be the best.

Cross-media planning

Print and digital media titles have specific technical requirements and separate production processes. However, if a media company is running a number of related titles, these need to be planned to be both visually and editorially compatible, so that the production teams can work cooperatively. You will need to establish a system of work practices that allow all those working on the titles to exchange information and support each other. It is important to ensure that the people working on the separate media communicate and share content and promote cross-media links between print and online titles. Print publications should include addresses for any related content on the website, and the website should promote the print title. Integrating all of a media company's cross-platform titles will help to establish the brand as truly convergent.

Source: Jamie Magazine

Source: jamiemagazine.com

Jamie Oliver's website and print magazine share a design look using a similar colour palette, type faces and imagery.

Page size and proportion

A print title is tactile – it has weight, texture and movement as the pages are turned. The dimension of a title conveys meaning through established conventions, some of which are based on tradition while others result from practical, economic or aesthetic considerations. The size of a title can place it in its market and identify its purpose. It can be based on the nature of the content or be a powerful design statement.

Planning a print title begins with its size and shape. There are various international standard paper formats that are used for most print publications. However, some magazines prefer not to use systems such as **ISO paper sizes** (A4 etc.) in order to make their publications stand out. A4, for example, is a relatively narrow rectangle that can be restrictive when designing pages. Magazines that want to convey a more exclusive message, or that are design led, often use a wider rectangle as this creates a better proportioned page in which to display content, and squarer shapes are considered to be more sympathetic to imagery (see the Golden Section, page 84). However, lower priced titles and those with small budgets may be restricted to the standard sizes. Some specialist titles with a small readership and mailed direct distribution magazines keep their costs down by using A4 as it is more economic for printing companies and mailing houses to handle.

Newspapers are identified by their paper size. Tabloid, compact and broadsheet sizes are considered to appeal to different audiences. Notoriously, tabloids are mass market; compact papers are actually much

Source: Before&After http://www.baamagazine.com

Before & After magazine uses a clean, open design that counterbalances blocks of colour and white space.

the same size but use a different name to separate themselves from the 'red tops' – a derogatory name for the lower end of the newspaper sector. The *Guardian* and its sister Sunday paper, the *Observer*, are the only newspapers in Britain to use the berliner paper size, more common in the USA. This was mostly a brand and marketing decision to give the publication an individual identity.

Newspaper page dimensions

The three main newspaper sizes are:

- **broadsheet**: 431.8 mm × 558.8 mm
- **tabloid** or **compact**: 289 mm × 380 mm
- **Berliner**: 315 mm × 470 mm

(These sizes may vary.)

Paper quality

The choice of paper (stock) will affect the identity and marketability of a title, as well as what can be done within the design and content. If you are involved in choosing the paper for a print title, you will need to consider both the quality of the paper and how the publication is to be printed. This is a complex decision as it depends on the print technology to be used, the reproduction quality you require and what type of paper your audience may expect. Most media companies will work with a consultant that specialises in paper and print and who will give advice on the right paper and size to use for the print process. Because paper is one of the most expensive elements when producing a print title, care has to be taken to ensure the correct stock is selected. This is particularly important because it can be difficult and expensive to change the paper once the publication has been issued. Swapping the stock can affect whether you can continue to use the same printing press, and the design may not work on another type of paper.

Large quantities of printed publications are surprisingly heavy to move. You need to consider the weight of the paper stock, as this has to be suitable for the method of distribution. The weight of paper affects the price and costs of distribution by road, rail and air, as well as the postage for direct sales publications. A print title will be planned to have a target number of pages per issue, and the weight of each issue needs to be carefully monitored to ensure it remains the same or distribution costs may increase. For instance, adding an extra eight pages might cause a magazine distributed by post to fall into a higher charging bracket.

Assessing the publication grid

How the content is positioned on the page has to be managed. The publication grid provides a structure that controls how the page is used and where the individual items should be placed. A title's pages will contain a number of separate elements, such as headlines and text blocks, and these are normally set up on grids made of vertical columns. When a page is made up, the grid guides the reader's eye through the content and up and down the page, and the number of divisions in the grid creates the contrast between staccato multi-item pages and the adagio of the two, three or more page features that set up the rhythm and pacing of a publication. The designer needs to be briefed on how the content needs to work both within each page and as part of the ongoing pattern of information. This will enable the designer to develop a grid structure for the publication.

As well as increasing the usability of the content, the grid will form the architectural frame of the publication and can give it a strong visual identity. There are a number of different types of grid that the designer may suggest, and you need to make sure that the style of grid you select matches the nature of the subject. It also needs to contain the amount of content that has been decided will be required for each page.

Paper quality versus paper weight

Paper specifying is an extremely complex area, as the design objectives can only be met by understanding how the paper, ink and printing press will work together. There can be serious production and financial problems if the wrong paper is selected. All papers have unique qualities and will react differently to the printing ink and press being used. Lightweight paper can suffer from **showthrough** – shadow patches of dark coloured ink appearing through from the reverse of the page. Lightweight papers may also become saturated during printing if the ink coverage is very dense, and the paper can split when dried (see page 322). Thinner paper can generate static electricity and this may make the pages hard to separate and turn. However, the incorrect choice of a heavyweight stock can also cause a range of problems.

Paper usage

Publishing media	Weight	Finish	Opacity (0 = transparent)
Newspapers	42.5–45gsm	Matt	50%
Glossy magazines	60–90gsm	Silk/gloss covers	75%
Mass market magazines	52–57gsm	Semi-silk/ matt	60%
Company reports	60–120gsm	Silk/gloss/ matt	75–100%

gsm = grams per square metre

Alexey Brodovitch was the doyen of magazine art directors in the 1950s and his style is still hugely influential. He created his cinematic page flow, similar to a film director's *mise en scène*, by alternating the shape, scale and position of text and images.

Brodovitch's design philosophy can also be applied to websites to create a sense of movement and continuity for the users as they move from page to page.

Grid design parameters

The size and proportion of the publication sets the other design parameters. All publications are based on a **grid** – the underlying architecture of the design that provides a logical structure for the content and gives visual balance to the pages. A modular grid system divides the pages into spatial units made up of the top, side and bottom **margins**, the space between the page edge and the **type or text area** (a rectangle within the page into which most of the content will fall), the **columns**, tall rectangles that organise the vertical flow of copy, and **gutters**, narrow vertical spaces between the columns that break the horizontal eye line. These are set up in ratios to the page size and each other and will, in turn, dictate the size of the type (see page 127).

'He [Brodovitch] believed that magazines and books, like films, are experienced sequentially and over time. Thus he was especially attuned to the flow of the layouts as they were to appear in the magazine.'

Andy Grundberg, *Brodovitch*

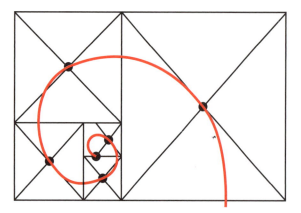

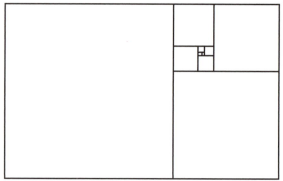

Fibonacci sequences are numerical patterns found in natural forms in which each number is the sum of the preceding two. Fibonacci sequences occur in the spirals of a snail's shell and the arrangement of flower petals. They are often used in conjunction with the Golden Section design principle.

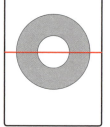

The Golden Section remains a key element in art and design and many pages both in print and on the Web follow its principles. The Golden Section is also used for product design, as well as the Rule of Thirds which can be seen in the design of the Apple iPod.

Idealised figures, such as Leonardo da Vinci's *Vitruvian Man* and Le Courbusier's *Modulor*, correlate spatial and numeric sequences to the human body. The resulting scale and proportions are used to create harmony and balance in art and design.

Numerical forms in nature

The belief that art and design should be based on mathematical systems has been held by many cultures throughout history. Leonardo of Pisa (*c*.1170-1250) discovered repeating patterns that can be expressed numerically and are present in the structure of natural forms such as snail shells, and can be found in music and poetry (Fibonacci sequences). These sequences are still used as a seminal aesthetic principle in European architecture, art and design.

The Golden Section or Ratio is a system of spatial division first identified by ancient Greek mathematicians (see the diagram above). The proportions are derived from natural forms, as with the Fibonacci sequence, and the Golden Section can be identified in the design of many classical buildings and objects. It was widely used during the Renaissance and employed by Leonardo da Vinci to create *Vitruvian Man*, his vision of idealised human proportions.

Sections and content division

The structure of a publication is made up of a sequence of pages, much like a film is made up of scenes. The grid that underlies the page provides the page-by-page pattern of reading and presents the content in a consistent way. The design of each page has to contribute to the overall brand identity and make the most of the material supplied, while allowing for the content to be laid out in a way that clearly defines the section or subject. The sections have to lead the reader through the publication and this is achieved by using informational indicators. The individual sections and subdivision also help a reader to locate content and identify related subjects or topics. When planning the sections for a title, you need to establish how all the material is to be arranged into subject areas and the order in which these will run. Publications use a number of traditional editorial subdivisions (see page 129) and these are often signalled by headings at the start or on each page of a section, or for each subject. For example, *Good Housekeeping* magazine calls its product pages 'Good Choices', the holiday section 'Good Breaks' and funny features 'Good Laugh'.

The most important factor is that it is obvious what a section or page contains when a reader scans through the title. There are a number of design solutions such as **page flags** or headers, which usually sit at the top of the page, and using a colour for the section can help catch the eye. The informational requirements of the design will dictate the size and prominence of page flags and headers. This may vary from title to title but should match the style of the publication. For example, a publication with a large number of pages or significantly differing content may use an entire page

to form a section break to separate topics. However, for magazines where space is at a premium, the flag may be just a small block of colour or single line of type at the top of a page. A designer should be asked to present a number of possible solutions for how each section might be identified. The page flags, headers and footers have a practical role and need to fit within the information flow of the title, but also have to add to the overall design appeal.

The front page or cover

The primary purpose of a front cover is to attract attention, and the cover page of magazines and newspapers employs a number of graphic or photographic devices that emphasise the contents and provide **entry points** – visual focus points in the layout that lead the eye into a page. The design and style of a cover is the visible demonstration of editorial identity and the means by which most readers recognise a publication. The imagery and typographic styling for a cover need to be carefully planned to ensure that the title and its content have an immediate appeal to the intended audience. It is normal practice to develop a number of design solutions for the front cover of a new title and to print several trial issues with different cover treatments to be market tested. However good the final dummy cover may look, you need to consider how the design will work and whether you will be able to source the necessary imagery on a regular basis. The design also must be flexible enough to allow the editorial and production teams to vary the cover for each issue and needs to be usable in print and online for promotional material, ads and websites.

The masthead (logo) is the main identifier and selling point for most publications and is usually type based. The masthead is a semiotic symbol for the title that conveys the name and nature of the publication, and its design needs to be strong enough to allow it to work in other media and in a range of sizes. The typographic treatment needs to be strong enough to enable the masthead to stand out on a busy cover and be readable on a background colour or image. Mastheads have to be instantly recognisable and are a key feature of the title's branding. It is best to select a masthead that is unified and uncluttered, with only one or two typefaces or type styles, simple graphics and the minimum of colours. The

Fashion

Fashion

FASHION

123 *Magazine Title* JULY 2010

123 Magazine Title

MT 123 July 2010

mag **123** July 2010

The standing items on a page should reflect the style of the magazine and clearly inform and guide the reader without becoming overly complex.

It is often necessary to experiment with the complex juxtaposition of design elements that make up a masthead or logo in order to achieve a well-balanced, strong brand identifier for a title.

majority of people view straightforward designs as more cohesive, and single items register more emphatically and promote better recognition memory.

The reason why a masthead is usually placed at the top of the front cover is brand recognition as readers are used to the masthead in that position. It is also to ensure that the title can be seen in retail displays. Newspapers are often folded in half to be put in racks or holders, and magazines may be stacked in front of one another on retail outlets' shelves. Some cult or lifestyle titles move their logo to other positions on the cover to make a statement that their non-conformist target audience will value.

Two leading designers who have been influential in the move towards breaking the 'masthead at the top of the page' convention are Neville Brody and David Carson. Brody, when designing covers for *The Face*, would shift the position of the magazine's logo around the cover to fit in with the main image for each issue, and Carson's *Ray Gun* magazine made a virtue of featuring both typographic and positional changes to the logo from issue to issue. Titles such as the Guardian's

G2 often vary the position of their logo on the page, using it to complement the cover picture or adapt it to form the cover image. A newspaper supplement does not have to ensure recognition in a retail environment as it is distributed inside the main paper. This enables a more flexible approach to using the masthead.

The design for a front cover, whether pictorial or text based, must match the nature of the content. What is important is that all cover or front page copy and images, whether for newspapers or magazines, carry good cross-referencing to the inside pages. Most magazines have picture-led front covers with **cover lines or sells** to attract potential buyers, while newspapers and text-led magazines use the front page headlines as the main signal to the readership. Newspapers usually carry an indication of the content somewhere on the cover as a list with page numbers and taster images, while others have a horizontal top or bottom **teaser strip**, with the full table of contents on the second page. Whatever approach is the most suitable for the editorial content, the treatment has to have a strong enough impact to market the title.

The contents page

The contents page provides a quick reference guide to the subjects covered in a title. You need to develop a look for the contents page that encapsulates the title's identity and establishes a link between the front cover and the inside pages. The contents may be presented as a factual list of content and page numbers, or by using images, graphics and typography in a way that sells the editorial content to the audience. Listings are more suited to a text-led or serious publication, while lifestyle and entertainment magazines often use cutout images and coloured typography to create an energetic introduction to a publication. The first few pages of a publication should be considered as an introduction to a title and can also be used for premium content such as the editor's welcome panel, high-revenue-generating advertising space and links to the title's website.

Print publications have a front to back linear structure, and the reader should be encouraged to stop and read the content as they progress through the publication. The reader also needs to be directed to the items that are of most interest to them. A reader will engage best with a publication that is well organised and signposted, and the design of the contents page should be visually linked to the rest of the title. The colours, imagery and typography should clearly indicate the separate sections, subjects and page headings and should reflect the current topics. The images used should be selected for their promotional value and not simply used for decoration. Contents pages need to create interest but should not be overly detailed as this can make them seem offputting and hard for the reader to follow.

Pacing and page balance

Each page must work as an individual design, against an adjacent page and as a series of continuing pages. It is the relationship between the pages that makes a title work as an entity and creates the flow of information that engages the reader and keeps them moving forward. The rhythm of a print publication comes from interspersing the more rapidly read sections with slower feature pages, and through contrasting busy, colourful layouts with simpler, calmer ones. The pacing of the content can be achieved by mixing pages containing a number of items with single page features, double page spreads and longer articles.

Publications require a structural flow that allows the topics to create a pattern and fall into the title's rhythm. Magazines normally begin with quickly read items such as news stories or a feedback page leading on to the main news, features, reviews and regular pages, and often concluding with a flick-through back section made up of offers, reader services and classified advertising. Newspapers' traditional balance of information is to have one lead and several secondary stories on each page, and to progress through national, international and finance news, with sports taking up the back pages. Many newspapers publish separate sports sections and supplements, and the final pages in the main paper can be used for non-news items such as reviews, weather forecasts and crosswords.

The contents of the ads need to work with the editorial as the look of the advertisements contributes towards the title's pacing. The run of editorial pages can be broken up by the visual juxtaposition of advertising and editorial, with ads use to separate sections and divide one feature from another. The overall pattern of editorial and advertising can be used to create the rhythm of a publication. For example, a magazine can separate two features by finishing one article on a right hand page and positioning an ad on the following left hand page facing the next article. The editorial pages need to be planned to allow for sufficient ad positions to generate the required revenue, and to permit the advertising department to approach suitable advertisers to ensure that the content of the ads reflects the editorial stance. The wrong placement facing of ads can cause bad **face-ups** – incompatibility between the design and the subject of facing pages.

> **Warning** It may damage the credibility of a title if the ads are not in sympathy with facing editorial pages, for example a feature exposé of poor private medical practices facing a private cosmetic surgery ad.

Website link to TED (see *http://www.ted.com*): *http://ted.com/talks/david_carson_on_design.html* Note Dave Carson's comments on the effect of poor face-ups at an emotional level (unsuitable use of advertising facing matter in *People Magazine*'s 9/11 issue).

'Because the competitive landscape of the web is such that the site which looks and works best gets the most traffic, developers and designers put a premium on the presentation of that content and let structural markup take a back seat.'

Mike Davidson, Disney Internet Group

Setting up a new website

Media websites should be thought of as a three-way product: the title publishes information to their visitors, the visitors respond and supply content to the title and also communicate with each other. With all these combined demands, a major decision has to be made on the scope of the site and the number of pages it should contain. Your site should both meet the expectations of your primary target audience, who may be extremely web-savvy, and remain accessible to the wider Internet community. If a website is to feature complex media and handle multi-functional data, you will need to identify the technical resources and level of maintenance that will be required to support it. The cost of sourcing and supplying content, and managing technology, has to be contained within the title's budget.

A new website needs a strong brand and a memorable name can help to establish the title. Internet brand names have developed their own frame of reference. They evolved out of the technology and programming languages and in reaction to the informal culture of the web. Names such as Google, Yahoo! and eBay typify the humorous, casual approach of web companies. Although many print publications have the sort of title that can work online, such as *OK!* or *Glamour*, you may need to assess whether the name will retain its relevance on the Web. A media product that is published both in print and online may use exactly the same name with just the locator added – themagazine.com – or the web version can have an original name and logo that will convey a different but related identity to a potential new audience. The choice of name should be based on market research and user testing.

Web technology

The design of a website has to work within the technical parameters of the Internet. Websites are basically collections of HTML and image files, applets, widgets and other items assembled into pages using programs such as Dreamweaver. Every time someone opens a page, the relevant set of files is sent from the server to a browser. The files are stored on servers and transferred

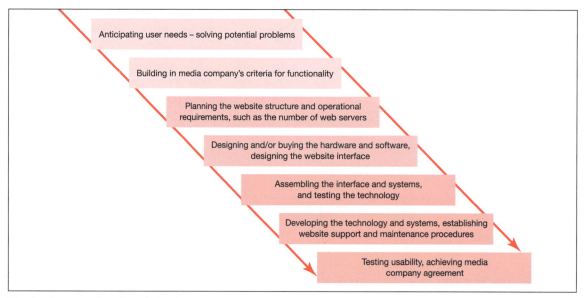

The development of media websites has to be carefully managed and subject to a system of review and revision, with goals set for each stage of the process.

to and from servers and PC by Wi-Fi, fibre optics or a high-speed telephone line. The most common form of access is broadband as it is widely available and can handle a large amount of data. It is important to understand the capabilities of the hardware and software to be used for your website (see Chapter 10, page 336).

New websites go through a series of initial developmental stages to determine how to combine the media company's editorial and financial requirements with Internet technology. The first step is to establish whether the media company's objectives can be met using the Internet, which means looking at both the target market in terms of users and the current developments in hardware and software. If a media company has a large enough budget, it can commission IT developers to create the programs it needs to launch a new product. However, it can take several years to fully develop new programs. The BBC took many years to set up the infrastructure for the iPlayer, but this timescale would not suit most commercial media companies' level of investment. More commonly, the development of a website design is set up around existing technology, and the site will be tested, redesigned and retested until it is ready for launch.

The site plan and navigation

The Internet is a very competitive place, and to succeed a website will need a degree of visual originality and a strong individual identity to stand out among the competition, while still maintaining those elements, such as clear sections, plentiful navigation and well-defined content areas, that will make it usable. But however well designed and innovative a website may be, the key factor is whether your visitors are able to use it. There is a balance to be achieved between the design and usability – the ease with which the site can be used by its visitors. The way people react to information on the Web is personal and immediate, and there is an expectation of more control. Most users like to be able to move quickly around a site and once they are familiar with how one website works, they tend to assume all sites will have a similar structure. Your web production team may have an established way of constructing websites, and you will have to decide whether to follow their system or create a new solution for your title.

However, if your site plan and navigation are unconventional, you should ensure that they do not befuddle visitors, as confused people do not stay around or return readily. Although it may be easier and cheaper to follow the normal web conventions, your designers should be directed to avoid producing yet another identical website and encouraged to consider how you can impress the title's desired audience.

The underlying page plan provides a mind map for the visitors to follow and has to be signposted so that they can navigate the website with ease. Planning the structure of a site begins with the **sitemap or spider** – a diagram that shows the underlying plan of the pages and their interconnectivity. The sitemap needs to be carefully planned to make sure the content is linked in a logical manner so the users can always find their way backwards, forwards and sideways through the information. There is no limit to the number of pages a website can contain, but the more pages there are, the greater the possibility of the design becoming confused. The principles of usability need to be applied, such as not making the visitor struggle to work out what to click on, or which page to move to next.

Reviewing the design suggestions

There are number of web design principles that should be applied when testing website designs:

- There should be several different methods of moving between related content, and these should be as clearly indicated as possible on each page
- Visitor interactions should be achievable in no more than three clicks and they should not have to scroll around a page to search for links
- Navigation features should be used liberally to provide repeated opportunities to move around the website and positioned in a way that will encourage the visitor to look at more pages and stay with the site
- The top and side menus, tabs, buttons, rollovers and clickable hyperlinks should give the visitor access to the site's content and beyond, and should be placed consistently on the pages
- For large, complicated websites, an easily accessible sitemap should be made available to show the entire structure and contents of the site
- Usability testing should be carried out by an external company or someone that has not been directly involved in the development process

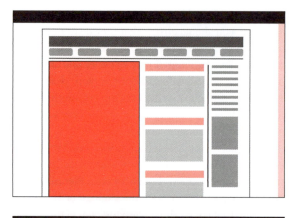

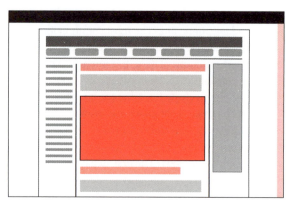

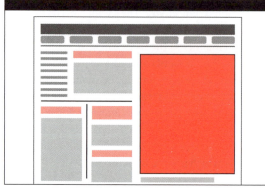

Web pages should be given a directional emphasis that creates a guide for the user to the purpose and informational value of the content. How items are positioned and sized is vital to how they will be perceived and their meaning interpreted. The most important information and/or the call to action should be positioned so that it draws the user's eye first. In countries where the convention is to read from left to right, users will tend to follow a web page from the top left downwards, and there is a positive bias towards information positioned on the left. Web page design conventions normally place the bulk of the content in a centre panel. Centred information can be seen as less weighted and users should follow the normal pattern of reading from the top down. Placing important items on the right hand side of the page can break users' expectations and catch their attention; however, it may also lead their gaze over and away from left and centred items.

'Less is more.'

Ludwig Mies van der Rohe

'Less is only more if more is no good.'

Frank Lloyd Wright

Planning a website design

Planning the design of a website requires balancing attracting visitors with dynamic and interesting content and not making the site overly complex, or the pages hard to follow. A good site needs to be easy to use and well signposted with intuitive links and clear, well-positioned navigation to guide the users to whatever they want to read, watch, do or buy. Both the design and the content of a site need to be very, very good in order to stand out on the Web. If there are thousands of print titles, there are tens of thousands of websites, and, for every successful site, there are many more that fail. The design of a media website should establish a strong look that will work for the brand and be attractive to the title's target audience, and so engaging that they will want to stay on the site and come back in the future.

A website's navigation has to be logical and easy to follow. It should be intuitive and tied to how people like to work with digital information, so that it guides users through the site, on to other media, and makes any interactivity obvious and accessible. Consistency of design and colour usage helps to indicate functionality and fixes a website's identity in the visitor's mind. While most media websites work with a fixed structure, you need to plan in how your site will be able to grow. This means ensuring that the pages can accommodate extra tabs and there is room to add categories to the menus and buttons. It is good practice, if you do amend the page structure, to make sure that the new graphics and navigation are in the style your visitors are familiar with.

User-centred design

A well-designed website should be planned around three main factors: how a user is likely to want to use it; where they will want to go first; and what particular actions and content they will use most frequently. A website needs to provoke *action* from its users, and the physical activity of moving the mouse and hitting the keys involves the user with the page more than eye action alone. On the Web, movement should not be linear but open-ended and interactive. The design of the pages and graphic elements should encourage the users to use the menus and click on buttons or links, and it is vital that there are plenty of navigation aids that inform the users where they are and will take them in any direction they want as well as allow them to navigate back home or to another page. The positioning, colour, tonality and scale of the page elements are important in leading the visitor's eye around the page and in creating implied directionality. The clickable items should be placed so that the visitor moves the mouse cursor from point to point through the content. These actions will engage visitors visually, physically and mentally.

The design of web pages follows the traditional principles of design, but other rules come from the technology and difference in online culture. For example, the way the early Amazon website presented tabs has been highly influential and, for a while, most websites used a similar style. You need to try to anticipate how graphic design and technology trends may develop, and how this will affect visitors' expectations of how a site should work and look. User-centred design should start from the visitors' experience, and all design decisions have to be targeted on providing them with the easiest, most enjoyable and accessible way of using a website.

The writing and visual content have to be media specific and a style should be developed to ensure they follow the title's editorial stance and employ the technology to provide visitors with the best possible experience. People use websites – they do not just read them. Copy should be punchy and lively – 300-400 words is as long as any web article should be – and features should be broken up into small sections of copy using images, cross-headings, links to video reports, etc. The key to structuring written content for the Web

Website page elements

When you are planning your website, you should brief the designer on the various options you wish to include, such as drop-down menus for country of origin. There are a number of conventions that are familiar to most visitors, and while these will be adequate for most requirements, you can also request customised solutions:

Advertisements	Links to sister titles
B2B links	Links to Twitter, Digg, etc.
Blogs	Media Player/streaming
Buttons	media
Classified ads	Multimedia, animation
Clickable/drop-down	Offers/downloads/
menus	subscriptions
Contact information	Picture gallery
Customer service	Retail/retail links
Home page	Rollovers
How to advertise on the	Search panels
site	Section pages
Hyperlinks/sponsored links	Splash screens
Index (sitemap)	Talkboards/forums/clubs
Interactive content	Ticker displays
Internal promotions	Web forms
Legal disclaimers	Widgets

is to simplify the information and vary the method of delivery, as well as including interactive hyperlinks (see Chapter 9, page 288). People react differently to information on-screen, and research has shown they prefer shorter pieces of writing, with links to a downloadable or printable longer version. A title's style of writing and visual presentation of online material need to match how the target audience would expect a page to look and how the audience will interact with the information. The updatable visual content also needs to be carefully managed and sourced to establish a consistent appearance for each page. Images in general should be direct and uncomplicated with contrasting colours that will stand out from the background (see *How to work with pictures*, page 216).

TIP A feature writing style should be developed that allows for cross-media hyperlinks that will assist the user to move around your site, access related archive material and provide connections to the media companies' other websites, blogs and print titles.

Web page dimensions

Before you initiate the design brief for a website, you need to research what types of computers your audience may have. Screen sizes vary, not only in size but also in proportion, and the differential can be extreme. You need to know whether your site will be accessed from small-screened mobiles and tablets, or larger screened laptops and desktops. As well as the size, the shape may also vary from square to wide screen. Web designers can create sites that adjust to fit the browser window and that allow the user to zoom in, but it is regarded as good practice to prepare a design for an average screen size so that the type and pictures are comfortable to read and view on most computer monitors. Whatever size and shape of screen the site may be viewed on, all the navigation and the main content should fall within the average proportions of the browser window.

Users are normally prepared to scroll downwards, but are accustomed to the page more or less fitting the width and do not like side-to-side scrolling. The total depth of a web page should be determined by an editorial decision on how much content the page is to hold and the subject of the material. For example, visitors to news media sites do not expect to have to scroll down on a home or section page, but may be prepared to scroll down to read a longer article. Users also tend to dislike having to scroll back up a page to access the navigation, and if you are intending to include longer runs to copy, there should be hyperlinks or 'return to the top' buttons placed at regular intervals down the page to return the user to the top of the page or the home page. You may also need to allow for down page menus to connect to other site features such as online TV, video reports and hyperlinks to external organisations.

Home pages in particular work best when functionality is directly associated to the content, such as making many items as clickable as possible. It is regarded as bad design practice to use scrolling windows within a page. Some titles go as far as splitting all the stories on the home page into independent content areas with their own scroll bars. This can result in a very busy and hard-to-use page.

Average base proportions for a website

Width	Length
768 pixels	634px or about one full screen
770 pixels	1,018px or about two full screens
774 pixels	1,334px or about three full screens

These measurements represent a range of useful basic page dimensions but it is recommended that the page design is dynamic to ensure that it automatically resizes in the user's browser window.

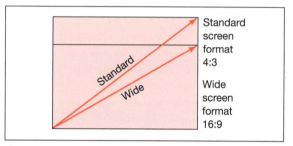

Source: Jakob Nielsen and Marie Tahler

Wider screens with an aspect ratio of 16:9 have largely replaced the earlier standard computer screen proportion of 4:3.

Grid usage

- The website grid has to control the vertical alignment of a page

- The grid needs to allow for margins and spacing between items and within content areas to prevent pages looking overcrowded, as this obscures rather than reveals the content

- The content areas should conform to the underlying grid to maintain consistent vertical alignments

- Type styles needs to be carefully sized to fit a given number of characters across each content area, and the leading chosen to fit the required number of lines of copy

- Text boxes should contain padding – space between graphic elements and text – to stop the text 'touching' the edges of the boxes

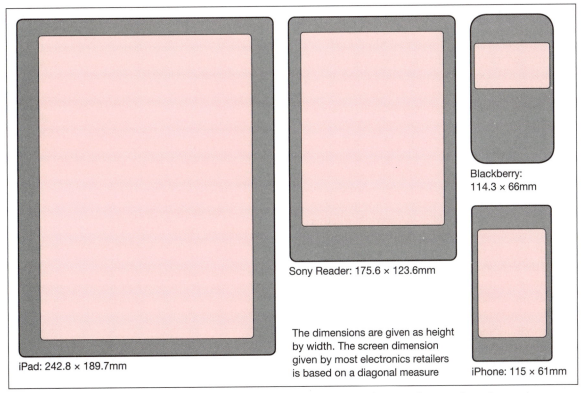

iPad: 242.8 × 189.7mm

Sony Reader: 175.6 × 123.6mm

Blackberry:
114.3 × 66mm

The dimensions are given as height
by width. The screen dimension
given by most electronics retailers
is based on a diagonal measure

iPhone: 115 × 61mm

The technical specifications of mobile devices can vary considerably with a wide range of screen dimensions and proportions, and the auto rotation means that pages may be viewed as portrait or landscape. Designs for each device require specific space for margins, scroll bars and control panels within the content area.

The website grid

However attractive a designer may make a website look, it needs a strong underlying grid structure to enable the live content to be positioned and updated by the production team. Although the essential nature of the Web is fluid and dynamic, using a grid gives websites a sense of order and provides a firm base that holds and balances the page elements. The grid creates visual consistency and aids users as it organises the content into a framework they can easily navigate. The title's grid should be designed so that the major elements – headings, menus and graphic units such as video players – follow a vertical alignment and maintain a logical visual relationship on the page. Most websites benefit from a formalised structure; however, you may require graphics that break up the regularity of the grid to emphasise particular elements. For example, having a style that enables you to use cutout pictures, or to run elements across two or more content areas, can achieve a more lively effect.

'The web is the ultimate customer empowering environment. He or she who clicks the mouse gets to decide everything. It is so easy to go elsewhere; all the competitors in the world are but a mouse click away.'

Jakob Nielsen, *Designing Web Usability*, 1999

TIP A commercial website's grid needs to be planned to accommodate the Internet Advertising Bureau (IAB, **http://www.iabuk.net**) standard web ads that are specified in a set range of size and shapes (pixel dimensions) (see page 70).

Technical and usability testing

You need to make sure that your website operates efficiently and that the technology works. Website designers and IT specialists should put new websites through rigorous testing to check that all the elements will download and appear as intended on a range of browsers, devices and operating systems. A web designer will continuously preview the pages as they are being worked on to see how they appear on a variety of browser windows. The final stage before the launch is for the designer, technical support team or company to set up a beta version – software or web pages to be tested by the public – to ascertain whether there are 'bugs' – problems with the programming or functionality. The results from the tests should reveal most of the technical issues, for example hyperlinks or forms not working as they are supposed to, or not at all. Once any problems have been resolved, the prototype site should undergo usability testing.

New websites should be subjected to testing by a selection of the target audience. The tests should examine whether this panel is able to access the content and navigate easily around the site. The design and media company teams can become so familiar with the product that it is hard for them to see any flaws that there may be in the design – it is very hard to imagine someone encountering the site for the first time when you have been involved with it from the concept stage. The testing should highlight any problems, and the testers' reactions to the design can be used as the basis for further amendments. The independent panel should continue to test the revised pages until you are certain that all the problems have been fixed. The website should not go live until all the technical problems have been resolved and the panel is satisfied that the site is usable.

The best place to assess your website design is to compare it with the other sites in your marketplace and to the most innovative websites on the Internet. There are many fantastic websites that can show how well it can be done; equally, there are a number of dreadful ones that make it clear what not to do. It is important to look at direct competitors and analyse their strengths and weaknesses, and to observe someone using their site. You need to have a range of experts and potential users involved from early on in the process as this will help you to make key decisions and reduce development time and costs.

Basic web page parameters

Web usability expert Jakob Nielsen has carried out extensive research into how people use the Internet. In conclusion, he has formulated 'Jakob's law,' which states that 'users spend most of their time on other sites than your site,' as his research has shown that people do not spend more than a small percentage of their time on any one site. His findings suggest that a website's design has to be easy to use with conventions that will be familiar to the user. The information covers optimal page dimensions, positioning and the value of functions to a user.

Optimal page dimensions

Page width: 770 pixels
Page length: 1,018 pixels, or about two full screens

These measurements represent a useful basic page dimension but it is recommended that the page design is dynamic to ensure that it automatically resizes in the user's browser window.

Average position of logo placement on websites

Upper left: 84%   Upper right: 6%
Upper centre: 6%   Other positions: 4%
Optimal logo size: 5,485 pixels (74 pixels × 74 pixels)

Most users will expect to look for a logo at the upper left corner of the window, which makes it the most effective place to position a logo. The size and proportion of the logo vary, and most logos are wider than they are tall, but a logo that fits within the 74 pixel square should be a reasonable size for the average page.

Optimal search box placement

Upper right: 35%   Upper left: 30%
Upper centre: 14%   Middle left: 12%
Other positions: 12%
Optimal search box size: 110 pixels or 18 characters

Some websites have more than one search box, while others do not offer a search facility. Where searching is available, it is better to position the box in the upper part of the page and towards to the sides – the research showed a very small preference for the right hand side. Users prefer to be able to see most of their enquiry, and a search box should ideally be long enough to accommodate several words of average length on a white background.

Most commonly used search labels

Search: 42%   Go: 40%   Find: 9%   Find it: 5%

Source: Jakob Nielsen and Marie Tahler

'Timing in life is everything.'
Leonard Maltin

Launching a new media product

Establishing the right moment to launch a title is essential. If the title is launched too early, readers or visitors may not be available to support it; too late and a competitor may have already established itself as market leader and locked in all the available advertisers' budgets. If you have had market research carried out, it may be time sensitive, and if there is too long a gap between receiving the results and the launch, the research may no longer be relevant. For example, changing consumer lifestyle aspirations and new developments in the title's intended market may make your title seem less appealing.

Selecting the optimum moment to launch a title can mean identifying the correct time of year, the mood of the moment and criteria such as the date of exhibitions or major sporting events. Another factor is that most companies and organisations set their advertising budget allocation a year in advance, and you need to ensure that the website or print publication is launched at the right time to tie in with their campaigns.

It is important to create and maintain a strong launch period. This is usually achieved by media companies offering advertisers discounted or free advertising space to build a substantial number of pages for a print launch, and to make sure all web ad spaces are filled. This helps the print and web titles to present a successful-looking product to the audiences and helps to establish their credibility. However, it is no good having 'a flash in the pan' first-print issue or launching a highly acclaimed website that cannot be sustained.

Presold advertising can be an indication of how well your title will be supported by the market. Having an annual financial forecast of advertising income will assist in planning the numbers of pages a print issue may carry, and how much can be spent on the continuing development of a website. It is vital that there is enough money to support the first year of publication. Readers and visitors need time to develop a relationship with the title and its contents, and advertisers may take a while to be convinced it will be worth investing in the product. Many first-time readers, visitors or advertisers will not make a permanent switch from their regular title. It is important that they can see a clear reason to change, such as the editorial content and design offering a completely new look at a subject. Advertisers need to see long-term readership or visitor loyalty developing before they will pay full rate card fees and commit to the title.

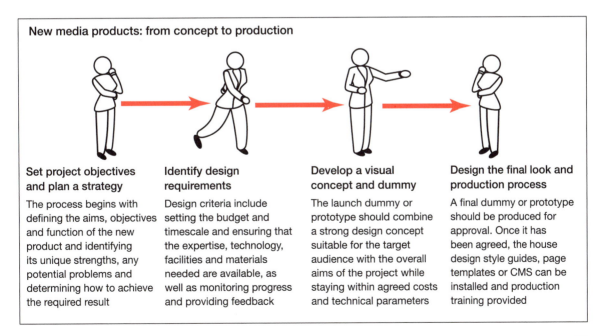

New media products: from concept to production

Set project objectives and plan a strategy

The process begins with defining the aims, objectives and function of the new product and identifying its unique strengths, any potential problems and determining how to achieve the required result

Identify design requirements

Design criteria include setting the budget and timescale and ensuring that the expertise, technology, facilities and materials needed are available, as well as monitoring progress and providing feedback

Develop a visual concept and dummy

The launch dummy or prototype should combine a strong design concept suitable for the target audience with the overall aims of the project while staying within agreed costs and technical parameters

Design the final look and production process

A final dummy or prototype should be produced for approval. Once it has been agreed, the house design style guides, page templates or CMS can be installed and production training provided

Launch objectives

Launches are normally planned in three distinct stages. The first stage is to involve the wider media industry, followed by a period of promotional advertising aimed at the target audience and finally establishing the title by running marketing activities.

The media industry and advertising associates usually cooperate with each other, since successful titles can produce mutual benefits. Some months before a launch, it may be worth setting up **contra deals** – offering other media companies and advertising agencies free ad space on the understanding that they will promote or support the new title. At the same time, to create a 'buzz' about the new title, PR companies or in-house departments will issue press releases and arrange for press, broadcast and online interviews to raise both industry and consumer awareness.

The second stage happens closer to the actual launch date. In order to make consumers aware of the title, the media company will run cross-media advertising and PR campaigns. This can include publicising the appointment of a high-profile editor or the celebrity endorsing the title. The advertising campaign should introduce the title's name and design to the public, and may well feature introductory offers or free gifts.

The third stage is to establish a long-term readership and returning visitor base through advertising and PR. You should also involve the title's editorial team to make sure that it produces strong content to back up the promotional activities. Each of these stages requires careful planning, and the promotional, advertising and presentation material needs to be consistent throughout the launch period. The first few months after the launch are crucial to building a brand, and a title needs to maintain the impact of the new design and content.

Launch tips

- Take advantage of a media company's other titles to support and advertise a new product launch

- Allow a generous amount of time for organising promotional events and producing related marketing material

- Ensure the launch runs to schedule as revising media information and rebooking advertising space will be time consuming and expensive, and venues and guests may not be available

- Offer promotional items

- Run a **teaser or tantaliser campaign** – a series of advertisements, mailing, offers or giveaways that lead up to and then reveal what is being promoted

- Use the launch to introduce the team members working on the title to their peers in the industry, financial backers, existing sponsors and potential advertisers

Three key stages in launching and establishing a new title

Involve the wider industry	Organise promotional activities	Establish the title
■ Instigate industry presentations ■ Prepare PR press releases aimed at the media used by the target market ■ Undertake consultation on the editorial programme with stakeholders ■ Develop advertising markets ■ Negotiate collaborative opportunities ■ Establish links with editorial contributors and build contacts ■ Seek endorsements from business associations and other organisations	■ Commission advertising campaign to create reader/user awareness ■ Prepare consumer PR press releases ■ Instigate launch marketing and promotional activities including parties and brand merchandising ■ Raise the title's profile through celebrity endorsements ■ Promote subscription offers for web and print ■ Entertain advertising clients	■ Establish and instigate a strategic plan to enhance the brand ■ Run competitions and interactive media to engage the target audience ■ Organise offers and giveaways to encourage audience loyalty ■ Strengthen relationships with advertising clients through entertainment and discounts ■ Develop point of sale and distribution channels

Building contacts

A special launch event can help a title's editors and writers to build a good relationship with any relevant news and specialist media agencies, PR and marketing companies. It is useful for a title to have close links with PR staff, and representatives of major brands can generate exclusive information and images and provide access to well-known people that the title wishes to interview.

The venue for the launch and the presentation material should be matched to the target audience. The decoration of the venue, style of the invitations, any promotional gifts and the catering are all part of the brand image and need to be carefully planned. There are a number of specialist event management companies that can be commissioned to handle the logistics of a large event. A major launch needs to be supported by other smaller presentations and one-to-one meetings to cultivate strong links with individual PRs and advertisers.

Well-known experts and leading figures in their field should be invited as their presence can add gravitas to a launch, and this may make them more likely to give interviews and advice on the title. A well-known celebrity may attract more people to the launch, but it is important their persona matches the brand.

A website launch may be a 'real-world' event or a virtual one, depending on the target market. New websites can be promoted by alternative advertising methods such as viral and guerrilla campaigns, and social media and AR websites offer opportunities for person-to-person promotions. Digital promotions can work in conjunction with traditional media such as posters, direct mail and press advertisements, as well as TV and radio campaigns. Information about a new website or publication should be sent to all those who might possibly be interested to coincide with the launch date, and websites published by relevant organisations, groups and bloggers should be encouraged to include links to your site.

'The more digital you are, the more global you can become. The more global you are, the more digital you can become.'

Keith Weed, CMO, Unilever

Audience profiles and reader services

You will need to register the new print or online title with **BRAD** Insight, the company that provides media and marketing data, and once it has become established the media company should apply for an ABC or ABCe rating. The media industry uses BRAD and the Audit Bureau of Circulation to provide advertisers with information on their titles, such as the audience profile, print circulation or number of website unique users. Most media companies submit the audience profile and other data on a title to the Audit Bureau of Circulation, an organisation that verifies the circulation and UU numbers and issues an accredited ABC or ABCe rating.

BRAD (British Rates and Data) Insight is the advertising industrys' preferred source of data on media products. The website covers almost every title published in Britain, and contains information on readership, circulation, UUs, advertising rates and technical criteria. This data needs to be made available to those handling marketing and promotions as soon as possible because it is used as the basis for persuading advertisers to continue to support a new title.

Print readership figures are normally derived from market research surveys carried out by companies such as the National Readership Survey that provide information on trends in readership as well as data on individual titles. Such organisations run continuous surveys across a large population sample to discover the number of readers either of one specific issue of the newspaper or magazine, or for consecutive issues over a given time period, for example January to June 2009, or April 2009 to April 2010.

Circulation relates to sales; however, the criteria by which a media company calculates how many issues it has sold may vary. For example, many newspapers controversially include **bulks**, the number of free issues given away at airports, in hotels, coffee shops, etc. The circulation of a magazine may just indicate the number of copies distributed to the public; however, the

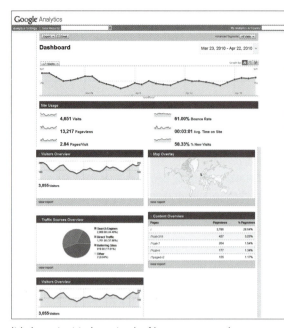

It is important to keep track of how many people are visiting your website, where they are located and which pages are most popular.

distribution of print publications is often handled by wholesalers on a sale or return basis, with circulated copies being eventually returned to be pulped, or delayed or destroyed in transit. There may also be a number of promotional copies that are given away to contributors and advertisers.

Circulation and readership can vary from issue to issue and season to season, depending on the nature of the title and external factors such as the weather. And the industry remains divided on whether the number of visitors to an associated website should be included as part of an overall circulation figure. Despite these variations, advertisers do consider these figures to be an indicator of a publication's success or failure.

UU numbers and page and advertisement click-on rates are used to judge which content is most popular and to identify the items on a website that are raising

revenue. The methods used to calculate the UU numbers for online media are based on identifying and counting each single visitor to a website. The visitor is counted only once, no matter how many times they revisit. This is achieved either by getting visitors to register a UU name and password or by attaching a cookie to the user's browser that generates an identifying code. The click-on or click-through rates are produced by web analysis companies and sites such as Google Analytics that measure how many times a user views each page and/or clicks on an ad. The rates are calculated as a percentage by dividing the number of click-throughs by the number of page visits.

The design brief for a title should be planned to include developing a solution for the media information that will ensure it is easy to find and follow. Media data can be made available to advertisers on a separate website, as well as by a link from the title's own site. This decision may depend on the subject and industry sector; for example, a B2B title may find it beneficial to have its media information directly available as a page on the main site, while some large companies run corporate media sales websites. Carefully written and presented advertising data can play a major role in establishing the value and trustworthiness of the title, and you should pay as much attention to the design and content of the media information as you would to the look of the actual title.

Key media information

Advertising costs	Paid-for or controlled
Advertising media	circulation
specifications	Price list
Audience profile	Reader/user profile
Circulation per annum	Readership/UUs (audited/
Contact details	not audited)
Deadlines	Status in industry
Longevity/newness	UU
Page hits	

Summary Pre-planning a publication and website

The subjects covered in this chapter are described as general principles and practices, and overall these will hold true. However, every media company handles research and development projects in its own way, and each new media product poses different design, editorial and technological questions that need case-specific solutions. While the rules of design and standard industry methods should always be applied where possible, they should not become constricting. It may be that, once all the market research and other practical criteria have been considered, a new concept may need a radical, rule-breaking design and innovation technology in order for it to succeed.

Design and development criteria

- Design gives substantive form to media concepts by visualising information in order to convey a specific message to a target audience.

- A business and market model for a new media venture has to be established before the visual treatment can be created. New products need a unique selling proposition (USP) and strong visual branding: a good title name and logo can convey the entire concept in a single word and be central to visualising the look.

- Market research and analysis must be carried out, and all new media products must be planned with cross-media links and for multimedia production.

- Titles that are to be published in more than one medium have to maintain a consistent brand identity in print and online, and the platform and paper (substrate) can have a substantial effect on the perceived value of a product.

- Media design should present the content in a manner that allows the reader or user to find their way with ease through the print publication or website. A well-organised and signposted title engages the reader or visitor and helps to build brand loyalty.

- An online or print title is made up of individual pages and their relationship to one another. Consistency in page design and typographic treatment serves to link sections and hold a brand identity.

- Establishing the right moment to launch a media product is essential, and it is important to create a strong launch period.

Website development

- A website needs visual originality and a strong individual identity to stand out on the Internet. A website needs to provoke action from its visitors and should be thought of as a usable product rather than just a publication.

- Websites should exploit the multimedia and interactive potential of the Internet to provide content that will make visitors want to stay on the site, and come back in the future, but should not be so complex or feature heavy that they become hard to use.

Advertising and content planning

- Advertising has traditionally been the greatest source of revenue for media companies. Advertising space is sold by ad dimension and length of ad exposure, and web advertising is also costed by ad views or click-ons/throughs. Audited readership, circulation and website visitor numbers are used by media companies' advertisers to attract and to fix the cost of advertisements.

- A media product has to be saleable to client companies as a good place to reach their customers. The features and other content for a title can be planned and issued a year in advance to attract advertisers and sponsors.

Activities and development

The questions and action points below have been designed to help you identify the key commercial and design criteria that should be considered when launching a new media product. You should review a number of titles in both media to ensure your choices reflect current market trends. Visit the *Design for Media* website for more fact and action sheets, sample templates, type schemes and colour palettes at **www.pearsoned.com/hand**.

Questions

Question 1

Below is a list of criteria that have to be taken into account when planning a new title. Numbering from 1 to 10, indicate which ones you consider to be the most important and which the least.

_The name
_The media
_The substrate
_The content
_The design style and underlying structure
_Potential advertising revenue
_Large target audience for the title
_Marketing and promoting the new title
_Distribution opportunities
_Secondary trading opportunities

Question 2

From the list choose 10 design and editorial features you consider to be the most important to mention in a new music webzine launch promotion. Look at existing music-related magazines, websites and digital editions for inspiration.

Logo/name – incl. locator	Streaming music
Target audience	Retail
Famous names/celebrities	Downloads/free giveaways
Future editorial contents	Forums
Latest news	Clubs
Product info	Social networking
Gossip	Personalisation
Reviews/listings	Interactivity
Multimedia features – video	User-generated content
Games	

Action point

You are going to launch a quarterly coastal lifestyle print publication, tablet apps and website that feature the British coastline and seaside towns. The title's purpose is to promote tourism and appeal to those thinking of relocating to the coast. Consider the following questions, and draw up a pre-launch plan.

- Would it be better to launch in the spring, summer, autumn or winter?
- Are there any TV programmes scheduled that may stimulate interest from the target readership?
- Are there economic circumstances that might create a need for the content?
- Are there environmental concerns that may be relevant?
- Are there secondary interests around the title such as exhibitions or events?
- Will there be any new products or services coming on the market that would be a good fit with your title?
- How could your title appeal to those who are looking for a career/lifestyle work balance change?
- What sorts of products and brands might wish to advertise their products, and when?
- How, where and to whom should the title be advertised?
- Should below-the-line marketing communication activities, such as direct mail or advertisements in local newspapers/magazines, be undertaken?
- Would an above-the-line TV campaign be appropriate?
- What other ways could you use to promote your new title?

HOW TO WORK WITH LAYOUT

- The digital workplace
- Page production basics
- The page production process
- Working with content management systems (CMSs)
- Print page design and construction
- Web page design and construction
- Tablet and iPad page design and construction
- Software integration

The *How to work with layout* pages provide you with a guide to developing visually appealing layouts using essential design techniques. These pages give practical advice on managing the page production process and integrating cross-media publishing computer programs. They also show you how to apply design concepts and create successful layouts.

The digital workplace

The page production work flow

Working in a shared digital environment involves understanding a media company's operating systems. Most publishers and advertising agencies employ central servers networked to individual work stations with Internet access. While some companies use a proprietary page management software, others prefer to establish their own system of folders to hold information such as page templates, standing artwork, images, copy and page make-up documents.

Whatever information structure is used, it is good practice to establish a job folder and agreed folder and file naming protocol to allow all of those working on a page to locate the associated copy and images (see page 270). Company practice may be to set up the job folder on the server or your work station. A job brief should be supplied that contains all the information necessary to create the job folder and associated subfolders, such as the title and publication date or client name, the number and/or size of pages, subject of the story/advertisement, section, etc. The first step is to set up a main job folder for the title/issue or client, and a series of subfolders to hold the standing artwork, copy, images and any other page assets such as video or audio files. Print folders should be broken down into individual subfolders for each section, spread or page.

Page asset folders also need an internal information structure. For example, an image folder might contain a subfolder for pictures sourced from image banks with another for commissioned photography. And within these folders there may need to be another series of subfolders containing a set of images for each target medium. As there may be several versions of the same image, the folder and file naming protocols have to be absolutely clear to allow for picture retrieval and prevent confusion.

The information structure: servers, folders and files

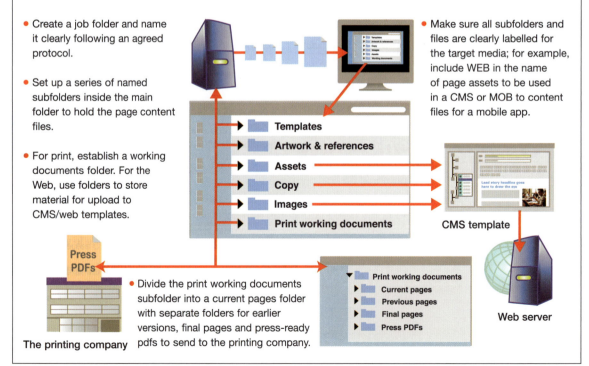

- Create a job folder and name it clearly following an agreed protocol.

- Set up a series of named subfolders inside the main folder to hold the page content files.

- For print, establish a working documents folder. For the Web, use folders to store material for upload to CMS/web templates.

- Make sure all subfolders and files are clearly labelled for the target media; for example, include WEB in the name of page assets to be used in a CMS or MOB to content files for a mobile app.

Templates

Artwork & references

Assets

Copy

Images

Print working documents

CMS template

Press PDFs

The printing company

- Divide the print working documents subfolder into a current pages folder with separate folders for earlier versions, final pages and press-ready pdfs to send to the printing company.

Print working documents
Current pages
Previous pages
Final pages
Press PDFs

Web server

The print template

Print templates form the hub in which all editorial content is assembled, with the page layout being built up from word processing documents, image and graphics files. When working on a page, it is good practice to rename and save earlier versions of amended page make-up, Word and image files as well as archiving all related material.

Page make-up programs embed the content of text files into the document so the original word processing files only need to be kept for reference once copy has been imported. However, image or graphics files should remain linked to the source program files and should be kept on the hard drive or an external drive during the page layout process.

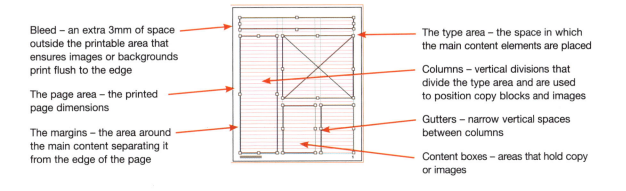

Bleed – an extra 3mm of space outside the printable area that ensures images or backgrounds print flush to the edge

The page area – the printed page dimensions

The margins – the area around the main content separating it from the edge of the page

The type area – the space in which the main content elements are placed

Columns – vertical divisions that divide the type area and are used to position copy blocks and images

Gutters – narrow vertical spaces between columns

Content boxes – areas that hold copy or images

Web templates

A website's design is stored as templates that hold the major page elements and usually provide some choice of type styles and image positions. Templates may be accessed through a CMS, a computer program that operates through an interface of type-activated fields,

drop down-menus and click options. CMS programs are used to create new pages, upload or enter and edit copy and images, update menus, control multimedia assets and embed hyperlinks. Web design programs may also be used to produce media websites.

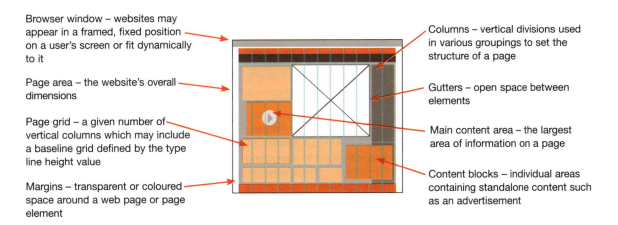

Browser window – websites may appear in a framed, fixed position on a user's screen or fit dynamically to it

Page area – the website's overall dimensions

Page grid – a given number of vertical columns which may include a baseline grid defined by the type line height value

Margins – transparent or coloured space around a web page or page element

Columns – vertical divisions used in various groupings to set the structure of a page

Gutters – open space between elements

Main content area – the largest area of information on a page

Content blocks – individual areas containing standalone content such as an advertisement

The page production process

Working with print templates

A print title's house design styles are stored in page make-up program templates that are used to assemble copy and images on the page. A title's design elements can be entered into windows: for example, the Paragraph Styles window which enables copy to be formatted from a list of styles for headlines, body copy, captions, etc., and the Colour or Swatches window which is used to apply house colours for type, box backgrounds and frames. You can also control the intensity (tint) and opacity (transparency) of the selected colour.

Print layouts are set up using content boxes – fields that allow you to position copy and images anywhere on the page. Content boxes are drawn using 'tools' accessed from the program's Tool Box.

To begin a print layout

- Launch the software program and open the template for the page or section and name and save it in a job folder, following the agreed protocol.
- Update headers and footers (title and issue date), folios (page numbers) and any other page furniture.
- Open and read through the copy file and amend it if necessary.

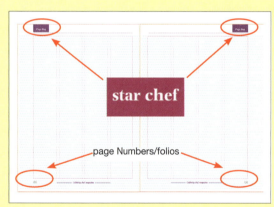

star chef

page Numbers/folios

- Open and assess the visual content files to make an initial selection of images.
- Place the content on the page using the margins, columns, gutters and baseline grid to set the width and depth of boxes.
- Use the house design style to ensure that the size, shape and position of the content boxes maintain the correct look for the title.
- Develop the layout by repositioning, resizing and reshaping boxes using the square 'handles' that appear at each corner and in the centre of each side.

Headline goes here headlin

- Use the baseline grid to set the horizontal alignment of boxes and to insert spaces (e.g. a two-line space between the headline and standfirst).
- Use the title's house style guide to apply the correct type styles.
- Draw a text box and place or input the headline, standfirst, caption, copy and other type elements.
- Select the copy to be styled, open the Paragraph Style window and click on the relevant house style.
- Check the house style guide and note how colours may be used.
- Open the Colour or Swatches window to see the list of house colours. To apply a background or frame colour, click on the content box, then click on the required colour from the list. To apply type colour, highlight the copy first with the type selected.

A range of trial templates can be downloaded from **www.pearsoned.com/hand**

Building the page

Step 1 Go through the material and select content that follows the title's design ethos.

Step 2 Work out the best position for the lead picture – consider the effects of alternative horizontal and vertical crops and different sizes.

Step 3 Apply the correct type style to the headline and standfirst and place the lead picture to ensure there are clear points of entry for the reader.

Step 4 Draw content boxes for the text, flow it in and apply the body copy Paragraph Style to see how much of the page it will fill.

Step 5 Import all necessary page content such as images, graphics, captions, picture credits, sidebars, boxed copy, quotes, etc.

Step 6 Liaise with the writers should there be insufficient written content or cut the copy if you need to use more images.

Step 7 Consider whether you need to use coloured backgrounds, tint or transparent boxes to separate and add visual interest to sidebars,

The layout of a page or spread can be developed by trying out various combinations of images, headlines and other copy elements to see how well they work together; this process may continue through several stages, from the preliminary sketch to the final proof, before a desired result is achieved.

boxed copy or captions, and to enhance the overall appeal of the page.

Step 8 Add design style details such as frames around picture boxes and dividing lines between type columns or separate stories.

Step 9 Check the completed page on-screen for style and editorial errors. Then print out a proof and check it on paper to make sure the layout works and all the copy is legible.

Step 10 If further changes are needed, revise and resave the page file, giving it another version number, and proof/print out the page again. Repeat this process until the content is correct and the page ready for press.

The points system

Type, leading (line spacing) lines and box frames in page make up programs and other software are specified in points. 1 point = 0.352mm or 1/72nd of an inch – the points system is based on the 6–12 scale.

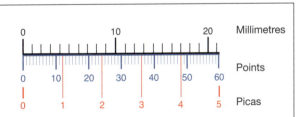

Horizontal measures such as column widths may be given in picas: 1 pica = 12 points or 4.233mm. Picas are the default width measurements in US print page make-up programs that use decimal inches for the depth. Measurement settings can be changed via the Preferences menu in most programs.

CMSs: the basics

Working with CMS programs

CMS programs are used by media companies to run websites on a day-to-day basis. The software provides a set of templates that are used as the basis for pages in each section or category (menu item) on a site. When a new page is set up, for example a home page with navigation, the metadata – information required by web servers and search engines to find the page – has to be entered into the CMS to ensure the page functions and is searchable.

CMSs allow those working on a website to key in headings and sells, place and edit copy from text editing programs and upload multimedia assets. The software's main menu manages the content with drop-down menus for inserting images, video, audio, animation files and copy. The drop-down menus give access to windows that enable menu categories to be changed, copy and visual assets to be edited, hyperlinks created and widget applications embedded.

Setting up a new page

- New pages require the metadata to be inserted so that web servers can identify and locate a page by name, page title and URL.

- The metadata must include a precis of articles and a range of searchable key words in order that pages can be found and key facts displayed by search engines.

- The initial set-up should record the writer's name and include a thumbnail image for the home page listing.

- A new page may need to be assigned to a category that corresponds to a menu choice.

- Access to new pages may be assigned to specific members of the production team.

The first step when working with a CMS is to select the template for the type of page you wish to set up.

Page management

Most CMS programs generally offer a choice of styles for headings and sells with standardised type styles for the copy. Page management menus often allow some further styling of the copy, such as inserting paragraph returns and for the use of bold or italic fonts.

The page management menu options normally include cutting and pasting copy into the CMS from a text-editing program. Copy should be fully subedited before being imported into the program to minimise the need for revisions.

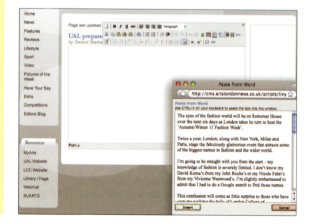

CMSs: the basics

Asset management

The asset management menu in a CMS controls how images, videos, sound, animation and other files can be inserted and positioned.

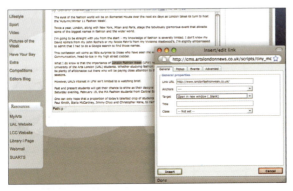

An image must have an identifying URL, a brief description of the content and a caption.

The size and position of an image on the page are controlled via the Appearance tab.

- The Image menu: the Appearance tab allows an image's size and position to be edited and adjusted.

  TIP Make sure the Constrain Proportions option remains checked.

- Most templates require images to be pre-prepared via an image-editing program to a default size or proportion in RGB at 72dpi as a JPEG or PNG.

- It is important to preview the image on the page to check that it does not 'crash' into the copy.

Inserting a text hyperlink

Use CMS text hyperlinks to create access points to other websites.

To make a text link active:

- Open the target web page and copy–paste the URL (http://. . .).
- Select the words in the copy you wish to make a link.
- Open the Insert/edit link window and paste in the URL, check 'Open in new window', then click on Insert.

The finished page has to be approved by the web editor or manager before it is published.

Print page design and construction

Creating a modernist layout

1 In this layout, the diamond holds the centre of the spread with the image filling the left hand page. The right hand edge of the image divides the diamond in two, creating a strong vertical emphasis. The horizontal vertices of the diamond move the reader's eye across the pages, linking the focal point of the image to the column of copy.

2 The circular wind vane is balanced asymmetrically against the diamond and, with the triangular support, creates a geometric form that is perceived as being in front of the diamond.

3 The horizontal tonal divisions in the background of the image conform to the Rule of Thirds, and provide texture as well as visual stability where they cross over the central diamond form.

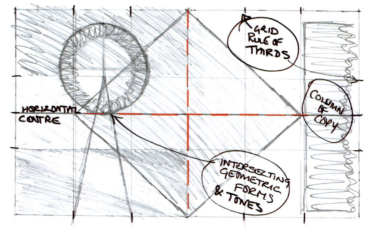

- The modernist look for this layout has been created by using a vertical three-column grid in combination with the Rule of Thirds design principle. The resulting nine-division grid and its interstices have been utilised to position and balance items and to set actual or implicit alignments.
- The spread balances both horizontal and vertical elements.
- The key to establishing the architectural style of this spread lies in controlling the geometric and tonal relationships between the type blocks, image areas and open white space.

Creating a type-based layout

1 In this spread, the type and background image merge on the page into one expressive whole. The written content is still accessible, but the layout is primarily designed to convey mood and emotion which here outweighs the need for immediate readability.

2 The large letters have been used as 'concrete language' to emphasise sensory experience over pure information.

3 The capital letters mostly fit into the grid and align with other characters, symbols and copy blocks.

4 The number 2 has been employed to indicate its synonym. The four icons can be interpreted as 'love message, play audio', and also add visual interest as well as counterbalance the arrangement of large capitals.

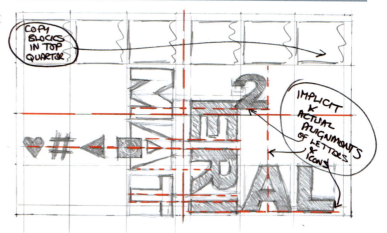

- Type used as image can convey both written and visual communication.
- Type-led layouts require well-defined typefaces with letterforms that will work in isolation as well as combination.
- When working with type only, changing the conventional position of words and letters can promote the reader's interest by challenging their expectations.
- The design of type is based on geometric forms that provide an in-built spatial relationship that can be exploited when creating type-led layouts.

Print page design and construction

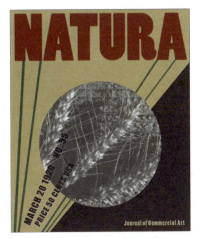

- Modernist mastheads are normally in a strong colour and sized to ensure they are the primary visual cover item.
- Images contain directional elements that can be used to lead the eye towards the masthead or other page content and to attract attention to the title, which is particularly important in a retail environment.

- Modernist pages most commonly employ asymmetrical balance, as symmetrical layouts tend to limit eye movement.
- It is best to keep the overall layout simple and uncluttered.
- When deciding on the colour scheme for a modernist design, use black and white as a base with one of two main colour combinations: either soft muted colours and tones or strong primary colours.
- Modernist design is most often associated with sans serif typefaces, but modern geometric serif type styles also work well when set against structural forms and angular patterning.

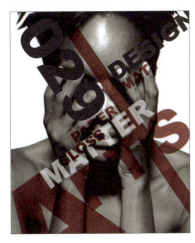

- Type-led covers apply the concept of type as image.
- Placing letters over the page edges creates entry points to the cover.
- Type at an angle adds drama.
- Transparent layers can create pattern and interest.

- Type-led designs generally employ an underlying grid to unify the content.
- An overall coloured, blended or textured background will function to hold type-led layouts together, particularly on pages without photographic images.
- Type-led layouts work well with a restricted colour palette. Keeping groups of characters in one colour maintains a visual connection even if they are in unusual positions or separated from other letters in the word.
- However complex the type design, the page content has to be accessible to the audience and allow readers to comprehend the text.

Print page design and construction

Creating a classical minimalist layout

1 This layout has been carefully planned and art directed so that the typeface, colours and photo shoot work as a whole to reinforce the design ethos of the title.

2 The use of white space is crucial as it frames the copy block on the left of the layout and defines its relationship to the large beige capitals. The white type links these elements to the letters and copy block on the colour matched image.

3 The typography has been positioned to form a frame around the focal point of the picture, which has been styled to contain details such as the mop-headed flowers that echo the typeface's elegantly rounded serifs.

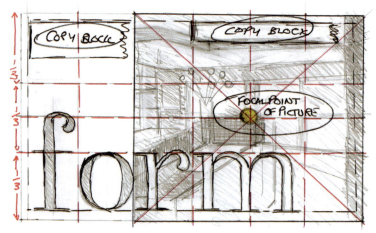

- Classical minimalist design is predicated on closely matched typography and photo styling.
- Minimalist layouts reduce the page content to the least number of items laid out in a clean, architectural style based on the geometry and content of the main image.
- Classical minimalism advocates the use of one typeface only in varying weights, sizes and colours for a layout or page.
- Layouts often employ one colour and black, but can use tints of the colour.

Creating a deconstructionist layout

1 This deconstructionist layout uses a visual language that invites the reader to become involved in discovering meaning, and invites reinterpretation.

2 The page area and margins have become absorbed into the layout, which is post modern in approach. The freeform design is intended to challenge assumptions such as the need for pages to follow a formal grid.

3 The page content has been interwoven to form a centreless, painterly design that follows an internal visual logic.

4 The shapes and structure of the letterforms, the spacing between words and characters and their position on the page have all been treated as part of the design, and break the classic typographic rules that direct how people read type.

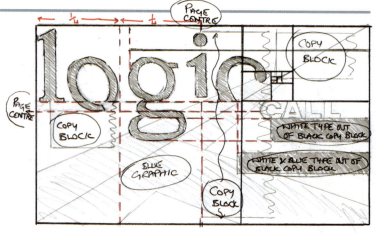

- The deconstructionist approach to layout is to regard a page or spread as an entity, with every element valid for change and re-presentation, from the completeness of letters to replacing characters with numbers or symbols.
- Deconstructionist layouts are more likely to be based on artistic composition rules such as the Golden Section than to employ a modernist grid.
- Deconstructionist page designers fully exploit digital technology and programs that permit them to manipulate and reconfigure classic page elements, and incorporate a radical post modern visual language.

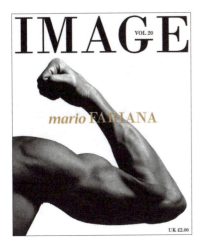

- The masthead on classical minimalist covers is often in a typeface designed specifically for the title.

- Classical minimalist covers normally feature one strong main image.

- Minimalist publications limit cover lines, relying on the strength of the title's ethos to attract their audience.

- The photography chosen for classical minimalist layouts should be technically excellent with simple but elegant photo styling.

- Classical minimalist layouts often work outwards from the main photograph or image, with page content balanced off or aligned to elements within the image.

- Classical minimalist layouts often use diagonal divisions or triangular perspective within images as positioning points for type and other page content.

- Although classical minimalist pages are visually simple, their balance, colour and mood have to be considered as part of the title's overall page flow.

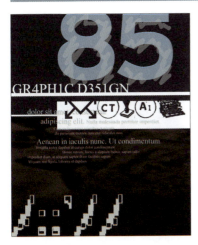

- Deconstructionist covers are always unconventional and the style is most often used for art and lifestyle titles.

- This masthead, with the name in smaller type than the issue number, illustrates the quirkiness of the style.

- The unique graphic language of post modern titles engages their audience.

- The overlaid and interlocking elements of deconstructionist pages should be positioned to direct the reader's eye through and around the layout.

- Deconstructionist layouts often involve readers by inviting them to solve clues or puzzles in order to gain access to the information.

- All items on a post modernist page are regarded as having meaning, so every graphic symbol, image, typographic element and spatial arrangement can be used to carry information or an emotional message.

- Deconstructionist use of colour is derived from the content or message.

Web page design and construction

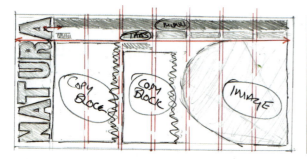

Creating a modernist web page

1 Modernism is widely used in website design as it provides users with a familiar framework that makes it easy to access information and follow the navigation.

2 Modernist web pages should be uncluttered and direct, with as few items on the page as possible and layouts that employ a multi-column vertical grid.

3 Modernist typography is normally subtle and used as background for the content. Type should be simply styled, clearly readable and left aligned.

- Modernist pages are based on regular shapes such as rectangles; here the image may appear to curve but it has been embedded within the green background box.
- It is a good idea to place logos on the left hand side, an area associated with brand imagery and navigation, and one of the first places users tend to look.
- Modernist type is best kept to one sans serif font, and any type and background colour combinations need to maintain readability and visual cohesion.
- Type styles and sizing should provide a clear visual hierarchy to guide the user through the content.
- This page uses a subtle colour palette that is typically modernist, with autumnal hues that echo the title's environmental message.

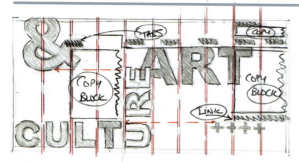

Creating a type-led web page

1 Type-led pages need a clear underlying structure to ensure usability – most web users are not prepared to stay on a site and search for information that is not instantly apparent.

2 For type-led pages to work, it is necessary to control the spaces between and around type elements: too much space breaks the association between letterforms, too little makes the page visually confusing.

3 Type-led designs work best when based on one font.

4 Sans serif typefaces fit particularly well into a grid.

- Type-led pages require a unifying graphic element such as a single background colour, texture or pattern to hold the letterforms, navigation and content blocks.
- The size and proportion of letterforms in type-led designs need to be planned so that the user's eye is drawn through the content by the typographic styling.
- In type-led pages, white space is used to counterbalance the cross-media elements by exploiting the fact that open areas on a page generate their own visual weight.
- Type-led pages can benefit from restricting the number of colours used and controlling their intensity.
- Layering, transparent type and animation of a few carefully selected type elements can help to add interest to static type-only pages. Letterforms can also be active and used for hyperlinks and mouseovers.

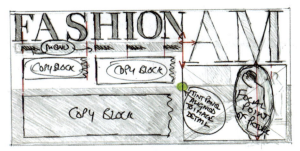

Creating a classical minimalist web page

1 Classical minimalism is well suited to the Web as the style's inherent sense of order and defined visual language provide clarity and consistency to a site.

2 The written content for classical minimalist pages should be concise with only one or two menus and as few links as it is possible to include without inconveniencing users.

3 Delicate serif typefaces or the softer sans serif humanist fonts best convey the typically restrained and sophisticated mood of classical minimalist pages.

- Minimalist pages that contain only a few items need at least one major element that is visually compelling or dramatic in order to gain and hold a user's attention.
- Minimalist page balance is achieved by establishing visual interrelationships between type, image and interactive media content that maintain the clean lines of the style.
- Classical minimalist typography relies on dramatic contrasts in scale which can require a web site template with tailored CSS for those elements, or, alternatively, large headings can be set up as text images.
- Minimalist pages normally use only soft colours, often with copy in grey, pale blue or white out of a tint panel, which is known to be relaxing to view on-screen.
- Minimalism's tendency to use very few page elements may enable rapid download speeds.

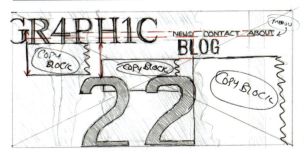

Creating a deconstructionist web page

1 Deconstructionist pages use tacit visual associations between the media elements to establish the connection of the page content to the navigation.

2 Deconstructionist designs should include overlapped and overscaled items to challenge users' expectations of how a web page should look.

3 Deconstructionist typography frequently features unexpected letter or word replacements, deletions and omissions to intrigue users and make the pages a little mysterious so that they want to stay on the site.

- Deconstructionist-style pages employ a montage of image, colour, pattern, type and interactive media to reinforce the mood and message of the site.
- The design of deconstructionist pages can be visually complex but should always make it clear how a user is to navigate through the site and interact with the content.
- Deconstructionist design uses non-linear spacing to move the user's eye around the page, and to offer a number of different opportunities and ways for the user to access the content and engage with the implied randomness of the style.
- Deconstructionist type is used not only to convey information but also as texture through the use of serif and sans serif fonts in differing weights and styles.
- Deconstructionist pages often employ multi-layering to create a sense of perspective or depth.

Tablet and ereader page design

Multi-dimensional layout

Devices such as the iPad tablet are able to convey a rich media experience that has changed the way audiences interact with titles. Pages for interactive, touch-screen devices need to be visualised in an immersive experience, similar to directing a film, with the added benefit of being able not only to zoom in and out, but also to move forward, backwards and up and down through the pages.

Page layouts have to be planned so that they can be viewed horizontally and vertically, and must allow for the interactivity on one page to be balanced against another. Features such as gyroscopic twist, tilt and the touch-controlled 360° image spin enable content to be presented through several different views and versions of each page.

Understanding how the audience physically engages with the devices and content has become an intrinsic part of

page design. The tactility of the user's experience can be managed through carefully placed scrubber bars and touch points that encourage the user to interact with the pages.

You now, even more than ever, have to consider the overall structure of a title and the interrelationship of the pages. Multi-viewers allow users to see every page at once at thumbnail size, as well as scroll through page by page. This means all layouts need to be visually harmonious and convey a cohesive narrative.

The effects of screen rotation have to be considered before content is produced, as pages have to be designed to work in both horizontal and vertical formats. The orientation of images and the deployment of interactive features should be broadly consistent to maintain the visual identity of the page.

The grid structure: visual cohesion and stability

| Contents/front page | News/interactive | Picture led | Text led |

A horizontal grid structure is used to place page elements at a consistent eye level. The regularity of the grid provides a formal structure to hold the interactive elements and guide the user through the pages. A grid can also help to stabilise the disorientating effects of zooming, multi-dimensional navigation and rotation.

News/interactive

Text-led feature page

The scrubber bar at the top of the contents page provides access to the title's sections, with a vertical navigation panel that employs thumbnail images as entry points to individual features.

This page uses a video of the writer as an introduction to a series of interviews, with the portraits acting as links to each of the interviewee's pages. The opening screen captures the mood while encouraging users to dive deeper into the content.

Relatively static pages can be used to introduce a topic. In this example, there are clickable arrows beside the picture that operate a slide show. Clicking on the chosen picture then takes you to another, more in-depth feature page.

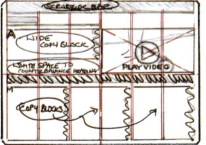

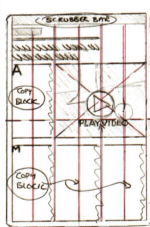

Creating page sketches

These preliminary drawings for the golfing title (shown on page 114) illustrate how sketches can be used when planning alternate horizontal and vertical layouts.

Developing a series of sketches can help to establish a cohesive layout scheme that will ensure design continuity no matter how the user moves through the pages. Pre-planning layouts can also help to ensure interactive pages work in visual terms, and that the functional elements are well placed within the design.

Adding personality and social media to interactive layouts

Contents/front page

A video message from the editor helps to personalise the content. The page also contains a link to his blog, Twitter and Facebook page to encourage users to build a relationship with the title and to become involved with its culture.

Software integration

Production technology: matching programs and platforms

Digital titles require every element of a page to conform to the technical criteria for the target media. Content files are produced through a range of specialist software and then used in a web design, CMS or print page make-up program. Each item of page content has to be processed to match the production platform and saved in the file type most applicable for publishing online, via a device or on a print substrate.

Image from source

Contact sheet in asset management software

Check resolution/resize

Image-editing software

Apply filter/effects

Adjust colour

Production-ready image

Import image into vector-based software

Apply text/additional design elements

Text from word processing software

FOOD COMPANY

Page layout/CMS software

Arrange all elements

Set type

Place images/ videos/audio clips

Publish

- It is good practice to source or create the best-quality imagery and multimedia assets you can obtain or afford. In technical terms, this means ensuring all software files match the production criteria for the output device.

- Asset management software is employed to open, review and select images, video and sound files, and also allows you to move items to related software for processing. At this stage, content files can be entered into work flow systems and catalogued or archived for ease of access.

- Media-editing software is used to check quality, exposure, colour accuracy and size as well as light and sound levels. This is the point at which any necessary adjustments and corrections are made.

- Editing software is employed to manipulate, construct and enhance media files. This may include 'Photoshopping', video and sound editing, including titling, transitions, timing, voiceover, music and adding special effects.

- In some circumstances, it may be necessary to combine digital files in one program to produce graphic, interactive or cross-media elements. For example, using a vector graphics program in conjunction with a database or image files to create graphs and charts, or adding interactivity to a series of still images to produce an animation or slide show.

- Once all individual asset files have been processed and prepared for publishing, they are imported into the specific page make-up program for their target media.

Technology, layout and production

The effective application of design and layout is underpinned by the right choice of technology and a well-considered work flow system.

A well-organised and managed process will make developing page layouts for any medium more efficient.

5 INFORMATION DESIGN

This chapter discusses:

- Information presentation – house design style
- Layout: placing content in a design
- The principles of layout
- Movement, shape and form
- Page layout conventions
- The baseline grid: print
- Designing with type
- Colour
- Substrate or screen colour
- Pictures on a page
- Cutouts
- Website design
- Web page structure
- Web images
- Picture and patterned backgrounds
- Convergent media

This chapter describes how you take a publication or website forward from the design concept stage, with advice on how you can use design and page make-up techniques to maximise the impact of your print publications and websites. It explains the role of the house design style and how it is applied to maintain the visual identity of media products. It also looks at how you can get the best results when working with type, colour and imagery.

'Style is merely the outside of content, and content the inside of style.'
Jean-Luc Godard, film director

'We seek visual reinforcement of our knowledge for many reasons, but primary among them is the directness of the information, the closeness of the experience.'

Donis A. Dondis, author and academic

The house design style will help you to operate within a set time scale (deadline), as it enables you to work quickly using pre-designed templates that contain all the title's design and technical specifications. Print and web templates provide a framework for applying the design structure and typographic style in a consistent manner. You will find the most efficient way to prepare a title for publication is to become familiar with the house style and work with the page guidelines.

Information presentation – house design style

There is a large number of titles across a wide range of media that all compete for audience attention, and any publication or website needs to present itself in an appealing and attractive manner to stand out from the crowd. Good design without interesting content may undermine the authority of a title, while well-written copy presented in a dull manner is unlikely to show off the information to best advantage. If you are working on content presentation you will need to develop information design skills and production knowledge that will allow you to maximise the visual impact of a title. In order to create print and online pages that convey the correct meaning to the reader and visitor, you will need to know how to plan and construct well-balanced layouts and understand how to work with a house* design style.

The house design style or website help pages will contain all the page layout specifications for a title needed by the production team. The designer or team who developed the design concept (see Chapter 4, page 79) should have provided a clear description of the overall design parameters, together with more detailed page layout instructions. This information becomes the title's style guide, with page-by-page details on how to apply the design, and advice on how to handle the day-to-day production processes. The house design style establishes a media product's brand identity, and you should always try to follow it as closely as possible, without allowing it to detract from the content.

Key house design style criteria

Print house design guide

Publication dimensions (page size)
Margin and gutter widths, number of columns per page
Page furniture: headers, footers, folios
Number of lines per column/page (baseline grid)
Average number of words per page
Design style rules
Typographic style rules: typefaces, sizes, colours and
  page-by-page usage
Typesetting: capitalisation, italics, em/en rules, bullets,
  hyphenation, justification, idents etc.
What each section and page contain
How items should be positioned on the grid
How and where to use boxed copy, backgrounds and
  other graphic items
How images should be chosen, prepared and
  positioned on the page
Colour palette(s)
Placing advertisements
Production specifications

Website CMS help pages

Website plan
Standard page content
How to create, edit and delete pages
Navigation: how to edit menus
Adding HTML: lines, backgrounds, coloured text
How to validate additional HTML
How to embed internal and external hyperlinks
How to place video and audio files in a media player
How to embed video and audio files
How to embed a widget
How to include visitor tracking scripts
Still image preparation
How to upload supplied advertisements

---

* House in this context implies the publishing house, but may
  refer solely to a particular publication's design style.

Extra: house style

Features

The features pages should be modular with an open layout which requires use of 'white space' that will create a balance between the headline, copy and pictures to keep a clean, modern look. Do not over complicate layouts.

Features need a strong headline and a good lead picture or 'hook' which should be larger than other images on the page. It is best to have a choice more than one headline and a selection of images as this makes page make-up easier.

All features are on the three-column grid. Pages 4-5 are a true spread and text and pictures can go across the spine and should follow the column guides and baseline grid. The house design and type style must be followed. Pages 6-7 form an untrue spread and text and pictures may not go across the spine. Where there is more than one article on a spread, 0.5pt cut and down rules should be used to divide the stories.

Sec... or f... sub...

columns, may be used to clearly differentiate between the main and side bar or tint box stories.

Colours

You can use the Extra Blue and Green house colours and Arts red for headline,s, boxes and side bar tints and frames. Only use one of the house colours and Arts red in an article, ie, Extra Blue and Arts red, or Extra green and Arts red.

Text

Main text is 8.5/12pt Stone Roman ranged left and with the first line indented, except for the first paragraph, which is full out.
A second story on a spread may be in 8.5/12pt Stone Bold ranged left with the first line indented, except for the first paragraph, which is full out.
The first par has a drop cap in the same font as the he...
th...
pa...
ca...
Yo...
Th...
fu...

H...

The basic font is Univers. Sizes run from 22/24.25pt to 66/68.25pt, but can be used larger in multiples of 11pt with a leading of +2.25pt.
You have three weights of type (Light, Black or Bold; the option of using house colours (Extra blue or green, Arts Red) allows for greater flexibility. Remember that headlines of 44pt and above have a minimum of a two-line space above and below; all others have at least a one-line space.
All headlines are ranged left. Text should not run alongside or above a headline

Standfirsts

The standfirst is in 33/35.25 Stone bold ranged left. Remember to leave a two-line space above and below. The standfirsts can be positioned beneath or above a headline. No full point (stop).

...ed in the main ...ead style) and ...ial demands

...ck to one-line ...ure pages

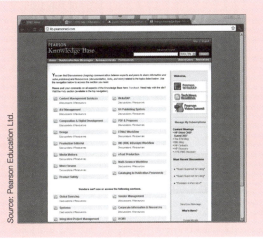

The house design style guide contains a detailed page-by-page guide to the publication's design with instructions on how to apply the style.

Online support services

Media companies that work cross-platform use the Web for operational purposes as well as publishing. Server-based websites can form a hub that contains information, assists with the exchange of knowledge and allows access to services, workflow systems and archives.

A website hub can be used to hold design, editorial and production materials such as templates, copy, images and multimedia assets. It can provide access to the content management system and publishing system, with direct links to printing companies. It can be used for other resources such as discussion areas, cataloguing and databases, and making relevant resources available to suppliers and partners.

Print titles often employ a standard layout for regular pages or sections to make them quick and easy to plan and construct.

Layout: placing content in a design

The convention of using a set pattern of content makes it easy for readers to find their way through any print publication, even one they have not read before, and using a standard model also aids navigation on a website. The layout of the content will vary with each issue or update, and the design for the pages and sections needs to be well organised and strongly defined to prevent the overall structure of the title being lost. The challenge for those designing and producing publications and websites is that, day by day or month by month, the visual presentation of the content must change, even though it covers the same main subject areas. Pages have to be constantly remade (to a greater or lesser extent) within the design parameters of the publication or website, and each new layout needs to make the title look fresh and inviting.

Individual pages should look interesting, no matter how often or infrequently the content is updated, but the layouts must always fit the overall structure of the title. A well-constructed page should enable a reader or visitor to follow the material in the correct editorial sequence and direct them onwards. This can be achieved by placing items in a way that establishes balance and implies movement. The placement of the graphic units – headlines, blocks of text, colour panels

and pictures – should be used to draw and direct attention. For example, a group of adjoined or overlapping objects, or having one much item much larger than others on a page, will attract the eye (see *How to work with layout*, pages 108 and 112).

There are a number of practical techniques that can be applied to set up the visual structure of a page and to control the way the information is presented to the reader or visitor. As well as fitting all the content, page layouts need to balance text and image, tonality and colour. The aesthetic principles that govern all two-dimensional art forms such as painting also apply to media titles. There should be a centre of focus that creates the main entry point; this might be a large, black headline or a visually strong lead picture. The mid ground should hold the next level of content, for example the standfirst and pictures that carry additional information. Items of lesser importance, such as the section headings or tabs, should form part of the background, which also consists of the colour of the screen and paper. Graphic units can be given a lower priority on a page by reducing the scale of an item or making it lighter in tone or colour.

All pages have an inherent visual tension that can indicate either movement or stasis. Some layouts focus the eye in one place, while others may contain the illusion of linear, diagonal, triangulated or circular movement. Directionality can be suggested by setting large against small, dark against light and bright against pale. These techniques should be used to encourage the reader or visitor to shift their focus from one item to another. A page without an implied direction, or one that has very symmetrical and similarly sized graphic units, may appear static or repetitious. While websites can take advantage of animation, web pages that overuse flashing images and special effects can become unsettling and uncomfortable to read.

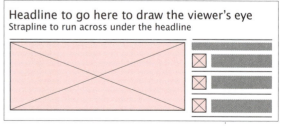

The positioning of graphic elements is critical to communicating the right message to the right audience.

TIP If you are producing a title for a specific regional audience you should research and use the design and layout conventions that apply to that group or location.

Balance comes from juxtaposing the size, tone, shape and directional emphasis of text blocks and images.

The amount of white space between items on a page can either unify or separate content.

'The challenge for the graphic designer is to turn data into information and information into messages of meaning.'

Katherine McCoy, graphic designer and educator

The principles of layout

People respond to visually pleasing designs more strongly than they do to efficient but dull ones. The attractiveness of the page, whether it is on the Web or in print, has an important part to play in communicating information. A fundamental design rule is to keep pages simple – do not overcomplicate or obscure the content. The urge to decorate and add 'interesting' effects is a temptation for some people involved in media production, and while this can result in a page that looks vibrant and lively, it may be inappropriate for the content. You need to consider your audience and its level of visual literacy. The fundamental purpose behind layout techniques and practices needs to be applied even if the title has an avant-garde design style. Whatever visual criteria are used, the ultimate aim is to make the content appealing, accessible, easy to read and easy to use.

The aim of layout is to present the page logically, and in an appropriate visual form, that communicates the editorial intention to the audience as they read and react to the content. If the look and content of a title are right, the audience should remain interested and invested in the medium, and will buy or visit it again.

Simple clean designs can be created by using white space and a limited amount of content.

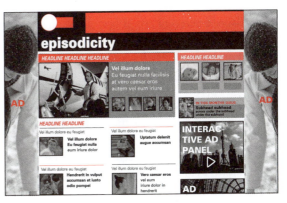

A page that contains many juxtaposed shapes and colours suggests energy and immediacy.

121

Movement, shape and form

When a reader or visitor first looks at a page, they will quickly scan the whole page, moving from item to item until they see something that focuses their attention. This rapid eye movement can be exploited and directed by the careful positioning of shapes, colours and scale, and by using the directionality inherent in imagery. There are set design conventions for pages that work with an audience's expectations. People are accustomed to reading pages from the top left to bottom right, and as the main headline is usually the first point of focus, it makes sense to place it at the top left. However, the practice of using the largest size of type for the main headline means that readers or visitors should be able to identify the most important heading, no matter where it is placed. A strong lead picture may

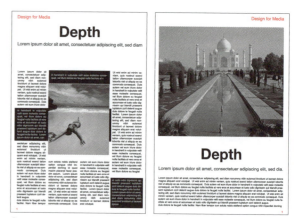

Convergent lines can create the illusion of depth.

Movement can be indicated by actions in imagery as well as multiple page entry points.

be positioned wherever it works best on the page, as long as it is has more impact than the other pictures and a clear relationship to the lead story.

Newspapers and magazines normally break their pages into a number of columns which have a down and up visual flow, with focal points such as headlines, images and graphics that stop the eye and indicate the importance of individual stories. The convention of reading from left to right creates a horizontal movement that works to counterbalance the verticality of the column grid. The reader's eye movement from left to right can be used to lead them through all the pages in an entire publication. Websites use the same principle with the main menu on the left, content in the

centre and advertisements on the right. They also use the eye's left to right movement to prioritise the running order of tabs.

Most pictures have an organisation of elements (composition) that leads the eye to the left or right and up or down. A picture with an off-centre **focal point** can be used to attract attention to a particular point on a page, or, by centring the focal point, attention can be held on the viewed page. The positioning and counterbalancing of items on the page can create a sense of movement and progression that guides the reader from item to item through the copy and on through the pages. Varying the position of content and graphic elements adds visual interest and helps to make it clear where a different topic is covered on the same page.

There are a number of basic designs that can be used to frame the content on a page. These can be used to create a structure that conveys a message in itself. The same content may provoke a different reaction depending on whether a symmetrical or dynamic treatment is used. If you are working on a news media product, the pages are likely to be carefully counterbalanced and geometric. Some magazines in print and online use the principles of understatement and economy of expression to convey authority or a sense of elegance, while others may employ exaggeration and spontaneity to capture an energetic and urgent feel.

TIP Humans react strongly to basic geometric forms, and especially well to circular shapes that remind them of a face. We tend to make eye contact with eyes in a picture – as we do with one another in real life – and then follow the direction in which the eyes are looking.

Symmetry/asymmetry

Symmetry in layout gives equal emphasis to comparable elements. Whether this works on a page depends on the relative importance of the items, as the information hierarchy may be unbalanced if the content is not meant to be equally weighted. Symmetry can be achieved by either balancing similar graphic units, or setting a picture against text blocks or open areas on the page. It works through tone and colour as well as dimension and proportion. Generally, repetition of size and shape, or mirrored positioning of pictures, type blocks or whole pages, should be avoided in layout unless it has a specific design purpose. However, if the purpose is to bounce the eye backwards and forwards between the items, or across the page or spread, then it might be an appropriate approach. Symmetrical layouts may appear static, and asymmetry can be a better way to suggest movement.

Most contemporary media titles use a modular design based on asymmetry, with layouts made up of contrasting graphic units placed on a formal grid. The style works through counterbalancing large elements against smaller items, for example creating a visual relationship between large type on or against a picture or open space. The contrast is achieved by controlling the scale, shape and colours of the content. Asymmetry opens up the possibility of exploiting the power of irregularity and visual dissonance to break with expectation, which should catch the reader's or visitor's attention.

Counterbalance

Where there is a contrast in size and shape, the relationship between the elements can be exaggerated and

White space

The open areas of a page are referred to as white space. These may be used to provide contrast to, and divisions between, the other page elements. Controlling the white space is as important as the positioning of the individual items, because it dictates the relationship between text and pictures. White space establishes the spatial boundaries of a page and is vital to the overall balance between all the graphic elements.

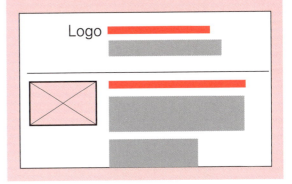

this can alter the perception of their proportions on the page. Offsetting a smaller block against a larger graphic unit, and using the rest of the page area as a frame can create counterbalance between contrasting elements. As a general rule, the columns of the main text should be positioned to create a structure of similarly toned blocks that will help to lead the eye through the copy. These can be counterbalanced against the larger type elements, images and other graphic items by balancing colour, tonality, size and shape to unify the page. Layouts work best where the graphic units are held in spatial counterpoise but still work in harmony with each other.

Symmetrically balanced layouts hold the reader's or viewer's eye within the page and can lack outward directionality.

Offset or irregular shapes can contribute a sense of counterbalance that moves the eye around the page.

Directionality

All graphic elements such as images have an internal directionality, and individual items may be used in conjunction with one another to influence the reader's or visitor's eye movement around a page. Within pictures, this can come from the subject matter, colour, tone and composition (see page 217), as well as where the image is positioned on a page. Directionality may come from the type style or a symbol, for example an italic typeface or an arrow, and it can also come from how items are positioned and counterbalanced. The techniques can be used to lead the eye around a page. For example, using a series of coloured boxes running left to right in increasing sizes can direct attention across the page.

Placing objects on a page in an implied or actual alignment will lead the eye, while interposing lines or rules can act as a barrier to break the eye flow. Colour can also influence direction, as the eye will track from red to red, or green to green. It is a common device in layout to feature matching colours that draw the reader or visitor through the content – for example, by linking the colour of the main headline to the cross-headings. Type alignment may also create directionality. Justified copy has two straight sides that

Lighter tones and graduation have a soft impact and can ease the reader's or viewer's eye across a page.

create verticality to guide a reader or visitor down the copy. The straight left hand edge of ranged left copy draws the eye to the left and down the pages, while the straight edge of ranged right copy can be used to emphasise the right of a column and to link to elements on the right hand side of a page. Centred copy has less directionality on the page, and a centred alignment should only be used where the focus of attention needs to be held in the centre.

Controlling the eye flow

The directed eye movement on the first two spreads leads the viewer's eye to the right to encourage them to turn to the next page. The main eye contact for the third spread is symmetrical, with the figures on each page centred to balance and arrest the viewer's eye to indicate the end of the feature. These techniques reduce any expectation that the article may continue, as there could be an advertisement or an article on a very different subject on the following page.

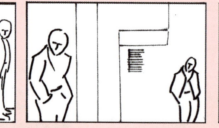

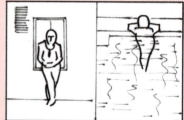

The first spread has a left to right emphasis. The figure standing on the right hand side draws the eye across the page and is turned to the right to indicate the page turn, but eye contact is maintained as the face is turned towards the viewer.

The second spread has a vertical emphasis with the contrasting scale of the two figures creating a downward and inward movement to direct the viewer's eye to the right hand corner and the page turn. Eye contact is maintained.

On the last spread, a seated, centralised figure looks directly out at the viewer and conveys stillness. Almost two-thirds of the right hand page is taken up by the foreground, which distances the figure from the viewer. Eye contact has been broken.

Page layout conventions

Page layouts normally follow established conventions. These are well known to readers and visitors, and using standard formats will provide ease of use and fulfil the audience's expectations of a media product. There is a strong case for using established layout practices that your audience is familiar with as these allow them to scan quickly through the content. For example, cross-heads lead the eye through the main text and by applying colour the text draws attention to a specific piece of information. This, and similar techniques, direct com-munication and are applied to both the layout of the page and the way in which the editorial material is presented.

A reader or user should be able to follow the visual clues you have supplied by the typographic and layout conventions of the house style. The audience will develop familiarity with the presentation of a title and most pages should be prepared within the house design style. While the set format has to be applied, the audi-ence will accept design variations as long as they still reflect the overall design of the title. Understanding the conventions and rules of page layout will enable you to create varied and attractive pages within a standard framework. The best way to engage the reader or visitor is to choose good images and employ strong typography, and to combine it with the title's design conventions within the page grid. The following pages provide a guide to the basic conventions used to create media products for print and online and cover how you can use the design elements of the title's house style to present the content in the most engaging manner.

The grid

Printed and online publications use grids that organise the page horizontally and vertically (see page 126). The grid consists of a number of set spatial divisions made up of margins, columns and gutters that can be specified for an individual page or a publication. Margins are the areas at the top, bottom, left and right of the page that create a border around the type or content area – the space inside the margins in which

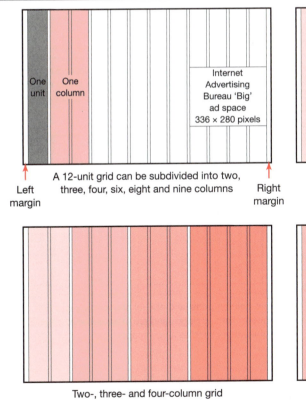

A 12-unit grid can be subdivided into two, three, four, six, eight and nine columns

Left margin

Right margin

Internet Advertising Bureau 'Big' ad space 336 × 280 pixels

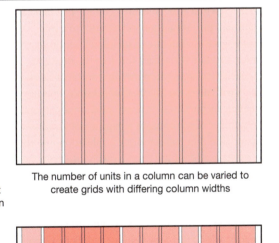

The number of units in a column can be varied to create grids with differing column widths

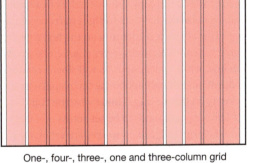

Two-, three- and four-column grid

One-, four-, three-, one and three-column grid

A 12-unit web page grid can be subdivided into two, three, four, six, eight and nine columns with the number of units in a column varied to create grids with differing column widths.

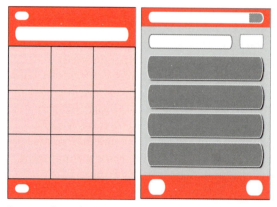

A range of standardised grid templates is available for smart phone apps.

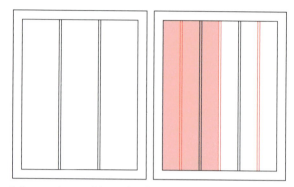

A three-column grid may be divided into six subcolumns. Subdividing a grid makes it more flexible as content can be placed across more than one column.

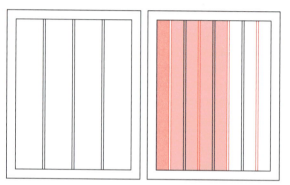

A four-column grid subdivided into eight allows content to be placed in one, two or four columns. A single eighth can be left empty of content to create vertical space on a page.

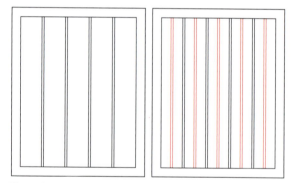

Five-column grids (and above) are normally used for news or listings pages and are more suited to larger-sized publications such as a newspaper.

the text and pictures are normally placed. This area is divided into a number of columns separated by gutters (the narrow vertical space between columns).

Templates for print and online are constructed on grids in the form of modular divisions (spatial units) in a defined two-dimensional space (the page or screen). The organisation and juxtaposition of the spatial units on a page grid – the margins, columns, gutters, text blocks and pictures – give structure and balance to a title. The grid holds the content and allows for continuity of placement to guide the reader through the material. The house design style will normally contain a range of templates with differing numbers of columns that are used to indicate particular sections or changes in topic.

The number of columns on a page is not just a visual design decision. The nature of the publication and the purpose of the content have to be taken into account, as does the width of the page or screen. Media designers set the 'pace' of a publication using the width of a column, in combination with the size and style of the type, to fix the number of words per line and therefore the speed at which the copy can be read. For example, newspapers normally have six to eight narrow columns per page. This allows a reader to scan the text rapidly as a narrow column contains fewer characters/words on each line, while wider columns will slow a reader or visitor down, and this should make them concentrate more closely on the writing. This is why the copy on website feature pages tends to be set across one wide column, and print magazine features are set on two- or three-column grids. Novels mostly use a single column per page, which should provide a slower paced, more relaxing read.

TIP Although the margin areas can be utilised for imagery and background tints, all text should remain within the type area (inside the margins).

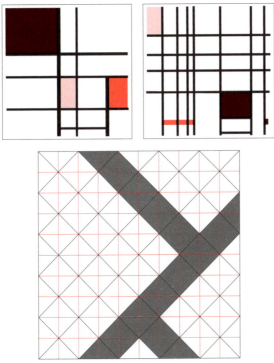

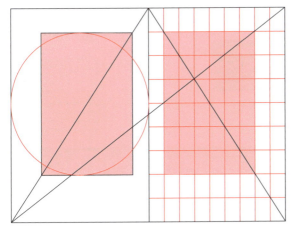

The modernist Dutch painters Piet Mondrian and Theo Van Doesburg founded De Stilj (1917–1931), an art and design movement that published a journal. The journal's design was based on a grid on a modular architectural framework of horizontal and vertical lines, with the regularity offset by open space and cutout images.

The twentieth-century typographer and graphic designer Jan Tschihold has been a major influence on publication design. His concept of the golden cannon of page construction developed the practice of designing on a grid using asymmetrically counterbalanced geometric shapes.

The modernist grid

Grids are used to design products and buildings as well as publications, and there is a wide range of historic and cultural influences that have led to the development of the style of grids currently used for both print and online. Western art, in particular twentieth-century modernism, has been strongly influenced by the square or double square modular grid that forms the basis of traditional Japanese architecture. The proportions of the *tatami mat* have inspired designers and artists to create paintings, objects and buildings that follow geometric systems of construction.

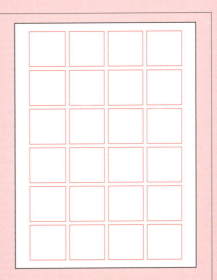

A modular grid divides the page into uniform spaces with dimensions set by the baseline unit. For example, a publication with a running text of 9pt on leading of 10pt has a baseline unit of 10, and the modular spaces might be 10 lines deep by 10 lines wide = 100pts square.

The depth of the type area is defined in lines of the baseline grid. Each spatial unit is separated by tall, narrow gutters that are also calculated in points, for example 5pts wide by the type area depth.

The orthodox or Swiss modular grid (1950s–1970s) has become an established way to design publications. The grid system used for media is based on regularly placed vertical and horizontal lines, with intersections and framed spaces used as locators for key elements.

Setting margin and gutter widths

- Margins have a proportional relationship to the printed page size or the dimensions of a digital screen – a large-scale page requires a wider margin than a small page or screen.

- The bottom margin should be deeper than the top margin, because if they are the same depth, an optical illusion makes the content area seem closer to the base of the page than the top.

- The basic proportion for left and right hand margins should be no less than 10% of the total width of a printed page, but because the decision is affected by editorial considerations, there is no strict formula to apply.

- The inner vertical margin of a print publication is usually wider than the outer one to allow for the centre fold.

- The horizontal margins of a print publication may not be of equal depth to allow for headers or footers.

- A margin should be approximately three times the width of a gutter (the standard gutter width is 4.2mm).

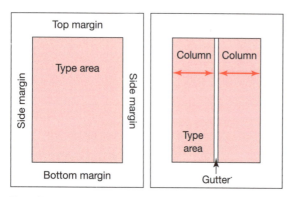

The print page area is the same as the final size of the trimmed (cutout publication). The type area is the main content space inside the margins which is normally divided into a number of columns.

Warning Sufficient width or depth should be left around the edge of the type area to prevent the text falling so close to the edge of the page or screen that it becomes visually uncomfortable to read. Margins of print publications should be wide enough to ensure that no vital information will be lost should the guillotine not cut the printed pages accurately.

Margins and columns

The margin and column widths will have been chosen to match the function of the title and the nature of its subject. A text-driven print publication with a large page size, such as a newspaper, will seek to have as many columns as possible to a page. The editorial purpose is to get as much information on the page as possible, and a design with a large number of columns encourages people to read quickly, creating a sense of urgency. However, if a column is very narrow, it will reduce the number of complete words that will fit on a line, and too few or too many broken words will make the text look disjointed and difficult to read.

The width chosen for the margins is related to the message of the design as well as fulfilling a practical purpose. Some titles use margins to control the amount of white space around a page for semiotic reasons. Using a wide or deep border around a type area will give the contents a strong presence by focusing attention on the centre of the page. An open margin space (a luxury margin) gives the message that here is a publication that is more visually led and design conscious. By allowing white space to separate and hold each page, the emphasis moves from just informing the reader to presenting a product that has higher design values and, implicitly, greater worth.

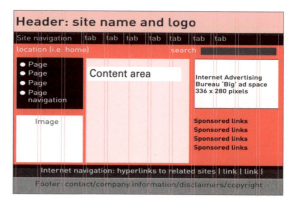

A basic web page consists of a header and footer, navigation tabs, links and menus, content and image areas, and industry-standard advertising spaces.

The size, tonal value, colour and positioning of pictures can be employed to direct a reader's or user's attention through the content.

Hierarchy and signposting

Layouts should be constructed with a clear information <mark>hierarchy to guide the reader or user through the information.</mark> The underlying structure provided by a grid provides a foundation for the page elements. A page hierarchy is achieved through assigning a level of importance to the content. The copy you receive may have an obvious running order or the writer or editor may request that some items are emphasised. Using particularly good images or powerful headlines will work best to create a strong entry point to a page.

Further signposting may be created using imagery. Well-selected images can encourage readers or visitors to read through the information in the desired order. The choice of subjects and the composition of the pictures, combined with their usage in the layout, is of fundamental importance in attracting a user or reader to a site or a particular story. One design axiom is the existence of image bias – people tend to look at pictures first. A strong lead picture can help to make a layout work, while a weak one can ruin the page or screen balance, or cause the reader or user to ignore the content or writing. The skill in selecting pictures that will act as signposts is to choose images that alert the reader or user to the nature of the content. It is necessary to be careful that an image, however beautiful or funny, does not give the wrong message about the content.

It is possible to create a page that has a good hierarchy but a confusing read path – the path the eye instinctively follows through the text. You should pay attention to the way in which a reader or visitor is most likely to track through the information and avoid disrupting the eye flow with pictures or graphics that divide the visual link between related text blocks, or which isolate small sections of the copy.

The hierarchy, signposting and read path have to combine editorial needs with the house design style and be used in a way that will produce an attractive layout.

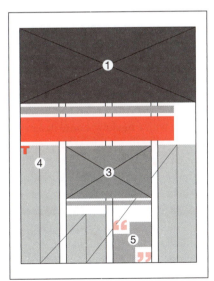

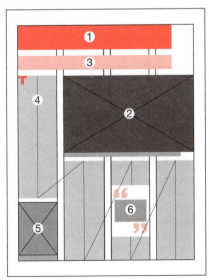

Warning Do not over prioritise an image or other page elements simply because it appeals to your personal taste or sense of humour.

The lead picture should attract the reader's or viewer's eye first, followed by the other page elements in a predetermined order of importance.

Writers will often supply overwordy headlines or too much copy for a story, and you may have to decide how to set up the hierarchy of headlines, pictures and copy logically in the available space. The wordiness of a headline should not dictate the type size, or the amount of copy how the page looks. Headlines can be rewritten and most copy can be improved by some judicious editing, but it is important not to sacrifice informational logic for visual impact.

The lead picture and headline should capture a reader's or viewer's eye and draw them into the copy.

Picture bias

Research into how people react to visual content has shown that there is a picture bias: people look at an image first, however briefly. This tendency is exploited in page layout by using one image that is significantly larger than other pictures on the page. This is called a lead or main picture. Selecting a powerful image that attracts and holds the reader's or user's attention can make the difference between a page that works well and one that lacks impact.

Chunking

Most people are able to absorb more information if it has been divided up into manageable chunks. Writers should have considered the media and style in which the information will be presented, but sometimes text is submitted as one long, unbroken run of copy. It is a good idea to read through and assess the text to see if it can be broken down into logical chunks by inserting crossheads, or separating some of the information into boxes or sidebars. For example, web content pages normally employ short paragraphs with one- or two-line paragraph breaks and crossheads at frequent intervals to fit the typical online reading pattern. If the copy does not lend itself to being subdivided, the editor or chief sub may be required to re write or subedit the text. You should avoid breaking up the text into too many chunks, as it may lose cohesion and appear to be a series of items on the same subject.

TIP There are three principles that should be followed when dividing up the content for a page: the layout has to look attractive as well as make informational and visual sense; the content should be easy to follow and entirely legible; and quotes, boxes and sidebars must relate to the text and fall in an appropriate position on the page.

Alignment and spacing

Many titles use a modular layout system where each page element becomes a rectangular or square graphic unit that is placed on the grid. The design style works by setting up an ordered balance of relationships that align the various layout elements on and between pages. Modular layouts are regarded as formal and authoritative. If you are working with a modular house design style, it is good practice to create a contrast between a horizontal emphasis on one page and a vertical emphasis for the next item or page. This can be achieved by using wide headlines and landscape (horizontal rectangles) pictures on one page balanced against portrait images (vertical rectangles) and deep columns of text on the facing page. Picture and text block alignments can be used to create a visual line of direction guiding the reader's or visitor's eye from left to right, or to encourage them to turn to or click on the next page.

Open spaces around, above and below the elements in a layout function to keep the items visually separate, and to catch and direct the eye. The space between items on a page can be used as a beat, pause or a stop. A wide space between page elements will hold the reader's or visitor's attention for longer than a narrow one. Where there is a direct link between two items, such as the headline and standfirst or sell, the space should be small enough to keep the read path intact, but large enough to communicate the separate functions of each element. However, leaving too much distance between related items may obscure the connection. The open space on a page creates lines and blocks that are an integral part of a layout and are useful for counterbalancing other graphic units such as text or image boxes. White space is seen as extravagant with connotations of exclusivity, and an open layout is considered cool and classy.

Text to picture ratio

When a title is designed, the overall balance between editorial pages and advertisements will have been considered as an aspect of the underlying design style. For example, the dimensions and proportion of the media product, the nature of the editorial and the style of the advertising all have an effect on how the content will be displayed. Each individual page also has an internal text to picture ratio, which will vary according to the subject of the publication or website. The text to picture ratio of most newspapers is weighted towards the copy, while visually led magazines may have a text to picture ratio of 40 per cent imagery to 60 per cent copy. The text to picture ratio helps to identify sections; for example, a product review page may consist of several short piece of text, each with a picture, while a Sunday supplement in-depth report on a serious political or social issue will have far more copy than pictures.

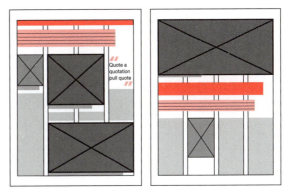

(a) The layout on the left is 'pic heavy', with too many graphic elements that overpower the amount of copy. The layout on the right is easier to follow as it has fewer items.

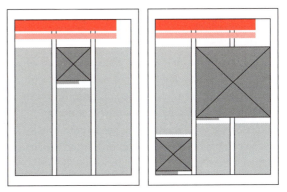

(b) The layout on the left is 'text heavy' with too few graphic elements, with the result that the copy looks dense and uninviting to read. The layout on the right counterbalances the copy against the large lead and smaller second points.

Deconstruction

Even with interpretive, free-flowing layouts, there is usually some underlying sense of alignment. Deconstructionist layouts that have few obvious visual boundaries still tend to be kept in some form of alignment for the text blocks – even if the lettering is flipped or reversed.

David Carson, Rudy Van der Lans, Scott Pakula, Neville Brody and April Greiman were major figures in the deconstructionist movement of the 1990s. Their radical approach to publication and website design broke with the modernist tradition and led to a revolution in graphic design. Visit:

http://www.davidcarsondesign.com/
http://www.emigre.com/EMagView.php
http://www.researchstudios.com
http://www.typotheque.com/site/article.php?id=99
http://www.barnbrook.net

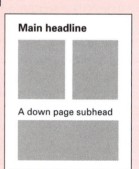

Headlines can be quirky and eye-catching.

Headlines

Headlines for both print and online not only must be cleverly written, but should also be in house style and suitably positioned on the page. The use of big, bold type to grab readers' attention is a well-established practice, but size and weight are not the only criteria to be considered. Headlines on a well-planned and balanced page with good type usage do not always have to conform to the standard convention of placing headlines. Positioning the headline lower down the page and using white space or an image at the top of a page breaks the formality and gives a softer lead into the layout. Moving the headline away from the top of a story or feature on facing or multi-item pages will help to avoid clashing headlines – two headlines parallel to each other.

If headlines are too similar in size, weight and positioned close to one another, they may cause the reader's or visitor's eye to jump across from headline to headline with the result that they read the text out of order, or they may read across the headlines, which will completely change the meaning. This effect can be overcome by putting a picture above the headline for one story and the headline below the picture for the adjacent item. This separates the headlines and will help prevent any confusion. You should also consider the position of the headings in adjacent advertisements when placing an editorial headline on a page.

Headline typography has both an informational and an aesthetic role in enhancing features and stories, and can add to the appeal of the publication as a whole.

There are business and technical titles that use the same headline style throughout, and in that case the headline type signals that all the content carries the same authority. However, most media products use a variety of headline type styles, sizes, weights and colour to emphasise the relative importance of each story and help the reader or visitor to know where they should begin to read. Headlines have a semiotic message.

The editorial content of most consumer publications normally covers a range of topics and will benefit from a choice of headline typography to build up the suggestion of differing content. However, introducing too many different styles, sizes and colours can destroy the visual cohesion and may cause confusion. For instance, changing the editorial headings for every feature may make it difficult for the reader easily to identify the editorial from the advertising.

Subheads and crossheads

A subhead may be either a small headline used for a secondary story on a page or a down page heading used to break up large areas of text. Subheads are normally in a smaller typeface and/or a different weight or colour to ensure the page's information hierarchy remains clear. A crosshead is one line of small text in a contrasting typeface, size and colour that introduces a different topic within the flow of text in an article or story. Subheads and crossheads provide secondary visual entry points on the page.

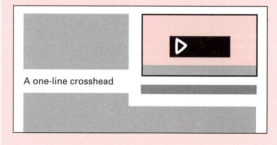

Standfirsts, straplines and sells

Headlines form a strong graphic element that attracts the reader or visitor to the story, but the first visual and informational contact with the copy is the standfirst, strapline or sell. This is a short précis of an article that introduces a story or feature. Its purpose is to catch the reader's interest by providing an introduction to the subject matter. Print feature headlines are often witty or punning rather than factual and descriptive, and the standfirst is used as an explanation of the headline, as well as an introduction to the copy. A strapline is a line of text that adds information to a news story headline and is normally only used for major news stories. A sell is the term for the short piece of explanatory copy that accompanies a web headline which gives more details to encourage the visitor to click through to the main story.

Standfirsts, straplines and sells are normally set in a typeface that is larger and bolder than the running copy and should be the second most visually important type element in the reading order. The type used must be smaller than the headline and should not be the same or a brighter colour, because if it is too strong or brightly coloured it will attract attention over the head-line and upset the page hierarchy.

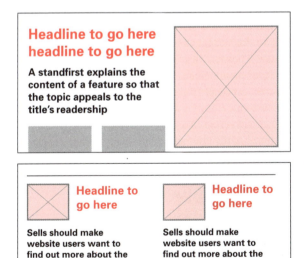

The standfirst or sell forms a visual bridge between the headline and lead picture and an informational link to a feature or news story.

Pull quotes and shout outs

A pull quote or lift-out quote is a direct quotation from the news item or article. It is normally in a larger typeface than the running copy and provides another attention-grabbing element that can be used to high-light what an interviewee has said or an interesting comment by the writer. It can be part of the house design style for a columnist's page and is a useful way of breaking long runs of text on a page when there are few pictures available. A shout out or call out is either a statement taken from the article or one written about it to add emphasis to a particular point. Pull quotes and shout outs help to promote the subject matter and give a feel for the tone of an article, and can make a page seem livelier as they 'speak' directly to a reader.

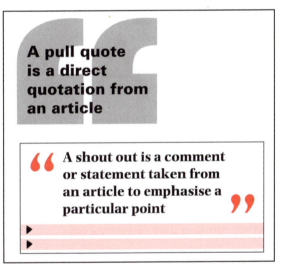

Pull quotes are used to draw readers or visitors into an article and emphasise important facts. Try to avoid placing quotes or shout outs exactly beside the same comment in the text as this can make the article seem repetitious.

TIP Print feature standfirsts should be visually associated to the headline, but, depending on the house design style rules, may not have to fall immediately above or below on the page. However, if they drift too far away from the headline, they might be confused with a 'shout out' or pull quote. Straplines are normally always set immediately below a news headline.

The body copy

The size and style of the main body of text are usually set to ensure that there will be a certain number of characters on each line across a given width. This is to ensure that there are enough words per line to maintain readability for all the sections, no matter whether the copy falls in a narrow column or on a wider space. If the type size is small and there is a large amount of information in each line, the copy may become uncomfortable to read as the eye and brain struggle to process the characters. Type designers will use their experience and run trials to determine the body copy style that will provide the most effective read for the target audience and media. They will produce a number of samples of different type configurations across various widths to work out the optimum proportion.

For most feature pages, the blocks of body copy provide the core of the design. The type style of the text forms a series of tonal graphic units that work with the other page elements and the white space to unify the visual relationship between the items. This exploits the fact that our eyes will focus on and move between tonally similar blocks, which has the effect of making us link areas of the same weighted type. You can use darker and lighter blocks of body copy to direct attention and control the read path, for example a block of bold copy will appear to come forward out of the page, while light typefaces seem to recede.

Main running text or body copy

Lorem ipsum dolor sit amet, amassoium consectetuer et adipiscing elit, sed diam nonummy nibh euismod hypocaust caud incidunt uttem adsum laoreet dolorissimus magna aliquam ertra volutpat. Ut wisi enim ad minim exerci tation ad ullam corper adarat veniam, quis nostrud exercitation ad ullamcorper suscipit lobortis nisl ut aliquip ex consequat.

Duis autem vel eum iriure dolor in hendrerit in vulputate velit esse molestie consequat, vel illum accumsan et iusto.

Ut wisi enim ad minim consectetuer et adipiscing elit, sed diam nonummy nibh euismod hypocaust incidunt uttem exerci tation ad ullamcorper.

The typographic style of the body copy or running text is kept consistent throughout a publication. The first paragraph of an article or story may be indicated by a **drop cap** – the first character increased in size to drop down a given number of lines – or the first one or two words may be set in bold and/or capitals.

Breaking up the body copy

Crossheads are used to break up large areas of text which may appear daunting to read. Writers often use crossheads to introduce new topics in the copy, but if they fall in a visually awkward place, such as at the bottom of a column or just above a picture or quote, it may be necessary to suggest an alternative position or to replan the page.

Captions and picture credits

A caption is normally one or two lines of copy that identify the people, places, events, times, etc. shown in an image. A caption is usually placed beneath the picture it refers to, but may also be placed in a group with directions to each picture (clockwise from...), or can be positioned near to the related image. Some publications' design house style may allow captions to fall directly on to a picture, or within the picture box. Wherever the caption is positioned, the most important rules are that it should be legible and that the reader or visitor can easily link it to the relevant picture.

A picture credit may be the name of the photographer, illustrator, source company/organisation, image library or licensing body of a picture or graphic. The image licensing agreement frequently stipulates that a credit be included (see page 283). Picture credits are usually in very small type and may be placed vertically in the margin or column to the left or right of a picture. They may also be written as part of the caption or placed on an image. However, readability must be ensured, especially if the credit is a legal requirement. The web convention is to place the credit on the image so that, if it is reused on another page on the website, the name of the photographer will appear on the new page. It also guards against illegal reuse of the picture.

Caption alignment can be used to direct the eye towards other page elements.

Photography by: picture credit

Picture captions provide further information on the image and can be used to link the picture to the copy.

Picture captions provide further information on the image and can be used to link the picture to the copy. Picture credits acknowledge the photographer, illustrator or source of an image.

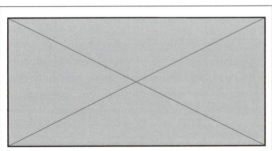

Caption caption caption caption caption

Box headline to go here

Boxed headlines, pictures, captions and body copy are inset inside the box by 1–2mm either side, and by one line down and one line up from the top and bottom.

The type style for boxed copy or sidebars is normally at the same size and leading as the main body copy, but can be in a different typeface and style.

The typeface used for boxed copy should be kept the same size and on the same leading as the main body copy to maintain visual consistency.

Boxed copy and sidebars

The term boxed copy is used for a content area separated out from the rest of the body copy, for example a fact file, contact details, web links or a case study. Sidebars or side columns are short stories or items that relate to the main article, for example a case study or vox pop (short interview) survey. The type style used for boxed copy is often in a different font and weight from the main article. All the type elements used for boxes will be specified as part of a title's typography, for example a box may contain a headline, crosshead in a range of weights and colours for the text styles.

Boxed copy and sidebars should have an identity of their own and be clearly separated from the body copy. This can be achieved by using vertical and/or horizontal lines, a frame or a solid or tinted background. The background of the boxes should be clearly delineated using hues from the house style colour palette, either as a percentage tint or opacity, or using solid black or coloured frames. Whichever box style is used, it is important that the type and pictures in the box do not touch the edges, as this will make the content of the box look crowded. Adding an insert or padding above, below and to the sides of the copy and images will ensure the box looks attractive and the copy remains easy to read.

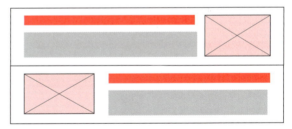

Background tints and frame boxes help website visitors to navigate through the information.

TIP When placing black type on a tint, it is best to keep below 30% of the background colour, and for white type the background tint needs to be 60% or higher. For a web page, it is important to make sure that type and background colour combinations used in a box do not have a disturbing optical effect (page 170).

135

Frames or keylines

Frames are used to define the edges of a picture or boxed copy. A fine black frame called a **keyline** is often used to give subtle definition to the edges of a box or an image, For example, a frame or keyline around a picture that contains clouds will prevent them merging with a white background. Frames can be applied in a variety of widths and in any colour (within the design guidelines), and in styles such as double, thick-thin or decorative, for example Victorian or Greek Key patterns. As a general design principle, keylines should be thinner than the uprights of the main text typeface so as not to draw attention from the copy. However, there are times when the frames are intended to be a noticeable design feature and need to stand out.

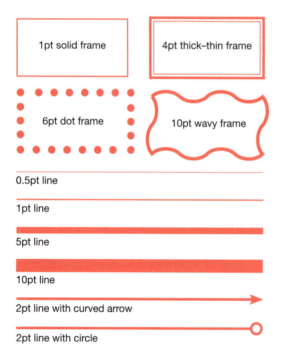

0.5pt line

1pt line

5pt line

10pt line

2pt line with curved arrow

2pt line with circle

Warning Some desktop printers cannot render keylines below 0.25 points, so very fine lines may not show on laser proofs but should output correctly from a printing press. Printing problems can occur with very thin keylines in a **CMYK** colour, as these may either change colour over the length of line or break up.

Lines or rules

The terminology may vary between computer programs, but a line or rule generally refers to a single stroke, for example a vertical line used to divide content areas. Lines are also used to section off stories on pages that contain more than one item and to separate advertising from editorial. The thinnest line is called a hairline but this is often too thin for practical use. A vertical line down the centre of the space between text blocks prevents the reader or visitor from confusing adjacent lines of type and helps direct their attention down the page. Horizontal lines are also used to divide separate content areas and lead the eye across the page. Lines may also be used as part of the page furniture to isolate headers and footers from the main type area.

Keylines are used to define the edges of an image and to prevent a pale image from fading into the page.

Angled type, type on a path, splats

Type is generally run in horizontal lines, but can be rotated or placed at an angle to create a dynamic page. Type can also be 'flipped' – turned around or over horizontally or vertically (mirrored or reversed). While these effects are fun, they should only be used if there is a good design or editorial reason. Many programs contain text tools that allow you to run copy along the outside of a shape, for example a circle, and to put type into shapes such as stars and sun bursts. These are used to emphasise an offer or special feature and are often referred to as splats.

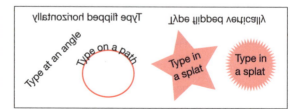

The baseline grid: print

The leading of the main text becomes the basis of the horizontal alignment and vertical spacing of printed publications' design and layout. The baseline grid in page make-up programs is a set of non-printing lines that resemble ruled paper and which can be kept visible while the page is being assembled, and hidden to pre-view the page. The vertical distance between each line of the baseline grid corresponds to the leading of the body copy. For example, for a main body copy size of 9pt, the baseline may be 10pt (9pt type size plus 1pt of extra space between each line). The baseline grid should be set to the same line depth on all the pages.

The function of the baseline grid is to fix the horizontal position of all type and picture elements across a page or spread and throughout a publication. The line unit of the baseline grid is normally used to establish the amount of open space above and below the content boxes. Page make-up programs include the option of locking type to the baseline grid. This sets an absolute

> **Warning** It is inadvisable to lock larger type elements that have a greater amount of leading than the body copy to the baseline grid.

alignment between the body copy, captions and any other same-sized styles, and the instruction can be applied as part of a style sheet.

Designing with type

The overall tonality of type affects the balance between the background, mid ground and foreground planes of a page. Denser, heavier typefaces are perceived as coming forward, while smaller, paler ones are viewed as receding into the background. The tone of the body copy should be chosen to ensure that it appears on the page plane (the mid ground) without any forward or backward visual movement. All the other type elements should be positioned on the level of the page plane in a way that will convey their importance in relation to the body copy. For example, a red box containing heavy white type will jump out of the page, while an introduction in a light typeface would fade back behind a bold headline and medium-weight body copy. The visual level at which type appears on the page plane can be controlled by altering the typeface style, weight, size or colour.

See *How to work with type*, page 168.

The baseline grid

Headline to go here

Standfirst to go here standfirst to go here standfirst to go here standfirst to go here

The baseline grid is a non-printing guide that establishes the horizontal alignment of a page.
  The distance between individual lines of the baseline grid is set by the leading of the body copy.

The leading of the body copy sets the measurement unit of the baseline grid. For example if the body copy is set in 9pt type size on 11pts of leading, the baseline grid unit would be 11pt. Smaller type styles such as the body copy, captions and boxed text styles are locked to the baseline grid to maintain the horizontal alignment. Larger type elements are positioned using the baseline grid but are not locked to it.

Colour

The basic colour palette for a title will have been established during the design stage and decided by the subject matter, brand identity and target audience. The way colour is employed for each individual page has to be considered in terms of the house style palette and the content to be used. The images chosen for a story need to be assessed for the semiotic colour message and how this will affect the overall layout. Pictures can be selected either because their colour trend matches the style of a title, or to suit a headline or topic. A dominant hue may be used to set the visual hierarchy on the page and for the colour of boxes, rules, drop caps, etc.

Generally, small type such as body copy, captions and picture credits is left in black or grey on a white or pale background as these are the easiest colours to read. And because black and grey type is so standard, it carries few semiotic implications. Once colour is applied to type it can affect the visual weight and even change how the copy is interpreted. Type colours need to balance the images and the page background colour to ensure the typographic elements maintain their page plane position and communicate the mood and informational focus of the content. If all the type and pictures on a page are pale and neutral, the message will be restrained and understated, whereas vividly coloured pictures and brightly coloured type are attention grabbing and can set an upbeat mood.

Substrate or screen colour

The underlying colour of the substrate or screen will affect the perception of all the colour elements on a page. The base colour of most paper used for print is off-white, and the background colours of web pages will vary, which needs to be taken into account when selecting images and colours. Background colours throw a subtle colour cast that affects how readers and visitors perceive coloured type, colour in pictures and the overall colour balance of a page.

See *How to work with colour*, page 247.

Pictures on a page

The theory of the picture superiority effect states that images are more easily recognised than words and are the key to memory recall – a picture is more easily remembered than words, even when only seen briefly. The lead picture is one of the first things that a reader registers when they look at a page, and it needs to have a really strong visual impact. The selection and placement of the main image becomes one of the key decisions that will influence the positioning and scale of all other page elements. Therefore it is absolutely critical that the best possible image is chosen for the specific purpose of the page. For example, the lead picture for a news website has to have enough visual strength to dominate the page, while capturing the essence of the story. It needs to be powerful enough to overcome the distractions of any secondary images, dynamic media and interactive elements.

There needs to be a balance between the size of the lead picture and the amount of copy on a page. It is important to make sure that a main image has sufficient prominence, while ensuring that the page elements still carry the correct visual and informational weight. As much of the copy as possible should be included – there are very few titles that attract a regular audience on the basis of images and layout alone. But it is equally inappropriate to over-reduce the images in order to squeeze all the text in.

It is normal practice to have more than one image on a page. There should be a significant difference in size between the main picture and any other images, with the secondary pictures descending in relative size. The pictures on each page should be positioned to create a contrasting eye flow, with a horizontal or vertical emphasis expressed through the shape of the images; for example, if the lead picture is landscape (horizontal rectangle), then the following image could be portrait (vertical rectangle). Images have an intrinsic directionality that is determined by the content which provides movement and forms part of the overall page balance (see pages 216–17).

You will need to keep the page balance in mind when selecting images. How many pictures can be used on a page has to be considered in terms of preventing a layout from looking too text heavy or becoming overcrowded. It is better to cut copy or drop images rather than let a page become packed with content, as this works against readability and usability. When sourcing images for a feature, you should obtain at least eight to twelve alternative pictures covering a variety of visual treatments and concepts, in differing proportions. News stories need four to six possible choices including landscape, portrait, close-up and long-shot formats. A multi-item page should have a number of alternative images sourced for each story to provide for maximum layout possibilities.

Working with pictures

- Avoid using several similarly sized pictures on a page as these tend to cancel each other out because, with no clear focal point, the eye keeps moving from one to another, leading to a less focused page.

- Pictures as well as headlines can clash (see page 132), and images should be positioned so that the shape and content of the pictures do not conflict

- Place sufficient space between images to avoid pictures merging together

- To create a unified block of images, reduce the space between images or allow the picture boxes to touch or overlap

- When presenting images to readers or visitors, you can bring a face or figure forward on the page plane by using a close-up of the face

- Full-length shots add depth to a page by moving the figures away from the reader or visitor

- If you need to differentiate between two very similar pictures, it is possible to use just part of one of the images to change the perceived page plane depth (cropping)

- Although most pictures on a page are rectangular, changes from the geometric norm will break the formality and catch the reader's eye. However, different box formats should be used in a way that is sympathetic to the rest of the design

- A page or spread that uses different shapes for the images can look busy and lively, but too many separate elements may create a visual cacophony

See page 202.

Cutouts

Cutout refers to the technique of removing the background behind an irregular area within an image and is used to create non-geometric page elements. A cutout can be used to isolate an element, such as a product, and to create image shapes that can add interest and movement to the page, for example a recipe with a picture of an ingredient dropped into the copy. Cutouts can be set up using imaging software, page make-up and graphic programs. These will create a clipping path that can be embedded in the picture that prevents the background from appearing. Page make-up software can work with images that contain clipping paths and has a facility that allows you to run the text around the cutout shape. If you are producing a cutout for the Web, it is better to remove the image's background completely and replace it with the web page background colour.

Cutouts create movement and can be combined with shaped type to enliven a page.

Website design

The Web has its own design rules for establishing website structures that are based on aesthetic principles and usability criteria. However, the design of websites is subject to wider fashion trends and changes as technology advances and design programs become more flexible. The introduction of font-face type and font-face-enabled browsers has the potential to free web design from the constraints of systems fonts, and the simplification of web and multimedia software has provided the opportunity to embed or provide links to a range of media. The greatest shift, however, has come from the need to include links to social networking media and the drive to personalise the web experience.

The technical demands of the Internet define what may be achieved, but the needs of the website user have to be the primary consideration for any design decisions.

The fundamental consideration when deciding what a website should include is: does it add to the visitor's experience?

All such design and technology issues should have been addressed during a website's development and testing stages, and those working on a published site generally replace content rather than make any major design changes. Website designers use programs such as Adobe Dreamweaver, but day-to-day content updating is normally handled via a CMS, an interface program designed to support media websites that allows production teams to enter and upload content.

Web pages consist of windows and panels, some of which contain the navigation systems, information points and advertising positions. These frame the updatable content areas, and the way in which editorial material is placed has to work in conjunction with the structural elements. The pages are normally set up as a series of templates for each type of page; for example, there may be one or two versions of the home page and

Web design award organisers

http://www.dandad.org/
http://www.webbyawards.com/webbys/current.php
http://www.designweek.co.uk
http://www.thenetawards.com/

a style for each section, such as finance and travel. The templates are accessed via the CMS and, depending on the flexibility of the design, it may be possible to choose where the headlines, copy and pictures fall in a content area. Using templates helps to keep the design consistent and makes the pages familiar to visitors, enabling them to use the site with ease.

Home page templates

Home pages carry the branding and act as an access point to the rest of the site and beyond, so they must provide clear and plentiful navigation points to the contents. The page layout also has to fit with any other related media products. For example, the *Vogue* website has a picture-led front screen with slideshow fashion galleries that can be frozen should the user want to look at a picture in more detail, and a *Vogue TV* media player as well as the usual logos, menus and buttons on a white background. When you work on a home page, you need to make sure that the colours in the images you choose work well with the colours used for the other graphics such as buttons and headlines. If there is a choice of template styles for the home page, it is a good idea to alternate them with each update so that the changes to the content are more apparent.

Section, content and functional pages

Section pages are secondary home pages that help the user navigate to the content pages and on through the site. For example, a news site may feature global, national, local and sports news, and each of these may have a base page, with menus and tabs to access the section's content or move on to other topics. Section pages follow a similar pattern to home pages, and it is important that you ensure there is forward navigation that clearly indicates any related articles, archived items and external websites.

A content page is the term for pages that contain an entire news or feature story together with pictorial, audio and visual assets in a central content area, as well as the menus and hyperlinks that transfer a user to the home and other pages. The templates for content pages may allow for a creative layout treatment. You may be able to choose where the pictures and videos are placed, decide how the text block divides, insert crossheads and select the position of hyperlinks.

There is another type of page that controls functions such as getting in touch, reader surveys and polls. These are often made up of fields that have to be filled in or radio check buttons and are connected to a program on a server at the media company or a partnered firm (web forms, see page 333). You may be involved, as part of the production team, in deciding what information you require from the form or interactive poll, and, although the technical side may be handled by web experts, you may need to check that a form is usable and that any other feedback items are functioning. For example, do the address fields hold enough characters for people to enter their details; are the instructions clear; and does the form look easy to use?

No matter which type of page you are working on, you will be responsible for the final look of the website.

The overall impact of a site comes from the attractiveness and visual strength of each individual page. Once you have developed an initial strong set of pages, it will become easier to continue to produce effective layouts, as it becomes more evident what does and does not work in the context of each page.

> **TIP** If you are working on a website from day to day, you are in the best position to identify whether there are any issues with the design or functionality of a page. If you do find something amiss, you should make a note of what has gone wrong and include the page URL so that the web designer or IT department can resolve the problem.

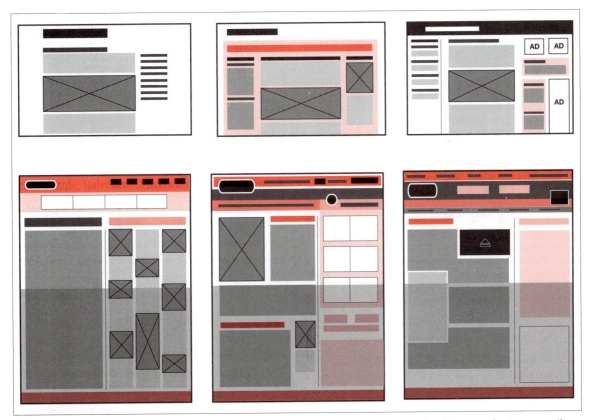

Standard pre-coded CSS web page templates can be obtained from web design companies. The greyed out areas on the lower diagrams indicate those parts of the page that would not be immediately visible to the website user on an average-sized monitor.

'Solving the design problem involves choosing the right medium (to carry the information), the right design elements and arranging them'.

Pina Lewandowsky and Francis Zeischegg, educators, artists and designers

Web page structure

A well-designed layout should display the information and visual content to the best possible advantage and in a way that enables the visitor to gain maximum use of the site's functions and facilities. A formal grid structure is particularly useful for web titles, as most online publication's designs normally use fixed positions for the main navigation and subject areas, with the position of the main typographic elements being kept consistent throughout. The standard format for pages is an upside-down 'L', although many sites have menus on both sides. When you are working on pages that do allow some freedom of positioning, you should try to direct the eye to within the content area and in relation to the fixed page elements. For example, if a portrait is positioned on the right of a copy panel, its gaze should lead to the left, across the copy and towards any menus or other items on that side. If the eye direction leads to the right, it can cause a visitor to bypass the copy and may suggest they look at an advertisement instead.

You need to consider how the viewing dimensions of the screen may affect the type and images on a page. Websites may have a fixed size at which they always appear, or include dynamic scaling that sizes the page to fill the screen. Type and images in a content area should be separated by open spaces and rules, and the spacing should be sufficient to compensate for the variations in view size. If the open spaces look narrow on a large screen, the page elements will definitely look too close on a smaller one. For example, a gap of 1–2 pixels above, to each side and below a picture set in the copy should provide a reasonable visual gap in most browser

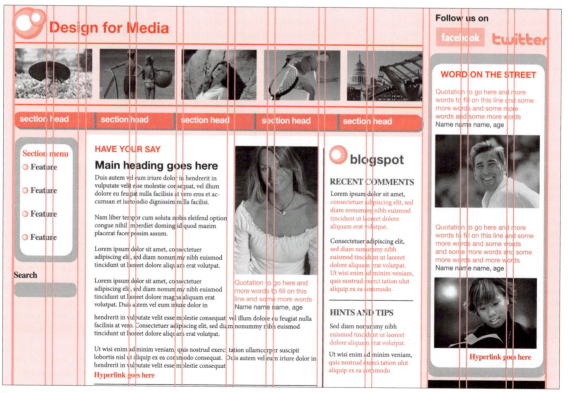

The web grid structure provides a framework for the contents; however, it is not necessary always to align the content, and graphic items can be positioned across the vertical divisions.

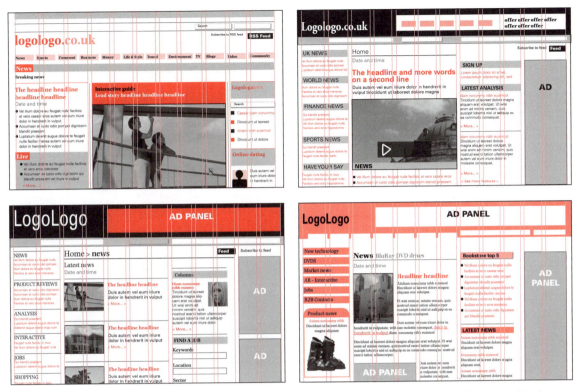

The web grid is a useful tool that allows content to be prepared and positioned quickly on websites that are updated at frequent intervals. Most media website grids have standardised spaces set aside for advertisements and promotions, allowing the marketing department to pre-plan online advertisement sales

windows. Many CMS templates regulate how much space is applied between text and picture and contain parameters such as the margins of content areas and whether the copy is centred in the width and depth, or divided into columns.

Once you have become familiar with the CMS template, you should be able to control the positioning and spacing between pictures and copy to create balanced layouts. As well as considering image content and directionality (see page 230), you need to work with general design principles, such as counterbalancing a large right-aligned image at the top of the content area against a smaller left-aligned picture lower down the page. You also need to ensure that the text blocks flow in a logical manner and to avoid any unsightly line breaks, for example the last line of a text block becoming isolated under an adjacent picture.

A feature page content area should maintain a visual and informational hierarchy. The headline and main image/video player are foreground items and will be positioned at the top of the content area. Other

Typesize and colour

Most Content Management Systems offer a range of type styles and colours to use on each page. If you are allowed to change the colour, typeface or weight, this can be a good way to highlight special items, but should not be overused, or the page may lose visual cohesion. A site that uses a large number of different colours, alignments and sizes can look unprofessional, and the user may become confused if a page looks radically different from the one before – possibly thinking they have accidentally moved on to another site.

pictures, captions and hyperlinks need to be placed so that they form a second level of interest, with the least important items such as picture credits and listings sited lower down the page so that they appear in the background. It is good practice to align the outside edges of items to carry the eye down the page as this defines the boundaries of the content against the surrounding windows and panels.

Web images and graphics

Most media websites use images, and some are strongly picture led with galleries of still and slideshow pictures. Many also incorporate video, multimedia, animation and music files. Web designers often create graphics for headers and menus using imaging software options such as drop shadows, 3D effects, inner and outer glows, while icons and buttons tend to combine type and picture, or letters as imagery. As with colour and typefaces, care should be taken to ensure that such effects do not dominate the content, and if you do place an image near to a very busy graphic, you should make sure it is not going to distract the visitor from the editorial content.

You will need to choose images that are suitable for the size at which they are to be displayed and to plan how, where and at what size the images will appear on the page (see page 222). Images on the home page need to work as a thumbnail, as well as a full-size image on the content page. If the image is indecipherable as a thumbnail, you should consider cropping it, or find a complementary picture to act as the entry point. Developing a variety of sources for images and videos will help you obtain a good selection of suitable material to resolve most visual problems.

Picture and patterned backgrounds

Many magazine websites have a coloured, patterned or pictorial background that helps to create its overall identity, and colour panels are used to highlight top and side menus and to direct the user's eye from item to item. If you are working on a site with vivid colours, you will have to make sure that the colours in the images or videos in the page do not conflict and will not disturb a visitor's concentration. Gradients, fades, 3D and other effects will add depth and movement, but these visual devices need to be treated with care, because if they are too strong they may overpower the content and distract the viewer.

It is vital to take into consideration where and how your design is to be viewed. A book cover, for example, has to work as a wrap for the actual book and in a variety of printed publicity material. It will also need to be suitable for viewing on-screen on tablets, smartphones, ereaders, and has to be scalable so that it will retain impact when positioned in an online bookstore app, as above.

Convergent media

The design of a web page needs to balance the textural elements with all these different elements. It also has to work alongside a number of other features, such as interactivity, blogs, social media, RSS feeds, advertising and online community links. The more conversant you become with the way people use the Web, the better able you will be to plan and manage your content and understand the most effective way to present content for each medium.

Summary Information design

The key to information design is clarity of communication, but media products are also brands that have to be sold in a competitive market. The editorial content has to be matched to an appropriate design and presented to readers, visitors and advertisers in an elegant and attractive manner. The design, layout and page make-up subjects covered in this chapter deal with how to target and tailor the visual elements that are used in print and online media so that every graphic or pictorial item, as well as the size, shape and structure of the page and the position of the type and images, conveys exactly what is intended to a specific audience.

- The style of a publication is pre-planned and described in a house design style guide or online help pages that record all the information on how a publication is to be put together.

- Publications mostly adhere to a set of layout principles and conventions that are familiar to their audience, such as the lead headline and picture being considerably larger than other text or images on the page.

- Print publications follow an underlying grid and have to be set up with regard to the technology of the production process and the substrate (paper) on which they are to be printed.

- Typography – the use of type – is a major element in publication design. It is used to create informational hierarchies, to ensure readability, to set a word count for an article to guide a writer, and for aesthetic purposes.

- The structure, typography, colour and graphic elements of a master design are held in web CSS pages or print master pages/templates.

- Page layout presents the content to the reader or user and must follow the house design style, be attractive and be suited to the publication and its audience. The techniques used include: using size and placement to indicate the information order; suggesting movement or providing interaction points; chunking information – breaking it into smaller units and placing these in boxes or sidebars; setting a ratio between text and pictures; cropping, sizing and positioning of pictures.

- Editorial images must be selected to match the publication's design style as well as for their visual content. They can be obtained from a variety of sources such as commissioned photography, photo and video libraries or be supplied by the readership/users.

- Colour is a vital element in most layouts and is used to assist navigation, signal importance, direct the eye and make a page look appealing.

- Websites follow a grid-based design formatted to the width of the average browser window screen and use cascading style sheets (CSS) to ensure that the design elements of a page appear in a consistent manner on any computer or operating system.

- Websites work as a media hub and need to have good connectivity.

- Images must be chosen that will be discernible at a small screen size on a variety of viewing devices.

Activities and development

The questions and research projects below will help you consider the role and function of design in the media industry. You should study the design of a range of websites and magazines, especially the visual presentation of the branding and content. Visit the *Design for Media* website for more fact and action sheets, sample templates, type schemes and colour palettes at **www.pearsoned.com/hand**

Questions

Question 1
How is a master design employed to hold the editorial structure of a publication?

Question 2
What graphic elements can be included in the structure and content of a page in print, online and in digital editions to encourage interaction with the target audience?

Question 3
What design and layout methods can be employed to ensure people read through the content in the order intended?

Question 4
What design elements can be included to brand a company's publications?

Action points

Action point 1
Analyse a monthly print magazine or newspaper and its associated website. Note all the house design style items you can see and consider the following:

(a) List what design items, if any, they have in common.

(b) Consider how the designs differ and explain why you consider the variations have been employed.

(c) Indicate whether any differences in the house design style between the media are reflected in how the written content is presented.

Action point 2
(a) Study a web-based publication and note the design features on the home and content pages and list any graphic elements that appear on each page.

(b) What features appear only on the home page?

(c) How does the design of a content page vary from the home page?

(d) Does the typography of a content page differ from the type usage on the other pages that make up the publication's website?

Answers to questions

Action point 1

(a) Masthead – logo, typefaces, content order, page structure, colours, news, editorial – comment, features, columnists, regular items (feedback, reviews, etc.), horoscopes, competitions, chat – feedback, offers – shopping, cross-media links, advertisers.

(c) Length of headline/sell, number of sections, number of stories, interactivity, video, audio, hyperlinks.

Action point 2

(a) Menus, buttons, hyperlinks – sponsored links, advertisements, images, headlines, sells, captions, copy, video, audio, interactivity, animation, web forms, key words, picture gallery, competitions, retail – offers.

6 CONTENT VISUALISATION AND STRUCTURE (1): TYPE

This chapter discusses:

- Visualising words
- Digital type
- Bitmap and vector type
- Sourcing and buying type
- Type designers
- Type naming
- Managing type
- Upper and lower case
- Serif and Sans serif
- Leading
- Type for purpose
- Readability and legibility
- Print typesize guide
- Choosing a headline type size
- Type on the printed page
- Web type sizing
- Cascading style sheets
- Graphic text

This chapter looks at **typography** – the art, craft and technique of working with **letterforms** – and discusses the use of type in the media. It will provide you with a description of typographic terminology and practices together with guidance on how best to use type for websites and in print. The chapter also explains the pitfalls and benefits of sourcing type from the Web.

'Typography is what language looks like.'
Ellen Lupton, author and academic

'Good typography will send the message to the viewer before he/she can read it.'

David Carson, designer

Visualising words

Type is a main component of media design, and having a good understanding of how type works can be a major advantage in prioritising the information on a page and when you come to work on page make-up. Most people will have some experience of using type through computer software such as Word but may not have any real understanding of what can be achieved with letterforms and the spatial arrangement of characters. The art, craft, psychology and technology of using type in design are called typography: a typographer is someone who employs type to communicate. Typography refers to both the creation of letterforms and how type is applied in a design. Letters can be used to convey all aspects of human interaction from hard facts to emotions by invoking the rhythms and patterns of speech, through their size, shape, style and tonality.

Typography is fundamental to the clarity of any published communication as it establishes how information should be ordered and how it is perceived. Typography is a quiet skill that when used well in a publication or website may be mostly unnoticed. But it is one of the most powerful means of directing attention, creating emphasis, shaping content and giving language form. It is a cornerstone of our cultural world, appearing throughout our daily lives where it directs, teaches, guides, entertains and provides information. Much of our society's constant cultural flow – whether high or low brow – is through the medium of type.

Typographic techniques have been in constant development since the fifteenth century, when Gutenberg introduced a system of printing with individual cast metal letters that could be reused (moveable type). Although there have been massive technological developments in how type is produced, the terminology and measuring systems used today by computer programs are based on previous industrial processes (see Chapter 3, page 47). Typographic rules, no matter what their origin, remain important in contemporary media design as they provide a basis for type usage that has been tried and tested. But if a discipline is to remain relevant it has to be able to accommodate progress, and new aspects of typography were developed to work with digital technology. Today, type is designed digitally and distributed via the Internet, and this has led to a global type culture with many specialist type websites and blogs. There are hundreds, possibly thousands, of **typefaces** already in existence, with more being designed every day. Each one conveys a unique visual meaning through its design style and cultural connotations.

Digital type

The computer has moved typography from an expensive industrial process to an accessible activity. Computer-generated type allows anyone to create and style their own digital environment and any material they produce, and people are now able to explore, experiment and extend their ideas and concepts with minimal expense. Whereas most people are happy to use existing fonts, there are type design programs available that enable you to generate your own typefaces to suit your own preferences. These programs enable you to design and originate alphabets or manipulate and

Type jargon buster

Typeface: a named design of type, for example, Times.

Glyphs: all the characters and symbols that make up a typeface.

Font: an individual style of a specific typeface, for example Times Italic Bold.

Type family: all the fonts that make up the range of a specific typeface including the different weights, styles and widths.

Type size: type for print is measured in points: 1 point = 0.376mm or 1/72th of an inch. Web typesize is measured in pixels and can be absolute (fixed) or relative (adjusted by the viewer's browser).

Leading (pronounced 'ledding'): line spacing. Leading is set in relationship to the type size.

adapt existing typefaces. Professional typographers also use the software to design typefaces for individual publications and websites, or even each page and article.

Specialist software, such as FontLab or Fontographer, uses **vector graphics** to draw mathematically plotted letterforms with smooth outlines. Every new typeface has to be designed to include all the characters, numbers, accents and symbols (**glyphs**). Once a designer has devised the overall look of a typeface, the digital type programs then create all the letters of an alphabet and work out the characteristics for each font, such as weight, size and proportion. The spacing between letters and other glyphs is also very important, and a well-designed typeface should have characters that work in visual harmony with one another.

Media companies may commission new type designs for a title in order to provide the product with a unique identity. The type style, once it has become associated with the brand, can then be used to create a strong visual link between platforms and for promotional material. A type design and how it is applied has a considerable effect on how a brand is perceived: for example, a fine, delicate typeface can be seen as feminine, while a heavy, techno-style type is thought of as youthful and masculine. If you are overseeing a project where you are either responsible for commissioning a new typeface for a specific use, or asked to choose from existing type designs, you should try to match the look and emotional message of the font to the target audience and market of the publication or website.

> **TIP** Although you may know the most commonly used keyboard commands for special characters, if you need to know how to type a symbol, such as a micron (μ), operating systems and programs usually have a facility that displays all the glyphs that make up a typeface. There are also freeware programs that do this, such as PopChar.

'Screen viewing will never be, and should never be, like reading printed text. Forcing typefaces to look like their printed counterparts shows no attempt to embrace the media for what it is. Screens consist of pixels, for better or worse.'

Craig Kroeger, www.minimi.com

Bitmap and vector type

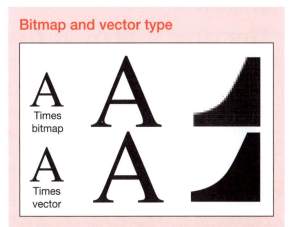

Vector type is created using tiny, precisely plotted points linked by fine straight or curved lines. Vector letterforms can be delicate and very small, or blocky and massive. They can be scaled up or down without any loss of quality and are resolution independent. Bitmap letters are built out of pixels and are resolution dependent, which may cause problems if they are rescaled. Bitmap-type curves have to be built up out of 'staircased' blocks, meaning it is not possible to make a true arch or circle. To conceal this, screen-based graphics use an effect called **anti-aliasing** that gives a softer outline to bitmapped type by sampling the colours either side of a letter and spreading pixels in graduated tones of the colours around the 'staircase'. Bitmap type looks good on-screen and therefore on the Web. Vector type is used for print as it produces a sharp, crisp image (see page 177).

Basic typeface characteristics

(9/10 Times Roman) The quick brown fox jumps over the lazy dog. The quick brown fox jumps over the lazy dog. The quick brown fox jumps over the lazy dog. The quick brown fox jumps over the lazy dog.

(9/10 Helvetica) The quick brown fox jumps over the lazy dog. The quick brown fox jumps over the lazy dog. The quick brown fox jumps over the lazy dog. The quick brown fox jumps.

The quick brown fox
(24pt Times Bold)

The quick brown fox
(24pt Warnock Bold)

The quick brown fox jumps   (12pt Tahoma Bold)

The quick brown fox jumps   (12pt Photina MT)

The quick brown fox jumps   (12pt Futura)

The range of letter shapes that make up a typeface define its identity. Times and Helvetica are examples of body copy fonts which are designed to give a standardised look to blocks of text. Body copy styles need to be legible at smaller sizes, so do not employ design features that would distract from the content.

Typefaces that feature exaggerated letterforms and notably individual characteristics, such as the lower case k in Warnock, help to create the mood and identity of a title, whereas a font such as Times that has uniform letter shapes and is very widely used may not convey an appropriate look and feel.

The character shapes of a typeface and the pattern they create can significantly change a reader's or user's perception of the text.

Sourcing and buying type

Typefaces are installed on computer operating systems as individual software files. Each typeface file must be present on the computer for the type to be visible on-screen and for it to print out. Computers and other devices come with some pre-installed typefaces – default system fonts. These have been specifically designed for viewing on-screen and for desktop printers. Website design may be restricted to default families of system fonts but many browsers now accept the more creative font-face typefaces. Print technology enables you to employ a much wider range of typefaces. The ability to buy a range of type means that you can choose fonts that are more suitable to the product and avoid having to select from the overused system fonts.

The design, advertising and publishing industries have always worked with higher quality fonts that provide a better result than system fonts, some of which are not particularly well designed and almost never use default typefaces for publication, graphic or advertising design. The Mac has always had a good reputation for type handling and display, and this is why it has become the platform of choice for the media and design industries.

There are a number of sources for type on the Web. Typefaces can be bought from specialist companies, commissioned from type designers or downloaded from type websites. Type manufacturers are sometimes referred to as **type foundries** (see Chapter 3, page 47). Linotype–Monotype (fonts.com), Adobe, Berthold, ITC (International Typeface Corporation) and Bitstream are large, long-established type companies that sell their own typefaces and versions of classic type such as Franklin Gothic or Caslon, as well as continuing to commission new fonts. There are a number of medium-sized type companies run by designers such as Carlos Segura, who founded and runs T-26, an American company dedicated to digital type design, and the British graphic designer Neville Brody, who is known for his typographically oriented work and who is associated with Fontworks (type.co.uk). There are also independent typographers and design groups, such as Alias, and websites like Veer that combines type, photographic and graphics libraries with lifestyle elements such as blogs.

When you purchase type, you need to consider whether to buy the entire range of styles available for a typeface or to select just those fonts you will be using on a regular basis. The budget set for the title may restrict the number of typefaces and styles you can use. Type manufacturers sell licences to use type, and it is illegal, as with any other computer program, to install or share type. Media companies are very careful not to infringe such restrictions and will expect you to comply with the legal requirements. The licence to use type may cover just one style, or you can buy them for sets or groups of typefaces. Companies that require a large range of type may purchase type libraries containing thousands of styles, which are also available on DVD. Type licences are issued for a given number of computers and printers, so you will need to know how many users there will be and how many sites your organisation will wish to use the type licences in.

If there is no budget to buy type, there are typefaces available from the Web for free. There are thousands of such typefaces and these can be extremely imaginative and sometimes even wacky. They can be suitable for quirky headlines and used for graphic text on the Web; however, the technical quality of free type can vary, and some fonts may simply not print out due to basic factors like software incompatibility and a lack of testing. There can also be problems with design nuances such as **letter spacing**. Commercial type manufacturers test all their fonts to ensure they are compatible with both PC and Mac operating systems and all the major software applications, and to guarantee that they will print out correctly from desktop proofers and printing presses. If you wish to design your own fonts, there are free type creation programs available on the Internet, such as FreeType, that enable people to design and distribute their own fonts. Free fonts may also be issued with certain restrictions, and you need to check that they can be used for commercial purposes.

Warning Any special effect or wacky typeface should have a design or informational purpose. You should not use unnecessarily complicated fonts or apply software effects that twist or distort type just because they exist, or because they appeal to you.

Free fonts

Individual type enthusiasts are responsible for many of the free fonts available for personal use on the Internet. However, some are offered as inducements to lure people on to software retail sites and you have to buy the typeface to obtain the full alphabet. Free fonts can carry viruses and, if they have not been properly tested, may crash or corrupt other type files or programs. When using a free font, it is often safer to convert the typeface into vector-based artwork through Adobe InDesign or Illustrator (Type menu > **Create Outlines**) rather than rely on the source font file.

1. ABCDEFGHIJKLMNOPQRST
2. ABCDEFGHIJKLMNOPQRST
3. ABCDEFGHIJKLMNOPQRSTUVWXYZ
4. ABCDEFGHIJKLMNOPQRSTUVWXYZ1234567890!
5. ABCDEFGHIJKLMNOPQRST
6. ABCDEFGHIJKLMNOPQRS
7. ABCDEFGHIJKLMNOPQRSTUVWXYZ12
8. ABCDEFGHIJKLMNOPQRSTU

1. Ventilate; 2. Steelcap Rubbing; 3. Rusted Machine;
4. Stone Age; 5. Steve Hand; 6. Dingos;
7. Metropolitaines D; 8. Arizona Airways NF

Type foundries, manufacturers and agents

www.adobe.com/type
www.bertholdtypes.com
www.itcfonts.com
www.linotype.com
www.monotypefonts.com
www.type.co.uk
www.fontshop.com
www.fonts.com
www.myfonts.com
www.fonthaus.com
www.virusfonts.com/

Free fonts:
www.dafonts.com
www.fontspace.com
www.freefonts.org.uk
www.identifont.com
www.1001freefonts.com
www.urbanfonts.com

Type designers

Type is as subject to fashion as any other area of the media. Some typefaces come in and go out of style, while others, like Helvetica, seem timeless. The first decade of this century has seen influences on type design from graffiti artists such as Banksy and from skater and street art that have come into mainstream type design through games packaging and website galleries. Another strong trend has been a return to hand-drawn and craft-based typefaces.

This is seen by some as a reaction to the increasing sophistication of digital type, as it reintroduces a human element into design. Type can also have political resonance as it is used for election posters and websites as well as on environmental and social campaign materials. Designer Jonathan Barnbrook is an activist who, through his designs and writing, campaigns to make graphic designers more aware of the potential misuse of words in type.

There is a large number of design specialists who are passionate about typography and who have built international reputations. There are some very well-known designers who have created the seminal typefaces that people use every day. Matthew Carter was commissioned by Microsoft to design Verdana and Georgia especially for use on the Web, the classic Avant Garde font was designed by Herb Lubalin and the Gill type family by the artist and designer Eric Gill.

If you are interested in finding out more about typography, you should look at the websites of The Association Typographique Internationale (ATypI), the leading international typographic authority, or the Type Director's Club, which is based in New York. TDC holds yearly global type design competitions and issues an annual of the winning and other top type designs. In Britain, the Typographic Circle runs talks on media design, and the International Society of Typographic Designers (ISTD) is a group of designers that work to promote links between education and industry.

Type designers and their typefaces

Alejandro Paul (Sudtipos): Marzo, Paz, La Protensa, Lynda

Bruno Maag (Dalton Maag): Metrolink, Dedica, King's Caslon

Christian Schwartz (SchwartzcoInc): Amplitude, Fritz, Pennsylvania

Craig Kroeger (Minimi): Ceriph, Classic, Mono, Kroeger

Erik Speikermann (Eden Speikermann): FF Meta, ITC Officina, FF Info, LoType, Berliner Grotesk (his FontFeed blog covers all things typographic)

Erik van Blokland (LettError with Just van Rossum): BeoSans, FF Hands, Trixie

Gerard Unger: Capitolium, Paradox, Vesta

Jessica Hische: hand-drawn typography and typographic illustrations

Jonathan Barnbrook (Barnbrook/VirusFonts): Bourgeois, Infidel, Moron

Jonathan Hoefler and Tobias Frere-Jones (Hoefler and Frere-Jones): Sentinel, Mercury, Gotham

Ken Barber (House Industries): Blaktur, Studio Lettering

Kris Sowersby (Klim Type Foundry): FF Unit Slab, Galaxie Copernicus

Ludwig Ubele: Marat Pro, Mokka, Augustin

Marian Bantjes: Restraint typeface, hand-drawn typography

Matthew Carter (Carter and Cone): Helvetica Neue, Verdana, Bell Centennial

Miles Newlyn: Democratica, Sabbath Black, Ferox

Neville Brody: Industria, Insignia, Arcadia, Tyson, World

Paul Barnes: Guardian Egyptian, Guardian Sans, Classics, Publico

Tal Leming: HouseGothic23, Mission + Control, Baxter

Wim Crouwel: New Alphabet 1, 2 and 3, Gridnik Alphabet

Wim Crouwel interview: http://www.youtube.com/watch?v=I5y3px4ovxE

Kris Sowersby article: http://www.designerinterviews.com/an-interview-with-type-designer-kris-sowersby/

Matthew Carter on Helvetica and neutrality: http://www.youtube.com/watch?v=2j2YQHECfPM

ABCDEFGHIJKLMNOPQRSTUVWXYZ
abcdefghijklmnoprstuvwxyz
1234567890!@£$%^&*()_+

The quick brown fox jumps over the lazy
dog

Erik Spiekermann was commissioned to design Meta, a
humanist sans serif font, to introduce an informal style of
presentation for the West German Post Office.

ABCDEFGHIJKLMNOPQRSTUVWX
YZabcdefghijklmnoprstuvwxyz
1234567890!@£$%^&*()_+

The quick brown fox jumps over
the lazy dog

Matthew Carter designed Verdana for Microsoft. The
typeface has maximum screen legibility and is compatible
with a range of operating system browsers.

ABCDEFGHIJKLMNOPQRSTUVWXYZ
abcdefghijklmnoprstuvwxyz
1234567890!@£$%^&*()_+

The quick brown fox jumps over the lazy
dog

Erik Spiekermann and Ole Schäffer designed the sans serif
font Officiana for use in business documentation.

ABCDEFGHIJKLMNOPQRSTUVWXY
Zabcdefghijklmnoprstuvwxyz
1234567890!@£$%^&*()_+

The quick brown fox jumps over the
lazy dog

Matthew Carter created Helvetica Neue for Linotype to
standardise its classic sans serif, Helvetica.

Main visual signifiers for typefaces

The key to distinguishing one typeface from another
is to look closely at the shape and proportion of the
individual letterforms. The lower case g, in particular,
is used as an important signifier in determining a
typeface's identity as its design can vary more between
typefaces than most other letters.

- g Text fonts (Times): for books and magazines
- g Script fonts (Apple Chancery): calligraphy, hand-
  writing fonts
- g Handwriting/grunge fonts (SteveHand): fonts with a
  personal touch
- g Corporate fonts (Meta): fonts for corporate design
- g Celebration fonts (Popular): events, birthdays,
  Christmas, sales to Halloween
- g Black letter fonts (News Gothic): gothic, Celtic fonts
- g Comic fonts (Marker Felt): kids and fun fonts
- ☺ Western fonts (Rosewood): inspired by the Wild West
- g Cool fonts (Skia): modern, technical look
- g Screen fonts (Verdana): optimised for viewing small
  sizes on-screen
- ✤ Symbol fonts (Zapf Dingbats): pi fonts and dingbats
  for symbols and graphic indicators

Type naming

There is no set convention for naming typefaces. Type
designers may choose a name for their own typefaces
that reflects a design movement or the publication
they were created for. Times is a **serif** font created for
and named after the (London) *Times* newspaper. Times
New Roman was designed by Stanley Morison, Victor
Lardent and Starling Burgess of Monotype in the 1930s
to replace the original nineteenth-century version. It
has become one of the most commonly used typefaces
in the world because it has been licensed as a system
font that is used by almost all hardware and software
manufacturers.

Typefaces may be associated with particular periods
and this can affect their semiotic message, and styles
are often linked to an historical era or art and design
movement. Claude Garamond, for example, created his
eponymous font in the sixteenth century, while William
Caslon and Giambatista Bodoni were typographic
masters of the eighteenth century. Baskerville is an eighteenth-century serif typeface created by John Baskerville,
the official printer for the University of Cambridge,
who has become associated with the Enlightenment,

an eighteenth-century philosophical and political movement that lies at the core of modern journalistic practice. Modernist typefaces such as Art Deco **sans serif** typefaces from the 1920s are still popular today, and several are used as system fonts because of their geometric elegance. The artist and designer Eric Gill developed Gill Sans in 1927, while Futura, which follows the modernist style of the Bauhaus art and design school, was designed in the same year by Paul Renner for a German company called Bauer. Many typefaces are named after their designer: Zapf Dingbats is a symbol typeface designed by the German typographer Hermann Zapf; and Adrian Frutiger created his Frutiger typeface in the 1960s for France's airport signage.

The history of Helvetica

A designer turned type salesman called Max Miedinger created the first version of Helvetica, originally called Neue Haas Grotesk (**grotesque** is the nineteenth-century name for sans serif typefaces), for the Haas type foundry in Switzerland in the 1950s. It has since become one of the most widely used typefaces in the world. Arial is Microsoft's version of Helvetica. In the 1970s–1980s, Linotype, the manufacturer of Helvetica, was wary of the idea of personal computing, which it saw as a threat to its income base. Consequently, Linotype did not cooperate when Microsoft and other software companies wanted to include its typefaces in their operating systems. As a result, many early digital technology companies designed their own (very similar but not quite the same) versions of the most popular typefaces.

Managing type

The key to working successfully with type is to marry the typeface to the media, the title and the audience. For example, a design for a print publication aimed at an older readership might employ an open, traditional-style font printed in black in a comparatively large size, while a website for a music title with a younger audience might use small-scale, brightly coloured type. The medium and the amount of information each page has to display dictate the size at which type can be displayed. Normally, the size of the main text is used to establish a base measurement, and all the other type elements, such as headlines and standfirst/sells, are chosen in relation to this size in order to develop a visual structure and hierarchy.

It is important to understand how typefaces will create pattern and tonality on a page. A thin, delicate typeface used for the main text can make a title look light and feminine, whereas a bold, chunky face will give a heavy and masculine appearance. The vocabulary employed to describe professional-quality typefaces covers the range of looks and sizes available. The two major categories of type are serif and sans serif. Serifs are fonts that have a line or arc that extends from the corner or foot of a letter; sans serif type is smooth (*sans* means without in French). Type is produced in a **type family** – a number of different styles that include variations such as light and heavy, wide and narrow, italic and normal. Type management also involves controlling the leading – the amount of white space visible between one line of type and the next. Leading affects the readability of the text and contributes to the pattern and tonality of a page. When you come to work on a title, you will find each type element has a style and size; for example, the news pages may only use a fixed set of headline sizes in a condensed sans serif typeface.

Type families and fonts

Type families include all the sizes, weights, styles and widths of a single typeface. In traditional cast metal type, a font was a single style of a type family; however, computer programs use the term to mean a typeface, and the two words are now synonymous. Type families can include a large number of different fonts, each described by its size, name, weight and style, for example 24pt Helvetica Neue Light Italic (see opposite). There are a number of system typefaces that are suitable for use on the Web. These come in groups that are categorised as serif and sans serif, with subsets in differing styles. Type style may also refer to other type practices such as strikethrough and underline.

The base style of a typeface is described as normal or roman (upright). Each individual font in a type family will be described using its weight, which affects the tonality of the letterforms and their density on a

ABCDEFGHIJKLMNOPQRSTUVWXYZabcdefghijklmnopqrstuvwxyz1234567890!@£$%^&*()_+
ABCDEFGHIJKLMNOPQRSTUVWXYZabcdefghijklmnopqrstuvwxyz1234567890!@£$%^&*()_+
ABCDEFGHIJKLMNOPQRSTUVWXYZabcdefghijklmnopqrstuvwxyz1234567890!@£$%^&*()_+
ABCDEFGHIJKLMNOPQRSTUVWXYZabcdefghijklmnopqrstuvwxyz1234567890!@£$%^
ABCDEFGHIJKLMNOPQRSTUVWXYZabcdefghijklmnopqrstuvwxyz1234567890!@£$%^&()_+*
ABCDEFGHIJKLMNOPQRSTUVWXYZabcdefghijklmnopqrstuvwxyz1234567890!@£$%^&()_+*
ABCDEFGHIJKLMNOPQRSTUVWXYZabcdefghijklmnopqrstuvwxyz1234567890!@£$%^&*()_+
ABCDEFGHIJKLMNOPQRSTUVWXYZabcdefghijklmnopqrstuvwxyz1234567890!@£$%^&
ABCDEFGHIJKLMNOPQRSTUVWXYZabcdefghijklmnopqrstuvwxyz1234567890!@£$%^&*()_+
ABCDEFGHIJKLMNOPQRSTUVWXYZabcdefghijklmnopqrstuvwxyz1234567890!@£$%^
ABCDEFGHIJKLMNOPQRSTUVWXYZabcdefghijklmnopqrstuvwxyz12
ABCDEFGHIJKLMNOPQRSTUVWXYZabcdefghijklmnopqrstuvwxyz1234567890!@£$%^&*()_+
ABCDEFGHIJKLMNOPQRSTUVWXYZabcdefghijklmnopqrstuvwxyz1234567890!@£$%^&*()_+
ABCDEFGHIJKLMNOPQRSTUVWXYZabcdefghijklmnopqrstuvwxyz1234567890!@£$%^&*()_+
ABCDEFGHIJKLMNOPQRSTUVWXYZabcdefghijklmnopqrstuvwxyz1234567890!@£$%^&*()_+
ABCDEFGHIJKLMNOPQRSTUVWXYZabcdefghijklmnopqrstuvwxyz1234567890!@£$%^&*()_+
ABCDEFGHIJKLMNOPQRSTUVWXYZabcdefghijklmnopqrstuvwxyz1234567890!@£$%^&*()_+
ABCDEFGHIJKLMNOPQRSTUVWXYZabcdefghijklmnopqrstuvwxyz1234567890!@£$%^&*()_+
ABCDEFGHIJKLMNOPQRSTUVWXYZabcdefghijklmnopqrstuvwxyz1234567890!@£$%^&*()_+

A selection from the extensive Helvetica Neue family that ranges from ultra light condensed to extra black expanded.

page or screen. Some typefaces come in a very wide range that extends from ultra light, light and thin, to medium and book (regular), and on to bold, semi-bold, black and extra black, while others may be limited to a few weights and styles, such as light, medium and bold. A typeface will have a base width to the characters. There can also be extended and condensed versions of the fonts that are designed so that they are readable in wider or narrow proportions. Type designers provide variations in width to ensure the font retains its characteristics and works visually without appearing distorted. It is possible to stretch or squeeze type by changing its horizontal or vertical scale, but this can make a typeface look unattractive and reduce its readability.

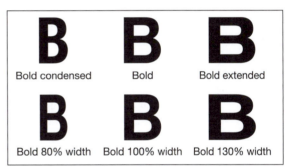

The top row shows how the weights and widths of a typeface are carefully designed to maintain an optimum balance between the thickness of the lines and the white space of the counters (spaces within the letters). It is as wrong to manipulate type as it is an image, as digitally stretching or squeezing a letter or picture can distort the proportions and unbalance the shape, which can look unattractive, as shown in the second row.

Example of a human figure demonstrating how when the horizontal proportions are distorted the overall effect is unbalanced.

Design for Media

Upper and lower case

Upper case is the typographic term for the capital letters and **lower case** refers to the small letters, which are also called the minuscule. The terms comes from pre-digital type production when all characters of every typeface were cast on metal 'pegs', with one for every letter of the alphabet in each size, weight, style and width. All the letters for a typeface were kept in a type composer's job case. This was divided into wooden trays with compartments for each letter, with the capitals on the upper level and the smaller characters in the lower one. The letters were transferred to a **composing stick**, a hand-held device that was used to make up lines of type at a fixed width.

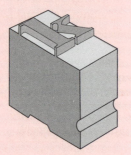

A hot metal, lower case letter.

Serif

Garamond	ABCDEFGabcdefg12345
Baskerville	ABCDEFGabcdefg12345
Didot	ABCDEFGabcdefg12345
Times New Roman	ABCDEFGabcdefg12345
Rockwell	ABCDEFGabcdefg12345
STENCIL	ABCDEFG12345

Serif type has four main styles that reflect the development of print and changes in visual taste. The first typefaces were created by hand, which gave the letters a particular shape and width, and the styles followed the look of written manuscripts. The practice of hand casting continued from the fifteenth century until the Industrial Revolution in the eighteenth, when the invention of new industrial processes allowed type to be designed with finer serifs.

■ **Old Style** or **Venetian** serif typefaces date back to the early development of type during the Renaissance. The capital letters were based upon chisel-cut Roman inscriptions such as those on Emperor Trajan's triumphal column. The lower case characters come from the medieval hand-written style of scribes who wrote letters for the general public, most of whom could neither read nor write. The early serif faces have a sideways flick, echoing the movement of a hand using a quill pen. Old Style serifs typically have round letters on a slight slope and heavy downstrokes. Aldus Manutius (c.1450–1515) was the most famous of the Venetian type masters and was credited with inventing the italic form.

■ Transitional serif typefaces come from the Baroque period (c. 1600–1750). Engraving was often used for print reproduction in the seventeenth century, and transitional typefaces reflect the effect of incising letters into metal with a steel cutting tool. The rounded letters are upright and use a combination of thin and thick crossbars and downstrokes. Times is the most famous typeface in this category; other styles include Plantin, Joanna and Perpetua. Baskerville (see page 153) is a transitional serif.

■ **Egyptian** or **slab serif** typefaces are heavy and square fonts, with little or no contrast between the elements of the letters, and feature blocks as serifs. The Industrial Revolution led to a growth in the use of print for packaging and advertising, and this encouraged printers to develop a greater variety of designs, including the slab serif type typically used for Victorian posters and playbills. Playbill, an Egyptian font, is based on Victorian theatre typography, and other slab serif styles include Rockwell and Clarendon, which was the first typeface to be registered as a copyrighted design.

■ **Modern** or **didone typefaces** were introduced during the eighteenth century. Modern serif typefaces are characterised by a geometric appearance with contrasting broad and hairline downstrokes and crossbars, and delicate serifs set at acute angles. The fine contours of the type were made possible by the mechanisation of the type manufacturing process, more accurate printing presses and smoother paper. Modern serifs include Didot, designed by François Didot (1689–1757), who also developed the printer's **points** type measurement system that has been adopted by software manufacturers for digital type. Bodoni, designed by Giambattista Bodoni (1740–1813), is a typical modern serif style. Other examples are Centennial, Century and Bernhard.

Sans serif

News Gothic	ABCDEFGabcdefg12345
Gill Sans	ABCDEFGabcdefg12345
Futura	ABCDEFGabcdefg12345
Arial	ABCDEFGabcdefg12345
Frutiger	ABCDEFGabcdefg12345
Blur	**ABCDEFGabcdefg12345**

Sans serif faces were developed during the Industrial Revolution. The first fonts, issued in 1816, were called grotesque as well as sans serif. The designs had a clean, mechanistic look made possible by new manufacturing techniques that meant the type could be designed with sharp corners and straight lines. The Bauhaus design school (1919–1933) developed the use of sans serif type as it expresses the architectural feel of modernist graphics. Sans serif faces have continued to be popular as the letterforms work well in the grid-based designs typically used for contemporary media titles. There are four categories of sans serif that include a wide range of type styles, from semi-sans that has slight serifs, to LCD and digital display styles.

■ **Grotesque** fonts are the earliest forms of sans serif and, while they are geometric, they retain some serif characteristics such as curved and upturned elements, for example rounded terminals. The style includes Trade Gothic, Helvetica, Univers and Akzidenz Grotesk.

■ **Neo-grotesque** is a development of the grotesque style. The typefaces are more geometric with letter shapes that do not always close on themselves and may have curved terminals. Arial is a neo-grotesque, as are some later versions of Helvetica. Other examples are Bell Gothic and Bell Centennial.

■ **Geometric sans serif** typefaces are made up of pure verticals, horizontals, circles and rectangles, and are visually mono weighted with a smooth outline. These faces are identified with the art deco movement and include Avant Garde, Futura, Eurostile and Lubalin.

■ **Humanist typefaces** were designed in reaction to the hard sterile look of the geometric sans fonts and make visual reference to the characteristics of earlier type styles. Humanist faces are softer on the eye and the letter shapes appear less formal. Examples include Optima, Gill Sans and Frutiger.

The designs of letterforms can be very dissimilar, even within the overall categories of serif and sans serif, as the dimensions and shape of the elements of a typeface can vary. Serif or sans serif type categories are not always clear cut, and the design of some typefaces may not fall neatly into one group. Typefaces are often associated with a particular design style and carry considerable cultural weighting, which should be considered when selecting a font. Serif styles are said to be better for body copy in print, as the serifs lead the reader's eye across a line of text. Sans serif fonts produce less interference on-screen, so are preferred for web copy. Sans fonts are more commonly used for headlines in both media than serifs, as their compact shapes are more legible, particularly from a distance. Print publications commonly used a mixture of serif and sans fonts in more than one style.

Height, depth and width

The height and depth of the letterforms are judged according to the **baseline**, the notional line on which typefaces 'sit', and all characters have a base width from which they would be expanded or condensed. How big a typeface looks is based on how tall we perceive the contrast between the capital letters and the **x-height** – the height of a lower case x – and the depth between each line of type. Some fonts have tall capital letters and ascenders, with correspondingly deep descenders, while others are more compact with short uprights and a low x-height (see page 166). The base width can also affect the usability of a typeface; for example, some fonts are designed to occupy less width, allowing for more words per line, while others are round and wide, reducing the number of characters that will fit across a line.

'Set a page in Fournier against another in Caslon and another in Plantin and it is as if you heard three different people delivering the same discourse – each with impeccable pronunciation and clarity, yet each through the medium of a different personality.'

Beatrice Warde, typography expert and author

Sans and serif: the relationship between style, size and leading

Lorem ipsum dolor sit amet, consectetur adipiscing elit. Integer adipiscing erat in enim lobortis interdum. Praesent egestas arcu quis lacus malesuada sed venenatis felis euismod. Curabitur placerat bibendum tortor ac imperdiet. Sed id sapien nunc, convallis elementum sem.

9/9pt Times New Roman: insufficient line depth with ascenders and descenders too close

Lorem ipsum dolor sit amet, consectetur adipiscing elit. Integer adipiscing erat in enim lobortis interdum. Praesent egestas arcu quis lacus malesuada sed venenatis felis euismod. Curabitur placerat bibendum tortor ac imperdiet. Sed id sapien nunc, convallis elementum sem.

9/10pt Times New Roman: adding 1pt of leading improves readability and legibility

Lorem ipsum dolor sit amet, consectetur adipiscing elit. Integer adipiscing erat in enim lobortis interdum. Praesent egestas arcu quis lacus malesuada sed venenatis felis euismod. Curabitur placerat bibendum tortor ac imperdiet. Sed id sapien nunc.

9/12pt Times New Roman: lightens tonality and reduces the perceived size of text

Lorem ipsum dolor sit amet, consectetur adipiscing elit. Integer adipiscing erat in enim lobortis interdum. Praesent egestas arcu quis lacus malesuada sed venenatis felis euismod. Curabitur placerat bibendum tortor ac imperdiet. Sed id sapien nunc, convallis elementum sem.

9/9pt Helvetica: cramped solid leading lacks space and breaks the eye flow

Lorem ipsum dolor sit amet, consectetur adipiscing elit. Integer adipiscing erat in enim lobortis interdum. Praesent egestas arcu quis lacus malesuada sed venenatis felis euismod. Curabitur placerat bibendum tortor ac imperdiet. Sed id sapien nunc, convallis elementum sem.

9/10pt Helvetica: increasing the leading separates the ascenders and descenders

Lorem ipsum dolor sit amet, consectetur adipiscing elit. Integer adipiscing erat in enim lobortis interdum. Praesent egestas arcu quis lacus malesuada sed venenatis felis euismod. Curabitur placerat bibendum tortor ac imperdiet.

9/12pt Helvetica: very open leading begins to make the font less legible

Lorem ipsum dolor sit amet, consectetur adipiscing elit. Integer adipiscing erat in enim lobortis interdum. Praesent egestas arcu quis lacus malesuada sed venenatis felis euismod. Curabitur placerat bibendum tortor ac imperdiet. Sed id sapien nunc, convallis elementum sem.

9/9pt Gill Sans: typefaces with low x-heights can be set on solid leading

Lorem ipsum dolor sit amet, consectetur adipiscing elit. Integer adipiscing erat in enim lobortis interdum. Praesent egestas arcu quis lacus malesuada sed venenatis felis euismod. Curabitur placerat bibendum tortor ac imperdiet. Sed id sapien nunc, convallis elementum sem.

9/10pt Gill Sans: plus points of leading can reduce the visual density

Lorem ipsum dolor sit amet, consectetur adipiscing elit. Integer adipiscing erat in enim lobortis interdum. Praesent egestas arcu quis lacus malesuada sed venenatis felis euismod. Curabitur placerat bibendum tortor ac imperdiet. Sed id sapien nunc

9/12pt Gill Sans: too much white space can fracture the line flow

Leading

As well as from the design of the typeface, the two critical factors that affect the legibility of typefaces are the point size and the line spacing. The typographic term for line spacing is **leading** (pronounced 'ledding'), which originates from when printers used thin strips of lead to create the spaces between hand-set lines of type. The lead strips were, like type, measured in points and used at depths that varied according to the size of the font (see page 159). The line spacing system used in print and web design programs automatically inserts digital space above and below the type, and the software will adjust the leading in relation to the chosen typesize. Print and web design software makes it possible to set the leading of each type element to suit the design.

The amount of leading depends on the style of the typeface and the size at which it is to be used. The judgement about how much space should be left between lines of type can just be a practical decision: a typeface set with too much or too little space around it can make copy hard to read, create extra text that will

Line depths

- Leading runs in ratio to the type size and is expressed as plus or minus points from the default size of each font (print) or as a percentage of the base type size (web). For example, +3pts of leading added to a 12pt type size = 15pts of leading (print) while +20 = more open leading , −10 = tighter leading (web).

- Word, web, graphic design and imaging program menus use standard type sizes with pre-set leading that adds + increments to the default type sizes.

- Print type size and leading is written as a fraction, for example 12/15pt = 12pt type size on 15pts of leading.

- Type size and leading can be adjusted manually, but should always be kept in ratio.

not fit on the page (overmatter) or cause it to run short. Headlines set in capital letters require less depth between lines than upper and lower case type which needs extra space above and below the ascenders (e.g. the upward stroke of an h) and descenders (e.g. the downward stroke of a y). The standard amount of leading used by programs should stop type ascenders and descenders 'tangling', but adding leading may improve the legibility of some fonts.

The amount of leading used with a particular size of type in a publication or website forms part of the visual identity, and line spacing can be as subject to fashion changes in graphic design as the style of the typeface. In aesthetic terms, the leading for a font is chosen in proportion to the type size to create an attractive effect. The white space leading inserts between lines of type is mixed by the eye with the black or colour used for the letterforms to alter the tone of a heading, introductory paragraph or block of text by producing graduations of grey or tints of a hue. Open leading – adding extra line spacing – lightens the grey tone or colour tint, while tight leading makes it appear darker. If a light typeface is set on very open leading, it may make the font 'float' on the page and can break the visual connection between the lines. Conversely, a heavy typeface on tight leading may become uncomfortable to read, or appear too dark against other items on a page and unbalance the design (see page 182).

Type for purpose

Most typefaces will have been designed with a particular purpose in mind. Typefaces are often categorised as text, display or script faces. A text face is one that will remain readable at a small size, while a display font is designed to look good from 18pts to much larger point sizes, and it may become illegible if used for **body copy** in smaller point sizes. For example, Times is a small-bodied serif typeface with short ascenders and descenders, and it is well suited for use as the main text typeface in a newspaper; however, its small capital letters make it less effective if used for a headline. Serif typefaces are visually complex compared with sans serif, and may be less suited for use on a background or picture.

Display type is often only suitable for headlines. For example, Impact is a very condensed headline face that can fit a large number of characters across a line. It has compact ascenders and descenders that allow it to be set on very tight leading. This reduces the visual open space above and below the headline; however, this means it is not suitable for use as a text face. Script faces usually resemble hand-created letterforms, for example calligraphy or graffiti. For example, Comic Sans may be suitable for a children's website as it suggests cartoon titling. The vagaries of informal type can make it hard to manage on the page using the normal leading, so it may have to be positioned by eye.

All type conveys semiotic messages. Serif type is considered formal and traditional, and using serif typefaces has the potential to add gravitas to a design, as they are perceived to be classical and historic, and can convey power and authority. However, not all serif faces are formal and the different shapes of serif change the meaning of the font. There are very fancy serif fonts with swirls and swash caps that are stereotypically

Warning Do not settle for a typeface just because it is available. The right typeface can enhance the attractiveness of a page or screen, but the wrong font or badly used type can ruin a design, no matter how brilliant the graphics and other imagery.

The magazine cover visuals have been designed using Didot, a highly stylised serif typeface.

Eurostile, a font that evokes the 1960s–1970s, has been used for the logo on this dummy website home page.

used for wedding invitations, and fashion magazines and companies use serif type to convey sophistication and elegance. Some advertisers of 'heritage' items use serif fonts to add verisimilitude to their allegedly traditional products. Type can also be decorative and fun.

There are thousands of variations of sans serif type ranging from schoolbook rounded to ragged deconstruction fonts. Websites that feature many different items on one page often only use sans serif faces because they are easier to make out in a busy setting (see page 188). Sans fonts carry the least semiotic message as they are mostly simple and clean, yet even this conveys a political and social inference, as a utilitarian bland typeface will still convey meaning through the designer's attempt to be universal. Sans typefaces are ubiquitous in modern life; in particular, Helvetica has become so widely used in the environment and the media that its popularity has reduced it to a background constant that few of us register. But the typographer Matthew Carter has pointed out that Helvetica had enormous impact when it was first launched, and its current ubiquity is due to its worldwide success.

The influence of modernism

Sans serif typefaces are strongly associated with modernism, in particular early twentieth-century art and design movements such as constructivism and futurism. One of the most influential figures in the development and popularising of sans type was Herbert Bayer, the leading exponent of modernism in typography at the German Bauhaus school in Dessau. His Bauhaus typeface is still in production (see below).

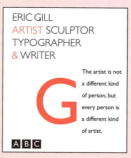

Gill Sans typifies the early twentieth century's sense of modernity and progress.

The rounded geometric shapes of the Bauhaus 3 typeface create strong graphic forms.

Deconstructionist designers moved away from established typographic convention and treated type in a more painterly manner.

See the DVD *Helvetica* by Gary Hustwit, 2006: *www.plexifilm.com, www.plexi.co.uk*

There is an interview and preview movie at: *www.pbs.org/independentlens/helvetica/makingof.html*

'Typography is two-dimensional architecture, based on experience and imagination, and guided by rules and readability'.

Hermann Zapf

Pictorial type

Type can be directly illustrative, as well carrying information and creating an impact from underlying signifiers. There are typefaces in medieval gothic, ornamental script and hand-writing styles, ones that look like stencils and even one that will type a traditional style blackmail note in what looks like cutout pieces of newspaper. There are also **Dingbats** –typefaces made up from symbols including arrows, stars, numbers in circles, copyright and registered trademark symbols, etc. These are used for signposting to assist readers or visitors to navigate through the content. And apart from basic pictorial fonts such as Symbol and Webdings, there are many far less sensible ones such as Dinotype that types in drawings of dinosaurs, as well as many others that key in images of butterflies or zoo animals and that are used purely for decoration.

Fabien Baron was the original art director on Andy Warhol's *Interview* magazine and is also famous for designing the Calvin Klein and Armani logos (www. baron-baron.com). He often uses typographic puns – sometimes referred to as concrete typography or the pictorialisation of copy – where the type takes on a shape or creates a visual echo of something in the article or picture (see page 177). A rebus is a style of visual communication. The word comes from the Latin for '[represented] by things'. A rebus combines symbols and images to represent words or ideas. An Egyptian cartouche – a panel of linked hieroglyphics – is a rebus, and Milton Glaser's famous i ♥ New York logo is another example.

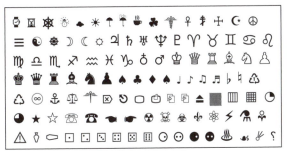

A rebus is a selling message or headline made up of a combination of type, pictures and symbols.

A selection from the Apple Symbols typeface.

Zapf Dingbats	✿✛✜✤✦✧★✩✪✫✬✭✮✯✰✱✲✳✴✵✶✷✸✹✺✻✼✽✾✿❀❁❂❃❄❅❆❇❈❉❊❋●❍■❏❐❑❒▲▼◆❖
Wingdings	☞☜☝☟✌☺☹☠⚐⚑✍✉✓☑✗☒⊗⊘⊙⊚er&⌨⌖⌗⌘⌙⌚⌛⌜⌝✄✍✎✏✐✑✒✓✔
Webdings	🏠🏡🏢🏣🏤🏥🏦🏧🏨🏩🏪🏫🏬🏭🏮🏯◀◁▶▷♥✈⚔⚕⚖⚗⚘
Emoticons	☺☻☹☺☻☹☺☻☹☺☻☹☺☻☹☺☻☹☺☻☹☺☻☹☺☻☹☺☻☹☺○€£$©☺?
FontForFree	☀♈♉♊♋♌♍♎♏♐♑♒♓☿♀♁♂♃♄♅♆♇☉☽☾☊☋☌☍⚹✦◇◈✿♨☯☮
Trekbats	♠🖖🖕🖐🖖🖕STAR TREK DEEP SPACE NINE🖖Ⓡ🖖STAR TREK ✹⊛⊙STAR TREK 🖖●♥↔←□←□→↓▼
Animal Tracks	🐾🐾🐾🐾🐾🐾🐾🐾🐾🐾🐾🐾🐾🐾🐾🐾🐾🐾🐾🐾🐾🐾🐾🐾🐾🐾🐾🐾🐾🐾✚
Techno Bats	♣🏁🏴🏳🏴🏁🏳◐♦☢☣5N⬅n🌀⍣⍙⍜casUa↓⚓⚔⚕⚖⚗⚘⚙⚚⚛⚜✈◼🏠♫♪
Ursa Bats	✳★✳✚✦◇◇◆★✦◇◆★★✦★★☆□□□□□□▲▲▲▲→+←↑↓⅛32○◉○○⅓☞●②☒☐

Dingbat fonts are available as standard system fonts, and a wide range of themed typeface such as Emoticons, Trekbats and Animals Tracks can be downloaded from type websites.

The language of type

Type can be used to communicate not only the written word but also speech patterns, and the communication style of a media product may need to convey an identifiable way of speaking, jargon or phraseology. For example, the choice of type for a computer arts website would need to blend the creativity of the audience to the computer industry. This would mean finding a font that reflects the visual aspirations of the visitor and the high-tech world in which they operate. Typography is a key element in creating 'vocal' designs as it can also help to indicate speech patterns through the use of punctuation – or the lack of it – bold or italic for emphasis, paragraph breaks and sentence length, indents, colour and the position of type on a page. For example, a youth-oriented magazine or website might use staccato sentences with the minimum of punctuation. This could be emphasised by setting the copy in a small type size in short paragraphs separated by line spaces (paragraph breaks).

Research has shown that some people modify the way they speak according to whom they are talking to, what they read and what they see. Social 'tribes' are strongly identified by how they speak and the words they use, and the products they consume. However, people may move between social and cultural groups during the course of a day, adapting what they say and how they say it as they do. This means that typefaces have to communicate at a number of different levels and reflect the norms and codes of social groupings.

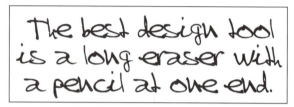

Quote by Marty Neumeier, set in SteveHand.

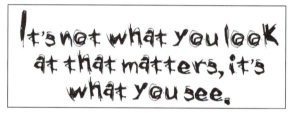

Quote by David Henry Thoreau, set in Grunge.

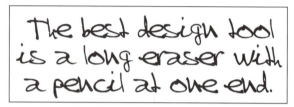

Quote by Jonathan Ive, set in Seeds.

Readability and legibility

People tend to read through recognition of character patterns. When children learn to read, they learn by identifying individual letters, but as people become accustomed to the shapes and how they are commonly grouped, they stop looking at each letter and begin to anticipate what each word will be. The space between characters and words affects the legibility of individual and grouped letterforms. When a typeface is designed, the spacing between the letterforms is optimised to maintain a balance of white space between adjoining letters. As a general design rule, upright letters are placed nearer to one another than rounded letters, but the actual distance is adjusted for each character in a style, weight, etc. for every typeface. This technique is called kerning and is automatically applied to typefaces. Automatic kerning is generally acceptable for body copy, but headlines may need manual kerning to remove space between characters that makes the words look visually unbalanced. Tracking is a software solution that can be used to reduce or expand all the spacing in between characters in a word, line, paragraph or for all linked copy in a document (see page 167). Minus tracking is often set as part of the typographic house design style as it may allow a few more characters to be fitted across a line, while adding tracking to some fonts can open up the spacing and increase legibility.

Type designers take into consideration problems such as a sans serif lower case l and upper case I being very similar, and will apply conventions that correct character clashes. However, the default typefaces on many computers are often poorly designed, and one particular weakness is that many of them have very bad character and word spacing. The factors that affect how evenly a typeface will space out across a page are the font, size, alignment, tracking and the width of the line. The wrong combination of choices may leave **open rivers** – excessive gaps between words in the line. Poor spacing may make it difficult to place a symbol such as a **bullet** because the gap between the words is too wide, or simply not consistent. Spatial disruption in a line can interrupt the reader's eye flow and break their concentration.

If you feel there are problems with the word spacing of the body copy, you can try adjusting the tracking to see if this improves the look of the copy. However, if you do change the tracking, this has to be a design decision for the entire publication, as it has a direct effect on the visual density of the copy and may potentially alter the word count per page. A related problem can affect type on the Web, as the anti-aliasing used to smooth out the appearance of a font may make the letters appear too close to each other. If you consider there is a problem

with the letter spacing, the web designer can be asked to adjust the tracking specification in the CSS. As with a print publication, this will alter all the body copy and you may need to check how this may affect all pages already published online.

One-year courses offer a shorter, sharper shock to the system. They are considered more heavyweight, in that students only have 12 months to cram everything in, but many graduates say they prefer this immersion method. It also means a return to the workplace more quickly and, therefore, perhaps, lower costs. There is no right or wrong length. Candidates must think carefully whether they want to take the time, and can afford the costs.	One-year courses offer a shorter, sharper shock to the system. They are considered more heavyweight, in that students only have 12 months to cram everything in, but many graduates say they prefer this immersion method. It also means a return to the workplace more quickly and, therefore, perhaps, lower costs. There is no right or wrong length. Candidates must think carefully whether they want to take the time, and can afford the costs, that a two-year course entails or if they prefer to immerse themselves into a one-year course.

The left hand example shows what happens if the typeface is too large for the column width. In the right hand example, the typeface is smaller but has wide characters, resulting in open 'rivers' – white gaps between words.

Using small type on a background

Print publications often use a sans serif typeface for boxed copy, sidebars, captions and subheads, even if the main text is in a serif face. This is to avoid the problems that can occur when small serif typefaces are used on a tint or solid colour background. Thin serifs can be difficult to print and there can be problems with the ink bleeding into the paper (see pages 168–9.). On the Web, small serif type can also become mixed with coloured background pixels, which can blur out the serifs and cause a third-colour 'halo' around the type. In general, it is advisable to use a sans serif typeface on coloured backgrounds as the uniform edges work better in print and on screen.

Type usage

12pt Helvetica black
using a heavy text font gives small typesize maximum impact for easy navigation through the magazine

30pt SteveHand
the hand-written font laid over the circular flash gives an air of friendliness and urgency

18pt Onyx
the ultra condensed serif face acts as a counterbalance to the Helvetica family used elsewhere on the page

84pt Curlz MT
the ornamental display font enables the headline to reflect the mood and subject matter of the editorial content

18/24pt Cambria
using a typeface with wide characters and open leading creates a light, inviting introduction to the article

12pt Helvetica bold and light
using contrasting weights for the byline, in a size that contrasts with the intro, acts as a visual break which is emphasised by the rule beneath

9/12pt Helvetica
the body copy is set in a clear text font with + 3pt line spacing to aid legibility and give an overall lightness to the text areas. All but the first paragraph is indented to make it easy for the reader to identify the start of each paragraph

8/9pt Helvetica bold
the caption style is in the same font as the body copy, but in a slightly smaller size and different weight

12/15pt Helvetica Rounded bold
the secondary intro is set in a bold sans font to contrast with the main page introduction

9/11pt Helvetica and Helvetica light italic
using the medium and light italic fonts of the same typeface clearly separates the questions from the answers. White Bold Condensed is used for the drop caps to reduce the space around the larger capital letters

12pt Helvetica Condensed and Wingdings
the condensed font separates the page number from the main copy, and the dingbat adds character to the publication

12pt Helvetica Rounded bold
the rounded edges of the crosshead font soften the overall look of the text areas

12pt Helvetica light and bold Condensed
the footer type face is condensed and the light font used for the web address throws emphasis on to the dateline

9/12pt Helvetica bold
adds contrasting weight to the address line at the end of the section

---

COOKING TIPS

Crazy Cupcakes

Cupcakes are so versatile, the teatime treat of choice. Go to town and add as many toppings as you can! They are a great activity for all the kids during those long summer holidays.

Kyla Middleditch Cookery Editor

Lorem ipsum dolor sit amet, consectetur adipiscing elit. Integer adipiscing erat in enim lobortis interdum. Praesent egestas arcu quis lacus malesuada sed venenatis felis euismod. Curabitur placerat bibendum tortor ac imperdiet. Sed id sapien nunc, convallis elementum sem. Nullam nec tellus dolor. Vivamus tincidunt adipiscing congue. Nulla facilisi. Nulla sit amet felis urna. Maecenas a justo et elit molestie rhoncus. Fusce dolor justo, rutrum ac egestas a, ultricies eu sapien.

Sed pharetra tempus mauris, in porttitor erat eleifend id. Maecenas varius libero vel arcu varius sagittis. Nunc nec

nunc ac dolor convalis vehicula non et magna. is tellus. Nunc malesuada, lorem vestibulum tristique volutpat, felis velit lorem.

Nunc suscipit, nunc facilisis hendrerit aliquet. Dui magna cursus lectus, id auctor quam elit eget elit. Suspendisse dictum laoreet dolor vitae ultricies. Suspendisse eget aliquet mauris. Sed ac tortor dolor

Maecenas lectus mauris, placerat ut mattisCurabitur placerat bibendum tortor ac imperdiet. Sed id sapien nunc, convallis elementum sem. Nullam nec tellus dolor. Vivamus tincidunt adipiscing congue. Nulla facilisi. Nulla sit amet felis urna. Maecenas a justo et elit mole.

▲123

Special offer

Lorem ipsum dolor sit amet, consectetur adipiscing elit. Integer adipiscing erat in enim

EDITOR'S CHOICE

Lorem ipsum dolor sit amet, consectetur adipiscing elit. Integer adipiscing erat in enim lobortis interdum. Praesent egestas arcu quis.

Lorem ipsum dolor sit amet, consectetur adipiscing elit. Integer adipiscing erat in enim lobortis interdum.

Qunc nec nunc ac dolor convallis vehicula non et magna. Suspendisse facilisis euismod tincidunt nam molestie.

Araesent egestas arcu quis lacus malesuada sed venenatis felis euismod. Curabitur placerat bibendum tortor ac imperdiet. Sed id sapien nunc, convallis elementum sem. Nullam nec tellus dolor.

ANibh nec ipsum ornare tincidunt. Etiam sodales, dui id ultricies sagittis, urna dolor rhoncus sem, sit amet tristique ligula nisi a nisi. Duis molestie feugiat turpis id feugiat. Donec lobortis aliquet enim, condimentum.

QVivamus tincidunt adipiscing congue. Nulla facilisi. Nulla sit amet felis urna. Maecenas a justo et elit molestie rhoncus.

QLeo euismod nec. Nunc ac turpis tellus. Nunc malesuada, lorem vestibulum tristique volutpat, felis velit porta nunc, et

Ausce dolor justo, rutrum ac egestas a, ultricies eu sapien.Sed pharetra tempus mauris, in porttitor erat eleifend id. Maecenas varius libero vel arcu varius sagittis.

Apharetra tortor eros a elit. Donec nec elit sed lectus laoreet eleifend et quis lorem. Nunc suscipit, nunc facilisis hendrerit aliquet, dui magna cursus lectus, id auctordictum.

Lorem ipsum dolor sit amet, consectetur adipiscing elit. Integer adipiscing erat in enim lobortis interdum.

www.magazine.com **January | 2012**

HOW TO WORK WITH TYPE

- The language of type
- Typesetting, leading and white space
- Body copy: tone and colour
- Print type and background colour
- Type on an image
- Adobe Photoshop type techniques
- Vector graphic type
- Web type and background colour
- Web and screen type

The *How to work with type* pages explore the ways in which typographic techniques can be applied to produce pages online and in print, and which convey information through the use of well-chosen and effectively handled typefaces. These pages explain how to work with type in colour, on backgrounds and on images, and demonstrates how to create type as image in both bitmap and vector computer programs.

Typographic terms and techniques

Typography is a long-established design discipline with a detailed terminology that describes all the constituent parts of a letter. The underlying anatomy of a character remains constant and is always measured and described in the same way, despite the fact that the capital A of one typeface may be radically different in dimension and appearance from one design to another. It is useful to be aware of the basic elements of type as this will enable you to analyse the strengths and weaknesses of a font, and establish its suitability for the media and the message. It is the detailed nuances of typeface design that define a font's identity.

Anatomy of type

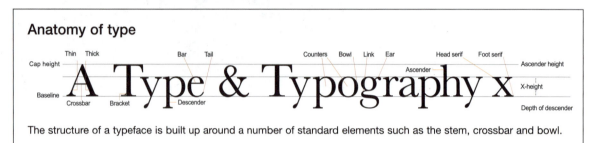

The structure of a typeface is built up around a number of standard elements such as the stem, crossbar and bowl.

Typeface characteristics

Letterforms in a typeface vary in dimension and proportion within a type size. It is the relationship between letterforms and the white space between characters that determines the individuality of a typeface and establishes how it will look on the page.

When choosing a typeface for a title, you need to examine the relative widths of the characters and letter spacing. Body copy typefaces generally have a uniform set of characters while the dimensions of display fonts' characters may vary considerably.

Helvetica Neue is a sans serif font design than has open, rounded letterforms that appear clean and neutral. The balance between the x-height and its compact ascenders and descenders forms a very even pattern.

Times New Roman is a serif font that has a uniform look with well-balanced letterforms. Compared with more exaggerated type designs, it has medium height ascenders and descenders and moderate lower case tails and crossbars.

Brush Script is a calligraphic font that, in order to represent brushstrokes, has little white space between the letterforms. The font's strong character can interfere with the authority of a message, which may restrict its usability.

Avant Garde Light is a sans serif font with wide, rounded letterforms that vary considerably in width. It has short ascenders and descenders and very little space between the lower case tails and crossbars (look at the e).

American Typewriter is a serif font with soft letterforms that have exaggerated serifs and tails, a uniform width and little white space between letters. Its historical inference needs to be considered when assessing its suitability.

Typesetting, leading and white space

Spacing letters to maximise readability

Letter spacing can be a powerful design tool that affects the way in which an audience interprets the page. Each typeface has default settings for letter spacing that can provide a good starting point when working out the best look for a title's type styles. However, it is often necessary to modify these defaults to improve the typeface's appearance and to ensure that the required amount of copy fits on a page. This is achieved by tracking (adjusting the space between all characters) or kerning (controlling the space between individual characters).

Applying kerning

Kerning modifies the white space between individual characters by increasing or decreasing the gaps between letters. Good kerning creates a balanced white space between each letter to maintain the visual cohesion of a word.

AVIATOR
AVIATOR
AVIATOR

Plus and minus tracking

The quick brown fox jumped over the lazy dog. The quick brown fox jumped over the lazy dog. The quick brown fox jumped over the lazy dog.

All typefaces are designed with a default amount of tracking that sets the letter and word spacing.

The quick brown fox jumped over the lazy dog. The quick brown fox jumped over the lazy dog. The quick brown fox jumped over the lazy dog.

Reducing tracking to –2 darkens the overall tone of a line or copy block.

The quick brown fox jumped over the lazy dog. The quick brown fox jumped over the lazy dog. The quick brown fox jumped over the lazy dog.

+23 tracking adds white space to lighten tones and is used to make typographic design statements.

Increasing and reducing leading

Leading set at more than twice the type size can be used to emphasise small type elements such as introductions and boxed copy.

The quick brown fox jumped

over the lazy dog. The quick

brown fox jumped over the

lazy dog.

Setting leading to a minus value can be used to create a contemporary graphic style (example shown: 14pt type size with 6pt leading).

Drop and raised caps

The quick brown fox jumped over the lazy dog. The quick brown fox jumped over the lazy dog. The quick brown fox

The quick brown fox jumped over the lazy dog. The quick brown fox jumped over the lazy dog. The quick

The quick brown fox jumped over the lazy dog. The quick brown fox jumped over the lazy dog. The quick

A drop or raised cap is a typographic design feature used to indicate and add emphasis to the beginning of an article. Matching the drop or raised cap's typeface and colour to that of the headline can help lead the reader's or user's eye to the start of the copy. Drop and raised caps can be set up using page make-up programs and CSS (Cascading Style Sheets) type properties.

Design for Media

Body copy: colour and tone

A

Body copy:
10/12pt Times
New Roman
Headline: 53/57pt
Bodoni in C29
M29 Y18 K0
Standfirst:
14/16pt Arial
Sidebar: C55 M29
Y38 K20

B

Body copy:
10/12pt
Baskerville,
Headline: 53/57pt
Baskerville in C29
M29 Y18 K0
Standfirst:
14/16pt Arial,
Sidebar: C55 M29
Y38 K20

C

Body copy:
10/12pt Gill Sans
Headline: 53/57pt
Baskerville in C34
M84 Y60 K24
Standfirst:
14/16pt Arial
Sidebar: C55 M29
Y38 K2

D

Body copy:
10/12pt Helvetica
Roman
Headline: 53/57pt
Bodoni in C29
M29 Y10 K0
Standfirst:
14/16pt Arial
Sidebar: C55 M29
Y38 K20

Figure A

Figure B

Figure C

Figure D

168

Body copy: colour and tone

Figure E

E
Body copy:
10/12pt Helvetica
Light
Headline: 53/57pt
Bodoni in C34
M84 Y60 K24
Standfirst:
14/16pt Arial
Sidebar: C55 M29
Y38 K20

Figure F

F
Body copy:
8.5/12pt Apple
Gothic
Headline: 53/57pt
Bodoni in C61
M19 Y92 K3
Standfirst:
14/16pt Arial in a
48% tint of C34
M84 Y60 K24
Sidebar: 48% tint
of C34 M84 Y60
K24

Maximising the legibility and readability of body copy

The typeface, size, leading and colour of the body copy affect its tonality and how it interacts with surrounding images and graphics; for example, densely set typefaces in heavier weights and dark colours will dominate a page, while lighter, more open fonts in paler colours recede into the background. It is a good idea to try out a number of variations in tone, colour and tint to determine the best combination to communicate the brand image of the title and content.

A Body copy set in Times New Roman has a traditional feel and is known to maintain its readability on a range of papers and screens. Its visual strength draws the reader's attention on to the main text.

B The contrasting height and weights of the characters in Baskerville allow more white space to show, creating a lighter appearance to the page so that the visual emphasis shifts to the other graphic elements.

C The compact angular shapes of Gill Sans make body copy appear relatively small and give the illusion of more white space between lines of type. It produces a medium tone that balances evenly against other graphic elements.

D Body copy set in Helvetica Roman provides a uniform strong tone due to the typeface's rounded simple shapes.

E Setting the body copy in Helvetica Light can soften the overall effect and draw the reader's eye into the design.

F Apple Gothic has an exaggerated x-height and wide characters that make the type look relatively large for its point size. This has the effect of reducing the number of words on a line, which increases the white space on a page and lightens the overall tone.

 Go to **www.pearsoned.com/hand** to download these body copy samples.

Type and background colour

Legibility on tint and coloured backgrounds

The way coloured type looks on a background varies not only from device to device but also on different types of paper, and how and where colours are used can drastically affect the appearance of type. When selecting colours for a title, it is important to ensure that the letters read out of the background and that there is a logical relationship between all the colours chosen for the page elements.

TIP It is a good idea to use a colour wheel and colour selection website to develop your skills in working out which colours will go together (see *How to work with colour*, page 255).

Controlling colour for type in boxes and panels

Complementary colours

Using two complementary colours can cause the type and background to compete for attention. Reducing the intensity or darkening the background colour will improve legibility.

Analogous colours

If the type and background colours are too similar to each other, the copy will be hard to read. Lightening the background colour will make the type more legible.

Tonal contrast

If your design is based around contrasting background colours, you may need to use a paler tint of the type colour to ensure readability.

Intensity of colour

The strength of a colour changes how typefaces are perceived. On vibrant colour backgrounds, the font may become illegible; applying a tint to the background will make type more legible.

Shades of grey?

Black type on a white background and white type out of black give the most readable contrast; however, using shades of greys can be easier on the eye, especially on-screen. The style and weight of a typeface also have to be considered: serif fonts have greater variances in line thickness and can be hard to read on black or grey backgrounds, while the more uniform design of sans serif typefaces is usually more readable in monochrome.

When choosing a percentage of grey for type on a background, you should make sure that there is at least a 30% difference in tonal values to ensure legibility: for example, 40% of the colour for the type on a background of 70%.

Type on an image

A Poor type choices can result in visually confusing pages.

B Careful type and colour choices improve legibility.

C Using graphic elements can emphasise type on an image.

D Creating strong visual groupings helps to unify a spread.

Choosing colour for type on an image

When positioning type on an image, it is best to select an open or single colour area to allow for maximum legibility. However, there are several typographic techniques that can be employed for 'busy' or highly coloured pictures to ensure the text remains readable.

A The magazine spread displays a number of common problems that can occur when placing type on an image: (1) the outlined headline and pull quote stand out against the blue sky but may be hard to read; (2) the white type used for the standfirst makes it almost impossible to read; (3) the white panel behind the block of copy on the left draws the eye because it looks like a hole in the picture.

B In this version of the spread, the picture has been opened in Photoshop and the Eyedropper colour sampling tool used to identify the main colours in the image and establish a palette for the pages. This has improved the visual harmonics of the image but not solved all the legibility issues as the yellow headline, the pull quote and the blue standfirst are still difficult to read. The use of a box coloured with a soft shade chosen from the smaller picture helps to frame the block of copy and link the two items, but the large transparent panel on the right hand side of the spread throws too much emphasis on to the columns of copy.

C In the third version, a drop shadow has been placed behind the yellow headline that subtly separates it from the image, with white type used for the pull quote that has been placed on a darker area of the blue sky. The standfirst has been changed to white type and placed in lines of background colour achieved by using the page make-up program command Paragraph Rules (lines) that places a rule above or below the text. In this instance, the blue rule is deeper than the type height and has been styled to run behind the lines of type. The block of copy beside the small picture has been coloured white and positioned on a darker area of the main picture. On the right hand page, another subtle shade has been chosen in Photoshop from the main image and used to colour the boxes behind the two columns of type.

D In the final version of the spread, a better balance has been achieved by moving the smaller picture, related block of copy and pull quote up into the top third of the pages, and by using a wide semi-transparent panel to link all the other typographic items together. Allowing the headline to cross over both the full-strength image and the semi-transparent panel connects the two main elements of the spread. The Paragraph Rule Below command has been used to add emphasis to the standfirst.

Adobe Photoshop type techniques

Creating transparent type

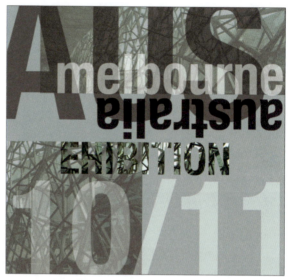

1 Open an image and go to the Layers drop-down menu: select Duplicate Layer (do not work on the Background layer), then New Layer to create more layers. Open any other images you wish to include and cut and paste them on the new layers in the first file.

2 Select the Type tool then click on the image to create a new text layer and give it a name.

3 Adjust the transparency of each layer using the Opacity slider. **TIP** Shifting layers above or below each other can help to achieve the desired effect.

4 Always save the editable layered image file (.ps, .psd). Use File menu: Save As to save a flattened copy (tif, jpeg), and File menu: Save for Web and Devices to save an optimised copy (jpeg, png, gif).

Placing an image into type

Positioning images inside type can be useful for headlines and special effects. There are several ways of doing this: you can either cut out the letters from a background image, or work with the Magic Wand tool to select the letters and cut them out of an area to reveal an underlying image, or use the Clone Stamp tool.

To cut type out of an underlying image: create a new type layer, enter your copy and select the type using the Magic Wand tool. Choose the base image layer and go to the Select menu: Inverse and then the Edit menu: Cut. This will remove all of the image outside the letters.

The Clone tool can be used to duplicate selected parts of an image and copy them into letters on a type layer. It can also be used to copy from a separate image or an image layer within a file. The effect is often employed for creating headlines and montage illustrations.

 For detailed instructions on how to place an image into letters, see **www.pearsoned.com/hand**

Adobe Photoshop type techniques

Organising the Layers window

Photoshop layers and layer groups should be carefully named. Well-considered labels will help you and your colleagues navigate through the layers and make it easier and quicker to edit the image should last-minute changes be needed.

Click on the layer thumbnail to activate a layer. Layers can be hidden or revealed by clicking on the eye icon, or locked (deactivated) or unlocked using the lock icon. Dividing layers into related subject groups reduces the number of items in the list.

Adding drop shadows into a type layer

- Create a type image (see Placing an image into type, page 172).
- To isolate the type from the layer background: use the Magic Wand and click on the background, then go to the Select menu: Select Inverse to select the type.
- With the type selected: go to the Layers window drop-down menu and open the Blending Options dialog box. Click on the Drop Shadow option and use the Blend Mode and Opacity to specify the mode and density of the drop shadow.

Applying a drop shadow to type

| The drop shadow default setting | Altering the angle of perspective | Increasing the distance and spread | Enlarging the shadow size |

You may find you need to amend the drop-shadow default settings to make the shadow more visible or to move it in relation to the type. The Layer Style window allows you to adjust the angle between the shadow and letters as well as the distance and spread – how far and the extent of the shadow from the letters. You can also change the shadow's size; a shadow that is larger than the letters will appear on all sides – the default is to one side only.

Vector graphic type

Running text around an image

Adobe InDesign's Text Wrap and QuarkXPress's Runaround features apply an offset/outset (space) that causes copy to run above, beneath or around an image. The ideal offset/outset needed to maintain a comfortable visual break is 3 mm; however, care should be taken to ensure lines of text running around an image do not become overly short and hard to read.

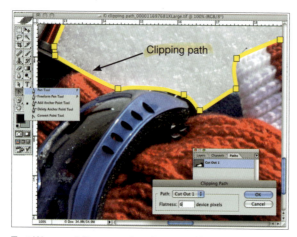

Text Wrap and Runaround are best used in conjunction with a Photoshop clipping path – a vector path that isolates an area of an image from its background.

Applying Runaround in QuarkXPress

QuarkXPress Runaround window   Adobe InDesign Text Wrap window

Circular type in Adobe InDesign and Illustrator

1 Select the Ellipse Tool from the Tool Box and draw a circle. Apply a stroke or fill colour (select None to make the circle invisible).

2 Select the Type on a Path tool and click on the top edge of the circle, then enter or import your copy.

3 Highlight the copy with the Type tool: select the type style and colour you want and centre align the copy.

4 If the type does not appear where you want it on the circle, you can adjust its position by moving the type positioning handles around the circle to the left and right.

Warning Take care to click on the line, not the Text import block.

5 Switch the copy to inside or outside the circle by moving the Type flip handle inside or outside the circle.

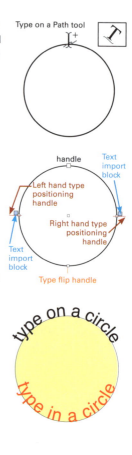

Create Outlines: converting type to vector image

Create Outlines is a feature of Adobe Illustrator that converts type into vector graphic images. Text items that are changed into graphic objects become independent of the type software that controls the appearance and editability of a font, and gain the advantage of being viewable on any digital device without the type program files being installed. Create Outlines is used by the media industry for logos and other artwork that need to be transferred between companies and used across media.

TIP Before you apply Create Outlines, use Save As to make a copy of the Illustrator file, as graphic text cannot be edited by keyboard.

1 Use the Type tool to enter your copy and format it using the Type menu, Character window or Control Panel. Once you are happy with the design, use the Selection tool to click on the text elements to be converted to outline.

2 Go to the Type menu and select Create Outlines.

Applying colour to strokes and fills

- Illustrator and InDesign apply colour to type in two ways: Fill – the colour inside a letter; and Stroke – the outline around the shape of a letter.
- Type colours can be applied using the Colour, Swatches and Stroke windows, and type can also be filled with effects such as gradients and patterns.
- Stroke width for type is given in points and can be set from the Stroke window or Control panel.

Drop shadows and transparency

1 Convert the type to graphic text using Create Outlines (see left).

2 Click on the type with the Selection tool: go to the Object menu: UnGroup to separate the letters so they can be individually manipulated.

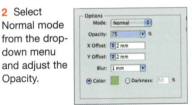

1 To apply a drop shadow, click on the graphic text with the Selection tool and go to the Effect menu: Stylize – Drop Shadow.

2 Select Normal mode from the drop-down menu and adjust the Opacity.

1 Click on each letter in turn with the Selection tool. Go to the Window menu: Transparency to adjust opacity.

2 Set the position using the cursor keys and Object menu: Arrange.

Web type and background colour

Designing with blue

Blue web palette

Blue is one of the most comfortable colours to read on-screen, with a range of tints and shades that work particularly well for type. The key when selecting a shade of blue is to ensure that the tonal relationship between the fore- and background colours maintains legibility.

Navy
RGB 0/0/50.2
Medium blue
RGB 0/0/80.4
Royal blue
RGB 25.5/41.2/88.2
Steel blue
RGB 27.5/51/70.6
Light slate grey
RGB 46.7/53.3/60
Cornflower blue
RGB 39.2/58.4/92.9
Light sky blue
RGB 52.9/80.8/98
Light steel blue
RGB 69/76.9/87.1

Designing with red

Red web palette

Red is the other most commonly used colour on the Web. As the colour can be visually very strong, you may find reducing the intensity or opacity of red type will help to control the eye flow and balance page elements.

Maroon
RGB 50.2/0/0
Red
RGB 100/0/0
Fire brick
RGB 69.8/13.3/13.3
Tomato
RGB 100/38.8/27.8
Salmon
RGB 98/50.2/50.2
Light coral
RGB 94.1/50.2/50.2
Rosy brown
RGB 73.7/56.1/56.1
Misty rose
RGB 100/89.4/88.2

Teal web palette

Lilac web palette

Green web palette

Yellow web palette

Orange web palette

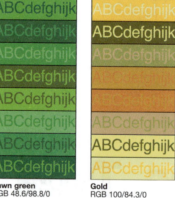
Magenta web palette

Medium aquamarine
RGB 40/80.4/66.7
Pale turquoise
RGB 68.6/93.3/93.3
Light sea green
RGB 12.5/69.8/66.7
Medium turquoise
RGB 28.2/82/80
Teal
RGB 0/50.2/50.2
Cyan
RGB 0/100/100
Dark turquoise
RGB 0/80/82
Powder blue
RGB 69/87.8/90.2

Indigo
RGB 29.4/0/51
Dark slate blue
RGB 28.2/23.9/54.5
Medium orchid
RGB 72.9/33.3/82.7
Medium slate blue
RGB 48.2/40.8/93.3
Medium purple
RGB 57.6/43.9/85.9
Orchid
RGB 85.5/43.9/83.9
Plum
RGB 86.7/62.7/86.7
Thistle
RGB 84.7/74.9/84.7

Lawn green
RGB 48.6/98.8/0
Green
RGB 0/50.2/0
Lime
RGB 0/100/0
Olive drab
RGB 42/55.7/13.7
Yellow green
RGB 60.4/80.4/19.6
Pale green
RGB 59.6/98.4/59.6
Spring green
RGB 0/100/49.8
Sea green
RGB 18/54.5/34.1

Gold
RGB 100/84.3/0
Olive
RGB 50.2/50.2/0
Dark khaki
CMYK 74.1/71.8/42
Goldenrod
RGB 85.5/64.7/12.5
Peru
RGB 80.4/52.2/24.7
Tan
CMYK 82.4/70.6/54.9
Khaki
RGB 94.1/90.2/54.9
Pale goldenrod
RGB 93.3/91/66.7

Orange red
RGB 100/27.1/0
Dark orange
RGB 100/54.9/0
Saddle brown
RGB 54.5/27.1/7.5
Sienna
RGB 62.7/32.2/17.6
Sandy brown
RGB 95.7/64.3/37.6
Light salmon
RGB 100/62.7/47.8
Wheat
RGB 96.1/87.1/70.2
Peach puff
RGB 100/85.5/72.5

Dark magenta
RGB 54.5/0/54.5
Magenta
RGB 100/0/100
Fuchsia
RGB 100/0/100
Crimson
RGB 86.3/7.8/23.5
Hot pink
RGB 100/75.3/79.6
Pale violet red
RGB 85.9/43.9/57.6
Pink
RGB 100/75.3/79.6
Lavender blush
CMYK 100/94.1/96.1

Web type and background colour

Bitmap and vector type

Bitmap and vector type can both be used for graphic text. Pixel-based type images offer the advantage of a wide range of effects. Vector type has fewer styling options, but the letters may appear crisper on-screen.

Resolution is another major consideration; bitmap type images are best created at precisely the target dimensions and resolution – but there are no specific restrictions on size or resolution for vector type.

Graphic text produced in Photoshop can exploit the full scope of the pixel-based program's features to create montages that effectively blend type and image.

Vector type can be enlarged or reduced without loss of quality. It is particularly good at producing smooth, sinuous lines and subtle typographic shapes.

Inappropriate use of colour

The yellow colour chosen for this website is too strong and looks unpleasant against the food – a serious problem for a business attempting to sell a dining experience.

This green/orange combination home page is strident and unsympathetic. The bright orange brand dominates the design, drawing attention away from the rest of the page content.

On this website, the pink is overpowering, too audience specific and unpleasant against the lilac background. It also clashes with the pineapple picture.

Good use of colour

The use of neutral shades has shifted the emphasis of the page on to the images, and the softer colours make the food look more appetising.

The introduction of grey has made the branding less intrusive, while the pink produces subtle warmth and looks elegant against the grey and black.

The use of shades of orange throughout the page harmonises the type and image content and also widens the appeal of the site.

Type handling and management

Saving type images for the Web and devices

JPEG is the most widely used web file format.

PNG8 is an adaptable format and compatible with most browsers

PNG24 does not compress data and can support transparency

If you are using type images on a website, you should save the files through Photoshop's File menu: Save for Web & Devices – an internal program that controls the file format, size, compression and number of colours in an image. The Save for Web & Devices window can display a series of options that allow you to compare different settings so that you can choose the best possible image quality in relation to download speed.

For more information visit **www.pearsoned.com/hand**

Source: Apple Inc.

Photoshop's Save for Web & Devices window

Managing your fonts

You are likely to find that most of the typefaces you need for page make-up are already installed on your computer; however, if you wish to add extra fonts you should use font management software. These programs install, store and allow you to organise typefaces, and are able to check for problems such as damaged font software and 'clashes' that can prevent typefaces from working.

Font management programs enable you to control the number of fonts that are active at any one time. This reduces the length of the type choice list, making it quicker to select a font. Most font management programs offer previews of a full character set for a typeface, and some allow you to input a test line of type to see how it would look in a specific font.

Source: Apple Inc.

Source: Fonts UK Ltd.

Above: Font Book, Apple's in-built font management program, can preview a full character set.

Left: Some font foundry websites allow you to enter a sample sentence to see how copy or headlines would look in your chosen typeface.

Emotive and interpretive type

Using type to direct audience reactions

Type has to convey not only information but also an underlying message or concept. The correct choice of typeface is crucial, as this will determine whether an audience can pick up on exact shades of meaning and understand the importance or mood of the words.

ABCDEFGHIJKLMNO
PQRSTUVWXYZ
abcdefghijklmnopqrstu
vwxyz

ABCEFGHIJKLMNOPQR
STUVWXYZ
abcdefghijklmnopqrstuvw
xyz

ABCEFGHIJKLMNOPQR
STUVWXYZ
abcdfghijklmnopqrstu
vwxyz

Feminine type

When choosing type for a feminine product or message, look for elegant curved shapes within the design. Thin uprights and contrasting crossbars give a light appearance and deliver a subtle, soft message.

Top to bottom:
Didot, Helvetica Ultra Light, Trebuchet

ABCDEFGHIJKLMNO
PQRSTUVWXYZ
abcdefghijklmnopqrs
tuvwxyz

ABCDEFGHIJKLMNOP
QRSTUVWXYZ
abcdefghijklmnopqrstu
vwxyz

ABCDEFGHIJKLMNOP
QRSTUVWXYZ
abcfghijklmnopqrstu
vwxyz

Masculine type

When choosing type for a masculine product or message, look for strong angular shapes within the design. Bold uprights and crossbars add weight and strength to the message.

Top to bottom:
Bodoni Bold, Helvetica Black Condensed, Verdana

SEARCH AND RESCUE
Search & Rescue

SEARCH AND RESCUE
Search & Rescue

SEARCH AND RESCUE
Search & Rescue

SEARCH AND RESCUE
Search & Rescue

Urban edge
Urban edge
Urban edge
Urban edge
URBAN EDGE
URBAN EDGE

Great Britain
Great Britain
britain tm
great britain

1 Baskerville Regular in upper and lower case: the font's small x-height and fine lines make the words look like normal text, rather than standing out as a sign or brand.

2 Lucinda Bright Regular in upper and lower case: this font is an ornate, rounded font with a large x height that does not have sufficient gravitas to encapsulate a service that deals with life and death.

3 Rockwell Regular in upper and lower case, coloured red: this font has square slab serifs that give it a distinctive personality, and the addition of red gives the type more urgency, but in a medium weight it still lacks impact.

4 Arial Black in upper case, coloured red: the use of heavy red capitals in a sans serif font equates to shouting the message and has the power to convey the importance of the emergency service's work.

1 Handwriting Plain: too personal a style.

2 Freehand 521: linked letters look too retro.

3 Living by Numbers: sketchy and calligraphic.

4 Grunge Regular: Irregular but not very readable.

5 Urban Scrawl Buttah Regular: graffiti-like but clearly legible.

6 Urban Scrawl Buttah Regular: a 2pt lilac stroke with a purple fill amplifies the street art message.

1 Garamond Regular: encapsulates the UK's conventional image.

2 Plantagenet Cherokee: less formal but still what the audience is most likely to expect.

3 Meta Plus Normal in grey: sans serif in lower case suggests rebranding or satire.

4 Blue Mutant Double Serif: the informality challenges preconceptions and implies modernity.

Web and screen type

CSS font and text properties

Font-family: Helvetica, sans-serif
Sets the main typeface grouping

Font-family: colour: #0066FF
Sets the hexadecimal HTML/RGB colour code

Line-height: 1.2px
Sets the space between lines of type in a headline or paragraph

Text-align: centre
Sets the horizontal alignment of a line or paragraph of type

Font-weight: bold
Sets the lightness or boldness of the typeface (font-weight: normal sets plain text)

Font-size: 37px
Sets the height of the typeface in pixels

Text-transform: uppercase
Sets the text in capital (text-transform: normal would set the text in lowercase letters)

Letter-spacing: 0.2px
Sets the space between the letters in a line

Word-spacing: 1.2px
Sets the space between words in a line or paragraph

DESIGNING WITH TYPE

CSS properties for type design are employed with background, border, classification and positioning CSS to define the design and layout of a web page. The CSS are pasted into a web page in a web design program and underlie CMS. When that page is opened on the Web, the browser refers back to the CSS properties which are held on a web server, and this maintains the page appearance.

The CSS that affect type are divided into two sets of mark-up indicators, one that controls the appearance of the font (typeface) and a second that sets the characteristics of a line or paragraph of text. Font properties define a typeface or family, type size, weight and colour. Text properties relate to the word and line spacing, alignment and styles such as shadow or over, through and underline.

Source: Creative Nights

The **typetaster.org** online application allows you to test how well a font will work on screen.

Source: CSS Typeset

Source: Panduka Senaka

Some CSS websites offer a service that supplies font and text properties for pasting in as code in a web design program, while others offer menus of pre-set CSS properties.

 http://www.w3.org/Style/CSS

TIP CSS obtained from websites should be pasted into a text edit program before being copied into a web page.

Type usage

Display fonts are designed to look good and read clearly at larger sizes. They are primarily used for headlines, big pull quotes and larger page furniture such as a section heading. Display type is also used in advertising, in particular for posters and outdoor promotional material as it remains readable at a large scale and from a distance.

Body copy fonts are designed to typeset cleanly and read well at smaller sizes. Body copy typefaces should be used for running text, captions, bylines, listings and results, picture credits, boxed copy, crossheads and small items of page furniture such as folios.

There are some type elements such as standfirsts and smaller 'In Brief' or box headlines that can be typeset in either a body or display font. The key to deciding if a font is suitable for use as a particular purpose and at a chosen size has to be whether it looks attractive with well-proportioned letterforms, works with the other type elements and can be easily read.

Warning Some display typefaces do not work well in smaller sizes and should not be used for body copy, while fonts designed as body copy may look clumsy when enlarged to a size outside the normal range used for running text.

Type size

Typeface sizes are chosen for both aesthetic and practical reasons. A media designer who has been commissioned to specify the size of the fonts for a publication or website will start by researching the nature of the contents. The designer needs to know the nature and length of the copy, the style and mood of the publication and the ways in which type might be used. All the fonts must look right in a range of sizes and allow the copy to be read comfortably by the target audience. Some youth-oriented publications and websites use what are teasingly called **under 40 fonts** – very small main text in vivid or clashing colour combinations that may exclude older readers or visitors. However, many titles fail to consider how type size, colour and spacing affect the usability of their website.

The amount of copy that needs to go on a page and the writing style have to be taken into consideration when deciding the typeface and size chosen for a publication or website. A technical or scientific journal or website may need to accommodate really long phraseology, so the body copy size may need to be small or condensed, while a children's title that has short, simple wording requires a large, plain, easy-to-read font. Not only do major news websites vary in the length of coverage of the same subjects, but also they use different type styles and sizes. The BBC News website uses a grey sans typeface for its running copy, while CNN's site employs a smaller black sans font and has comparatively more information on each subject. Sky News online employs a more commercial treatment that uses larger heavier fonts and loud reds and yellows with big chunks of text reversed out.

Headline sizes vary from very large (200–300pts) for the front of a tabloid newspaper to relatively small (14–24pts) for boxed story headings. The sizes used relate partly to the nature of the media product and will also have been chosen to accommodate the headline writing style. Tabloid newspapers, such as the *Sun*, are famous for pithy, witty headlines, while more serious papers like the *Guardian* tend to have longer, explanatory headlines. Web headings are often fairly long as they have to include searchable key words while following the editorial style. This may restrict the possible size differential, but there are many other interactive features that can be used to attract attention, such as animated type and vibrant coloured backgrounds. Print headlines need to make a more immediate visual impact because the pages are static, whereas web headlines work in a different way as they are navigation aids that provoke action, drawing the visitor on through the pages.

Type sizing guide

Type sizes vary from title to title and platform to platform. The chart gives a general guide to the relative sizes used for individual type elements:

- The smallest readable size for print is 5–6pt, the proverbial small print, which is used for supplementary information such as terms and conditions.

- 8pt is the smallest type size at which it is comfortable to read a document.

- 8–9.5pt is the average range for body copy sizes in newspapers.

- 9–11pt is the average range of body copy sizes in magazines.

- Captions are normally set in the same type size as the main text or just one size smaller.

- Picture credits are usually in very small type (6-8pt), depending on the design style.

- Boxed copy and listings type are often set in a sans serif typeface, even when the main body copy is serif, as most people find sans type easier to read out of a coloured background.

- 12pt is the **default type size** in Word and for most print and web design programs, but this size is too big for columns of body copy in newspapers and magazines.

- HTML web type sizes range from size 1, the smallest, up to size 7, but because operating systems and browsers build type in different ways, these sizes will not necessarily produce a standardised result.

- Web type size 3 is the equivalent of 12pt. Many websites use size 2 for the main text, 3 for lists and set sells and headlines in sizes 4 and above.

- 10–14pt sizes are used for crossheads to ensure they are slightly larger than the body copy to provide pauses for the eye in the copy flow (see Chapter 5, page 132).

- 12–18pt type sizes are used for standfirst, intros and sells. The size chosen should be significantly larger than the body copy size and somewhat larger than the crosshead.

- 14–18pt type sizes can be used for secondary headlines, 'In Brief' column headings and subheads.

- Main headline sizes for magazines start from 18pt but may be any size up to 72pt or larger.

- Tabloid newspaper headlines can be sized up to 150pt.

TIP When using type above 150pt, it is advisable to convert the type into vector outline.

Helvetica Medium
6pt 8pt 9pt 10pt 12pt 14pt 18pt 24pt 36pt 48pt 60pt 72pt

Times Roman
6pt 8pt 9pt 10pt 12pt 14pt 18pt 24pt 36pt 48pt 60pt 72pt

Standard type sizes follow a mathematical progression largely based on multiples of 3pt that show an obvious change in scale that still maintains the relationship between each pre-set typesize.

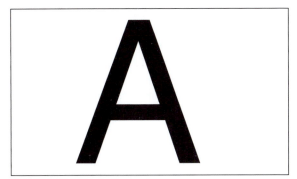

150pt Helvetica Medium.

460pt Myriad Roman converted to outline.

The size of a typeface is expressed as a standard depth that includes space above and below the letters. The characters in different styles of type may appear to vary in height depending on the design of the font.

Choosing a headline type size

The headline typeface must be large enough to clearly differentiate the heading from the running copy, standfirst or sell. It has to indicate the importance of a story and accommodate enough words for the writer to compose a good headline across a given number of columns, or within a content area on a website. Too large a type size reduces the number of words per line and will limit where a headline can be positioned, and can make it very difficult to write a sensible heading. Too small a typeface placed across a wide measure may result in a headline that could be taken for the standfirst, sell or an introduction. You should make sure you are aware of any story hierarchy before you select the heading size, to ensure that there is a contrast in size that gives the lead story the most prominence and that directs the eye through the preferred reading order (see page 301). You also need to consider how the heading works with the other elements on the page and throughout the title.

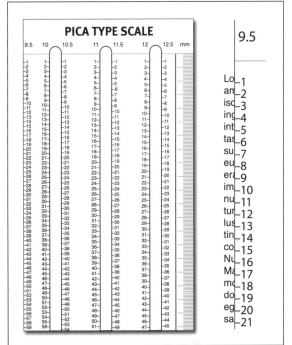

A printer's type scale (*left*) is used to measure leading and establish the line depth of printed copy. The inset (*right*) shows how to use a type scale to measure leading by aligning it to the baseline of printed text.

'Anyone looking at a printed message will be influenced, within a split second of making eye contact, by everything on the page.'

Erik Spiekermann and E. M. Ginger

Type on the printed page

The body copy forms the building blocks around which all the other elements are structured, and its size and leading form the basis for the title's **baseline grid**. This functions to keep the horizontal spacing consistent throughout the publication (see page 137). Each baseline unit is equal to a line of body copy. It is common practice to leave a set number of baseline units between each element on the page, in order to establish a system of vertical spacing. For example, the house style may specify that two baseline units should be inserted between a headline and a standfirst, and one baseline unit added between the standfirst and the main text. The body copy is locked onto the baseline grid to maintain a horizontal alignment across the page. Any other typographic styles with the same leading are also locked to the grid (see Chapter 5). The baseline grid is used in conjunction with the margins and columns to fix the position of headlines, pictures and other graphics into a coherent structure.

A publication designer derives the baseline unit from their choice of body copy typeface, size and leading, and will use it to set the size of headlines and other

typographic styles. For example, on an 11pt baseline grid, the headline sizes might be specified as 22pt, 33pt, 44pt, etc. The baseline grid is also used when laying out pages to establish content structure and copy flow. The body copy usually falls on the grid in columns of equal line lengths, with shorter stories kept in neat, rectangular blocks. Longer multi-page articles can benefit from subdividing the body copy into balanced, visually linked sections using pictures, quotes, sidebars, etc. as breaks in the run of text can help stimulate interest. However, you should avoid creating layouts with bad breaks – graphics or pictures positioned so that the blocks of body copy are no longer clearly associated – as this can cause the reader's eye to 'jump' across items and interrupts their concentration.

Type and other elements on a page can be locked on to the baseline grid to ensure a consistent horizontal alignment.

Headline goes here
The quick brown fox jumps over the lazy dog.

Lorem ipsum dolor sit amet, consectetur adipiscing elit. Integer adipiscing erat in enim lobortis interdum. Praesent egestas arcu quis lacus malesuada sed venenatis felis euis-

mod. Curabitur placerat bibendum tortor ac imperdiet. Sed id sapien nunc, convallis elementum sem. Nullam nec tellus dolor. Vivamus tincidunt adipiscing congue. Nulla facilisi.

Headline goes here
The quick brown fox jumps over the lazy dog.

Lorem ipsum dolor sit amet, consectetur adipiscing elit. Integer adipiscing erat in enim lobortis interdum. Praesent egestas arcu quis lacus malesuada sed venenatis felis euis-

mod. Curabitur placerat bibendum tortor ac imperdiet. Sed id sapien nunc, convallis elementum sem. Nullam nec tellus dolor. Vivamus tincidunt adipiscing congue. Nulla facilisi.

If a heading or block of copy appears too close to other type, despite its being on the correct leading, page make-up programs have a facility called baseline shift that moves both locked and unlocked type up or down in relation to the baseline grid and can be used to reposition a single word or line as well as larger text blocks.

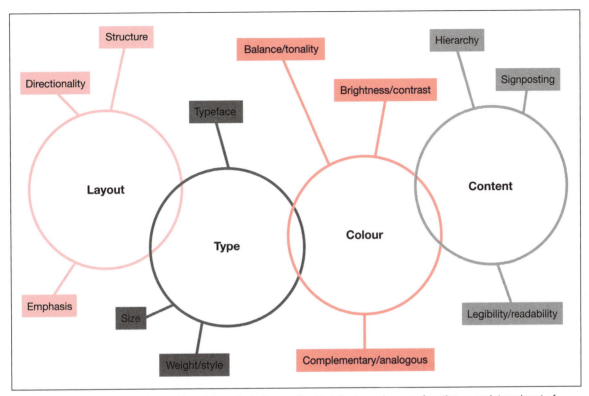

Criteria to consider when working with web type include ensuring that the type elements function as an integral part of the page structure, making certain that the typefaces are easy to read and consistently legible, and judging how well the colours match and whether the tonality of the type balances on the page, as well as determining that the choice of font clearly signals the subject and importance of the content.

Web type

If you do become involved in a web design project, you may need to make decisions on what the typographic treatment should be. Even if you are not designing the website yourself, having some knowledge of how the technology which underlies web design programs can help you to make informed decisions and control the type elements of the site. Understanding web typography is also useful for working with CMS type style menus, or if you need to commission graphic text. Many typographic conventions, such as sizing and spacing, apply equally to online and print. The technology of the Web and the devices used often require the application of media-specific criteria and a screen-based visual treatment.

Most websites feature a standard range of system typefaces that work with most computers and browsers. Website design programs offer these type styles and

a set of fixed sizes and related line heights. In fact, any typeface could be used on the Web, but it is common for websites to stay with the default type families to ensure the website looks the same on as many computers as possible. The safe sans serif fonts for websites include Arial, Helvetica, Verdana and Trebuchet; and the serifs are Georgia, Times New Roman and Courier. These are used because browser and operating systems do not always include the same typefaces. The aim behind supplying a selection of commonly used browser typefaces is that, when a page is opened, the viewer sees something broadly similar to what the designer intended.

Warning If a font not included in the web safe set is used for a website, it may not be available on the viewer's computer. The browser will be forced to use a substitute font and the page may not appear as intended.

The quick brown fox — Size 1

The quick brown fox — Size 2

The quick brown fox — Size 3

The quick brown fo — Size 4

The quick bro — Size 5

The quick — Size 6

The qu — Size 7

HTML standard web type absolute sizes.

Type sizing

Web type sizes are listed by number, where the smallest size is 1 and the largest 7. Size 3 is the default size and is the approximate equivalent of 12pt in print. However, web type sizes are set in pixels, not points, and the points system is not suitable for specifying type in CSS and **dynamic HTML (DHTML)**. Type is resized by adding a percentage increase to the default size; however, the amount added may vary on some browsers, so it is always best to preview a selection of different type sizes on a page. There are two ways of setting the size of type for a web page. One is called **absolute text sizing**, which fixes the type size for the text and overrides an individual's browser preferences. For example, even if a person has increased their browser type default to a large size, an absolute sized typeface will still appear at its specified size. The advantage of absolute type sizing is that the page should remain as it was designed. Unfortunately, because of the variations between operating systems and browsers, and the need to accommodate those with visual disabilities, this is not necessarily a good way to work.

Resizing type

In web design programs, the relative text sizes run from 1 to 7 > +1 to +1 > −1 to −7. For example, moving to +1 from size 3 = size 4.

The other method is called **relative text sizing**, which uses the default type size. The type is adjusted in a browser by a fixed percentage for all type based on the dimensions of the letter M (an **em**) of the default type size. Relative text sizing should ensure the type appears as you want, but if someone has changed their browser type preference, the type will display at a different size. However, relative text sizing can help to minimise the variations that can occur between the Mac and PC, and the way different browsers work. This method of type sizing will not interfere with visually impaired visitors' ability to increase their browsers' default type size.

Cascading style sheets

Cascading style sheets (CSS) are web pages that contain all of the instructions for the structure of a web page, including the typefaces, styles, leading, colours and all other text formatting options. CSS offer a far more precise way of ensuring that type does appear exactly as wanted, by forcing the viewer's web browser to override the user's size/font default preferences. All major browsers support CSS, and once a CSS page controlling the type usage is uploaded to a website, anyone updating or adding pages can apply the type styles from a menu in a web-editing program or CMS. CSS can also be used to assign styling to all the graphic elements used on a website.

CSS styles should be set up for all the coordinated type used throughout a website, including the main text, headings, subheadings and any other graphic items. CSS are used in conjunction with web editing software and

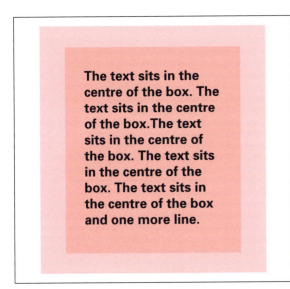

The CSS box model provides space around the text so that it sits within the background or frame.

CMS so that the person updating a site can apply consistent type styling. However, CSS are only editable through web design software and remain fixed unless the website design is updated. CSS cover not only the typeface size and weight (normal, bold), but also all the styling information such as line spacing, **indents** and **outdents**, upper or lower case and any colours applied to the type. CSS contain other instructions including the size and styling of text boxes, for example whether they have a border (frame) or **padding** – space around the text and the background colour.

Graphic text

There can be occasions when the system typefaces are not suitable or lack character, and it is possible to use other typefaces as graphic text – type converted into an image. This is often used for logos and decorative elements, as well as for fixed navigational graphics such as buttons or tabs, menus and panels. Using type in an image format eliminates the need to have matching typefaces on all computers. Web designers and graphic artists use programs to produce still and animated graphic text and can apply effects such as lighting glows, looped sequences and 3D (see pages 172–3). Although graphic text allows for a creative use of type, it will increase the memory needed for each page and make it slower to download. Graphic text should never be used for body copy or content that requires frequent updating.

Websites are not immune to typographic design rules, and just because it is possible to construct visually elaborate pages using graphic text, you should consider whether this is appropriate for the media company or website's image. It is generally inadvisable to clutter up a website with a large number of type styles, colours and busy graphics as visitors may find the pages confusing. The cardinal rule of type design is simplicity, and it is best to restrict the use of type for your site to two or three fonts and to ensure that they are used in a consistent manner on all graphic material.

The original and imaginative way in which individuals use standard typefaces to customise their own websites and blogs has influenced mainstream designers.

Advances in web typography now allow designers to work without restraint and to use a wider range of typefaces to target their audience.

187

Standard web type fonts

Style	Example
Cursive	Comic Sans MS
Monospaced	Courier Courier New Lucinda Console Monaco
Sans serif	Arial **Charcoal** Helvetica Lucinda Sans Unicode Lucinda Grande MS Sans Tahoma Geneva Trebuchet MS Verdana
Sans serif condensed	**Impact**
Serif	Book Antiqua Georgia MS Serif New York Palatino Times New Roman Times
Symbols	Symbol (abc = αβχ) Webdings (abc = ✔ ⚙🏭) Wingdings (abc =☜♌☝) Zapf Dingbats (abc = ❁❂❊)

ABCDEFGHIJKLMNOPQRSTUVWXYZ

abcdefghijklmnopqrstuvwxyz

1234567890!@£$%^&*()

ABCDEFGHIJKLMNOPQRSTUVWXYZ

abcdefghijklmnopqrstuvwxyz

Verdana and Georgia were commissioned for the screen and contain hinting data that ensures the letters align to the monitor grid.

'95% of the information on the web is written language. It is only logical to say that a web designer should get good training in the main discipline of shaping written information, in other words: Typography.'

Oliver Reichenstein, Information Architects
informationarchitects.jp

Web type codes and languages

Standard web pages are constructed using a collection of mark-up codes and languages, such as HTML, that are static, and script-based languages, for example JavaScript, that enable actions. The code is text based, made up of letters, words, numbers and symbols, and contains instructions for the position of each element on the page, the type size and styling, as well as any interactive functionality. The web browser reads the code and constructs a web page based on the instructions. Each coded element is called a tag and carries instructions: for example, <p> is the tag for a new paragraph, <strong> indicates bold copy and <font face="Helvetica"> is the symbol for changing a typeface to Helvetica. The tags are placed in front and at the end of every element on the page. For example, <title>Design for Media</title> would insert a heading.

Web design programs are WYSIWYG, but they all use HTML or a similar programming language as the basis of 'what you see'. The software has a range of website design options that can be accessed from drop menus. However, it is a good idea to learn some basic

Basic HTML Code

Opening tag   Contained text   Forward slash

<EM>designincontext</EM>

Angle brackets   Closing tag

Each element of the page is contained within tags (opening and closing brackets)

<FONTSize="4">

Default font sizes can be specified. "4" is one of the sizes of the standard set of sizes (sizes range from 1 to 7)

TEXT="#1F9AD7"

To add colour to the type enter the hexadecimal reference for the colour you wish to use, in this case cyan

<IMGSRC="image.location">

An image can be included on a page by inserting a link to the server where the image is stored

<WIDTH=250HEIGHT=180IMG SRC="image.location">

The size of an image is specified in pixels with the link to the image location

---

ABCDEFGHIJKLMNOPQRSTUVWXYZ
abcdefghijklmnopqrstuvwxyz
1234567890-=!@£$%^&*()_+
Museo sans 500

ABCDEFGHIJKLMNOPQRSTUVWXYZ
abcdefghijklmnopqrstuvwxyz
1234567890-=!@£$%^&*()_+
Museo slab 500

ABCDEFGHIJKLMNOPQRSTUVWXYZ
abcdefghijklmnopqrstuvwxyz
1234567890-=!@£$ ^&*()_+
Quicksand

ABCDEFGHIJKLMNOPQRSTUVWXYZ
abcdefghijklmnopqrstuvwxyz
1234567890-=!@£$%^&*()_+
St Marie

Several OpenType fonts are font-face compatible and can be used on the Web.

HTML tags in case the effects you require have not been included in the CMS. A range of HTML tags is available online that can be hand-coded into the software to add functionality. The type for web copy has to be in HTML, XML or another text-based code

Web type: font-face embedding

Here we have discussed the general principles of using type on websites and how the technology is applied. However, while the key to all type design is usability – ultimately, type's function is to convey information to the user and explain any actions they may be required to take – functionality needs to be balanced against the aesthetic appeal of a page.

One major recent development to note is that all major browsers are now being produced with CSS 3 font-face selectors that allow type and web designers to create and use individual typefaces and type families outside the usual web safe selection. Font-face embedding was developed in response to web designers'

continued requests for fonts that would permit them to match a website's typefaces to its content and audience. The result of recent browser versions' inclusion of font-face selectors is that type foundries are now producing a wider range of commercial web typefaces, as well as growing numbers of free fonts designed by open source contributors. The result is likely to be a radical change in the appearance of the Web. While you may be working with a CMS that has a fixed design, it is always a good idea to be aware of such technological and typographic trends, in order to know when to suggest that a website needs to be redesigned.

TIP It is important to remove all formatting applied to text in word processing or print design programs before copy is pasted into a CMS. This is because the instructions for type positioning such as line returns and tabs will be applied to the type when it appears in the web software. The simplest way to do this is to paste the copy into a program such as TextEdit or WordPad to eliminate the formatting.

'Typography has an important place in the web at the moment. Social interaction, and how to design for it, is a hot design topic... the medium of social interaction is language, and the way language is shaped and looks is typographic design. Web 2.0 is all about typographic design.'

Mark Boulton

Type in other media

The type design rules for websites can also be applied to iPhones, iPads, ereaders and other digital media. Most devices allow people to zoom the page view size, and the screen view can also be adjusted to see one or two pages at once, which means the type may be viewed at any size. All have different requirements related to screen size, and how and where people might use them, and these have to be considered when planning an epublication. E readers and iPhones normally have relative type sizing that adjusts the proportional spacing of type size and leading, and looking at how this works on websites can be a good guide to what might work with a variety of screen enlargements. In general, the best type size is between CSS size 2 and 4 (10 and 14pt) as this is easy to read on a small screen, and choose clean sans fonts, similar to the default typefaces that work well online. Type for epublications should have an open leading to allow for maximum zoom flexibility, as white space helps character recognition on smaller screens. For the same reason, it is better not to reduce the spacing between characters or use minus tracking. The text should be in black or a dark colour on a white or light background and positioned on a template with margins, and possibly columns, to maintain readability. At present, however, there is little standardisation in how these devices display type, and often the standard of typesetting is poor, with open rivers breaking up lines and plenty of widows and orphans (see page 163).

The move to epublishing

The increasing use of devices such as the iPad, ereaders, tablets and smart phones offers new opportunities for media groups to provide people with epublications. As the hardware and software advance, it is likely that more and more media groups will move into epublishing. Several are looking at manufacturing their own A4 or A3 ereaders and many, including the *New York Times*, have launched iPad editions. Although it will take time, the signs are that the social shift towards ereading is now fully under way. In the future, you are likely to be asked to produce material for a range of eproducts, and you will need to be aware of how to adapt your use of type to the latest technology and devices.

Above: A reader using an iPad has the option to select the type size and zoom, allowing them to set the page view to their own personal preferences.

Right: The Kindle DX E-Ink technology, together with specially designed fonts, improves the screen legibility and replicates the experience of reading printed type.

Source: Amazon.com, Inc or its affiliates

Summary Content visualisation and structure: type

Type on a page is the visual representation of the spoken word, and typography is the technique used to indicate tone of voice, character, inflexion and emphasis. The type design for media products is part of their branding and the style of type can indicate to a reader or visitor not only the overall identity of the title, but also the purpose and function of individual items. The ability to control type and how it works on a page allows for the precise manipulation of visual meaning and therefore how the textual elements will be interpreted. It is the interaction of type with pictorial elements in a defined space that forms the basis of page make-up for online and print.

- Typography can be an art, craft, psychology and technology and is an important aspect of many other design disciplines.

- Typography is fundamental to the clarity of any media product as it establishes how information should be ordered and how it is perceived.

- Type exists as a digital file that must be installed on a computer's operating system for the specific typeface to be visible on-screen and print out. OpenType fonts can be installed on both PCs and Macs.

- Type can be bought from specialist companies, commissioned from type designers or downloaded from free type websites.

- All typefaces have identifying names and build into type families made up of type styles (fonts) described by their characteristics.

- Type is designed with a variety of dimensions, weight and width to be fit for a purpose, and letterforms may be differently proportioned within one size.

- Leading is the typographic term for line spacing. It is measured in ratio to the type size, and given as plus or minus points from that size.

- All type conveys semiotic and emotive messages as well as being illustrative. It is important that the typefaces chosen for publications and websites match the identity of the media company and its target audience, and reinforce its market position.

- Website design programs offer a standard range of type styles, sizes and related line heights that display consistently in most browser and operating systems. Some browsers include a CSS 3 font-face selector that allows for the use of a wider range of fonts.

- Cascading style sheets (CSS) force the viewer's web browser to override the user's size/font preferences to stop the typefaces being replaced by browser default settings. CSS should be used for any other coordinated type usage throughout the site.

- Web type sizes are listed by number: 1 = smallest, 7 = largest. Web text size can be absolute – fixed by the designer – or relative so that the type size adjusts to match the viewer's browser or computer set-up.

- Standard web pages are constructed using a mark-up language code based on letters, words, numbers and symbols that tells a browser how to display a web page's type.

- Consistency of typographic style and usage helps the target audience of a website, print or epublication to identity and mentally organise the content.

Activities and development

Undertaking the questions and action points below will help you to interpret the subtle meanings that can attach to type and to select typefaces for a media product. Note especially how the shape of letterforms interacts with other elements on a page or in the environment. Visit the *Design for Media* website for more fact and action sheets, sample templates, type schemes and colour palettes at **www.pearsoned.com/hand**

Questions

Question 1

Analyse a print, web and tablet publication and describe how the topics in the following list are demonstrated by the choice and use of type for each platform:

- Subject matter of the title
- Current social and cultural trends
- Geographic location of the media company
- Cultural identity or political alignment of the title
- Visual content and graphic style of the title
- Technical requirements and platform-specific limitations

Question 2

Visit a shopping centre and look at the typefaces used for shop facia and company logos. Analyse and describe how the type styles reflect the nature of the company, its products, typical customer profile or name of the shops (e.g. a techno style of type for a computer games shop).

Question 3

Visit three of the type websites and blogs listed below. Identify and note any typographic themes or trends, for example calligraphic or hand-writing influences, gothic lettering or modernist/Bauhaus styles. Examine the type handling in a range of mainstream print publications and websites and describe any influences or common treatments of the typefaces and styling.

Type blogs:

http://spiekermann.com/en/
http://tdc.org/
http://Ilovetypography.com
http://Typophile.com
http://Ministryoftype.co.uk
http://typographica.org/
www.typography.ir
www.fontfeed.com
www.typetheory.com/
http://nicetype.blogspot.com/
www.typographyserved.com/

Action points

Action point 1

Type your name, or that of a friend or colleague. Copy and paste the name three or four times and change the typeface, size, weight and style for each version. Free-associate to add a list of words you might use to describe the persona suggested by the way the name looks in a particular typeface. For example:

Di Hand – informal, casual, relaxed
Di Hand – formal, stylish, traditional

Action point 2

Visit a free font website such as dafont.com that allows you to preview the type styles. Enter the same short phrase of three or four words in the custom preview field and see how it looks in three different typefaces that evoke the following themes:

Techno

Traditional

Retro

Romantic

The environment

Business and finance

7 CONTENT VISUALISATION AND STRUCTURE (2): PICTURES

This chapter discusses:

- Communication through imagery
- Photojournalism
- Social photo reportage
- Celebrity, style and fashion photography
- Visual morality
- Image manipulation
- Pictures and privacy
- The semiology of images
- Picture usage theories
- Selecting images
- Graphics: the visual presentation of data

- Visual analysis
- Icons and illustrations
- Cartoons and caricatures
- Buying graphics and illustrations
- Moving images
- Image handling
- Optimising images for the Web
- Picture composition
- Picture depth
- Close-up or long view
- There is no true image
- Media players and audio files
- Stills from videos for print

This chapter discusses the cultural weight and significance of imagery and how this both affects and is used by the media, as well as the ethical and moral questions raised by photojournalism and digital photo manipulation. It will help with commissioning and selecting the different types of visual imagery you might use to illustrate a story or feature, and offers advice on how you can employ pictorial material, with practical guidance on the technical aspects of imaging for print and online.

'Photography is an immediate reaction, drawing is a meditation.'

Henri Cartier-Bresson, founder, Magnum Photos

'Our notions of how we understand images have undergone substantial changes as we come to realise there are no neutral images.'

Robert Hirsch, artist, author, educator and historian

Communication through imagery

Imagery is a key factor in modern media. More than ever before, both serious and entertainment titles rely on video and still images to grab their audience's attention. When thinking about how to visualise a story, you should reflect on the pictures you have found interesting or amusing, and consider the techniques that have been used. These might be good composition, how the subject has been placed in the frame or the use of colour in the image. Understanding why an image works in a particular setting will help you develop the ability to make picture choices that match the editorial ethos of a title and capture the mood of a story, as well convey as information.

Up to 80 per cent of our comprehension of the physical world is based on the information our eyes feed to our brains. This data provides us with much of our understanding of the immediate environment we live in, as our brain absorbs visual experiences to build up our view of the world. When we talk about perception, we are referring to the way in which we establish the size and scale of an object, how far away or close it is, and our sense of visual balance and proportion. The concept of beauty is drawn from observations filtered through knowledge, cultural influences and social conditioning. So strong is the visual imperative in our lives, we cannot prevent ourselves making assumptions about people based solely on the way they look, and we are generally drawn to those whose appearance comes closest to cultural archetypes.

Pictures can be aesthetically pleasing, develop a narrative or make a separate point from the copy; they can also illustrate a concept, create an emotion, inform, amuse, criticise and entertain. Where words alone cannot completely convey all aspects of a subject, images will highlight facts, identify people and provide views of places and events. A picture may, on the surface, be no more than a literal representation, but as with type there are deeper semiotic levels. Most photographs are sized, cropped and positioned to influence how they are interpreted in a design and in relation to other page content.

This nineteenth-century illusion induces the eye to switch between the images of a young woman or an old woman.

A classic visual illusion that, through the juxtaposition of positive and negative shapes, causes the viewer to perceive either a vase or two profiles.

'The images that mobilise conscience are always linked to a given historical situation. The more general they are, the less likely they are to be effective.'

Susan Sontag, author and academic

Photojournalism

Photography has been used as a way to create imagery for publication since the mid nineteenth century. Early picture-based magazines, such as *The Illustrated London News* (1842) and *Life* (1883), used photography as well as engraving and wood block illustrations, and, as photographic techniques improved, the photograph became the main form of visual content for newspapers and magazines. The photographers of the Victorian and Edwardian eras were able to use their large, heavy cameras and tripods to provide images of almost everything on the planet, from Arctic expeditions to Amazonian exploration. They also began to record pictures of daily life that showed the life of the poor in the slums as well as shots of the aristocracy in their stately homes. Photographers also travelled the world to cover battles that were formerly only seen as artist's impressions that tended to glorify war. Roger Fenton (1819–1869) was one of the first photographers to travel with the British Army. It was the realism of his photography that captured the troops' terrible living conditions during the Crimean War, as much as William Howard Russell's campaign reports in *The Times*, that mobilised public opinion and forced the government to improve the soldiers' situation.

Most newspapers continued to use black and white photographs until the late twentieth century, as pre-digital colour printing was time consuming and expensive. The more expensive, high-end magazines began to use colour photography and illustration almost as soon as colour printing came into commercial use in the 1890s, as colour pages attracted readers and advertisers. Because of the expense, publications often limited full colour pictures to the front cover and a few inside pages, with most other pages printed in black and white.

Link to Web – Library of Congress: Roger Fenton: *http://www.loc.gov/rr/print/coll/251_fen.html*

The century also saw the evolution of photographic reportage, which quickly became a powerful communications tool for news media, reformists and propagandists. **Photojournalism** was first recognised as a separate profession from photography in the 1930s. The ability of photographers to take shots *in situ* had been greatly helped by the invention, in the 1920s, of hand-held cameras that could take images good enough for print publications. These made it possible for photographers to capture informal scenes as the camera's small size made it more discreet than a large camera mounted on a tripod, which was a large intrusive object that could intimidate the person being photographed. The photographic plates they used required a long exposure time that meant the subject often had to remain still while the image was taken.

The period between the two world wars saw massive industrialisation and the growth of mass media. There was a large number of newspapers and magazines being published and these all required a constant supply of visual material, most of which was photographic. Newspapers and magazines employed staff photographers and would also commission freelance professionals who specialised in particular areas such as fashion, travel or war photography. While many photographers were represented by agents who sold their work to the media on commission, one group of well-known photographers decided to form their own agency, Magnum, which became the most famous photographer's agency in the world. The founder members were Henri Cartier-Bresson, Chim (David Seymour), George Rodger, William Vandivert and the war

Portable photographic equipment

The first photojournalists used professional-quality Rollei 21/4 × 21/4 inch square film format cameras or Speed Graphic (1912) 4 × 5 inch film format cameras with large flash guns – the type of camera press photographers used in 1930s' classic black and white movies. Leica was the first company to introduce 35mm compact film cameras (1925), which were easier to use than the older models. The 1920s also saw the development of flash bulbs that could be used in portable flash guns, which, together with the high-quality, lightweight Leica, provided photographers with the equipment they needed to take photographs in almost any situation.

photographer Robert Capa. Magnum and other photographers would often cover events at their own expense and chose to take images that they felt were important, as opposed to a staff photographer who would be sent to record situations by an editor. The many titles being published at the time provided a market for their work.

Social photo reportage

Twentieth-century photojournalists recorded people's daily lives through still images that froze and perpetuated an event or action. The best of these moments in time and life captured a universal truth and gave an insight into the human condition, something that had previously been the sole province of art. The power of photography to portray people's lives and highlight suffering had long been used to attract public attention to social injustice and the horror of war. Alfred Stieglitz (1864–1946) was a pioneer in the use of photography to record ordinary life. He established an American tradition of social documentation through photography. This was employed to striking effect when, in the 1930s, the photographers Dorothea Lange (1895–1965) and Walker Evans (1903–1975) were commissioned by the US government's Resettlement Administration to publicise the terrible situation of the people who had lost everything in the worldwide economic crash of 1926 known as the Great Depression. Lange's photographs, particularly *Migrant Mother* (1936), a portrait of a starving woman with her children, became a symbol of human suffering.

War photography has always been politically charged, and both sides in a conflict use photographs and film to present their own version of events. Governments will send official war reporters so they can control what is shown to their public. However,

Source: © Nigel Tanburn

Observer photographer Jane Bown (*left*) photographing the late American playwright Arthur Miller (*right*) with Dame Helen Mirren (*centre*) (Wednesday 4 January 1989).

there is also a tradition of freelance photographers who either want to make their own statements about a conflict, or see it as a source of income or excitement. Images from the First World War were highly censored and slanted to portray a successful campaign, but by the Second World War a number of photographers were working independently and they created striking images of all aspects of the conflict. Bill Brandt (1904–1983) photographed people in London Underground stations sheltering from the bombs during the blitz, Robert Capa (1913–1954) recorded hand-to-hand fighting while Lee Miller (1907–1977), one of the first female war photographers, took a series of iconic images of the liberation of Europe at the end of the war. Later twentieth-century war photography continued to have a significant impact on public opinion and government policy through the work of photographers such as Don McCullin (1935–), who covered the Vietnam/US conflict in the 1960s for the *Sunday Times*. The conflict produced one of the most iconic images of war, through the photo taken by AP photographer Nick Út (1951–), of napalmed, screaming children running naked on a road.

Photojournalists provided the newspapers and photo-news magazines with sensational images, as they would roam around looking for exciting images of every day events and compete to be first at the scene of accidents or fires. One of the best known of the

Link to Web – photography archives and libraries: *http://www.artsmia.org/get-the-picture/stieglitz/index.html*
http://www.loc.gov/rr/print/list/128_migm.html
http://www.billbrandt.com/
http://www.leemiller.co.uk/
http://www.flickr.com/groups/old-photos/
www.nationalmediamuseum.org.uk
http://news.bbc.co.uk/1/hi/world/asia-pacific/4517597.stm

Link to Web – Jane Bowen gallery: *http://arts.guardian.co.uk/flash/page/0,,2176315,00.html*

1930s–1940s street photographers was New Yorker Weegee (Arthur Fellig), who gained the reputation of having a sixth sense, as he always seemed to arrive just after a drama such as murder had taken place. His collection of photographs, *The Naked City*, was adapted as a film in 1948, and the influence of his heavily shadowed style can still be seen in modern noir police dramas.

There were a number of twentieth-century magazines that specialised in photo reporting, such as *The Picture Post* in Britain and *Paris Match* in France, both of which were launched in 1938. Picture-led magazines and photo-spread stories in newspapers proved extremely popular and helped to establish large circulations. Many of the photo magazines featured political as well as cultural content, with commentaries and writing by leading authors such as George Bernard Shaw and Dorothy Parker. The thousands of images commissioned during the 20-year history of the *Picture Post* were used to form the basis of a photo library by its proprietor, Sir Edward Hulton. He bought several other photographic collections over the years to form one of the largest photo records of popular culture and events from the 1900s to the twenty-first century. The library is now in private hands and the images can be purchased online.

Source: Library of Congress, Prints & Photographs Division, FSA/OWI Collection, LC-USF34-9058-C

Migrant Mother (1936) by Dorothea Lange. This portrayal of destitution and hardship captures the social mood of the time.

Celebrity, style and fashion photography

The nineteenth and twentieth centuries saw the development of an image-based celebrity mass culture that made popular icons of film and sports stars as well as politicians, socialites and entertainers. Magazines and newspapers reflected the huge popular interest in celebrity romance and gossip. The 1920s–1940s were known as the golden age of cinema, and the era saw the launch of picture-led magazines that specialised in images of the rich, famous and/or glamorous. The market for images of well-known people, their clothes and homes, led to new photographic specialities including celebrity and society portraits, interior and fashion photography. One of the most famous was Eve Arnold, the first female member of the Magnum agency, who was especially noted for her photographs of movie stars and society figures. The photographer Cecil Beaton was

Links to Web:
http://museum.icp.org/museum/collections/special/weegee/
Magnum Photo agency: http://www.magnumphotos.com/C.aspx?VP=XSpecific_MAG.PhotographerDetail_VPage&l1=0&pid=2K7O3R14AZX1&nm=Eve%20Arnold
World Press Photo: http://www.worldpressphoto.org
Press Association: http://www.pressassociation.com
British Association of Picture Libraries and agencies: http://www.bapla.org.uk
National Press Photographers Association: https://www.nppa.org
Hulton Picture Library: www.hultongetty.com
National Portrait Gallery: http://www.npg.org.uk/collections/about/photographs-collection.php
The Photographer's Gallery: http://www.photonet.org.uk/
http://www.pbs.org/wnet/americanmasters/episodes/annie-leibovitz/photo-gallery/19/
http://www.mariotestino.com/search.php?q=princess+diana&submit=1

the main portraitist of Britain's film stars and the leading figures in society, fashion and the arts, including the royal family.

Photographers such as David Bailey and Terence Donovan, who came from working class backgrounds, introduced a more informal approach. Their images including fashion shoots brought to fame models such as Twiggy, and they produced iconic images of rock stars such as Mick Jagger. Their lifestyle was as glamorous as their subjects, and was captured in Antonioni's 1966 film *Blow Up*. Celebrities and PR companies are well aware of the power of a portrait and will work with photographers to produce iconic images. Fashion photographer Mario Testino created several famous images for Princess Diana, including the 1997 cover for *Vanity Fair*. Another photographer who takes images for *Vanity Fair*, Annie Leibovitz, is the best known of today's portraitists of music, film and fashion stars. She has been taking photos of popular culture icons since she began her career working for *Rolling Stone* magazine in the 1970s.

Visual morality

There has always been an editorial code that news images should not be staged or manipulated. Where it does become known that events were set up, it can adversely affect the reputation of a title (see page 200). People expect news media to be truthful and that the same moral and ethical standards should be applied as strongly to pictures as to writing. There are questions about whether suffering, disease or death should be shown in unedited detail, as to do so might infringe the human rights of those pictured *in extremis*. There is a fear that making public such images encourages prurient, 'car crash' reporting, with the additional problem that exposure to such sights may desensitise the viewer or reader and inure them to atrocities.

If you are selecting news images of sensitive subjects, you do need to take into account the distress they may cause a reader or viewer, and anyone connected with the event. When violent or potentially distressing scenes are shown on television, a warning is solemnly issued that there may be unpleasant images

in the report, but such images are still broadcast 'in the public interest'. Newspapers need to compete with other news media, but obtaining a powerful image of an event that would make a good front or home page is not necessarily an automatic reason to publish. Another consideration with a news picture is whether it is acceptable to editorialise the image to fit a particular point of view. The picture of the injuries suffered by Professor John Tulloch in the 7/7 London Underground bombings was used by news media around the world. He later complained about the use of his picture in association with editorial opinion that did not represent his own political views.

The layered nature of online content means that a website has the option of issuing a warning on the home page with a link to violent or shocking content, and access can be password restricted. However, the moral issues still apply, and the fact that it is easier to publish a wide range of visual material on the Web should not be taken as an unquestioned right to do so. However, the global nature of online news means that, even if there are reporting restrictions applied to

The Falling Soldier

The war photographer Robert Capa first gained international renown in the 1930s for his coverage of the Spanish Civil War. He became notorious for publishing *The Falling Soldier* (5 September 1936), a highly controversial image of the moment a Spanish militiaman was killed by a bullet. Capa's justification was that the public should be shown the full truth of what was taking place. However, there has been a continuing debate about the image, as it has been claimed the picture was not genuine and that the 'death' may have been staged. Recently, José Manuel Susperregui stated in his book, *Sombras de la Fotografía*, that the hilly landscape in the background of the picture is actually 25 miles (40km) from the Cerro Muriano battlefield where Capa claimed the event took place. It is now widely accepted that Capa staged the image.

Link to web – Magnum archive:
*http://www.magnumphotos.com/Archive/C.
aspx?VP=XSpecific_MAG.PhotographerDetail_VPage&l
1=0&pid=2K7O3R14YQNW&nm=Robert%20Capa*

the use of certain images within one country, a victim's family may still be confronted with the sight of a relative's death or serious injury on an international website or in a foreign publication.

Image manipulation

There is often a discrepancy between the actuality of an event and its portrayal in the news media. Image manipulation is a thorny issue, as photo- and video-editing software makes it possible not just to edit, but also to change significantly the content and meaning of a picture or film. There is a moral issue whether it is ever acceptable to alter the content of a news image if a picture reveals something at odds with the publication's editorial stance. This also affects news media sites that might be tempted to consider selectively manipulating a video news package or even staging a scene to support their point of view. In reality, it is a truism that both filmed and photographic news imagery is carefully framed and editorially directed, and on occasions the events filmed or photographed are, if not actually staged, enacted with a consciousness of the presence of cameras. A good deal of effort will go into finding sympathetic or aligned pictures, even if a photographer or film-maker has not been briefed to ensure that the images convey a particular political or social message. And it is not just the content of images that is controlled by the media in order to give a specific impression: the manner in which pictures are cropped, the size at which they are used, the way they are positioned and juxtaposed with other content on a page, all affect how a target audience may interpret them.

Photomanipulation has a long history; in early twentieth-century Soviet Russia it was not uncommon for politicians who had fallen from favour to be removed from official photographs. There have been less sinister instances in Britain where politicians have employed photomanipulation, such as the cabinet minister who missed a photo call so had himself 'Photoshopped' into the publicity shot, and the controversy surrounding the publication of a local football team's photo with the one

Link to web – BBC News:
http://news.bbc.co.uk/1/hi/uk/5118048.stm

'*Digital imaging has destroyed the unwritten arrangement between photographers and audiences by giving image makers the ability to seamlessly alter the picture of "reality". In the 21st century, seeing is no longer believing.*'

Robert Hirsch, artist, author, educator and historian

black player edited out. But what has the most negative effect on the public's relationship with visual imagery is not just the glaringly obvious examples, gleefully exposed by newspapers and websites themselves, but the awareness that such alterations can and are being made. Photomanipulation raises the question of trust, and whether the public can have any expectation of truthfulness, in either imagery or written content, from news and other factual information sources – even if they are aware that the news outlets have a particular political affiliation or are subject to outside financial influences.

There are other issues that involve areas such as image retouching. It is a well-known fact that almost all celebrity, fashion and advertising images will have been altered. As with political image manipulation, the removal of blemishes and signs of ageing, as well as adapting backgrounds and enhancing colours, have been practised since photography began. Advertising uses these techniques to present a product in the most

Link to web – Wikimedia:
http://images.google.com/imgres?imgurl=http://upload.wikimedia.org/wikipedia/commons/9/91/Voroshilov,_Molotov,_Stalin,_with_Nikolai_Yezhov.jpg&imgrefurl=http://commons.wikimedia.org/wiki/File:Voroshilov,_Molotov,_Stalin,_with_Nikolai_Yezhov.jpg&usg=__WuN1UYGdjQO-IWbaoTf5KTae9Fg=&h=326&w=484&sz=47&hl=en&start=7&sig2=OJqZmnmyeAj7ocaJpJpqiQ&um=1&tbnid=Z8xFcMbC31k6JM:&tbnh=87&tbnw=129&prev=/images%3Fq%3Dstalin%2Bphotomanipulation%26hl%3Den%26client%3Dsafari%26rls%3Den%26um%3D1&ei=D_QcS9OXLpTI-Qbcz7nUDw

attractive manner; editorial photo-editing employs similar methods to ensure there are no elements in the picture that contradict the story or distract the eye from the main subject, such as removing a lamp post or tree. However, manipulation can also be used to alter the viewer's interpretation of an image. This can be smoothing out the creases in clothes for a fashion piece to imply they hang well, or adding a brighter, bluer sky to the pictures for a holiday feature or brochure.

Source: Courtesy of Unilever PLC and group companies

DOVE EVOLUTION is a viral advertising campaign created by Ogilvy and Mather for Unilever that demonstrates how image manipulation is used to distort reality and create an expectation of beauty that is unattainable for most women.

Pictures and privacy

Privacy is another awkward subject. There is an area of contention between those in the public eye and the media about the extent to which anyone owns the right to their image and how it can be used. There are laws covering defamation that apply to pictorial representations as well as copy, and there have been a number of cases where celebrities have taken publications and websites to court for using a derogatory picture, or reproducing images without permission.

There have been several test cases, and generally it is possible for someone to restrict the use of their image where a legal contract has been agreed. Michael Douglas and Catherine Zeta Jones had sold exclusive publishing rights to photos of their wedding to one publication, but another magazine obtained and published images of the wedding without permission. The couple brought and won an image infringement case. The illicit photos had been taken by paparazzi using telephoto lenses. While it is legally possible to prevent someone entering a private area to obtain a picture, long-distance lenses are capable of taking detailed pictures from more than a mile away. Modern lenses together with satellite surveillance, CCTV and mobile phone cameras encourage people to record every aspect of life and make enforcing any visual privacy difficult, let alone in the media. However, the existence of advanced camera and imaging technology is not sufficient justification for publishing pictures obtained by stalking celebrities or other dubious means. A group of paparazzi were alleged to have contributed to the accident that caused the death of Princess Diana. The photographers defended their behaviour on the grounds that they were acting to fulfil the public's interest in the princess. They were not prosecuted for their part in the tragedy.

If you do encounter a situation where you want to use a potentially controversial image, you will have to balance the need to show the image against moral and ethical considerations such as: is the person already well known or might the image be intrusive or defamatory, and could using it infringe any legal restrictions such as time embargoes? Video and image sharing websites mean that millions can view everything from world events to domestic trivia, and most individuals who use social networking sites are happy to upload their self-portraits; however, cultural and legal differences between countries affect what may be published by a media company in print or online.

Link to web – Kate Winslet GQ cover: *http://www.independent.co.uk/news/media/pixel-perfect-why-you-shouldnt-believe-your-eyes-when-it-comes-to-those-glossy-images-829196.html?r=RSS*

Picture usage theories

There have been a number of research studies into how people react to imagery, and some typical visual behaviour patterns have been identified. It is known that most people have a **picture memory bias**: the majority of people remember images more easily than they do words, and pictures or scenes are a significant trigger for recall. This is the basis of brand and product recognition, and the speed and ease with which humans develop visual familiarisation is also relied upon when designing for media.

There are other common visual criteria that include reactions such as **baby-face bias** and **regular feature bias**: people have a preference for faces with small, childlike features that comply to a culturally accepted ideal. The **body–face ratio bias theory** states that the more of the body shown, the lower the intelligence of the individual is rated, while a close-up view of the face increases the expectation of high intelligence. This rule should be kept in mind when deciding whether to include a full-length figure. These and other picture usage theories can be a useful guide, as readers and viewers are known to be most comfortable with standard archetypes and brand types as they can recognise them at a glance. However, you should not rely solely on conventional interpretations and generic imagery, but should try to use those elements of the pictures you feel will work best on a page.

The semiology of images

Every image or video has a semiotic value: we attribute meaning and derive a message from everything we see – including still or moving pictures – and this applies to both an entire image or frame and its constituent parts. Images should be closely examined to make sure they do not contain anything that somebody, somewhere, could misinterpret. All aspects of imagery can be signifiers: the shape, tone, shadow, highlights, colour and scale of any or all the parts of an image may alter how it is read. For example, bright, highly coloured pictures may convey cheerfulness and good humour, or seem

Source: Guardian News & Media Ltd.

The Guardian newspaper's 'The Whole Picture' TV advertisement showed that the way in which an event is presented can challenge stereotypes and audience expectations. http://youtube.com/watch?v=SMKScopMnKl

childish and obvious, while dark shadowy scenes may convey menace or a relaxed, sophisticated mood.

Imagery is subject to cultural weighting, as people place a value on what they see and how it is displayed, and the quality and usage of the image carries weight. A feature with large-scale images and little text can be seen as being indicative of a high-end magazine or marketing brochure, while a busy page with a large number of pictures is regarded as more typical of a mass market title. The use of non-professional images can convey immediacy and newsworthiness, and audience-generated content is used to suggest inclusion and participation. However, both may also indicate cheapness and a lack of respect for the reader or viewer.

Warning Images can show as much as the text of an article or story, and it is important they are used in a believable manner or the audience can lose trust in the publication or website. People have a world-view garnered mostly through media images, and readers and viewers mentally cross-reference what they see, quickly spotting misuses, mistaken attributions and manipulation.

Link to web:
http://photoshopdisasters.blogspot.com/

Carelessness in the use of imagery, either in informational or technical terms, can be as damning as bad subediting. Using poor-quality or inappropriate images can look like a mistake, or be taken as indicating a lack of knowledge or care, if there is no news value or relevance to the picture.

Every image has an impact on an audience's emotions, and even when the picture represents something well known the context in which it is viewed may change its cultural weighting. Sometimes this is deliberate and calculated, but in other circumstances it may be accidental and unfortunate. It is important to analyse the pictures that a publication or website plans to use, and to try to anticipate and control the viewer's reaction. There can be some subjects for which it can be very hard to find appropriate visuals, for example health case studies and reports into violent crime where realistic imagery might be gruesome. In such a situation, it is generally better to use a diagram or illustration rather than medical or crime scene photography.

Selecting images

It is likely that the online or print title you are working on will have a particular style of imagery, and this should be borne in mind when choosing visual material to match the editorial stance of the title. When selecting photographs, videos or illustrations, the overriding concerns should be: does the imagery fulfil the brief and will it add to the content quality of both the title and the page? Interesting and visually stimulating images can provide additional information and add to the audience's enjoyment, while using weak or irrelevant pictures may distract from the written content. It is best to work with a selection of still and moving imagery that represents various aspects of a feature or story, and to ensure there is a choice of image shapes and sizes, colours and tone. This provides for flexibility in picture sizing and placement when making up print and online pages.

The production process can be pressured and it is common, when faced with a difficult subject or tight deadlines, for an image to be chosen just because it was the only thing that could be found within the time

Close-up shots can create a sense of intimacy by providing a detailed near view of the subject.

Mid shots introduce foreground space that reduces the immediacy of the visual contact and makes the viewer an observer.

Long shots with the subject in the background can employ the visual content of the foreground area to direct the eye into the image plane.

Distance shots employ a panoramic view to capture a sense of place and scale.

TIP The lead picture for a feature should be planned at the same time as the initial editorial story concept and must visually summarise or encapsulate the subject of an article. A lead picture's dimensions should be sufficient to match the largest possible image size for the title at the correct resolution. For example, the ideal specification of an image file for an A4 (210 × 297mm) magazine full bleed cover picture would be 216 × 303mm at 300dpi (see page 298).

Strong architectural forms can be used in composition as patterns of light and dark, and structural elements can generate dynamic graphic forms within an image.

available. To avoid this problem, especially for features where there should be plenty of time to pre-plan the content, it is a good idea for the production person or team to obtain a synopsis of an article or story from the writer, and to source or commission as many alternative images or videos as possible prior to page make-up. Photographers, videographers and writers who are supplying their own images should be given early deadlines to ensure the visual material can be checked and prepared in good time. Collating images in advance also allows time to correct or alter images in Photoshop, and for pictures to be re-sourced or recommissioned if what has been supplied is not suitable.

Choosing images or videos for a news story should be straightforward. They must be factual – it is regarded as bad photojournalism to stage a news picture (see page 199). However, unlike features, news pictures may come from a variety of sources and differ in quality. Professional news photographers and photo agencies produce high-quality material in sharp focus, with excellent framing and properly balanced colour. But if the only picture available of an event was taken on a bystander's camera phone, then that is what should be used as the news value always outweighs technical consideration. News images may come from the journalists themselves, CCTV, photographic and video sharing websites or from 'citizen reporters'. The major editorial considerations are still the same: does the picture tell the story and will it have impact on the page?

The Rule of Thirds has been applied to the close cropping of this image to enhance the interior angles and create visual drama.

TIP Images on a page work well when there is a variety of contrasting shapes, as this helps with the patterning of a layout and can indicate information hierarchies. It is also a good idea to vary the picture composition between close-ups, full- and mid-length shots. The tonality and colour trend of pictures should be considered as colour and shade can be used to place emphasis or direct the eye and affect the impact of images on a page (see page 218).

Graphics: the visual presentation of complex data

There are a number of other types of imagery apart from photography. These include graphics – charts and graphs that represent data – which can make factual or numeric information easier to understand, icons which are employed as visual signposting and illustrations which can be used to make a comment on a story, set a mood or create a visual look. You may also consider using cartoons and caricatures, as these can be either light-hearted or serious and political.

Graphic devices can reduce the visual density of a page and make the information seem more accessible. It is a good idea to make sure technical or scientific articles include charts, tables, graphs and diagrams as this can make it quicker and easier for readers or visitors to assimilate complex information. An entire page of unbroken copy can give the impression of textual heaviness, and even scientific and technical titles benefit from an approach that combines a percentage of visual information with type. You should ask the writers to suggest a list of possible imagery or source information. If no imagery or information is available, you should read through the copy and identify any possible areas for illustration, then liaise with the writer to confirm the suitability of the ideas and their visual treatment before commissioning any artwork.

Icons and illustrations

Icons are graphic symbols used to provide brand identity and for recurring subject headings or topics in a publication and website. These may be kept in the same or a very similar style for titles that are to be published in print and online, as icons and other artwork can form part of the overall branding. Alternatively, the two media may need to use different styles, as web icons and illustrations are often animated or employ effects that work only on-screen. Icons can be used throughout a media product, sometimes in conjunction with other graphic elements, for subjects such as news that are common to many media. Small images or icons can be used as a semiotic indicator, to inform or emphasise; for example, an icon of a film camera is often used to indicate the 'star' ratings for film reviews.

Icons can act as an international visual language to communicate information and instructions, for example the shadowed click buttons on a website.

Visual analysis

Diagrams, maps and plans, shown either as 2D schematics or 3D projections, are often the best way to situate stories and explain a sequence of events. Cutaway diagrams and computer-generated models can be used to give a clear visual explanation of complex technical and scientific processes such as machinery, the human body or architectural structures. Many sports publications and sites prefer to use a visual approach to written descriptions for the analysis of match play, results charts or medal tables.

Illustrating numbers and measurements can make it easier to visualise comparative size, distance and scale – for example, using a familiar object to provide a comparison for height or thinness.

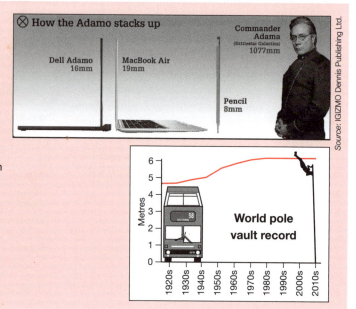

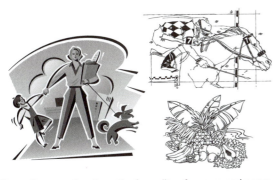

Illustrations can break up the formality of a page and come in a range of picture styles and shapes that can be tailored to the subject or mood of a title or article.

Illustrations (drawings, paintings, sketches, etc.) can be informative, interpretive, set a mood and/or be decorative. Illustrations may be used as an alternative to photographs but they have a purpose and semiotic content of their own. They are more readily connected to art and may be used to convey subtle social and cultural values. For example, many people connect illustrations with children's literature, as they are regarded as softer and more emotive than photographic imagery and therefore do not carry the same expectation of accuracy. An illustration can be used to tackle subjects that might otherwise be distasteful or where a photograph might prove upsetting. The best illustrations elucidate something extra from the copy, something that the words might struggle to convey. They can introduce an element of imagination, brighten a page with unreal, vivid colours and may even be poetic and beautiful.

However, if an illustration is to be used with a more serious item, you should take care to commission an image that matches the journalistic weight of the piece. When briefing an illustrator to produce an image you should be very clear about the visual information to be included and what may not be shown. News illustrations are often used for situations where photographs cannot be taken; for example, cameras are not allowed inside courtrooms while a trial is in progress. Courtroom drawings have become an established way of showing trials, but because they have to be done very quickly, the sketchiness may seem inappropriate if a trial is dealing with sensitive issues.

Cartoons and caricatures

The British media has a long-standing tradition of using political cartoons to pillory the government and society of the day. In the eighteenth and nineteenth centuries, artists such as Rowlinson and Gilray visually excoriated what they regarded as the corruption and decadence of government figures and royalty, and their drawings, published in leading journals and newspapers, had real political clout. Cartoons can carry a serious message and have a considerable influence on how the events and personalities of the day are perceived, and the parodies they create can cancel out any carefully orchestrated persona concocted by PR agents and spin-doctors. Today, cartoonists are often far more vituperative than a journalist could legally be, and Steve Bell and Gary Trudeau are particularly well known for their hard-hitting political cartoon strips.

Caricatures are deliberately distorted drawings of people that emphasise physical features and personality traits. These are often created to mock famous individuals and are used to accompany news stories, articles, interviews and gossip pages. You can use caricatures to illustrate unflattering, controversial or even hostile copy where a photographic portrait could not carry the same visual bite. A caricature may be unkind but it can also be affectionate; it can portray someone in an ugly or false light, or highlight an otherwise hidden attribute. Some publications use them as part of their visual style, while others resort to a caricature when they know the subject of their article would be unwilling to let them use a photograph. Gerald Scarfe is the best known caricaturist in Britain. He has been lampooning those in the public eye, including politicians and pop stars, since the 1960s.

Cartoons and caricatures can be amusing or subversive.

Source: Kevin February

Buying graphics and illustrations

You should consider what may be the most appropriate look for any visual material and how it will fit in with the house design style and the tone of the article or story. There are specialist illustrators and design groups that can be commissioned to create graphics, illustrations, cartooning and caricatures in a wide range of styles. It is useful to build a network of reliable freelance artworkers and illustrators through websites, social media and agencies.

There are a number of websites that display examples of both individual and design group work through online galleries and portfolios, such as the Central Illustration Agency (CIA) which features top British names such as Alan Aldridge, famous for his airbrushed illustrations to *The Butterfly Ball*, and Sir Peter Blake, doyen of British pop art, who created the Beatles' *Sergeant Pepper* album cover. The website illustrationweb.co.uk shows work from many countries and can be searched according to subject or style, for example food illustration or a loose style. Icons and graphics can also be bought directly from illustrators, designers or agencies, and there is a large number of artwork libraries, some of which offer free downloads. Getty, Corbis and other image banks offer generic stock illustrations in a particular style or on a subject that can be purchased to download individually or as themed collections on DVD.

Moving images

The boundaries between broadcast and web media have become increasingly blurred, and online news reporting now fully utilises video and sound to give a richer form of delivery. If you are working online, you will need to understand how video and audio content is originated and sourced. Media companies may employ their own video crews, or expect reporters to create their own footage or sound reports. You can also commission or buy video and audio content from freelance film-makers or news agencies. Thomson Reuters and Associated Press (AP) are the best-known sources of news footage, while image banks, such as Getty Images Footage and Corbis Motion, also offer news videos as well as films on generic subjects.

There is a great deal of public video news available on the Web, and media companies often canvass their audience for material. When using video or audio from open or non-professional sources, you may need to develop another set of skills in order to establish the authenticity and technical usability of any material. It is also necessary to be certain that you obtain the rights to show the footage and that it complies with any legal requirements or restrictions.

Convergent media skills

Convergent skills are becoming increasingly important for anyone looking to build a career in the media, and it is now common practice for photographers to learn direction and video camera skills. Journalists and other media contributors who formerly provided just written content are now frequently expected to be able to film a news report or feature segment, as well as record and edit sound.

Image handling

It is possible to enhance the images you receive and adjust them to fit the size and shape you require for your page. Pictures and video can be adapted or edited to compose and frame the content to ensure it conveys the story in the most visually effective manner. It is also necessary to consider how all the individual elements fit together on a page. There are, however, technical limits set by the devices used to create video and imagery, and the nature of the presentation media.

When you come to prepare an image or video, the way in which you are able to use the material is affected by the media specifications of a title and the technical quality of the images and videos you have to work with. The criteria you need to be aware of include the resolution – the amount of data used to create a digital file; the dimensions – the physical size of an image or a video; the frame rate – the number of frames per second; the file type and colour mode (see page 233). The resolution of a file defines the output quality and establishes how large you can use an image or video, and the dimension is related to the size at which a file can be used at a fixed resolution. Videos are governed by their resolution, the frame rate and the physical size of each frame. Both still and moving images have to be in the specified colour mode and file format for the designated media.

Low and high resolution

In order to work on both print and web titles you will need to understand pixel imagery. The resolution of a video or image is made up of a grid called a bitmap that is measured horizontally and vertically in inches (1 inch = 2.54cm). The number of pixels that make up a grid defines the resolution and therefore the quality of an image or video. The more pixels there are per inch, the more information there is in a file. Print requires a large amount of file data to print pictures accurately on paper, while computers and devices need less information to display good screen imagery. When you come to specify imagery, it is important to be aware of the media in which it is to appear, and any target dimensions. This information is the basis from which you calculate the resolution needed to prepare images for print or online. Printing presses require high-resolution images and web technology and software uses low resolution:

- **High-resolution** images have 300 or more pixels per inch (ppi) and are used in print on higher grade coated papers for magazines and media collateral such as posters, brochures and leaflets.

- **Medium-resolution** images (150-200ppi) are used for publications that are printed on more absorbent paper, such as newspapers.

- **Low-resolution** images are suitable for use online and with other digital devices. The most commonly used resolution for the Web is 72ppi.

points
pixels per inch

- Unedited **data capture** – a scanned image or camera download – is described as **full resolution** to indicate that all possible visual information is being displayed.

Cross-media picture conversion

It is possible to alter an image that has been prepared for one medium and use it in another. Adapting a 300ppi print image for online is fairly straightforward, as print images have more data than is needed for displaying on a 72ppi monitor, and you can easily discard the extra pixel data. Choosing an online picture for print is more complicated as there may not be enough pixel data in a web image for it to reproduce accurately in print. This is because pictures prepared for the Web are normally small both in dimension and memory size so they use as little data as possible in order to download quickly.

Pictures found using a search engine and those on image resources websites should display the pixel dimensions and memory size. These specifications, together with the overall quality of the image when viewed at full size (100%), are the best indicators of whether an online image is suitable to be adapted for print. If the pixel dimension is less than 500 × 500 and the memory size under 500k, or the image is a **gif**, then the picture will almost certainly be too small and lack sufficient data for print. However, it is not possible to be categorical about images above that limit, as the actual size of the picture can depend on a number of other factors. The only way to be sure whether an online image may be used in print is to open it in Photoshop or another professional standard imaging program to check the dimensions and resolution are suitable.

Warning The British and American media and design industries have always used inches, and image specifications for titles are usually given in ppi or dpi (dots per inch). Photoshop can give image resolution in both pixels per inch and pixels per centimetre. It is important to check that you choose the correct measuring system when you prepare an image file.

TIP When sourcing pictures from the Web for print, it is good practice to check whether there is a choice of file size and/or resolution.

If necessary, you can offer the option to your audience of viewing high-resolution 300ppi images via a website download link.

Image capture

The resolution of digital cameras is specified in **megapixels** (a megapixel = 1 million pixels). A high-megapixel capacity means the image contains a large amount of information and can therefore hold greater detail and have a wide colour range. However, the higher the resolution, the more memory is required to generate, store and edit an image. Cameras normally have a control that allows the amount of megapixels to be adjusted to take a higher or lower resolution picture, either through a menu choice or by increasing/reducing the **pixel dimension** (the width and height of the image in pixels). The type of lens also affects the standard of the image, and an image taken on a 12 megapixel professional-quality camera will be better than one taken on a 12 megapixel mobile phone.

Selecting the right camera

Digital compact cameras 4–12 megapixels.

Digital compact cameras 8–12 megapixels fixed internal optical zoom lens.

Digital single lens reflex cameras 8–25 megapixels will take a wide range of different focal length and zoom optical lenses.

The megapixels of a camera define the size of image it can take (see *How to work with pictures*, page 214). However, the final image quality is dependent on the sophistication of the lens. When selecting a camera, as well as checking the file memory size, physical size (width and height) and resolution that it can achieve, you should also ensure the lens is able to capture the detail required for the target media.

Viewing size and actual size

An area that often causes confusion is the difference between the size and appearance of a digital image file on-screen and its actual dimensions and true quality. The first step when you come to judge the usability of a picture is to open it in a professional photo-editing program such as Photoshop to check the resolution (ppi/dpi) and physical size. Most imaging software opens files so they fill the viewing window, so you may be looking at a picture shown at a percentage of its actual size if it is larger than the viewing window. All images should be checked at 100% view to decide if they are good enough to use in a specific medium, and whether they are suitable to be enlarged or reduced. If you open an image file and the entire picture fits into a small viewing window, you are seeing the actual dimensions (size = 100%). If an image that is larger than the monitor screen is viewed at 100%, you will only see a section of the picture.

You should normally have an idea of the size at which you want to use an image on a page. It is important to keep the final size in mind when you select imagery, as clarity and detail can be lost if a large image is over-reduced and the pixels may become visible if a small image is greatly enlarged (see page 209). Many low-resolution images that look good at 100% on-screen will appear **pixellated** – the pixels will be visible as blocks or blur the image – if used for print publishing, as presses require smaller pixels to produce a smooth-looking image. This effect becomes even more noticeable if the image is enlarged.

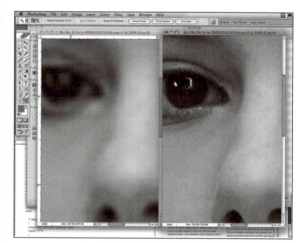

Enlarging the image on-screen shows the difference in quality between low- and high-resolution versions.

Image file format

Digital images are captured in a number of file formats, some of which retain the original pixel colour data better than others. The most commonly used media image file formats are JPEGs, tifs, pdfs, pcx, eps and gifs. Each file format saves the colour information using a different method. **JPEG**, the standard online picture file format, automatically compresses and discards information to reduce the file size, while the tif format, which is used for print, retains all the original data. The acronym JPEG stands for the Joint Photographic Experts Group – the committee that originally developed the JPEG as a file compression system specifically for use on the Web. JPEGs employ a method called **lossy compression** to reduce the file size, but as long as the original image contains sufficient colour information this has little visual effect. However, if the JPEG is over-compressed, an image may degrade noticeably as lossy comprehension loses colour each time a JPEG is opened and closed, and when a file is resaved. Uncompressed file format such as tiffs and Photoshop psd should be used to retain the image quality.

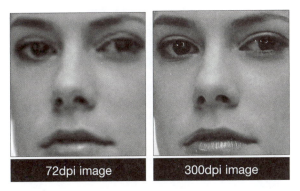

72dpi image   300dpi image

Low-resolution images should be used on the Web, but are not suitable for print as they can reproduce poorly and may look blurry and flat.

Enlarging and reducing images

Good image management relies on controlling the resolution (pixel size). The best possible results on screen and in print depend upon matching the correct pixel dimension for the media to the size at which the image is to appear. For the Web, this means making sure the image is at the exact width and height it will appear so the browser does not need to rescale it. The other key reason is to keep the memory size as small as possible to enable the quickest download time.

Images for print require as much colour information as possible, and while the amount of memory a file takes up is not as critical as for the Web, it is good practice to prepare images that are close to the final reproduction dimensions. Matching the image's dimensions to the printed size will limit each file's memory size and reduce the amount of data used by each image placed in a page make-up program. It also means that you will need less disk space to store all the images for a publication.

Although there may be a temptation to avoid the extra steps needed to rescale images, there are a number of technical reasons why you should not do this. When an image is enlarged, the physical size of the pixels is increased and this can blur and degrade an image. How much a picture can be enlarged in a page make-up program is defined by the relationship between the image file's dimensions and its resolution. Most print publications have a fixed image resolution (see page 207), and the size at which pictures are imported into the software is described as W100% × H100% – the width and height of the image file. The majority of print titles specify that an image may not be enlarged by more than 120% over the import size of the image file. Reducing the import size is not as critical, as pixels do not noticeably fill in unless a very large image, for example 210 × 297mm (A4), is taken down to a minuscule size, say 20 × 24mm.

Cropping

Image management may also involve altering the dimensions of a picture, selecting a specific area that reflects the focus of interest or removing extraneous details. Cropping – selecting an area of an image – has two purposes: one is to make the best visual use of the elements of a picture, while the other is practical and involves matching the dimensions and proportions of an image to the space available on the page. For example, if a portrait shot has been taken against a busy background, cropping to the head and shoulders will focus attention on the subject.

The arrangement of content within a picture affects the way in which the image is interpreted, and reframing the subject can alter how the viewer reads the image. Cropping can be used to position the main element in relation to the frame edge. A subject placed in the middle of an image holds the focus in the centre, while choosing a crop that positions the main element near to the edge of the image gives directionality.

It is good practice to match the cropped area of a photo or graphic to how it has been scaled and positioned on a make-up page, and to any fixed picture dimensions on a CMS template. Cropping is also used to remove those areas of an image that are not going to be seen inside the picture box or holder in order to reduce the memory size of a file.

Photoshop montages using stock imagery are a popular way of combining several elements of a complex story, especially where it would be difficult to source a single picture that would illustrate the overall topic.

How to crop and save images

How to crop images for print page make-up:
- Print a proof of the final page to show the shape, position and crop of the picture content and make a note of the width and height of the page make-up picture boxes.
- Open the press-ready versions of the images in photo-editing software and use the cropping tool to draw a shape over the pictures to match the picture box on the page (using the width and height fields on the option to constrain the proportions). Crop the image file.
- Rename the cropped image file (key word_picture number_PR (press ready)) and save the file in a separate folder.
- Replace the images on the page with the cropped versions to ensure maximum reproduction quality.

How to crop an image for a CMS template:
- Determine the pixel dimension of the image boxes (normally given on help pages).
- Open the web-ready versions of the images in photo-editing software and use the cropping tool to draw a shape over the pictures to match the image box on the template (using the width and height fields on the option to constrain the proportions). Crop the image file.
- Rename the cropped image file (key search word_CMS image tag number) and save it in a separate folder.
- Upload the image on to the web page via the CMS.

The cropping above shows how carefully selecting details from a picture can make an effective thumbnail for the Web.

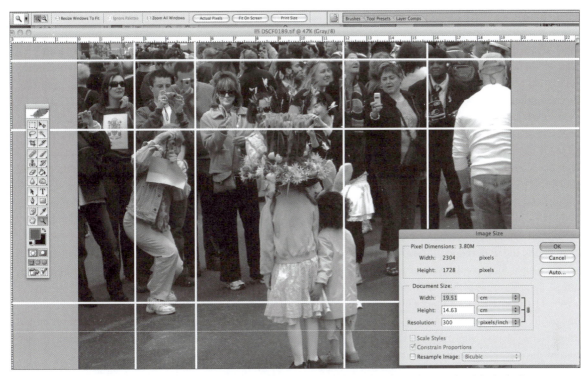

A photograph will often include extraneous visual information, such as the back of the man on the right in the image above, whose white shirt leads the viewer's eye away from the key figures.

Tight cropping can emphasise one particular element of an image.

The image should be cropped to frame the main focus of attention within a horizontal or vertical shape that suits the image and will be usable on a page.

Cropping can achieve a number of different effects from an image within the same frame.

211

Resampling and interpolating

Most images that you source or receive will have to be adjusted to fit the technical requirements of the media. This could be because the image is physically too big or the resolution is too high or too low. When you enlarge or reduce a picture, you need to consider how this will affect the size of the pixels, and any alterations should be made using photo-editing software so that the changes affect the image's underlying pixel grid. Resizing a picture involves controlling both the physical size and the pixel dimensions.

Photo-editing software resizes images through a process known as **interpolation** – an algebraic method of adjusting the underlying 2D pixel grid. Interpolation software looks for repeating colour patterns in the image, samples areas of differently sized pixels and reassembles them into a scaled up or down version of the image file. Photoshop, the main program used to resize images, uses bicubic interpolation: the changed image is made up of pixels that have been repositioned on the pixel grid and compressed to ensure that the image's dimensions adjust in ratio. Genuine Fractals, a plug-in that works with Photoshop, is the professional photographer's preferred resizing software. It uses algorithms to create the new resolution by recalculating and resizing the pixels that make up an image.

> **TIP** It is good practice to resize images to the dimensions they will be used in a print layout, on a web page or in a CMS template.

Link to web – resizing and resampling:
http://www.photoshopessentials.com/essentials/ resizing-vs-resampling.php

http://www.adobe.com/designcenter/ photoshopelements/articles/concept_resample.html

http://tv.adobe.com/show/learn-premiere-pro-cs5/

http://www.adobe.com/support/photoshopelements/ gettingstarted/index.html

Optimising images for the Web

The aim when working with online imagery is to achieve the smallest possible file size for downloading and to minimise any subsequent image scaling by the browser software. The correct preparation of image files will greatly enhance a visitor's experience, as fast-loading web pages make it far easier to engage with the pages and reduce the potential of a visitor leaving the site. When you prepare images for the Web they need to be converted to RGB (Red, Green, Blue) mode and scaled to the exact size that the image is to appear on page at 72ppi resolution. They also need to be **optimised** to ensure they download in the fastest possible time. Optimisation is a process of reducing the memory size of an image file by discarding colour and other data. Photoshop and other imaging programs optimise images by reducing the number of colours used, combining layered images on to one layer and adjusting the amount of compression (deleting unused digital information from a file).

Optimising images has the benefit of reducing the file size, but care must be taken when reducing the file size to ensure that visual definition is not lost. Photoshop can show how long it will take to download an image at the most commonly used connection speeds. The software allows you to reduce the number of colours, which increases the download speed. Most browsers and search engines automatically optimise uploaded images, while some devices, such as the iPod, will optimise pictures unless the 'include full-resolution image' option has been chosen.

> **TIP** Optimised image files should be resaved with a new web searchable file name.

> **Warning** On no account should images that have been processed and compressed to web safe colours be used in a print publication, as most of the colour information needed to get a good result on a press will have been destroyed through the compression process.

HOW TO WORK WITH PICTURES

- Photography: the basics
- Image content: form and structure
- Working with images of people
- Focus and depth of field
- Vector graphics
- Working with images for the Web and digital devices
- Working with images for print and slideshows
- Layering images
- Correcting image files
- Photo-editing: colour adjustment
- Image handling

The *How to work with pictures* pages describe how photography and other graphic elements can be created for and used in the media, and demonstrates how to apply the principles of pictorial composition. These pages introduce photo-editing, colour adjustments and working with image manipulation techniques including layers, healing and cloning. They also summarise the processes involved in preparing visual material for the target media such as image handling, filing and archiving.

Photography: the basics

Digital photography

Digital cameras work by capturing light and converting it into millions of coloured pixels. The pixel capacity of a camera image is given in megapixels (1 megapixel = 1 million pixels): the higher the number of megapixels, the larger the image a camera can generate. The maximum number of pixels available and the quality of the camera lens set the quality of photographic imagery that a camera can record. A good camera lens is made up of several

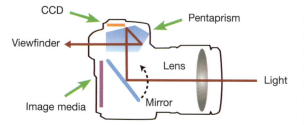

When a digital single lens reflex (SLR) photograph is taken, light passes through the lens and is reflected 90° upwards by a movable mirror on to a pentaprism (a five-sided component made of glass) which redirects the picture three times to ensure the image is viewed the right way round. The CCD (charge-coupled device) converts light into electrical signals that create the pixels which make up the image and visual display.

elements that reduce distortion and direct light with a high level of accuracy. These enable the camera to capture a high degree of focus and clarity.

Professional photographers use cameras with 8 megapixels and above, which produce photographs at a large dimension that hold detail well. Professional-standard cameras can be set to take images at a particular resolution to match the target media in which they are to be published.

A camera's pixel capacity is important as the resolution of an image must match the requirements of the target media, and the pixel dimension determines not only image quality and size, but also the file's memory size, which can be vital when up- or downloading. Resolution is also fundamental to how well details, colour and contrast will hold on screen or in print.

Resolution	Target media		
*Low **56-72ppi**	Avatars	Mobile apps	Websites
Medium **150-200ppi**	Newspapers	Business documents and communications	Presentations
High **300+ppi**	Media for printing on a press	Publications: books and magazines	Print-based advertising

Camera type and usage

Point and shoot: compact and mobile phone cameras

Point and shoot: photos of family & friends, children, pets, parties and celebrations; portraits & pictures for blogs and social media pages; personal experience: overseas holidays, sports, trips & outings

Standard mid-price-range cameras are often described as 'point and shoot'. They normally have auto focus, auto flash and auto exposure features that allow a non-expert to take a competent photograph. While such images are not of a professional standard, there can be occasions when the importance of what a photograph or video shows overweighs technical quality.

Professional level: single lens reflex cameras

Professional photographers use SLR cameras that have both auto and manual controls for focusing, flash and setting exposure. SLR cameras can be fitted with a range of detachable lenses such as telephoto or wide-angle lenses and may handle high definition. The cameras produce images that display well on-screen and look good in print.

User generated photo content: public events, celebrities, eyewitness record of daily life (street fashion, working day)

Single lens reflex cameras: professional photography and photojournalism: news, sports, fashion, portraits, celebrities fashion, advertising, marketing, PR, mood shots, pack shots, land & cityscapes

F-stops and shutter speeds

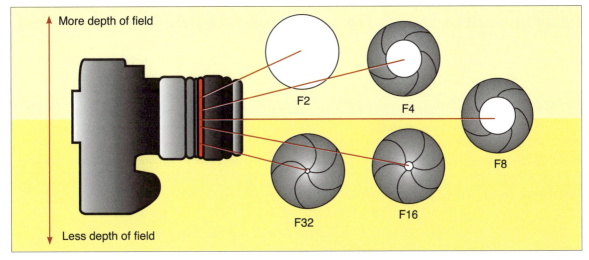

More depth of field

F2

F4

F8

F16

F32

Less depth of field

The amount of light passing through a lens is controlled by the size of the aperture – the centre of a circle of adjustable metal leaves. Aperture settings are measured in f-stops: opening the aperture by an f-stop allows twice as much light through the lens; reducing the f-stop lets half as much through.

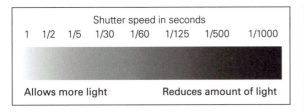

Shutter speed in seconds

| 1 | 1/2 | 1/5 | 1/30 | 1/60 | 1/125 | 1/500 | 1/1000 |

Allows more light   Reduces amount of light

To achieve the optimal photographic result, you must take the camera exposure and the subject matter into account when selecting f-stops and shutter speed. In order to control the exposure you need to balance the size of the lens aperture against the length of time that the shutter is open. Fast shutter speeds are used to freeze moving images and avoid blurring. If you want to increase the depth of field and achieve greater definition, choose a long shutter speed in conjunction with a smaller aperture. Higher f-stops usually record images with enhanced detail while lower f-stops record images with less detail and depth of field.

WARNING Keeping the shutter open for too long may result in motion blur if the subject moves and camera shake if the camera is not supported on a tripod.

1/60 second: the default shutter speed on most cameras. It is suitable for average light conditions including overcast days and well-lit interiors.

1/125 second: a good shutter speed for shooting outside on bright days and for capturing slow action such as images of people walking. Also suitable for use with flash.

1/500 second: this shutter speed can be used to freeze fast action such as passing cars and players at sporting events. It may also be used to capture children or pets in motion.

215

Image content: form and structure

Planning a pictorial composition

When photographers take a picture, they will consider both the composition of the shot and the message to be communicated. When that picture is used on a page, it may be chosen to convey other concepts, and how it is handled and its interaction with the rest of the content can modify how it is viewed. How the audience interprets the image can add more layers of meaning.

Photographers and artists use a number of techniques to ensure that each image has a strong underlying structure that directs the viewer's attention on to the subject. A pictorial composition is built from the relationship between all the elements of an image. The photographer will consider the scale of the elements within an image, the sense of visual depth, lines of direction and the overall balance.

The other key compositional element is the mood of the image. Photographers will attempt to juxtapose the location and the position of the subject within a frame to create a feel or provoke an emotional response. The way in which elements are arranged and the angle at which a photograph is taken can make an image appear static or active, dynamic or cool, and this can alter a picture's impact.

Spatial relationships

Each element of an image needs to be positioned within the frame, in terms of both where it sits and how large or small it appears in relation to the other items. You may find that techniques such as the Golden Section that divide the image plane into one-third/two-thirds can help to create structure and establish the best position for the focal point of the picture.

Left: The acute angles, placement of accessories and use of the Golden Section create a strong dynamic.

Triangulation

Photographers often base their compositions on a pyramid structure. Triangulation within a frame can help unify the elements and concentrate the point of focus on to the central group. Upright or inverted pyramid shapes also enhance the main part of the image and define its relationship with the surroundings. You should look for, and if necessary crop to emphasise, A-frames within an image, as these provide visual strength.

Left: The figure, bow and violin form a double-A shape that unites the violinist and his instrument while creating a strong shape against the background.

Left: The still life is arranged in an inverted-A composition that provides a formal structure for the 11 separate items.

Balance

Most images conform to the human sense of natural balance. Symmetrical balance is quiet and still, implies stability and is reassuring to most people. Asymmetrical balance has more movement and energy, and you can use it within a frame to play one element against another to create a sense of equilibrium. Balance can be achieved through contrasting scales, between the foreground and background, and the left and right hand sides of an image. It can also be established using harmony or emphasis on particular key colours.

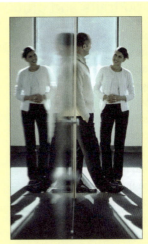

Above: The asymmetrical positioning balances the fore and background.

Left: The mirrored image enhances the sense of symmetrical balance.

Perspective

Perspective can be used to add visual depth to images through controlling the lines and angles within the frame. The natural point of focus falls on the central vanishing point but you can alter this by introducing figures or other elements that will draw the eye away from the horizon line.

Left: The buildings on the horizon line, the railing and path all converge on a central point.

Emphasis

A central focal point within an image can be created by utilising the surrounding elements to drive the eye towards the main subject. You can achieve this by using dark and light shapes, textural contrasts and positioning within the picture frame to throw emphasis on to a key visual feature. This enables you to draw attention to a specific area of an image even if it is relatively small in scale.

Above: The buildings in the foreground create a sense of convergence that directs the eye to the central image.

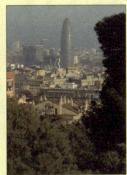

Above: The distant, misty view of the tower is strengthened by the dark foreground.

Working with images of people

Making the most of portraits and group shots

When preparing a portrait picture you should make sure that the viewer can interpret the look in the subject's eyes, as media audiences read facial expression and body language in the same way they would if they met the person in real life. When working with group shots, ensure that there is a clear interaction between the figures that can be created by placing them close together in an A-frame shape.

Portraits and groups should be carefully cropped to concentrate interest on the figures, and to suggest movement and create shapes within the picture, for example using the subject's head and shoulders to form a triangle. The key to preparing effective portraits and group shots is to ensure that all facial expressions and relative positions convey the intended meaning of the photograph.

Left: The image is flat and lacks a focal point or implied movement, while the subject appears distant and has an impenetrable expression.

Right: The high-angled shot and tilted head evoke movement, and the warm, direct gaze is reassuring.

Same picture, different crops

Use the original picture as a starting point: crop it to remove unwanted items and focus attention on the key elements, and make the most of the allocated shape on the page.

Left: The gap between the figures allows the background to dominate the centre of the image; it also separates the subjects, whose body language suggests they are not interacting with each other.

Right: An inverted A-shape is created by the handshake that provides a central visual point between the subjects, and the sense of connection is strengthened by eye contact.

Full length shot: the full height of the figure against the background angle makes the most of the perspective.

Three-quarter length shot: using a tighter crop helps to disguise the awkward angle of the subject's arm.

Head shot: employing a close-up can capture mood and concentrate attention on the subject's expression.

Focus and depth of field

Establishing a visual priority

When taking a photograph, you can apply emphasis to a particular area of an image by choosing a focal point and controlling the depth of field. Selecting how much of the image is in focus enables you to highlight the key element of an image and separate it from the background or competing or complex visual content. Depth of field helps to guide the viewer's eye towards your chosen subject or key feature, whereas if you keep all of an image in sharp focus, there is no variation in emphasis.

The gull has been emphasised by focusing on the foreground and selecting a wide aperture that produces a narrow depth of field, leaving the background out of focus.

Focusing on the figure in the background, selecting a wide aperture and repositioning the narrow depth of field results in a foreground that is out of focus.

Depth of field

The depth of field is the distance from the camera lens that will be in focus at any one time. This can be used to lead the viewer to focus on a specific area of an image and can enhance the perception of depth within a photograph.

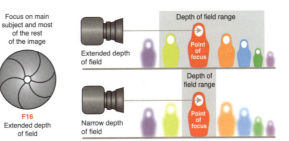

Adjusting the size of the lens aperture controls the extent of the image that falls into the focal area. Reducing the aperture size increases the visual depth that will appear in sharp focus, while a wide aperture restricts the distance from the lens that will be in focus.

F32 aperture: the focus is on the cup and the background remains in focus.

F2 aperture: the focus is on the cup with the background out of focus.

Narrow depth of field

A very narrow depth of field can be used to isolate the main subject from a cluttered background. This can be achieved by selecting the widest possible aperture to give you a condensed depth of field and focusing on to the key element.

Vector graphics

Working with vector illustrations

Vector graphic programs are used to create graphic elements such as illustrations, icons and buttons for websites and print publications. The two key advantages of vector over bitmap images are that, because the images are formed from mathematical coordinates, they can be resized without loss of quality, and as vector artwork does not contain pixels, media-specific resolution requirements do not apply.

Vector artwork is constructed from adjustable control points linked by paths that produce smooth, crisp edges. Each point isolates a section of path, making the shapes easy to adjust: corner points form right angles, while smooth points operate through Bezier curve handles that manipulate the degree of curve in a line section. The points and paths combine to form vector objects that can be filled with and/or given an outline (stroke) colour.

You should plan your design as a series of interlocking shapes and place each element on a layer – a separate transparent level within a document that can be named and modified. Layers can be locked or hidden, making it easier to edit an image, as they allow you to work on each element of the design in turn.

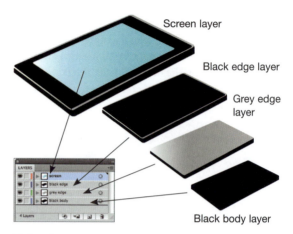

Screen layer

Black edge layer

Grey edge layer

Black body layer

Using layers

1 Open a new document and enter the settings for your target media, name and save the file.

2 Select the Layers window (Window menu) and draw the first element of your design. The image will appear on the default layer in the Layers window.

3 Go to the Layers drop-down menu and select New Layer (or click on the new layer icon at the base of the window). Name the layer and draw the second element of your design on the new layer.

4 Continue adding new layers and drawing/placing the elements on separate layers until your design is completed.

Combining vector type and images

Download the Wings file and instructions from **www.pearsoned.com/hand**

1 Open, rename and save the Wings file.

2 Go to the Layers window and change the name of Layer 1 to Wings 1.

3 Set up a new layer and name it Circle.

4 Keep the Circle layer active, select the Ellipse tool, hold down the Shift key to constrain the proportions, and then

draw a circle. Go to the Swatches window and fill the circle with yellow.

5 In the Layers window, move the Wings 1 layer below the Circle layer to position the wings behind the yellow circle.

6 Create a new layer and name it Type 1. Type in *Sun Holidays* and *Fly away today!*

7 Go to the Character window and choose the fonts, weight, tracking and/or kerning. The alignment can be altered using the Paragraph window. Go to the Swatches window and experiment with different colour fills and outlines for the type.

Fly away today!

8 Duplicate the Type 1 layer and name the duplicated layer Type 2. Click on the eye icon beside the Type 1 layer to hide it. Select the Type 2 layer and convert the type to outlines (see *How to work with type*, page 175).

TIP Keep the characters close together as tight spacing looks more professional.

Vector graphics

Live Trace: converting bitmap images to vector graphics

Live Trace is a feature of Adobe Illustrator that can convert photographic pixel-based images and hand-drawn sketches into vector graphics. The software creates simplified shapes by adjusting the tone, resolution and colour of a bitmap image and drawing a vector path around each element. The process creates size- and resolution-independent vector graphic files that can be used cross-media and scaled without loss of quality. Live Trace operates through a Tracing Options window that allows you to control

exactly how an image is to be traced, and makes it possible to specify how many and which colours are to be used, how much detail retained and the definition and smoothness of the lines and fills.

> **TIP** It is a good idea to reduce the amount of detail and/or remove the background of the image in Photoshop before Live Trace is applied.

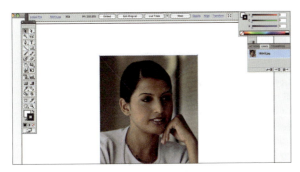

1 Select an uncomplicated photograph with good contrast.

2 Open Adobe Illustrator and go to File menu – New to set up, name and save a file for your target media.

3 Go to File menu – Place to open the photograph (bitmap image). Click on the Live Trace button in the Control bar or go to Object menu – Live Trace.

4 Select a Live Trace option: Live Trace has a selection of default settings such as Simple Trace, Photo High or Low Fidelity and Greyscale

5 Go to the Object menu – Live Trace – Tracing Options and use the Tracing Options window to adjust the tracing effects that control the degree of vectorisation.

Left: The colours in the vectorised image can be stored in the Swatches window and edited using the Live Paint Bucket and Selection tools.

> **TIP** The best way to work with Live Trace is to keep the Photoshop file linked to the Illustrator version as this allows you to continue to edit both the original and the vectorised image files.

Above: Live Trace identifies each area of similar-coloured pixels and combines them into vector shapes with varying amounts of detail and smoothness of line.

For more information on how to use Adobe Illustrator visit *Adobe.com*

Images for the Web and devices

Evaluating and preparing images for viewing on-screen

When working with images to be viewed on-screen, you need to ensure that the visual material conforms to the technical specifications of the web page or device. You should choose images that will work at a small scale and bear in mind that, on some devices, the colour range may be restricted. The overall aim should be to prepare images that will download quickly while maintaining the highest possible visual quality for the device or bowser.

There are a number of actions that you need to apply in order to achieve the best possible result. The first is to prepare the image to the exact size and proportion for the page or device, then you should optimise the image to reduce the file memory size and decrease the time it takes for an image to appear on-screen. It is also important to enter keywords for the metadata for the image that enables search engines to find pictures and pages.

Managing image size and resolution

1 Open a copy of the original image in Photoshop and resave it with a different name. Use the Crop tool to select the most suitable area of the image in proportion to the target page or device.

2 Go to Image menu – Image size to check the pixel dimensions, document size and resolution against the specifications for the target page or device. If necessary, use the window controls to adjust the image to conform to your requirements.

3 If the image resolution is not 72ppi, uncheck the Resample Image button while keeping the Constrain Proportions button checked. Alter the resolution *only* to 72ppi – the document size will increase if the original image was at a higher resolution.

4 Recheck Resample Image while keeping Constrain Proportions checked. Enter the target pixel dimension (image size) matched to either the width or height. Click on OK and Save.

Optimising images using Save for web and devices

1 Open the cropped and resized file. Go to File Menu – Save for web and devices.

2 Select the 4-Up tab to view the download speed and memory size options. Compare the image quality against the download speed and make adjustments to reduce the file size and improve the download time using the control buttons on the right hand side of the window.

3 Choose the required file format (JPEG, PNG or gif) and select a quality that produces a low file memory size but still maintains a clear image.

4 Use the Colour Table to lower the number of pixel colours, which normally reduces the file size, and compare the results against the original.

TIP Always leave the sRGB button checked.

5 You can select the Preview drop-down menu to check how the image may look on the main two platforms.

6 Once you have reduced the file to the smallest memory size at the best possible quality, save and rename the optimised file.

TIP Choose a file name that combines relevant subject information with 'search engine friendly' key words. This data should always be entered into CMS or similar production systems.

Images for print and slideshows

Preparing for print

Images that are intended for printing should be at the highest possible quality for the paper or substrate to be used on the press. You should make sure that the images you choose are suitable for print reproduction, and that any image editing and adjustments maintain the maximum amount of colour information and picture detail.

Ideally, the pixels that make up print images should be at the optimum size for the output media; that is, at the correct resolution and in the exact final printed dimensions. You need to bear in mind that there is always a difference between the screen and printed versions of an image, and that it is necessary to check the size and resolution before deciding whether pictures can be used for print.

Changing the colour mode

You should use Image menu – Colour mode to save images in the correct colour mode. CMYK is the only image colour mode used by traditional web offset litho printing presses. Digital presses can use RGB; however, it is important that when working on a project for digital output, all images are prepared in either RGB or CMYK colour mode and not a mixture of the two.

Resizing images for print

1 Make a copy of the original image and open it in PhotoShop. Resave it with a different media-specific name. Use the Crop tool to select the most suitable area of the image and to remove unwanted pixels.

2 Go to the Image menu – Image size to check the pixel dimensions, document size and resolution against the print specifications. If necessary, use the image size window controls to adjust the image to conform to the target media requirements.

3 If the image resolution is not 300ppi in the image size window, uncheck the Resample Image button while keeping the Constrain Proportions button checked. Alter the resolution *only* to 300ppi – the document size may decrease if the original image was at a lower resolution.

4 If you wish to make a 300ppi image smaller, recheck the Resample Image button while keeping the Constrain Proportions checked. Enter the width or height in the Document Size fields. Click on OK and Save.

Preparing a scrolling slideshow for tablets

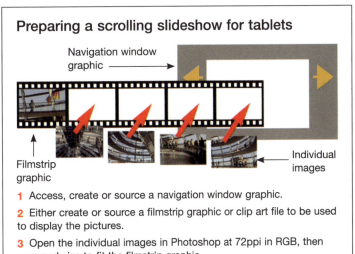

Navigation window graphic

Filmstrip graphic

Individual images

1 Access, create or source a navigation window graphic.

2 Either create or source a filmstrip graphic or clip art file to be used to display the pictures.

3 Open the individual images in Photoshop at 72ppi in RGB, then crop and size to fit the filmstrip graphic.

4 Open the filmstrip graphic, place the images on a series of layers, save and make a flattened JPEG copy of the file.

5 Import the filmstrip JPEG into the tablet publishing software, select and number each frame to link it to the navigation arrows, and enable touchscreen scrolling.

223

Layering images

Creating a montage

There are some topics that cannot be clearly communicated using a single photograph, and there may be times when you are unable to find a relevant image. This is where using photo montaging can help to develop powerful graphics from existing images. Combining images allows you to create an illustration that can capture various elements of a complex story. A montage of images on separate layers can convey a number of messages and bring together several themes within one picture.

How to combine images using layers

1 Open the background image file and check the resolution is correct for the target media. The dimensions should ideally be at least twice the size it will appear on page to allow for retouching. You may also need to increase the background (canvas) size.

2 Open a second image file and check that the resolution matches the background picture. If the second image is overscaled at that resolution, you will need either to resize it, or if it is undersized, to source a larger picture.

3 In the background image file, open the Layers window and set up and name a new layer. Copy and paste the second image in position on the new layer. Go to Edit menu – Transform and if necessary reduce the image until the desired effect is achieved. Remove any unwanted background from the second image layer.

4 Duplicate and rename the second layer. Click on the layer copy and move it behind the second layer. Go to the Filters menu and apply Blur – Motion Blur, using the sliders to adjust the degree of blur.

5 Open a third image file and follow step 2. In the background image file, open the Layers window and set up and name another new layer. Place and scale, then eliminate unwanted background areas as described in step 3.

6 To align images, create and name a new layer in the background image file. Go to the View menu and make sure Rulers and Extras are activated. Click on the top or side Ruler in the program window, hold down the mouse button and drag ruler guides into position on the image canvas. Then follow steps 2 and 3 for each additional image (see main image above).

7 Save the layered image file. Go to File menu – Save As and make a flattened copy. Close the layered version and open the flattened copy. Make sure that it is the appropriate size, correct resolution and colour mode for the target media.

The Photoshop Layers window

 For more information on how to use layers, go to **www.pearsoned.com/hand**

Image retouching and adjustments

Sourced or supplied images rarely match your exact requirements and you may need to make an aesthetic and editorial judgement on the picture's suitability. There can also be exposure problems that need correcting using photo-editing software to improve the image. Where there are features that need enhancing, retouching techniques can be applied to modify details and eliminate blemishes. Some photo corrections are quite easy, but if an image needs considerable work you may find it requires the skills of an expert retoucher.

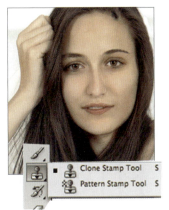

Healing
The media's search for physical perfection often leads to cosmetic retouching in order to idealise an image. In this example, the Healing tool has been employed to eliminate a crease in the model's cheek on the right side of her face by selecting a range of pixels in that area and blending them together.

Cloning
Images are also enhanced to conform to fashionable concepts of beauty. Here, the Cloning tool has been used to reshape the model's eyebrows.

http://www.dove.us/#/ features/videos/default. aspx[cp-documen- tid=7049579

Applying tonal adjustments

Levels
The Levels window has three main controls, namely highlights, mid tones and shadows, that are adjusted using sliders. The right hand example (*below*) was improved by adjusting the highlight and mid tone arrows to the right.

Curves
Curves allow you to customise the tonal ranges by displaying a histogram (graph) that represents the original image. The tonal gradient of the right hand image (*below*) has been modified using the linear curve adjustment.

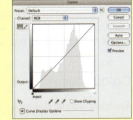

Left: The original photograph was overexposed with bleached-out highlights.
Right: Tonal levels have been restored using Photoshop.

Left: The figures in the foreground are underexposed.
Right: Photoshop's Curves adjustment has been used to lighten the figures.

225

Photo-editing: colour adjustment

Colour control and manipulation

Photographs may have an overall colour bias which may be caused by weather conditions, the amount of sunlight or by other coloured objects and elements in the environment around the subject. As a result, the image can have a colour cast that does not suit the object of the picture, the message of an article or advertisement, or can contain a colour clash that might distract the viewer. Rather than retaking the photograph, colours can be amended using Photoshop or a similar image-editing program to adjust the colour balance, and, consequently, alter how viewers interpret the image.

Applying Photo Filters

Above: This photograph was taken on an overcast day; the effect of light from the grey clouds bouncing off the water and the pale misty surroundings have created a very cool image that makes the buildings look distant and dull.

Right: Applying Photoshop's Warming Filter emphasises red and yellow tones while blocking out most of the blues and greens. The result is a visually warmer image that makes the scene more attractive and appealing.

The Photoshop Photo Filters window provides access to a range of preset filters that can correct or change the colour cast of an image.

Colour balance, vibrance and saturation

Applying Colour Balance

Photoshop's Colour Balance window sliders can be used, individually or in tandem, to add or subtract the amount of each colour in an entire image, or just for shadows, mid tones or highlights. The window allows you to 'fine-tune' the colour of an image to produce a specific effect, such as a golden glow or sepia tint.

Applying Vibrance

The intensity of an image can be adjusted by altering the amount of vibrancy and the degree of saturation of its colours. In the image on the left, the vibrance and saturation levels have been increased to give the colours more brilliance and boost the impact of the image.

TIP Some colour adjustments only work with RGB images.

Photo-editing: colour adjustment

Colour channels

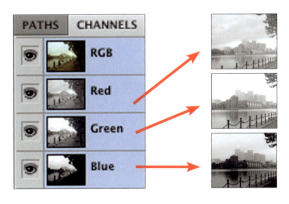

Red colour channel

Red and green colour channels viewed together

Green and blue colour channels viewed together

Red, green and blue colour channels combined

Viewing an image split into individual channels enables accurate evaluation of the density of each colour.

All digital images are made up of colour channels that store the pixel information of each individual colour, and it is the amount of colour information in each channel that builds the detail and intensity of the whole image. Channels can be viewed and edited using Photoshop's Channels window.

RGB images consist of three channels and CMYK of four. Image channels can be edited individually by clicking on a channel and selecting a colour adjustment function such as Levels or Curves that controls brightness and contrast.

Advanced image editing – working in Camera Raw

Most professional cameras can take photographs in Camera Raw file format, an uncompressed mode that allows the metadata of an image (exposure, colour temperature, hues and tones) to be edited in great detail. Camera Raw works with first-level data capture and, when used in conjunction with photo-editing software, makes it possible to fundamentally alter or rescue an image.

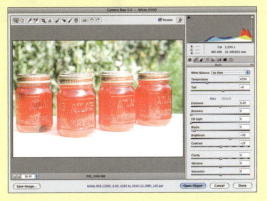

The original photograph was overexposed with the colours and tones bleached out by the bright sunlight.

The Camera Raw recovery sliders have been used to restore the image by recapturing lost data.

Image handling

Image management and archiving

Working with media imagery requires a well-organised approach because producing a title can involve sourcing and commissioning a large number of images to be used in print, online and for mobile and other devices. You, or your company, needs to have put in place clear, media-specific image and/or asset handling work practices. There are several proprietary media management and archiving computer programs available, or a systems specialist can be commissioned to design a customised web- or server-based folder and filing system.

Media production requires careful process control and file tracking to ensure that the image and target media match. The same picture may be prepared for more than one platform and it is advisable to keep a detailed record of the specific image production criteria for the various media. Once the requirements have been established, image preparation time can be speeded up by using Photoshop and other image-editing programs to record sets of actions for repeated tasks, such as setting the resolution, colour mode and file format of pictures for use in print or online.

Building content

- Develop a list of image sources and suppliers.
- Plan ahead: be aware of media specifications before obtaining images.
- Ensure that image suppliers are well briefed and continue to liaise with them during production.
- Obtain a choice of imagery for each subject.
- Be platform agnostic and take a flexible approach to what can be used to illustrate a subject or story.

Picture editing

- Check and double check that all images are suitable and of sufficient quality for the target media and/or for cross-media use.
- Use a photographic media management program such as Adobe Bridge to view several images at once.
- Establish a standard set of image adjustments and filters such as Brightness/Contrast and Unsharp Mask for each medium.

Placing images

- Form your own judgement: make sure you are happy with the images before commencing page make-up and be prepared to request alternative pictures if necessary.
- Consider the images individually and as page elements: tones, colours and shapes should balance.
- Maintain the narrative: images should support the written information as well as entertain and decorate.

Archiving

- Store separate sets of both original and edited image files.
- Make sure all file tags are subject specific and searchable.
- Use Photoshop's File Info to store the caption, copyright and other relevant data and/or archive a text document.
- Keep two sets of backups on different forms of external media and store them in separate places.

http://tv.adobe.com/watch/learn-photoshop-cs5/auto-mating-tasks-with-actions/

Print imaging round-up

- Print images should be high resolution (300dpi), in CMYK and scaled or cropped to match the final target reproduction size.

- All images placed in page make-up programs are initially shown at the same width and height as the original image file (expressed as W 100 per cent × H 100 per cent percentage enlargement, usually referred to as same size (S/S)).

- Page make-up programs are normally set to a screen display performance that uses a low-resolution version of the original image file as a position guide. This is the reason why page make-up pictures 'drift' and look poor in relation to the Photoshop version. While it is possible to increase the display performance, viewing images at a higher resolution may slow down the program.

- Page make-up programs do not embed image files. The software creates a link to the original file.

Print pages may contain a range of picture sizes and shapes. All images must be saved in CMYK and of good enough quality at high resolution to allow for enlargement to the required size.

- Page make-up programs represent enlargement or reduction by increasing or reducing the size of the pixels in the low-resolution version of the image. As the pixel size increases, the image quality and clarity will degrade, making it difficult to 'read' the image.

- It is important to note that enlarging an image in Quark or InDesign does not affect the size or resolution of the image digital file. This can only be done in Photoshop or another image editing program.

Online imaging round-up

- Images for the Web should be composed or chosen with the target dimension and size in mind. Most picture holders are square or shallow rectangles, so landscape format is normally more suitable than portrait, although the shape of images on feature pages and in blogs may use a more vertical rectangle.

- Smaller picture boxes require simpler image compositions.

- Using close-ups or details from a large image can be very effective, particularly for thumbnails.

- Digital photos for use online should be saved as JPEGs or PNGs at 72ppi and should be resized to an average pixel dimension that matches or is a little bigger than the website's largest possible picture usage.

- Images for a website must be cropped, sized and optimised to match fixed picture holder sizes before they are used in CMS or blog templates.

- Most websites and CMSs store images in a database and it is important to tag all pictures so they are searchable and retrievable.

- Photoshop's 'Save for Web and Devices' facility can be used to reduce an image file's memory size, which speeds up the download time, but care should be taken to ensure the image quality does not degrade.

Web pages often use imagery from a variety of sources. All image files have to be RGB and the resolution and size must be correctly formatted for the page before they are uploaded.

Picture composition

All pictures have an intrinsic shape and structure. This can be either formal, as in the case of a posed studio fashion shoot, or informal – a crowd or candid street scene. If you are briefing a photographer for a front cover shoot for a magazine you may want to ask them to take images with a particular direction, angle or tilt, as well as where to allow space for the logo and other cover typography. When researching news pictures or looking through supplied images, you should look for informal patterns and shapes or lines that will interact with the other page elements. These help lead the eye around the objects within the image and either contrast or balance it with other pictures on the page.

Triangulation and pictorial direction

Images have most impact when they have a strong, underlying geometric form that holds the image and its subjects together. Two figures standing side by side, even if symmetrical, can have the effect of diffusing the viewer's attention because they lack a focal point. To indicate which figure takes priority, it is better to use an underlying shape to create visual connections and direct attention, for example a strong triangular 'A' shape to unify a group. Political leaders and movie stars who are experienced with photo calls will stand close to each other before shaking hands or interacting. In a photograph or video, this has the effect of creating a sense of purpose and can give the initiator of the handshake a dominant presence.

Background patterns and architectural features can also be used to give a still or moving image 'shape'. A skyscraper's receding verticals, or internal design features such as the central curves of balconies in the Guggenheim Museum (see page 203), can be used to add impact to business portraits or location shots. There are other techniques that can be used to direct the viewer's eye to a designated point on an image. These include perspective, for example road lines disappearing to the horizon or looking along a tree-lined street, **pictorial direction**, which can be achieved by tracking a racing car to keep it in focus while allowing the background to be blurred by camera movement, and graphic elements, such as looking for the patterns and shapes created by rows of marching soldiers.

Foreground, mid ground and background

Images occupy three planes – the foreground, mid ground and background. Any or all these can be in or out of focus, and the main point of visual contact – the focal point – can be on any one of these planes. The visual depth of an image affects the involvement of the viewer. If the focal point is in the foreground, the subject is more prominent and the viewer gains a greater sense of immediacy, while if it is in the background the viewer may feel drawn into the image.

Images can be viewed as a sequence of these planes: the **foreground** (close to the camera), the **mid ground** (the area within the picture frame a viewer feels most connected to) and the **background** (the distance elements that are normally filtered out by the conscious mind as being of little or no importance). A photographer can use these planes to describe the relationship

In this image, the wind turbines are distant from the viewer and they appear to blend into the environment.

This image portrays a neutral view as it gives equal emphasis to both the wind turbines and their surroundings.

This image shows the blades dominating the sky and landscape and emphasises the intrusive nature of wind turbines.

The way in which an image is composed should reinforce the intended message.

Source: Sean Power

Above: The close-up creates a strong graphic image that focuses attention on the key issues and conveys the photographer's point of view.

Far left: The mid-range view of the staged pat-down provides a feel for the political intent of the protest.

Left: The long-shot overview combines the size of the event with its famous public location.

between themselves, the viewer, the subject of an image and their position in relation to the background. A shot that emphasises the foreground, or moving the camera in for a close-up, brings the subject into intimate proximity with the viewer. Bringing the mid ground in to focus places the viewer and the subject of the image on an equal and participatory level. The mid-ground shot can direct attention on to a particular part of the image while still being in control of the foreground and background. Framing that directs most attention to the background can create a sense of distance from the subject that isolates the viewer and turns them into an observer, so that they lose any sense of personal contact. Or it can hint at possibilities over the horizon.

I'm a photographer, not a terrorist!

More than 2,000 photographers attended the 'I'm a photographer, not a terrorist' protest in Trafalgar Square, London, in January 2010. The mass rally was held to draw attention to the police employing the 'stop and search' Section 44 of the Terrorism Act (2000) to prevent photographers from taking pictures in public places, something that most people consider to be a human right. Media organisations, and those working for them, had raised concerns with the Home Office about how counter terrorism legislation was being applied after a number of photographers were stopped and questioned by the police.

'If your pictures aren't good enough,
you aren't close enough.'

Robert Capa

Close-up or long view

It is a truism that the better the camera, the higher the quality of the image it will take, but even with the most sophisticated of modern cameras it is still down to the photographer's 'eye' to interpret and capture the best images. There are a number of techniques that can be used to control the level of importance that the viewer will assign to any or each part of an image. These include which areas and how much of a picture are in focus and how they are lit.

Focus

It is a commonly held view that photographs should be in pin-sharp focus. This is based upon preconceived ideas about what makes a good photographer and how a camera should be used. But images with a softer focus or deliberate camera movement can be used as creatively as hard focus pictures and can add impact to a page. However, it can be difficult to argue the case for using soft focus pictures if readers' or visitors' expectations of image quality contradict the editorial ethos. As a result, care has to be taken when selecting images that are out of focus or blurred, and they should only be used where the effect will bring a definite benefit to the page, or there is another good communication reason to do so. 'Arty', out-of-focus or blurred images can be seen as the result of poor printing as well as bad or pretentious photography or videography.

There are occasions when focus quality is not relevant. Mobile phone camera shots or films can have a distinct edginess about them that can capture the nature of the moment. The G20 riots in London in 2009 generated a whole range of UGC videos and photographs that were quickly seized upon by the mainstream media as well as by individuals and groups with political agendas. The images published on the Web varied enormously in quality but their purpose was to provide evidence and to authenticate claims, rather than achieve technical perfection.

Capa and the D-Day landings

Robert Capa took a series of seminal, out-of-focus images of the D-Day landings in Normandy in 1944. The blurred photographs were used by all the news media as they captured the danger and tension of the moment. Capa was quoted as saying he experienced 'a new kind of fear, shaking my body from toe to hair, and twisting my face', while taking the photos, which may be reflected in the final images.

Depth of field

Depth of field is a technique where the sharp focus is concentrated in part of an image, for example a portrait shot focused on the face with the background out of focus. Alternatively, shifting the focus off the foreground and on to elements in the background can help create a sense of involvement with a topic, for example the crowd at a music festival. The technique is based on either using a wide **aperture** (largest hole in the shutter), known as **f-stops** on the lens, which reduces the amount of the picture in focus, or using a small aperture (smallest hole in the shutter), which gives a deeper range of image focus (depth of field).

Above: Looking past the out-of-focus foreground figure draws the eye to the main subject.

Left: Focusing on a cake in the top left of the composition softens the picture and leads the eye over the foreground.

Controlling the depth of field can throw emphasis on to a specific element of a photograph.

Point of interest – centre of focus

A good photograph has a 'point of interest' – an area of the image that encapsulates and communicates an editorial statement. A clenched fist on the edge of a table may demonstrate the frustration of the subject, while a twinkle in the eye implies a certain mischievous streak in the character of the speaker. A good video is one that frames the action so that the viewer's focus remains on the subject, by making sure that the background or other activity within a frame does not distract the viewer. The other factor that can make or break a video is timing, and this has to be tightly controlled in order to tell a succinct but complete story.

There is no true image

Most images are 'editorialised' – cropped and positioned on a page to amplify a point of view in support of an article. Today, a photographer's and film-maker's role has changed from **data capture** – composing, filming and taking pictures – to working on data management – editing and manipulating the digital material. The zoom lenses on modern cameras allow photographers and film-makers to frame (crop) the image when taking a photo, which can be further editorialised through digital manipulation in Photoshop or video-editing software.

While there has been a shift in photographic practice (which now includes videography), and although imaging software has become cheaper and more widely available, it still takes a trained eye to recognise the most meaningful part of the image to use within a given space. Images should be carefully analysed to identify those elements that support the story – a second between two shots of the same subject can present images with totally different meanings. A slight movement of the subject's lips or eyebrows can communicate a totally different message from that of the written content, and photographers may have to take many frames of a politician delivering a speech to get one acceptable image that can be used appropriately to support a journalist's story. It is common practice for fashion and advertising photographers to take hundreds of shots in order to get the one 'perfect' image, which is then further enhanced using photo-editing software.

Media players and audio files

Websites employ a variety of media and there are a number of books and websites that will help you handle and upload video and audio files (see Contacts and resources, page 347). Where you are required to work with multimedia, it is likely you will be supplied with edited material that is ready to be uploaded to the Web via the CMS. Website templates may either have fixed video and audio windows, or allow for a choice of position for a feature page. Some media companies host all of their own videos, while others rely on using links to content on other websites or services.

Video and audio files require **media players** – additional software plug-ins for web browsers that enable the digital files to be viewed or heard. Media players process the audio and/or visual content downloaded from the Web and can add program-specific features to the browser, such as Flash animation. Most browsers include media players, but it is a good idea, for those people that have older computers or slow Internet connections, to offer a hot link from a multimedia website to a mirrored HTML version – the same website without rich media such as animation or video.

Audio files are edited, compressed and saved as wav, wma or mp3/mp4 files. The files can be heard immediately through a streaming media player or downloaded as a podcast for listening at a later date. An audio player plug-in begins to play the file as soon as a sufficient amount of data has downloaded, while the rest of the data continues to download. Advances in file compression and telecoms bandwidths have reduced the amount of time **buffering** (downloading manageable-sized chunks of data) takes. The BBC iPlayer is almost instantaneous, with live program streaming running only seconds behind the broadcast reception.

Warning There is always a temptation to use the very latest video editing and interactivity, but care should be taken when introducing new features, as visitors may not have or be able to run the latest media players.

Thumbnails and stills from video

Videos require a strong thumbnail still image to appeal to the audience and induce it to play the film. Video-editing programs normally offer an auto thumbnail function, but it is a good idea to choose your own still as this allows you to make a judgement on which frame best reflects the content. Images can be captured from video content by either downloading video or HD video files, and from online browsers. A video can be paused so that either a screenshot or image grab program can be used to extract a single frame. Screenshots for web pages can be processed and saved at the same size as the screen grab. However, if still frames are required for print, the video files should be downloaded before the frame is selected and resaved as an image file. The resulting 72ppi image will need to be resampled, which will reduce its dimensions to 33–25% of the original video size in order to achieve a 300dpi resolution image (see *How to work with pictures*, page 222).

WARNING Although a print resolution version of a video frame can be created, the quality and colour information may not be sufficient for print media reproduction.

Video screen capture

Videos should be viewed several times to find the frame that best captures the subject and mood of the film. In this example, the frame chosen appeared three-quarters of the way through the movie.

The auto capture selection for this movie was not suitable as the first frame did not give a clear view of the subject of the movie.

While some frames might produce interesting images, you need to take care that an unusual angle does not convey the wrong message about the content

TIPS

- Screen captures are subject to copyright restrictions as with all other media formats and permission should be granted by the author before use.

- It is best to make thumbnails and stills from the original video using film-editing or specialised thumbnail programs.

- If you create a screen capture using a generic video player, you need to ensure the image on the monitor is large enough to be adapted for the target media.

- It is better to use portraits or close-up details than a general view.

- If you do use a picture of a face, make sure the person's eyes are open and their mouth is not gaping in an unattractive manner.

- Make sure the image is at the required size and shape, and that the subject is well positioned in the frame by applying the Rule of Thirds or Golden Section to the composition.

- You should consider how the thumbnail image will work with the rest of the content on the page; for example, whether the colour and tone of the picture will balance against the type and other page elements.

- Special effects can be used to indicate the image has been captured from TV or CCTV.

The media industry employs both still and moving images and there is a wide range of pictorial material available, from hand-drawn illustrations to interactive animation. Whatever method of visualisation is chosen, it should represent the best possible way of conveying the most relevant information and enhance the communication of the subject. Images have to meet the technical requirements for whichever platform they are to be used on and meet the individual specifications for each media product. The inclusion of well-considered and appropriate visual content can improve most titles.

- All imagery must be chosen to match the editorial stance of the title and must follow a specific visual house style.

- Images must be suitable for the media they are to be used in, and the picture content should be considered before selecting visual material.

- Every image has a semiotic value and should be analysed to make sure it cannot be misinterpreted. Imagery is subject to cultural weighting that may be changed by the context in which the pictures are viewed.

- Photojournalism is a powerful communications tool used by the news media, governments and other organisations.

- Image manipulation is a truism, as moving and still imagery are carefully framed and editorially directed, and may actually be staged or enacted with a consciousness of the presence of cameras.

- Graphics can make 'dry' information more acceptable for the audience of generalist publications and can enliven specialist magazines and websites.

- A good photograph has a 'point of interest' – an area of the image that encapsulates and communicates an editorial statement.

- A well-directed video has tightly composed framing that tells a fluid story and maintains focus and attention on the subject.

- Many photographers use both still images and video cameras, and journalists are often expected to film a news package or feature segment, and to edit and record audio reports.

- Photographs should be selected with the reproduction size in mind, and the base size (width and height) and resolution (pixel dimension) should be matched to the reproduction size for both print and online.

- Resizing an image changes the dimensions without affecting the pixels. Cropping isolates one area of an image so the rest can be deleted.

- Web images must be in RGB (Red, Green, Blue) colour mode or web safe hexidecimal colours at 72ppi and sized to the exact size (XX pixels high by XX pixels wide) that the image is to appear on the website.

- Images for print must be in CMYK (Cyan, Magenta, Yellow and Black) mode, at high or medium resolution – depending on the nature of the substrate – and sized to the exact dimensions (XX height by XX width) that the image is to appear on the page

Activities and development

These questions and action points are intended to increase your knowledge and help you study still and moving images. Visit the *Design for Media* website for more fact and action sheets, sample templates, type schemes and colour palettes at **www.pearsoned.com/hand**

Questions

Question 1

Choose a current news story and follow it in a newspaper and on its related website. Examine the photography used to illustrate the story or news item:

(a) Are any of the same photographic images used in both media? If they are, does the size and crop of the images vary?

(b) Do the photographs have the same impact in print and online? If not, describe why this might be.

(c) If a different set of pictures has been chosen for print and online, outline the possible editorial and production reasons behind the alternative selection.

Question 2

Select a fashion, celebrity or sports magazine or website. Examine the editorial and advertising images and try to determine whether they have been photo manipulated (look for smoothed-out, airbrushed skin without blemishes or wrinkles, unnaturally long, slim necks and limbs, heightened colours and lighting effects). Consider the semiotic message of these changes and how they might influence the readers' or viewers' reactions to the images. Are there any wider social implications that arise from the use of manipulated imagery?

Question 3

(a) What resolution, colour modes and file types would you use to prepare an image for the Web or devices?

(b) What resolution, colour modes and file types would you use to prepare an image for a printed publication?

Question 4

(a) You are working on a mass market women's title that has a print issue, website and digital edition, and you have been asked to find illustrations for a feature on violent crimes against women. What type and style of imagery would be best suited for such a sensitive subject?

(b) You are working on a building industry title that has a print issue, website and digital edition, and need to find images for an article on safety at work, but you have been asked to avoid the obvious clichés. What type of imagery and pictorial subjects would you choose?

Action points

Action point 1

Study the composition of a selection of images from a range of media and note the composition of the subject:

(a) Has the main subject been centred in the frame both horizontally and vertically (i.e. equal space all around), positioned more to one side, and/or moved into the top or bottom half of the frame?

(b) Is the main subject in the foreground, mid ground or background?

(c) Is the subject in sharp focus or in a softer view?

(d) Is the subject in an environment that has been tightly cropped, or removed from the background?

Action point 2

Carry out a Google image search. Note the pixel dimensions and file memory size (shown underneath the picture). View the image at full size to see the dimensions, clarity and colour depth of the picture. Open a new search window and, using the same subject, select the advanced image search. Enter 'large' in the file size field, jpg for the file type, and select full colour from the drop-down menu in the colour field. Choose an image and note the pixel dimensions and file memory size. View the image at full size and compare the larger picture's specifications and image quality with the original search.

236

8 CONTENT VISUALISATION AND STRUCTURE (3): COLOUR

This chapter discusses:

- Colour in culture and society
- Colour in information design
- The colour industry and colour branding
- The theory and science of colour
- Colour technology and calibration
- Web colour
- Red, green, blue (RGB)
- The print four-colour process (CMYK)
- Choosing and specifying a colour

This chapter looks at colour as a cultural and commercial phenomenon. It describes colour theory and the colour industry and examines how colour perception can be used to create an emotional impact as well as to indicate meaning. The chapter will provide you with useful information about colour technology and guidance on how it is applied for print and online.

'Man needs colour to live; it's as necessary an element as fire and water.'
Ferdinand Léger, artist

'For most people, much of colour "knowledge" is based on instinctive responses, cultural conditioning and those aspects of colour that we seem to absorb without much conscious thought.'

Leanne Eiseman, executive director,
Pantone Color Institute

Colour in culture and society

Colour is both the physiological experience of light and a cultural construct. When selecting colour for media products, you need to consider the effect your choices will have on your audience. People interpret colour based on their experiences and personal preferences. The skill in choosing colours for a specific media product is to match the audience's expectation to the nature of the content. Colour can direct or alter the perception of words and images on a page and of publications and websites. It can be used to provoke a strong emotional response or to evoke a sense of calm. Colour can help an audience identify with a particular brand or lifestyle. In the media, colour is a powerful visual tool that can be used for styling, trend setting and decoration.

Colour interpretation is subjective and may change from one culture to another, a fact that needs to be considered when designing a publication for an international audience. Civilisations throughout history have used colour for communication and identification, and it has a major role in establishing modes of taste and fashion. The historic, cultural, religious and geopolitical symbolic uses of colour include national flags, team colours and the Red Cross/Crescent symbol. How a culture reacts to colour at any one time reflects its current economic status and national mood.

Preferences for colour start in babyhood and will change from childhood to adulthood as people build life experiences and as the physical ability to perceive colour develops and then declines. There have been a number of studies that have looked at whether there are biological factors to colour choice, and it is has been discovered that there are differences in men's and women's colour vision. Babies and small children are thought to respond more to bright colours than pastels, but this may be due to an underdeveloped ability to see lighter hues. American studies have claimed that adult men prefer yellow and women blue, but any research into colour preferences may be affected by a number of factors. These may include ethnicity, geographic location, social and religious background, family taste, an individual's state of health and the fashions of the time.

There has been extensive research into the medical and psychological effects of colour. The association of colour with emotions or feelings of illness or well-being is grounded in the natural sciences. It is well known that the human body is highly sensitive to light and colour, and exploiting this physiological phenomenon offers access to a very potent form of communication.

Social change and colour fashions

Colours are strongly identified with time and place. Each decade of the twentieth century is associated with specific colours, and these can be linked to the

Colour timeline

1950s	1960s	1970s	1980s	1990s	2000s
Brown and tan	Primary colours	Brown, orange	Silver and red	Neutrals	Flip-flop and heat-
Pastel shades	Black and white	and white	Pink and grey	Blue greens	sensitive colours
Bright colours	Psychedelic	Deep purples	Strong colours	Multicolours	Green, brown
Jazzy patterns	Eastern influence	Pinks and greens	Black and white	Candy colours	Muted colours
Postwar austerity	Swinging sixties	Deep recession	Economic boom	Slump to recovery	Boom to bust
Economic revival	Space age	Revivals 1950s	Yuppies	Rave culture	New Labour
Dior New Look	Pop music	and art deco –	BMWs	House and Brit	Environmentalism
Late 1950s' boom	Quant/Corrèges	Biba	Shoulder pads	pop	Green activism
Jazz/R&B	Hippies,	Club 54 Halston	Giorgio Armani	Princess Diana	Stella McCartney
Rock and roll	socio-sexual	Glam rock	Duran Duran	Modernist –	Rap – bling
	revolution	Punks and goths	Madchester	minimalist revival	

events of the period. In the 1940s, the devastating effects of the Second World War led to shortages, food rationing and austerity, and the colours of that era are predominantly browns and beige. By the late 1950s, the world's economies had recovered and the popular colours were pastels and bright hues, reflecting the 'never had it so good' claim of British prime minister Harold Macmillan (1957–1963). The British social revival was a reflection of a booming economy in the USA. The resurgence in industrial output and growth in consumer confidence following the Second World War led to high employment and introduced the notion of the American dream of a suburban utopia. The newly affluent workers bought mass-produced goods and automobiles in colours that reflected the optimism of the era – pastel home and electrical goods, brightly coloured clothing and the iconic pink Cadillac.

By the 1960s, the postwar boom was running out of steam and, as the decade progressed, there was increasing social and political unrest. The Cold War and the American wars in the Far East undermined consumer confidence. There was a growing unhappiness with the political establishment, and a counter culture developed, where 'psychedelic' rainbow shades became the emblem of the anti-establishment hippie movement. The 1960s' fashion used bright, strong artificial shades influenced by modernism and the technology and space race, and the development of new synthetic fabrics.

The 1970s were an era of international political crises, terrorism, industrial strife and economic recession. The mood changed from the energy of the 1960s to a more sombre, restrained view of life. Favoured colours were brown, purple and orange, leading on to punk black.

In the 1980s, the economy recovered and lifestyle became the catchword. Young, urban professionals – yuppies – wanted to show off their success and money, and did so through their purchasing power. Their tastes were caricatured in the film *Wall Street*, where they were portrayed as liking flashy metallic or black cars and wearing red-framed glasses and braces. Another 1980s' trend was the new romantic style that featured flamboyant colours both for clothes and make-up.

The early 1990s saw yet another economic downturn and the rise of indie grunge culture, with clothes

The meaning of colour

Colour has emotional resonance, and associative memory is often evoked by colour. Even within one culture in the same time period, colour interpretation changes according to context; for example, while a red light may indicate danger, a red heart means love, red roses romance and red lipstick or clothes may suggest passion.

and media designs in browns, neutrals and teal green. The end of the decade saw incomes rise and a more positive national mood, with the result that colours brightened with the returning optimism. Environmental issues began to be a mainstream concern, and there was an increasing use of green and natural fabrics and colours.

The first decade of the twenty-first century saw a return to economic growth and high consumer spending, only to hit the familiar bust that follows a boom. Despite a worldwide banking crisis, colours remained bright, and green and blue continued to be popular choices as companies wished to project the image of being environmentally aware. The development of new ranges of coloured plastics and the adoption of vibrant screen-influenced colours encouraged the use of intense, vivid colours. During the same period, manufacturers and the media became more sophisticated in the way they used colour as a marketing tool to motivate continued consumer spending.

Colour FX

Advances in colour pigment technology have brought in new effects such as flip-flop colours that change from turquoise to blue to violet, and red to copper to gold, depending on the angle from which they are viewed. Special effect inks have been developed that can replicate metallic and pearlescent finishes, and there are heat-sensitive inks that remain invisible until exposed to a heat source such as the sun, or change colour in reaction to the wearer's and/or the ambient temperature, or when touched.

Colour in information design

Colour in the media can command attention, signal importance by indicating the hierarchy of information and direct eye movement to follow the flow of information. Because colour is so culturally and emotionally weighted, it can substantially alter the way in which a reader or visitor reacts to and interprets a print publication, website, the editorial content and advertising. The way in which people respond to colour is employed in publishing media to attract an audience and market their products. If you become involved with the development of an online or print title, you will have not only to select a palette of hues intended to appeal to the target audience and advertising market sector, but also choose colours that can be used to editorialise the content. This can mean selecting colours that indicate the importance of an item, such as using a bright red for the main headline (find sample palettes for media on the website).

Most media companies develop palettes of harmonious colours as an aspect of a title's branding that will be used throughout a magazine and website (see *How to work with colour*, page 253). Colour is used for signposting and to reflect the subject and establish continuity in the design of a title. For example, using the same tab colour for all the pages in a section will help the reader or visitor identify and follow a subject.

Colours selected for typography should enhance readability and connect the written content to the imagery (see page 171). Colour can give impact to headlines without the need to use large letters and can also be employed to place emphasis on particular areas or items in the text. This can be useful for a page that contains a large amount of complex information. Boxes with tint backgrounds and coloured lines can help to compartmentalise the page and ensure the content remains readable. Colour can also give depth to a page as it can create the illusion of a third dimension. This is because reds and oranges appear to advance out of the page, while blues and greens remain static or seem to recede. Mid greys and neutral hues stay within the eye's focus on the page plane, which can be used to hold the gaze in one place.

The colour industry and colour branding

Colour is a global industry that is regulated by organisations such as the Commission Internationale de l'Eclairage (CIE: www.cie.co.at/index_ie.html), the international authority on light, colour and **colour spaces**. There are companies that trade in colour in the form of dyes, paints and inks, with a sub-industry of specialist colour consultants advising on trends and colour selection. Design agencies may commission consultants to work with their clients on selecting corporate colours, and to offer advice on how to match the colours to the target market. Colour consultancies and designers involved in developing brand colours will consider the psychological aspects and subliminal meaning of each colour or combination, and assess how well they might stand the test of time.

There are also companies which specialise in 'colour futures'. They carry out research into consumer behaviour and identify key cultural indicators and also keep track of the latest technical developments in pigment and ink manufacture. They combine this information with other emerging trends to forecast the colours most likely to be fashionable up to two years in advance of the retail season. Designers and manufacturers employ these reports to develop products, for example clothing and accessories. Colour forecast companies work with specialists from chemical industries, manufacturing companies, retail and the media to help them pre-plan the colour for a wide range of products and materials. This is particularly important in industries such as fashion where companies often invest considerable sums developing new clothing ranges, and in the automotive industry where colours for cars are selected several years in advance of production.

Link to web – colour trends/forecasting sites:
www.pantone.com
www.eisemancolorblog.com
www.internationalcolourauthority.org/
www.colormarketing.org/
www.colourlovers.com/
www.globalcolor.co.uk/home.php
www.view-publications.com/content.html
www.colorassociation.com/

'There are not more than five primary colours (blue, yellow, red, white and black), yet in combination they produce more hues than can ever be seen.'

Sun Tzu Wu, general and philosopher

Colour matching systems

How colour is described can be subjective and individual, and we can struggle to convey a precise shade or colour. English, like many other languages, only has words for the main colours with descriptive qualifiers such as apple green or hot pink used to describe **tones and tints** for all **hues**. While such terms as sapphire blue or summer rose can be very expressive and beautiful, they are open to wide interpretation. This makes it very important that there is a universally understood method of communicating and specifying the exact colours to be used.

Most media companies work with external partners and other businesses, and colour information may need to be passed on to other companies, for example the brand colours for editorial, advertising, events and exhibition design.

In the early twentieth century, Albert Munsell, an American professor, invented a system of identifying a range of colours using a numeric code. This method of naming has been adopted and adapted by companies such as Pantone (www.pantone.com) and Focoltone (www.kikuze.com/focoltone/index.html). These companies produce colour guides, colour matching charts and calibration devices that can be used for media, fashion, home and product design. The media and related industries use colour matching systems to identify the colours specified for a product or title, and to communicate information on how the colour is to be used.

Jargon buster The natural spectrum is a colour space, as is **RGB** and **CMYK**. See *How to work with colour*, page 246.

The colour references are available from the Colour Matching System companies' websites and also printed in books showing chips of the colours with the corresponding CMYK, RGB and HTML values. Companies and organisations use Colour Matching Systems to specify their brand colours, and to make certain that the colour of their logos and other corporate material is applied consistently in print and online and for any other marketing material. For the process to work, all the parties involved must use the same Colour Matching System reference for viewing, selecting and specifying.

There are some differences between the Colour Matching Systems. Pantone has a wide variety of colours including pastels, metallic and fluorescent ranges, while Focoltone Colour Matching System has a smaller range but features deeper and more subtle colours. The colour palette for a print publication is entered in and selected from the page make-up program's Colour or Swatches window. Spot colours may be labelled using their original Pantone or Focoltone codes, or may be renamed with customised publication names such as Glamour purple or Closer pink, together with their colour matching reference. See *How to work with colour*, page 256.

Colour identification

The Colour Matching Systems work by assigning a set of numbers and letters, and a trade name, to a colour, for example Pantone Orange 021C or Focoltone 1161, a rich vibrant orange, or Pantone 715C or Focoltone 3389, a warmer, more subtle shade of orange. This allows designers in all media, and especially those involved in the production process, to communicate clearly about colour.

Computer screen colour calibration

Designers who are preparing material for print should not rely solely on their screens for a colour match, as even a calibrated monitor may not show an accurate representation of the colour. There are colour spectrometer readers available that calibrate monitors to ensure colour accuracy throughout a production cycle, although the fundamental technological differences make it impossible to eliminate all variation (see *How to work with colour*, page 247).

Source: Pantone LLC

Pantone's colour spectrometer reads colour and gives the closest Pantone/RGB/hexadecimal and CMYK mix.

Brand colours

Colour can be used to describe a product generically, such as brown for a chocolate bar wrapper, or identify an individual brand such as Cadbury's Dairy Milk that comes in a purple wrapper. This guides a customer to purchase an item by category or brand. Media products can also be identified by generic colour: for example, tabloid newspapers are also called redtops as most of them have red logos. Consumer magazines are marketed on their name and reputation, and most prefer to have picture-led front covers with logo colours chosen for each issue to complement the images, while using brand colours on the inside pages. Websites, newspapers and print business titles normally keep to a single brand colour for their logo or masthead. The logo colour is not usually included in a title's colour palette as this may dilute the brand identity, where colour is also used for letterheads and advertising, promotions and marketing material.

Media companies generally set up individual colour palettes for each print publication and may have a range of palettes for each title's sections or topics, while websites have at least one key colour combined with a palette that is used for tabs, lines, boxes and backgrounds. Many media companies recognise the value of a title's brand colour and will apply it across all their platforms. Brand colour is particularly important online, as visitors react extremely quickly to their first glimpse of a site, and colour can help to identify a brand's website at a glance (see page 240).

The companies and organisations that publish house magazines or newsletters employ corporate colours to maintain brand communication and visual consistency. Contact publishers design titles that employ their client's well-known brand colours, as customers will be familiar with these, and this can help identify the publication or website to the core brand. Leading supermarkets' *Waitrose Magazine* and *Sainsbury's Magazine* follow the consumer model of matching their logo to the image or other typography on the cover, while the *National Trust Magazine* and newsletter logo is always in the National Trust's brand colour.

While graphic and type styling may be updated, the company colour usually remains the same. Brand colours can be replaced, but normally this is done slowly over an extended period of time, as customers and audiences can be resistant to sudden change. 'Evolution not revolution' is a mantra within the media, indicating that alterations should be made gradually and slowly. Colour may be so strongly identified with one item that companies may struggle to sell their products if they do not use accepted market colour combinations. Red and white have become so strongly associated with cola that other brands, such as Virgin Cola, have used the same colour scheme. *The Economist* has invested heavily in marketing over a number of years using its red brand colour, and any change of colour might wipe out the recognition achieved through its advertising campaigns.

TIP Examples of corporate identity manuals may be found on the websites of major brands and organisations.

'To compose in colour means to juxtapose two or more colours in such a way that they jointly produce a distinct and distinctive expression.'

Joseph Itten, artist and educator

The theory and science of colour

Colour is not an absolute. Colour vision is a physical and biological phenomenon triggered by the human nervous system reacting to light falling on the eye – we detect objects through light. A person looking at a colour in a print publication is seeing waves of light reflected from the paper. If the person is looking at a website on-screen, the colour is being generated by projected light waves. The varying frequencies or wavelengths of light are interpreted as different colours, and the quality and intensity of colour appear to change depending on whether it is projected or reflected. There are other factors that affect colour perception, such as the position of the viewed object and the visual capacity of the individual, as well as the location of the observer and the prevailing atmospheric conditions.

Light has no meaning until the brain has processed it, but the brain and eye are not able to identify all colours in every situation and light conditions with absolute certainty. Our perception of colour is based on what we extrapolate from the immediate sensation of light, combined with previous knowledge of why that sensation might have occurred. Colour interpretation is affected by accepted associations – the sky is blue – and the knowledge that an individual acquires of the world: if the sky looks grey, expect rain and carry an umbrella.

Sir Isaac Newton (1643–1727) was one of the first scientists to carry out experiments into the nature of light, and from his observations using a triangular prism he developed a number of theories concerning the nature of light and colour. In his book *Optiks* (1704), he observed that the eye sees colour through three forms of light, although he did not resolve the science underlying this. It took another 200 years before the physician Thomas Young made a link between the wave theory of light and how the eye works, and realised that colour is a variable sensation. He was the first to describe correctly that colour vision is based on three colours: red, green and blue (trichromatic vision). His ideas were accepted and expanded by later scientists such as Hermann Helmholtz, who carried out detailed investigations into the science of colour, and James Clerk Maxwell, whose colour matching device and chromaticity diagram became the basis of the CIE standard. Modern electronic medical scanning techniques have confirmed that the human retina operates through light-sensitive receptors called rods and cones, and that there are three kinds of cones that absorb long-wavelength light (red), middle-wavelength light (green) or short-wavelength light (blue).

Reflective light is affected by the nature of the substrate and how it reflects light and absorbs ink. Paper comes in a variety of colours, tints, textures and surfaces, and any of these factors can change the appearance of a colour. The variation in how the ink is reflected may be small, or it can totally alter the colour. For example, a rich, dark racing green may look good on a high white, smooth finish **gloss** or **silk-coated paper**, but on a recycled, course-grained **matt**

Media technology and colour

The science of light is the basis for the colour systems used by computers, cameras and scanners. Digital colour is created using red, green and blue (RGB) light mixed in numeric proportions to generate tints (colour plus white) of 256 colours. Adding white creates the luminescence of colour on a computer screen, as hues with a higher luminance value appear brighter. Printed colour is created using cyan, magenta, yellow and black (CMYK) in numeric proportions to generate shades (colour plus black). Adding black increases the tonality and decreases the vibrancy of colour.

Colour perception alters according to the purity of the hue compared with grey (the **chroma**), and colours on-screen or in print are described in degrees of **saturation** that indicate the purity of a hue. The strength or **luminosity** of a colour can vary, as can its shade or tone, and different colour density changes the attributed meaning. A strong, luminous red invokes heat and danger; a weak, flat red looks drained and insipid. See *How to work with colour*, page 249.

uncoated paper the subtleties of the colour may be lost and the resulting shade look close to black.

Transmissive light stimulates the brain, and this attracts and holds the viewer's attention. On-screen colours are brighter and have more relative perceptual depth than coloured ink on paper. However, screen colours can be affected by the make of a monitor and its individual colour and brightness settings. The tone or colour of the paper and brightness/contrast or colour cast of a screen may also alter a colour. Bright or dark colours appear more vivid when surrounded by white paper or screen, while pale colours will look even paler and may lose impact (see page 258). The platform and operating system also vary, as colours viewed on Windows appear darker than the equivalent shade viewed on a Mac. Web colours can be set up as part of the CCS and may be dynamic and change as the user moves from page to page by clicking on links or rolling over buttons.

Some people find looking at colour on paper easier over longer periods than colour on-screen. Ink colours are flatter and softer than their digital counterparts. LG, Philips, Sony and other electronic companies have developed **epaper** and **eink** for **ereaders** that simulate the effect of ink on white paper.

Colour theory

Colour theories have been developed to describe how colour works and can be a useful tool in choosing colours. Understanding the principles of how colour is organised into complementary or contrasting groups will help you to select those colours that work well together and to use them effectively on a page.

Most media software colour selectors and the palettes developed for titles are based on the work of Johannes Itten (1888-1967), a colour theorist and teacher at the Bauhaus School (1919–1923) in Germany. Itten developed a series of **colour wheels**, sets of progressive hues that link primary to secondary to tertiary colours and provide a guide to which colours go with each other and those that clash. The wheel was based on opposed **complementary colours** – colours

Colour theory basics

- Primary colours: red, blue, yellow
- Secondary colours: green, violet, orange
- Tertiary colours: yellow–orange, orange–red, red–violet, blue–violet, blue–green, yellow–green

which when mixed together as pigments produce grey black, and when combined as light produce white (see *How to work with colour*, page 255). When complementary colours are placed against each other they cause the human eye to see a third colour between them. Itten chose yellow–violet, red–green, blue–orange, as the basis of his colour wheel or triangle. Colours that fall close to each other on a colour wheel are called **analogous colours**, and as these generally work well together they are often used for colour schemes and palettes in online and print publications.

Colour wheel basics

The colour wheel is split into **active colours** that seem to come forward when set against **passive colours**, which visually recede when placed next to active hues. Colours are also said to have **visual weight**, but the effect may vary depending on the colours combined. Cool, bright colours can have less weight than warm, pale ones. The colder and darker a colour, the more it will recede, which is why the main text typeface colour is most often black, grey or similar.

Software colour selectors

Many programs have point and click colour selectors based on the colour wheel, and there are specialist online colour wheel programs that can be used for web design. Artists' colour wheels are useful for choosing colours for print design and can be purchased from most art shops and on the Internet. They are made from a number of joined circles of card with cutout windows that can be spun around to show the colours in various combinations.

For help with choosing a colour palette visit: *http://www.colorschemedesigner.com*

HOW TO WORK WITH COLOUR

- ■ Colour modes
- ■ Colour calibration
- ■ Pixels and screens
- ■ Image colour correction
- ■ Selecting and specifying colour in Photoshop
- ■ Colour images and tints
- ■ Project mood boards
- ■ Selecting complementary colours
- ■ The colour wheel and colour combinations
- ■ Sourcing colour ideas and inspiration
- ■ Colour gamut
- ■ Selecting and specifying web colours
- ■ Colour reproduction: print

The *How to work with colour* pages give advice on using colour for both media platforms, with diagrams and illustrations that show how to create colour palettes which will evoke mood and appeal to a target audience. These pages contains instructions and information on some easy colour management techniques used for both print and online titles that will provide a good basis for the confident application and control of colour.

Colour modes

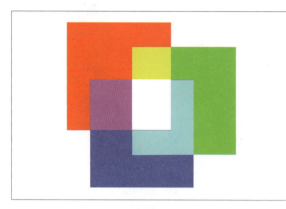

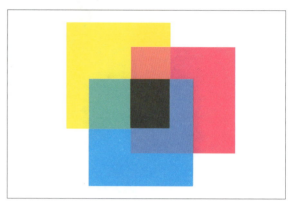

RGB (Red, Green, Blue): the native colour space used by computers for capturing and displaying digital images. RGB is based on human colour vision – the 'cone' photoreceptors in our eyes are sensitive to red, green and blue.

CMYK (Cyan, Magenta, Yellow, Black): the coloured inks used for wet ink printing. In theory, CMY can print most colours, but blacks tend to become muddy. An artificial black (K) is used to give a denser black.

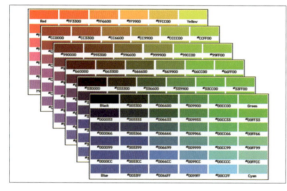

Source: Pantone X-Rite

CSS colour codes ensure that colours look more or less the same when viewed on a Mac or PC, in different browsers and on other devices. The palette is based on the three-channel RGB colour space, and is made up of combinations of six graduated colours, with two for each channel.

Pantone Colour Formula swatch guides for 'spot' or 'special' print colours. Pantone colours are specified by numbers and letters, such as Pantone 253C, that identify the colour and output substrate (C = coated paper). The printer's ink mix formula is also shown.

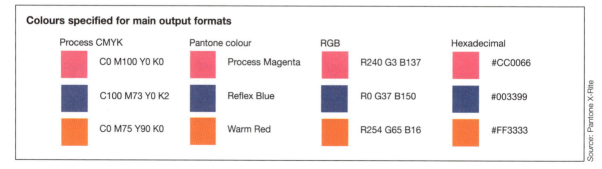

Colours specified for main output formats

Process CMYK		Pantone colour		RGB		Hexadecimal	
	C0 M100 Y0 K0		Process Magenta		R240 G3 B137		#CC0066
	C100 M73 Y0 K2		Reflex Blue		R0 G37 B150		#003399
	C0 M75 Y90 K0		Warm Red		R254 G65 B16		#FF3333

Source: Pantone X-Rite

Colour calibration

All the devices used for colour production should be accurately calibrated if you wish to achieve colour consistency. The media industry uses standard colour calibration target charts and software to check devices, create colour profiles that enable a computer to compare digital images with standard calibration charts and correct any colour discrepancies. The calibration process for monitors and scanners involves taking colour readings from the devices and comparing them with target charts. Printing companies can normally supply colour profiles to match other devices to their presses.

Colour accuracy

The Pantone ColorMunki is a spectrophotometer that checks and calibrates the colour accuracy and consistency of computer monitors, cameras, printers and projectors throughout the design and production process.

Source: Pantone X-Rite

ColorMunki training videos: *www.xritephoto.com/ph_learning.aspx?action=videos&litid=1570*

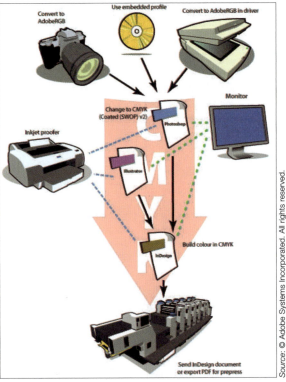

All digital devices in the colour production process need calibrating.

Scanner

Kodak produces standard colour calibration target charts for digital scanners. To calibrate a scanner: (1) scan the Kodak target chart at high resolution (300dpi); (2) send the scanned image file to Kodak; (3) Kodak checks it against the company's colour charts and returns a colour profile for the scanner linked to the computer.

Digital camera

The X-Rite Colour Checker is the industry standard for calibrating digital cameras. To calibrate a camera: (1) take a colour photograph of the X-Rite chart under controlled lighting conditions; (2) send the image file to an accredited X-Rite agent; (3) the agent creates a colour profile to be installed on the download device.

Inkjet/laser printer

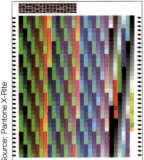

Source: Pantone X-Rite

Printer target chart files can be downloaded from the web. To calibrate a printer: (1) print the target chart; (2) post the printout to a lab for checking; (3) an ICC colour profile is returned for the linked computer.

Pixels and screens

In order to achieve maximum picture quality, it is important that all images used for online and print are at the correct resolution (dpi/ppi) for the media.

Image at 100% enlargement, shown at actual size, 300dpi print quality.

Image at 100% enlargement, shown at actual size, 150dpi newsprint quality.

Image at 100% enlargement, shown at actual size, 72dpi screen quality.

Bitmap image colours are displayed as square pixels of colour. Small pixels in a given area of the image contain more detail and have greater colour accuracy.

CMYK printing halftone screens

 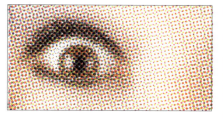

Combining varying sizes of dots of four transparent printing inks creates the CMYK printing colours. Dark colours have a high percentage of large dots, and light colours a lower percentage of smaller dots, for each process colour. Allowing all of the paper to show creates white.

Images can be resized in Photoshop's Image Size window: it is important to leave the Resample Image box unchecked to retain image quality when increasing or decreasing a picture's resolution or size.

Guide for file and image sizes captured by digital cameras at different resolutions

Pixel size (mega-pixels)	MB (RGB)	MB (CMYK)	MB	CMS 72ppi	CMS 200dpi	CMS 300dpi
1600 × 1200	2	6	7.5	56.5 × 42	20 × 15	13.5 × 10
2400 × 1800	4.3	12.5	16.5	84.5 × 63.5	30 × 22.5	20 × 15
3000 × 2000	6	17.5	23.5	94 × 70.5	37.5 × 25	25 × 17
3500 × 2500	8.75	25	33.5	123.5 × 88	44 × 31	29 × 21
4000 × 2850	11.4	32.5	43.5	141 × 100.5	50 × 36	33 × 36
5000 × 4000	20	57	76	176.5 × 141	62.5 × 50	42 × 34

Guide for file sizes for print and screen rulings

Output use	Screen ruling	File	MB greyscale	MB cmyk	kB
A3 newspaper single page	85lpi	170ppi	5.5	21.5	n/a
A3 newspaper single page	120lpi	240ppi	10.5	42.5	n/a
A4 magazine single page	120lpi	240ppi	5.3	21	n/a
A4 magazine double page	120lpi	240ppi	10.6	42.5	n/a
A4 magazine single page	150pi	300ppi	8.3	33.2	n/a
A4 magazine double page	150lpi	300ppi	17	66.4	n/a
Web banner (468 × 60 pixels)	n/a	72ppi	n/a	n/a	82
Web skyscraper (120 × 600 pixels)	n/a	72dpi	n/a	n/a	211

Image colour correction

Images may need to be colour balanced to improve their quality, correct a fault in the original image or prepare them for a specific platform, such as adjustments for the absorbency and colour of paper. Colour correction, as with many of the other production tasks covered in this book, is a specialist subject. Fortunately, the range of editing features available in imaging software such as Photoshop makes it easy to deal with basic colour issues.

The colour production process

| Original image | Camera/sensor blurring | Scanning process loses quality | Halftone screening printer/press quality |

Each time an image is transferred, colour quality can be lost.

Colour correction

The principle underlying colour correction is to balance colours against their complementary colour, that is red against cyan, green against magenta, and blue against yellow.

The Photoshop Variations window can be used to modify individual colour highlights, mid tones and shadows.

Tone and contrast

Images to be printed on a press need a wide tonal range from shadows to highlights, while how well images will display on a screen or the Web depends upon their light to dark contrast. Photoshop's image adjustments, such as levels and curves, can be used control and modify image tone and contrast.

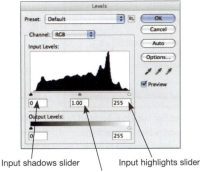

Input shadows slider   Input highlights slider
Gamma slider

The Photoshop Levels window inputs and adjusts the levels of shadows, highlights and gamma (brightness).

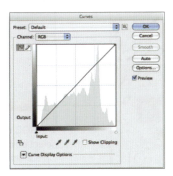

The Curves window allows the highlights and shadows to be modified by changing the shape of the curve graph that represents an image's tonal range.

Raw format for cameras

Most professional grade cameras take images in Raw format. This file type holds all the information captured when the image was shot, including the date and time, whether the flash was used, etc. An image in Raw contains more data than a tif or compressed JPEG, and this means that it is the best format to use for adjusting an image. The modified file can then be resaved to the specifications for online or print.

249

Selecting and specifying colour in Photoshop

Photoshop supports a range of colour management techniques for online and print. The Colour window allows colour to be added manually using the colour picker or colour value sliders, and colours can be sampled from on-screen images using the Eyedropper tool. The Swatches palette allows you to create new colours and store them, and gives access to Pantone and other colour systems.

The Photoshop toolbox gives access to colour management functions such as setting and swapping the foreground and background colours, the Eyedropper tool that can take a precise colour reading from an image, a range of brushes, including an airbrush for spraying smooth colour, and the Paintbucket and Gradient tools.

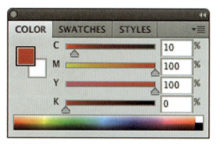

The CMYK colour specifier window allows a numeric percentage of each process colour to be added for print. This is best done using a four-colour-process ink specification book.

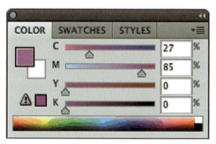

The CMYK colour window with RGB colour ramp (multicoloured bar) selected: the warning symbol is an alert that the colour is not suitable for screen-based work.

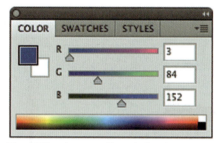

The RGB colour specifier window is used to select colours for screen-based graphics. Colour selections for print should not be based on RGB screen images unless the monitor has been calibrated to eliminate the visual difference between the colour modes.

The RGB colour specifier window with Web Safe colours ramp selected. The warning symbol indicates that the chosen colour is not web safe. Selecting Web Safe colours ensures the colour ramp can only be used for selecting web-suitable colours.

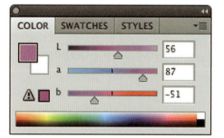

The Lab colour space, in theory, describes all the colours the eye can see – going far beyond anything any digital device can handle. The alert is a warning that the selected colour is not web compatible.

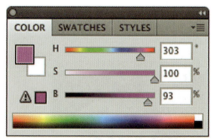

The hue (H), saturation (S) and brightness (B) colour picker.

Selecting and specifying colour in Photoshop

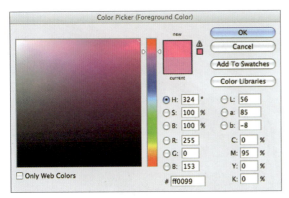

The Colour Picker window: features controls for all colour modes and access to the Swatch and Colour libraries.

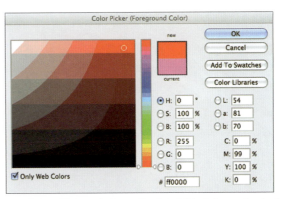

The Colour Picker window with Only Web Colours checked restricts the colour picker to RGB/hexadecimal colours.

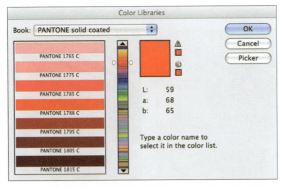

The Swatch Libraries window: colours can be selected with the slider or by typing their code number.

The Swatches window holds default colours, stores mixed or sampled colours and displays Swatch and Colour Libraries.

Using the Photoshop Eyedropper tool

The Photoshop Eyedropper tool and Colour Sampler tool sample and display the colour values of an area or individual pixel from an image open on-screen. The sampled colour appears as the foreground selection in the toolbox and the colour sample can be saved as a swatch. The colours shown below have been taken from the image to create a colour theme that could be used for a feature.

C18/M0/Y0/K27 R123/B123/G123 #FF1234567	C42/M28/Y19/K0 R123/B123/G123 #FF1234567	C31/M62/Y54/K9 R123/B123/G123 #FF1234567	C0/M49/Y32/K0 R123/B123/G123 #FF1234567	C3/M77/Y43/K0 R123/B123/G123 #FF1234567	C5/M5/Y84/K0 R123/B123/G123 #FF1234567	C0/M47/Y100/K0 R123/B123/G123 #FF1234567	C22/M100/Y100/K15 R123/B123/G123 #FF1234567

251

Colour images and tints

CMYK 300dpi tif file that has been changed into greyscale using Photoshop's colour mode converter and printed in black ink only.

RGB 300dpi tif file with colours rebalanced to black and white using Photoshop's image adjustment controls, resaved in CMYK mode and printed using all four process colour inks.

RGB 300dpi tif file that has been changed to CMYK using Photoshop's colour mode converter and printed in all four process colour inks.

Chalk and charcoal filter applied to an RGB image and resaved in CMYK mode.

Rough pastel filter applied to an RGB image and resaved in CMYK mode.

Magenta tint chart

10% tint	20% tint	30% tint	40% tint	50% tint
60% tint	70% tint	80% tint	90% tint	100% tint

Process colour shades are achieved by varying the percentage screens of the colour. It is good practice to use a shade palette of at least 10 steps to allow for colour drift in the printing process.

Posterise filter applied to an RGB image and resaved in CMYK mode.

Cutout filter applied to an RGB image and resaved in CMYK mode.

Design project mood board

House style colour palette CMYK

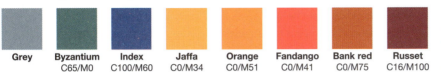

Grey	Byzantium	Index	Jaffa	Orange	Fandango	Bank red	Russet
	C65/M0 Y23/K34	C100/M60 Y0/K27	C0/M34 Y91/K0	C0/M51 Y87/K0	C0/M41 Y59/K0	C0/M75 Y100/K6	C16/M100 Y65/K15

Sample textures and patterns

Design notes

All the colours, textures and imagery used in a design should reflect the mood and target market of the title. The examples here are for a publication aimed at high-income earners in the business and financial sectors.

Sample photography and illustrations

Graphic elements

Sample typography

Main display typeface

26pt Apple Gothic

A sample of the introduction typeface

14pt Apple Gothic

Lorem ipsum dolor sit amet, consectetuer adipiscing elit, sed diam nonummy nibh euismod tincidunt ut laoreet dolore magna aliquam erat volutpat. Ut wisi enim ad minim veniam, quis nostrud ullamcorper.
Body copy type style example: 9.5/13pt Photina MT

Illustration John Gosler

> " *The quick brown fox jumps over the lazy dog. The quick brown fox jumps over the lazy dog. The quick brown fox jumps over the lazy dog.* "

Pull quote type style example: 14/18pt Photina MT italic on 100% grey background

Selecting complementary colours

Colour matching

Colour palettes can be built around the main image using the Photoshop Eyedropper tool to select small areas of colour on the source image.

Placing the photo and masthead on a background of each sample colour will normally work well, as the selected colours are already in the photograph. This technique should avoid any unfortunate colour clashes, and can also help reflect the subject matter of the product – warm for fashion, cool for business.

 To download colour palette samples go to
www.pearsoned.com/hand

Warm colour selection

C10/M19 Y28/K0	C24/M60 Y38/K9	C34/M88 Y77/K42	C12/M86 Y100/K0

Cool colour selection

C22/M11 Y9/K0	C26/M17 Y16/K0	C40/M33 Y36/K0	C29/M30 Y380/K0

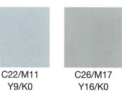

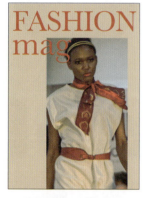

The colour wheel and colour combinations

Tints and shades

In CMYK, shades are created by adding black, tints by reducing the percentage of each colour.

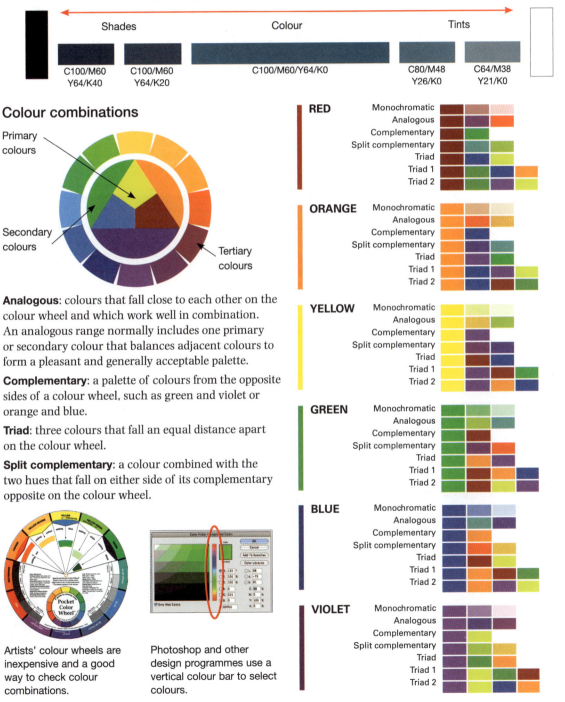

	Shades		Colour	Tints	
	C100/M60 Y64/K40	C100/M60 Y64/K20	C100/M60/Y64/K0	C80/M48 Y26/K0	C64/M38 Y21/K0

Colour combinations

Primary colours

Secondary colours

Tertiary colours

Analogous: colours that fall close to each other on the colour wheel and which work well in combination. An analogous range normally includes one primary or secondary colour that balances adjacent colours to form a pleasant and generally acceptable palette.

Complementary: a palette of colours from the opposite sides of a colour wheel, such as green and violet or orange and blue.

Triad: three colours that fall an equal distance apart on the colour wheel.

Split complementary: a colour combined with the two hues that fall on either side of its complementary opposite on the colour wheel.

Artists' colour wheels are inexpensive and a good way to check colour combinations.

Photoshop and other design programmes use a vertical colour bar to select colours.

RED
- Monochromatic
- Analogous
- Complementary
- Split complementary
- Triad
- Triad 1
- Triad 2

ORANGE
- Monochromatic
- Analogous
- Complementary
- Split complementary
- Triad
- Triad 1
- Triad 2

YELLOW
- Monochromatic
- Analogous
- Complementary
- Split complementary
- Triad
- Triad 1
- Triad 2

GREEN
- Monochromatic
- Analogous
- Complementary
- Split complementary
- Triad
- Triad 1
- Triad 2

BLUE
- Monochromatic
- Analogous
- Complementary
- Split complementary
- Triad
- Triad 1
- Triad 2

VIOLET
- Monochromatic
- Analogous
- Complementary
- Split complementary
- Triad
- Triad 1
- Triad 2

Source: © The Color Wheel Company: www.colorwheelco.com

Sourcing colour ideas and inspiration

Colour palettes can be created for titles by producing mood boards from sourced material such as magazine tear sheets, fabrics, paint chips and other forms of textural and visual stimuli, or by referring to specialist colour consultancies.

Colour consultancies are companies that research and forecast developing colour trends, using their consumer and industry knowledge to produce inspirational images, themes and colour palettes that can be used or customised for individual projects.

Pantone View Colour Planner showcases palettes for use in a range of design disciplines.

Source: Pantone X-Rite

Source: Pantone X-Rite

Molecular: an exploration into a mood that is not sombre, but vibrant and glowing and in constant reinterpretation of itself. It represents a whole world built and organised around a mosaic, with faceted and unified parts. Deep, deep darks have never been more enticing, more positive, more promising and exciting to play with.

Multiple Identity: think of the physical changes in skin, of how emotional or corporeal responses alter states. The texture mutates and temperatures rise or fall. Think of eye colour.

Source: Pantone X-Rite

Source: Pantone X-Rite

Mimetic: at close range, this can look like a disorderly arrangement of bits and touches of colours, but seen from a distance they form an organised whole image.

Universe: visions of dynamic waves and veils of saturated, layered colours are studded with starry accents, all set against the beauty of black – a versatile and unusually rich palette that delivers real design gymnastics.

Source: Sven Laurent. Pantone LLC

The Pantone Hotel state of the art accommodation allows guests to choose a room colour to match their mood. The designers have demonstrated how a carefully chosen palette of colours and textures can communicate a modern, design-led lifestyle.

Visit these colour websites
www.pantone.com
www.globalcolor.co.uk
www.internationalcolourauthority.org
www.view-publications.com
www.dcipherfm.com
www.nellyrodi.com

Source: © Global Color Research

Global Color Research: concepts and inspirations

Sourcing colour ideas and inspiration

Mood boards: building visual references

Daria Kubacik & Ellina Buksa

Mood boards are often created for a new media product to develop ideas for the design, type and colour styles.

Colour psychology: cultural perceptions and emotional signifiers

Colour psychology involves the experience of colour – the associations we make between events, impressions and emotions. It is based on the Jungian philosophy of the collective unconscious – the theory that people, societies and all humankind share information on the subconscious level.

Source: X-Rtie

The myPANTONE website offers a wide range of colour palettes developed by professionals and enthusiasts. These can be used as they are, or can become a useful starting point for developing further colour palettes.

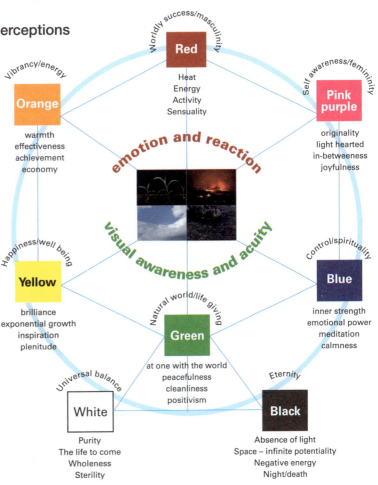

Worldly success/masculinity

Red
Heat
Energy
Activity
Sensuality

Vibrancy/energy

Orange
warmth
effectiveness
achievement
economy

Self awareness/femininity

Pink purple
originality
light hearted
in-betweeness
joyfulness

emotion and reaction

visual awareness and acuity

Happiness/well being

Yellow
brilliance
exponential growth
inspiration
plenitude

Control/spirituality

Blue
inner strength
emotional power
meditation
calmness

Natural world/life giving

Green
at one with the world
peacefulness
cleanliness
positivism

Universal balance

White
Purity
The life to come
Wholeness
Sterility

Eternity

Black
Absence of light
Space – infinite potentiality
Negative energy
Night/death

Colour gamut

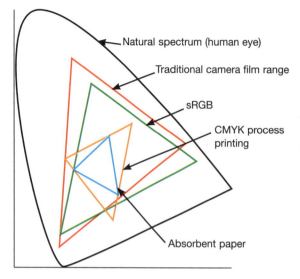

- Natural spectrum (human eye)
- Traditional camera film range
- sRGB
- CMYK process printing
- Absorbent paper

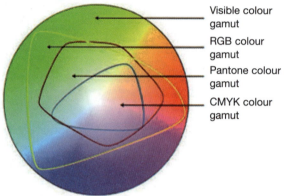

- Visible colour gamut
- RGB colour gamut
- Pantone colour gamut
- CMYK colour gamut

A colour gamut is the complete range of colours available on a device such as a monitor or printer. The RGB gamut is used for monitors, smart phones, tablets and digital cameras. It usually consists of more colours than are available for CMYK-based devices, such as presses. An 'out of gamut' warning would indicate that a colour cannot be achieved in that colour mode.

Computer monitors generate colour through three light sources – RGB (Red, Green, Blue). In theory, every colour that exists can be created using RGB. However, although most monitors can produce millions of colours, this is still less than the visible spectrum.

Monitors work through transmissive (projected) light, while printing with ink on paper is viewed through reflective light. This means we do not see the colours in the same way. Printing inks are made from dyes, earths and chemical colours that do not produce the same extent or subtlety of colour as RGB monitors, and glowing, brightly lit colours attract the human eye more strongly than flat, matt ones. The differences in the underlying physiology, physics and chemistry mean that a colour on a monitor can never look exactly the same as it does in ink on paper. This is why it is so important to ensure all images are in the correct colour mode for the output media. However, because not all devices are properly colour calibrated,

printers often prefer to be sent RGB images that they can convert using their own ICC colour profile, in order to be sure the colours are correct for their press.

The diagrams above show CMYK, RGB and other colour gamuts. The main point to observe is the differences in scale between the gamuts, the largest being the natural spectrum, the smallest one- or two-colour printing. When an image is converted from RGB to the smaller CMYK gamut, some colours will be lost.

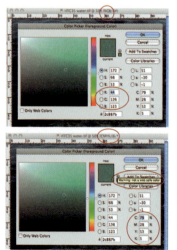

The colour gamut warning dialogue box can be activated in Photoshop to warn when colours are out of gamut.

Top: The Photoshop Colour Picker window showing an RGB colour reading in gamut.

Bottom: Converting the colour mode to CMYK may activate the 'out of gamut' warning.

Selecting colours for the web

Colour Hex code	Colour Hex code	Colour Hex code
#FFFFFF	#CCFF99	#99FF99
#FFFFCC	#CCFF66	#99FF66
#FFFF99	#CCFF33	#99FF33
#FFFF66	#CCFF00	#99FF00
#FFFF33	#CCCCFF	#99CCFF
#FFFF00	#CCCCCC	#99CCCC
#FFCCFF	#CCCC99	#99CC99
#FFCCCC	#CCCC66	#99CC66
#FFCC99	#CCCC33	#99CC33
#FFCC66	#CCCC00	#99CC00
#FFCC33	#CC99FF	#9999FF
#FFCC00	#CC99CC	#9999CC
#FF99FF	#CC9999	#999999
#FF99CC	#CC9966	#999966
#FF9999	#CC9933	#999933
#FF9966	#CC9900	#999900
#FF9933	#CC66FF	#9966FF
#FF9900	#CC66CC	#9966CC
#FF66FF	#CC6699	#996699
#FF66CC	#CC6666	#996666
#FF6666	#CC6633	#996633
#FF6633	#CC6600	#996600
#FF6600	#CC33FF	#9933FF
#FF33FF	#CC33CC	#9933CC
#FF33CC	#CC3399	#993399
#FF3399	#CC3366	#993366
#FF3333	#CC3333	#993333
#FF3300	#CC3300	#993300
#FF00FF	#CC00FF	#9900FF
#FF00CC	#CC00CC	#9900CC
#FF0099	#CC0099	#990099
#FF0066	#CC0066	#990066
#FF0033	#CC0033	#990033
#FF0000	#CC0000	#990000
#66FFFF	#33FFFF	#00FFFF
#66FFCC	#33FFCC	#00FFCC
#66FF99	#33FF99	#00FF99
#66FF66	#33FF66	#00FF66
#66FF33	#33FF33	#00FF33
#66FF00	#33FF00	#00FF00
#66CCFF	#33CCFF	#00CCFF
#66CCCC	#33CCCC	#00CCCC
#66CC99	#33CC99	#00CC99
#66CC66	#33CC66	#00CC66
#66CC33	#33CC33	#00CC33
#66CC00	#33CC00	#00CC00
#6699FF	#3399FF	#0099FF
#6699CC	#3399CC	#0099CC
#669999	#339999	#009999
#669966	#339966	#009966
#669933	#339933	#009933
#669900	#339900	#009900
#6666FF	#3366FF	#0066FF
#6666CC	#3366CC	#0066CC
#666699	#336699	#006699
#666666	#336666	#006666
#666633	#336633	#006633
#666600	#336600	#006600
#6633FF	#3333FF	#0033FF
#6633CC	#3333CC	#0033CC
#663399	#333399	#003399
#663366	#333366	#003366
#663333	#333333	#003333
#663300	#333300	#003300
#6600FF	#3300FF	#0000FF
#6600CC	#3300CC	#0000CC
#660099	#330099	#000099
#660066	#330066	#000066
#660033	#330033	#000033
#660000	#330000	#000000
#CCFFFF	#99FFFF	
#CCFFCC	#99FFCC	

HTML and CSS web colours are based on RGB colour values and specified using three sets of two figures and two numbers, running from 00000 (white) to FFFFFF (black), and headed by a hash sign (#). The possible permutations result in more than 16 million different colours. The hexadecimal system is also used to create the range of web shades of grey.

> **TIP** There are 150 web colour names that are used by all makes of browser. To see the full list visit: *http://w3schools.com/html/html_colornames.asp*

Web colour wheels that give both the RGB and Hex values for a colour are a useful way of selecting colour for screen-based media. The wheels display web colours in a similar way to traditional artists' colour wheels, showing the analogous, complementary, opposite and triadic colour relationships (see page 255, *www.colorwheelco.com*).

Websites and apps, such as the Color Scheme Designer, allow you to select RGB/Hex combinations and assess the colour relationships on-screen.

Colour reproduction: print

Working in print with two colours

If a print title's budget is limited, two-colour printing can be a less costly alternative, as a good range of colours can be achieved using just tints of black and a process colour.

Yellow–Black

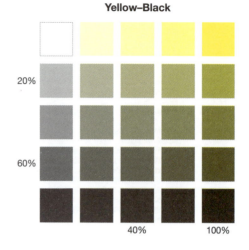

A duotone is a photograph printed using only two colours, usually black plus one other. To keep costs down, use a process colour (Cyan in the example) for the second colour.

Magenta–Black

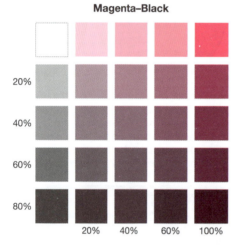

Cyan–Black

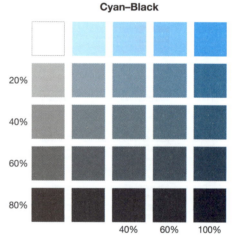

The final check

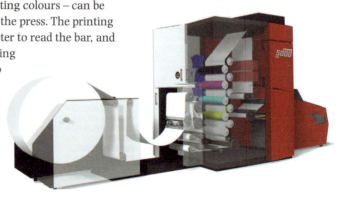

A colour bar – a test strip that shows all the printing colours – can be added to final artwork to check colour inking on the press. The printing company uses a device called a spectrodensitometer to read the bar, and information about ink density, dot gain and slurring (ink blurring) is sent to the computerised press to ensure that the printed colours will be accurate.

You should check with the printing company to make sure that the colours in your document are suitable for the press to be used. It is good practice to obtain a contract colour proof from the printers that shows the expected colour standard for your title.

Colour temperature and visual movement

The way in which a colour is used, its extent and where it is placed on the page in relation to other items can affect how a title's contents are perceived. The viewer's reaction to a colour varies according to how much of a page it takes up; larger areas of a colour are seen as lighter than the same colour in a small space. The proximity of one colour to a second alters the focus of the eye. This effect is referred to as the 'figure and ground relationship' – a visual theory that divides perceived objects into the *figure*, the dominant element that the eye will focus on, and the *ground*, any element that recedes into the background, which may be the paper or screen. This can be used to direct attention to a particular item, for example a red headline in a bright yellow-tinted box will always attract the eye. See *How to work with colour*, page 176.

There are some neutral colours that do not suggest movement, and which can be used to calm and counterbalance the visual activity induced by dominant, recessive or complementary colours, for example beige, taupe, dove greys and lilac.

Reds and oranges are described as **warm colours**. Red on the natural spectrum falls close to infrared (which the human eye cannot see), and looking at a red object or being in a red room provokes an increase in heart rate and corresponding feelings of warmth and excitement. Blues and violets are **cold colours** and have the physical effect of lowering the heart rate, so can soothe and pacify. Public buildings such as hospitals and schools are often painted in soft shades (hue plus a percentage of black added) of blue or blue greys to keep people calm and relaxed. The colour temperature is an expression of the physical effects of a colour, and the term also refers to associative values such as red – blood, fire and hot chilli peppers – or blue – ice, skies and sea. Yellow to violet has the greatest temperature contrast.

The juxtaposition of colours affects the visual movement between coloured objects and the background, as does the density of the hue and the shape and dimensions of the colour areas. Red type surrounded by white space is strong, for example the classic Coca-Cola logo, while Harrods store's brand colours, deep green with gold, convey stability, sophistication and luxury. Blue type on white will recede, and a pale blue will fade if it is close in tone to the background. However, the right tone of blue on white can imply cool efficiency. Royal Philips Electronics, a firm that uses simplicity as its slogan, has a mid-blue logo and uses the colour to brand its website. Greys are recessive colours and are rarely used for logos, apart from high-tech and car companies that use metallic effects. However, plain neutral backgrounds are useful to bring bright colours forward in the field of vision, for example a yellow square on a mid-grey background would come forward, while a similarly sized violet or purple shape would recede (see page 170).

Colour jargon buster

Brightness/contrast: the intensity of a colour in relation to its background

Chroma: the purity of a colour (hue) in relation to grey

Complementary/analogous: complementary colours oppose each other on a colour wheel; analogous colours are adjacent to each other on a colour wheel

Luminosity: the amount of light a colour reflects (+ white = higher luminance)

Shade/tint: variations of a hue (shade = + black, tint = + white)

Temperature: the heat value of a colour (+ red = hot, + blue = cold)

Colour spaces

A colour space describes a range of colours. The natural spectrum is a colour space, as are the colour modes used for digital and print technology. Computer processors and monitors, desktop printers and printing presses employ set colour spaces, as does photographic and broadcast equipment. The term for a range of colours that a device is able to produce using a particular technology or in a specific instance is a gamut. See *How to work with colour*, pages 246 and 262.

Colour technology: gamuts

Gamuts describe colour ranges such as those used by a monitor, the entire palette that a computer program can record, and may be used to define the colours in an individual image. However, there can be considerable variations in the way devices, software and systems generate and output colour, with the result that the same colours viewed on a Mac can look completely different on a PC, or when printed using a laser or inkjet printer compared with a digital or traditional press. Even as basic a colour as black can look inconsistent in tone on the same platform where the type, graphics or images on a page have been created in separate software programs. Image-editing programs such as Photoshop can be set to give out gamut warning alerts, for example if the range of colours used in an RGB image file means it cannot be converted to a CMYK output file (see page 250).

Every make and model of any device that uses colour may have a different colour bias. The wide range of colour variance can be seen in any shop display of TVs tuned to the same programme. This is partly due to differing manufacturing techniques and software, but is also because the brightness and contrast settings can be altered to suit the viewer and the lighting conditions. This may not really matter for TV viewing, but can cause critical differences between devices where accurate cross-media colour matching is required.

Most computer monitors have default colour settings for the display. This may be adequate for most purposes, but is rarely accurate enough for media titles. If you are using your monitor to select colours that will be transferred to other devices, you will need to calibrate the monitor display. This is to ensure that the colour remains the same on the output device – a printing press or browser. The monitor and any desktop printers and image scanners should be **colour calibrated** – a software-based method of aligning colour gamuts to achieve consistency in appearance and final production.

There are a number of programs available that can match the look of colour on-screen to the output of proofing printers and commercial presses, or to industry-standard RGB or hexadecimal colour values (see *How to work with colour*, page 247). While it is not always possible to match colours completely, even within the same medium, calibrating the hardware and software will help prevent any nasty surprises when the title is printed or published on the Web.

Colour calibration and profiles

Colour calibration adjusts the colour of a device (input and output) to match that of a standard colour space (RGB or CMYK). There are various ways of calibrating colour for different devices, but usually an industry-standard colour digital file or a printed target colour chart is used as a comparison to assess a device's colour accuracy. A software patch is created using this information to enable the page make-up and imaging software to match the colours to an agreed standard. To achieve an accurate colour rendition throughout the production process, all of the digital devices used, including cameras, computer monitors, scanners, proofing and printing presses, should be colour aligned.

Most desktop computer monitors and tablet screens have some basic colour controls that improve the results on an individual screen. If you wish to coordinate all of the devices used for production, you will need to create a colour profile – a set of software equations that transfer from one device to another. The profiles used for monitors show the variances in colour compared with a set of International Color Consortium (ICC) standards. A monitor is calibrated by using a meter that contains colour sensors. The meter comes with software that runs a colour-calibrated selection of images and colour targets on-screen. It will detect any display variants from the standard colour set. The software then creates a colour profile that can be used to adjust the monitor so that it displays ICC accurate colours on-screen.

The method used to calibrate individual input and output devices such as scanners and desktop printers involves industry-standard **colour charts** (see *How to work with colour*, page 247). The ICC profiles used to adjust scanners and digital cameras are based on supplied sample **colour target charts** – a series of accurate standard colour patches. The target charts are either scanned or photographed using the device to be tested, and the image file created is sent to a colour lab that checks it for accuracy. The colour lab creates an ICC profile to be used with that scanner or camera.

Specialist colour labs and some printer paper manufacturers will check the colour accuracy of the printouts from desktop printers against a standard target chart. To calibrate a printer, a target digital file has to be obtained from the colour lab or manufacturer, and run on the device. It is then sent to the company to be checked. The printout is analysed using a **spectrophotometer** – an optical instrument that measures the properties of light – to detect any discrepancies between the printout and the target chart. The information is used to build a software profile for the printer. You may need to have several profiles done for each printer, with one for each type of paper (glossy, matt, etc.). All the devices used in the production process should have ICC profiles written for them and these should be installed on all computers used for production. ICC profiles are specific to individual paper stocks and the brand of printing ink to be used. See *How to work with colour*, page 258.

Web colour

Pixels are small squares of light that are made up of percentages of each RGB colour in higher or lower proportions. RGB colour on a computer monitor is generated by red, green and blue light waves. White is created by projecting the maximum amount of all three-colour light waves into 1 pixel, grey by all three colours in equal proportions, and black on-screen is the total absence of light – no colour projection at all. This way of working with projected light is called **additive colour** (see page 264).

There are two digital colour spaces. RGB is used for computer monitors, digital cameras, video and TV, while web browsers use the hexadecimal system. Web colours are represented as a three-part number or letter code: 255 (RGB) or FF (hexadecimal colour) indicates maximum colour saturation, minimum saturation by 0 (RGB) or 00 (Hex). So an RGB bright red would be R255 G0 B0, or FF0000 in Hex colours.

Modern devices have the ability to display millions of colours, while older mobile phones and PDAs only had 16-bit processors that supported thousands of colours. Early computer colour monitors could only display 256 colours, and there was a noticeable discrepancy in 40 of these colours between the PC and Mac operating system. There were also differences in how the first browser programmers coded colours. These factors resulted in the computer industry developing a standard browser, cross-platform palette of 216 web safe hexadecimal colours, and this became the standard colour range used for web pages.

Now that Macs and PCs are both Intel based, and the companies that produce browsers have made them more compatible with each other, there are fewer discrepancies or colours that jump or shift. Hexadecimal colour is no longer a technical requirement, but using the system will guarantee that colours work consistently on both platforms and in all browsers. It has the advantage of being well established and widely

To find out more about the browser-safe web palette visit:
http://www.lynda.com/resources/webpalette.aspx

supported, and it provides a colour resource within the structure of the computer operating system that takes up little memory. This is an important factor as it means a hex-coloured website or page should be quicker to download, and many web designers still prefer to use hex colours as they can be sure that these will work well, even on older machines, other devices and most makes of browser. There may also be some older versions of computers, smart phones and tablets still in use that have 256-colour displays.

Browsers display the colour of pixels for a web page based on colour coding instructions in CSS or HTML source files. The browser software compares the colour code with a standard web safe colour chart, and if it does not correspond to an existing shade, the browser may **dither** the pixels or change the colour to the nearest standard hue. Dithering refers to placing two pixels of a similar colour next to each other and relying on our eyes to blend them to create another colour. However, the flickering eye movement that makes the colours merge can also make them appear blurred.

If the target audience for your website is likely to have the latest computer equipment, then the full range of RGB colours can be used. However, an image file with millions of colours can only be displayed at its full range of colours on devices that can render those colours. Web design and content management system programs can handle most images as long as they are in the correct colour mode, file format and at 72ppi. Photoshop has a Save for Web command that ensures a JPEG's colours can be rendered in HTML and CSS and that prevents the JPEG colour profile being embedded. Video and animation software also works in RGB.

Red, green, blue

RGB colours are **additive primaries** used for computer hardware and cameras, scanners and digital printing. Additive colours are created on a scale that begins with black and moves towards white; as more colour is added, the amount of white increases and therefore the colour lightens. The RGB numeric code

for red is R255 G0 B0, blue is R0 G0 B255 and green R0 G255 B0. All other RGB colours are created by adding or subtracting proportional amounts of red, green or blue: for example, R225 G225 B0 is yellow, R225 G0 B225 is magenta and R0 G225, B225 is cyan, although these hues differ from the print process colours. In imaging software, colour spaces are also known as colour modes, and each colour in a mode is split into a channel. The RGB colour mode has three digital channels (one for each colour). Web gif files are often saved using Index colour, a low-data single digital channel **colour mode**. The CMYK colour mode consists of four digital channels. See *How to work with colour*, page 246.

Hexadecimal colours for CSS

The hexadecimal cross-browser colour system provides an agreed set of colour values that will be accurate when viewed on most computer screens. The hex colours used for CSS follow the RGB system described in the above paragraph to create colour using a code of numbers, ranging from 0 to 255, combined with letters (see chart on page 259). Under this system 0 equals hex #00 and 255 equals hex #FF. For example, red is #FF0000, green #008000 and blue #0000FF. There is a list of 16 **W3C standard colour names** with corresponding hex values that can be safely used in CSS. These are aqua, black, blue, fuchsia, grey, green, lime, maroon, navy, olive, purple, red, silver, teal, white and yellow. The most commonly used browsers support approximately 150 standard hex colours.

Key hexadecimal colours

aqua	#00FFFF	green	#008000
navy	#000080	silver	#C0C0C0
black	#000000	grey	#808080
olive	#808000	teal	#008080
blue	#0000FF	lime	#00FF00
purple	#800080	white	#FFFFFF
fuchsia	#FF00FF	maroon	#800000
red	#FF0000	yellow	#FFFF00

Four-colour process: cyan, magenta, yellow and black

The colours cyan, yellow, magenta and black (CMYK) used in four-colour printing are **subtractive primaries**. Subtractive colours are created on a scale that begins with white and moves towards black; as more colour is added, the amount of black increases and therefore the colour darkens, eventually becoming black (see page 246). K stands for key colour and is always black. Process colours (CMYK) are expressed in percentages that relate to the size of the dots in a halftone screen (see page 248). The printing process creates the illusion of a large number of colours using percentages of each of the four process inks. Most printers' colour guides offer up to 24,000 colours made up of CMYK dots, but the process can achieve millions of colours:

■ Cyan is a greenish cold blue: when mixed with percentages of magenta it becomes deeper and warmer, for example 100% cyan with 70% magenta results in a rich, purplish blue. CMYK printed greens are created by mixing percentages of cyan and yellow, with black for darker shades.

■ Magenta is a vivid mauve pink: mixed with cyan it creates purples and with black added it provides a range of crimsons and plums. Bright red for print is made up of 100% magenta with 100% yellow, with the percentage of magenta reduced to produce orange. However, certain colours such as vibrant oranges are difficult to achieve using process ink mixes.

■ Process yellow is vibrant and bright. It can be turned into gold, orange and warmer shades by mixing in percentages of magenta. Adding small amounts of black and magenta creates browns.

■ Black (K) ink forms a crisp contrast with white paper that makes small type easy to read. Reducing the percentage of black produces a simple grey that can be changed to dove grey by adding magenta, or to gunmetal by adding cyan.

Channels and file size

Every digital image is made up of coloured pixels. Each individual colour is made up from percentages of the channels used by the colour mode – a bright blue image will have a high percentage of pixels in the blue channel. The memory size of an image increases if it uses more channels and if the channel is made up from a greater number of pixels. This means an image file saved in CMYK mode contains four sets of colour data, and the file would have a greater memory size than the same image saved in RGB, although it may not hold any more colour information. See *How to work with colour*, page 227.

Greyscale

Greyscale is a colour mode made up of one channel that uses 256 shades of black, which is used for black and white printing. Printing companies normally refer to this as mono printing. If a black and white image falls on a print colour page, using a block made up of the four colour process inks will give a richer tone to the picture (see *How to work with colour*, page 252). It is not advisable to use greyscale online. Black and white web images should be saved in the RGB colour mode to create the appearance of black.

Percentage tints

A reduction in the relative size of each dot within the screen and the amount of paper left to show through gives a tint – a reduction of the solid colour that is created by smaller dots of ink on the substrate over a given distance (see page 252). All tints allow a degree of white paper to show through: for example, 0% ink coverage reveals all the paper, while a 50% dot screen lays down 50% ink coverage so that 50% of the white paper shows through, while 100% ink stops any paper showing through and gives a solid colour. White type reversed out of a colour relies on the whiteness and quality of the paper together with accurate registration to appear crisp and clean.

Spot and special colours

If you wish to achieve a 100% match to a brand colour or feature metallic effect type, you will need to specify an additional spot-coloured mixed ink to be used with the four CMYK colours. Certain colours are hard or impossible to achieve using just the four-colour process. Colour Matching Systems such as Pantone, offer pastel, neon and metallic special or spot-coloured ink ranges. These are specified using swatch books that contain samples for each colour and give the ink formula to mix the colour. If a special colour is used in addition to the four-colour process, for example to print in gold on a magazine cover, the publication would have to be printed on a press that can handle the extra colours. Spot colours can be printed on their own, replacing black as the mono shade, or on a two-colour press in combination with black or another spot colour (see page 322). Pantone produces a spot and CMYK selector that shows the solid ink and its equivalent CMYK printed side by side to show the degree of shade variance.

Separations

The printing process operates by separating the pages or images to be printed into individual colours. Each separation requires a **halftone screen** – a pattern of inked dots of differing sizes. Larger dots make a colour appear darker, smaller dots make it appear lighter. For example, all blue elements appear on the cyan **separation**, but as blues may also contain percentages of other colours, some elements of a blue image may also appear on the other three separations. A dark, midnight blue might consist of 100% cyan, 90% magenta, 30% yellow and 60% black. Overlaying four sets of semi-transparent coloured dots in higher or lower percentages, and varying the sizes (halftoning), creates the illusion of a wide range of continuous colours (see page 320). In imaging programs, each separation is represented by a digital channel. See *How to work with colour*, page 227.

Colour influences and media bleed

Colour used in the media is highly influenced by trends in wider society. Fashions in colour for clothing, products and interiors have an effect on publication and

Colour on paper

When specifying colour for print, the texture of the paper or nature of the substrate should to be considered. Pantone has a range of Colour Matching Systems for different papers and other surfaces. The company produces printed colour selectors that show ink colours on matt and gloss paper, and which can be fanned out so colours on different paper types can be viewed side by side. Colours for matt papers should be specified using an **uncoated colour selector** that shows how ink on matt paper absorbs light and appears flat. Colours for silk or gloss paper should be specified with a **coated colour selector** that shows how ink drying on top of glossy paper reflects light and creates a shine. See *How to work with colour*, page 241.

website design. The palettes used by websites and leading print publications also filter back into other areas through a colour version of media bleed, as media companies interchange ideas from the Web, computer games, films, TV, books and magazines. There is often a *zeitgeist* consensus on what colours are 'in', and there is plenty of cross-cultural bleed. Japanese colourising, in particular colour work for computer games, animé films and manga comics, has been hugely influential.

Films and film technology have had a large role in setting colour trends. The Technicolor film system, developed in the 1920s, became synonymous with vivid, hyper-realistic colours that have influenced image colours as consumers have come to accept, and possibly expect, enhanced colourisation. Colour alteration, correction and adjustment have become commonplace, particularly for fashion or interior images, and photo-editing techniques are used by many printed publications and websites as a standard method of making a picture look as good as possible on the page or screen. You should be open to colour trends that are relevant to your product. The ability to understand the cultural message of colour and good use of colour can increase readership and visitor numbers, and improve the audience's experience of a media product. You may work on print publications that can exploit full colour in print and on websites displayed on brightly lit monitors that produce vivid colourisation. Gaining an understanding of the colourising possibilities offered by digital technology is vital in controlling how colour can be used as a communication medium within and outside a title. See the *How to work with colour* pages.

Summary Content visualisation and structure: colour

Colour in the media reflects wider cultural influences and is used to brand titles across platforms. It is an important aspect of information design and can signal subtle and sophisticated messages that convey the importance of content and influence how readers or visitors perceive the quality of the media product and value its authority. It is important for those working in media productions to have an understanding of the technical processes that are employed by the various media, and of the way in which each platform displays and outputs colour.

- Colour is both the physiological experience of light and a cultural construct and colours are strongly identified with time and place.

- Colour is a vital component of brand identity. Media companies employ individual colour palettes for each publication and may have a range of palettes for each title's sections or topics, while websites have at least one key colour or a palette.

- Colour in the media can command attention, signal importance by indicating the hierarchy of information, direct eye movement to follow the flow of information and, because colour is so culturally and emotionally weighted, substantially alter the way in which someone reacts to and interprets a print publication, website, editorial, content or advertising.

- Colours selected for typography must function not only to maximise readability, but also to connect the written content to the imagery.

- There is a strong commercial sector built around colour overseen by the Commission Internationale de l'Eclairage, the international authority on light and colour.

- Pantone and Focoltone are companies that provide colour matching systems.

- Computer processors and monitors, desktop printers and printing presses employ set colour spaces, as does photographic and broadcast equipment. Each make and model of any digital device may vary in how it renders colour. Colour calibration is a process that adjusts the colour of a device (input and output) to match that of a standard colour space (RGB or CMYK).

- Colour on a computer monitor is projected in red, green and blue light waves. These are generated through pixels that are small squares of light which transmit percentages of each colour in higher or lower proportions.

- The hexadecimal system, used for web colours only, represents colours as a three-part number or letter code.

- Browsers work out what colour the pixels for a website should be from colour coding instructions in CSS or HTML source files.

- Printing uses a four-colour system based on cyan, magenta, yellow and black (CMYK). Four-colour printing operates by separating the page or item to be printed into the four CMYK colours that relate to four halftone screens, with one separation (digital channel) for each process colour.

Activities and development

The questions and action points for this chapter will provide you with an opportunity to examine the use of colour in the media, note how media titles employ colour and the effect colour can have on branding, marketing and the audience's experience. Visit the *Design for Media* website for more fact and action sheets, sample templates, type schemes and colour palettes at **www.pearsoned.com/hand/**

Questions

Question 1
Select a print magazine and its website: analyse how many colours have been used and how they are employed in specific sections. What is the main brand colour? Is there one overall colour palette, or is colour used in different ways for different subjects? Are varying shades of one or more colours used in particular ways and places? Is the colour use consistent in both media?

Question 2
Note the corporate identity colours used by a large company with several trading areas and/or products. How has the brand colour palette been used for its business and promotional material, such as a house magazine, newsletter, brochure, logos, typography, clothing tags, packaging, store fitments, posters, print advertisements, TV ads, videos, own website and web ads on other companies' sites?

Question 3
Select a magazine, website and an item of packaging. Analyse why, in terms of the target audience and competitive marketplace, the colour palette used may have been chosen. Is there a connection between the subject matter and the colours selected for each medium or item?

Question 4
Examine a media title's print publication and website and note any visual difference between the RGB screen colours and printed CMYK inks. Discuss how perceived change in hue, brightness and tonal values might alter the readership's or user's reaction to the title in either medium.

Action points

Action point 1
Download and print the viewfinder file from the *Design for Media* website and cut out the window indicated in the black and white squares. Choose a colour and first view it through the window in the black area, then through the white area cutout. Note if the colour seems stronger through the black or white window. This technique can be used to judge whether a colour is being used to its best advantage.

Action point 2
Obtain the print issue of a title that also appears online and compare on more than one computer monitor the colour of the masthead (logo) and the palettes used for the pages. If possible, look at the difference between the colours on both a PC and a Mac, and in a variety of browsers.

Action point 3
Create a mood board using imagery, type samples, graphic design styles, colours and textures for a travel company that is going to launch a website and associated print material to promote a music festival or major sporting event.

Action point 4
Using either a page makeup program or PhotoShop, select a number of images with a clearly dominant colour trend, then choose samples of type in red, blue and black and use these in various combinations on the images. Note which colours work well together and those that clash or become unreadable.

9

BUILDING A PRINT OR WEB PAGE

This chapter discusses:

- Collaborative working
- Editorial production practice
- Editorial schedules for page production
- Web and blog schedules
- Page and copy handling
- Editorialising the image
- Working with imagery
- User-generated content
- Copyright
- Working with advertising
- Page creation design rules
- The role of the grid

- Layout skills
- Working on web pages
- Searchability
- Understanding and managing the site plan
- Usability
- Content on a page
- Web assets
- Web advertisements
- Print page production
- Print page flow control and proofing

This chapter covers the production process. It describes the work you may be expected to undertake as part of a media team, including the tasks and systems used to create online and print publications. The chapter gives practical guidance on how to collate, prepare and plan content handling, and on using page creation software and web content management systems to build a page for print and online.

'To design is to communicate clearly by whatever means you can control or master.'

Milton Glaser, graphic designer

*ea may be given any visual form.
...sk before the designer, in collaboration
with the publisher, is to determine which form
will be best.'*

Timothy Samara, educator and designer

The hardest dilemma you will encounter when you start working on a new project is where to begin. The facetious reply is always 'at the beginning', but in a continuing process how do you decide where that is? The goal of media production is to get the final product into the marketplace and to the target audience, and the actions taken by all those involved must be aimed at achieving this. There are established working practices employed in publishing and related areas such as advertising, PR and marketing. These systems have been developed to ensure that those working on printed publications and websites are able to operate as an efficient team to set up well-constructed pages.

Most media companies are team-based businesses, and titles are normally put together by a group of people working in cooperation on specific tasks. The teams are traditionally hierarchical, with a senior manager or editor taking final responsibility for the overall look of both the publication and the website. They oversee the quality of the content and layout of individual pages, both in print and online (see page 25). The team involved with page make-up will liaise with the editorial, management, production, subediting and legal departments, as well as IT and website managers. They will also commission freelance writers, filmmakers, photographers, graphic and web designers.

Working in a team requires good communication skills, as a large number of people can be involved in putting together a single page, let alone a whole newspaper, magazine or website. Small teams also need to talk to each other, as the fewer people there are on a title, the more important it becomes that they all understand each other's role in the process. You also need to be able to work cooperatively with freelance content and service providers.

The media industry has moved towards undertaking more production in-house, resulting in editorial and page production teams now carrying more responsibility for a wide range of page creation activities. Media

companies require people with the training and skills necessary to produce a title or update a website, and prefer to employ those who are competent in a number of areas. This means that you will need a broad spread of skills and knowledge that will allow you to work efficiently with media technology and software.

Collaborative working

Media companies run their websites and print publications from central servers. These are large-capacity computers, or groups of processors, that are used to store and share files, and may administer the computer programs. The server manages the whole editorial and production system and is the hub through which writers, photographers, advertising and marketing departments and production teams exchange information. You will therefore need to become familiar with working with a server, as it is a key element in the running of efficient editorial and production teams. A well-organised server and online system with clearly named files is vital to ensure that the content for pages is easily accessible and the production work flow runs smoothly. Other departments such as advertising, marketing, conference and event organisers may use the server to work on collaborative projects. Servers are also used for functions such as backing up and archiving data.

Some media companies use server-based editorial work flow software that allows several people to work on a page of a print publication at the same time, with various levels of access assigned to each individual.

Server systems

The server is where key data and source files are kept, such as the house design style guide and the folders containing shared material such as templates/master pages and standing artwork files. It is also used as the base for the page production process. Those working in a particular area will be given a password that accesses only those parts of the server relevant to them. Senior editors and managers may be the only people with open access that allows them to make changes at any stage and the right to publish the final pages.

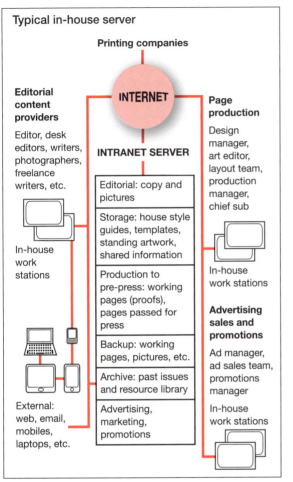

Typical in-house server

Printing companies

Editorial content providers

INTERNET

Page production

Editor, desk editors, writers, photographers, freelance writers, etc.

INTRANET SERVER

Design manager, art editor, layout team, production manager, chief sub

Editorial: copy and pictures

Storage: house style guides, templates, standing artwork, shared information

In-house work stations

Production to pre-press: working pages (proofs), pages passed for press

In-house work stations

Advertising sales and promotions

Backup: working pages, pictures, etc.

Ad manager, ad sales team, promotions manager

Archive: past issues and resource library

External: web, email, mobiles, laptops, etc.

Advertising, marketing, promotions

In-house work stations

Servers are used for data storage and file exchange.

Websites are produced as a series of pages made up from text and picture files stored in a database or folders on the main or a dedicated web server. Web teams normally use a server-based content management system (CMS) – a user-oriented program that does not require an IT or computing background. A password is normally, required to work on and to publish the pages.

Editorial production practice

The purpose behind any production process is to communicate the information to the audience in a timely and interesting manner, within the media company's budget. The editorial process involves several stages that require a balance of organisational and practical skills. The editor is responsible for planning the content and of monitoring the progress and cost of each page. They also manage all those involved and will make sure everyone in the team is aware of what has to be done, who is expected to carry out the work and when it has to be done by.

The first stage for the editor and team is to set the objective for the pages. This means identifying what the content will be and how it will be sourced, as well as deciding how to present the information to the target audience and which media will be used. The

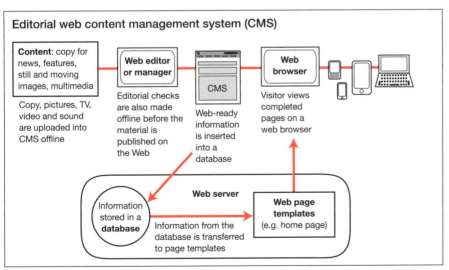

Editorial web content management system (CMS)

Content: copy for news, features, still and moving images, multimedia

Web editor or manager

Web browser

CMS

Copy, pictures, TV, video and sound are uploaded into CMS offline

Editorial checks are also made offline before the material is published on the Web

Web-ready information is inserted into a database

Visitor views completed pages on a web browser

Web server

Information stored in a database

Information from the database is transferred to page templates

Web page templates (e.g. home page)

CMSs represent the front end of a web server and are used to upload and format content into CSS templates, as well as providing access to functionality such as widgets and for archiving.

second stage is to draw up a schedule of when the material has to be completed and to assign the work to the appropriate people, making sure that they have full instructions on the tasks and that the resources needed are in place to allow them to complete their work within the required time.

The next stage is to organise all the material for the page production process in a clear and logical manner. The content for both media should be assessed for editorial relevance and technical suitability prior to the pages being assembled and the selected items prepared for page make-up. The pages are set up on templates that contain the house style for the structure and type, and each page then follows the design rules for the title. Layout skills (described in Chapter 5) are used to present the content in a visually interesting way. The final stage is where the pages go through a process of copy checks. Print pages can also be subject to a series of layout adjustments and there may be several versions of a page before it is approved. An editorial system needs robust version control as it is extremely important to ensure the correct version of a page is used.

> **TIP** It is important to make sure that everyone understands and follows the title's production systems. These are used to control the process and ensure that the content generated is consistent with the house editorial and design styles and technical requirements.

Planning and progress meetings

However good the working systems are, the key to successful production is good communication between the teams. Media titles hold regular editorial planning and production meetings, prior to a print publication or website being produced, to decide how to handle the material for specific pages or articles. As well as the main editorial planning meeting, there will be regular progress meetings between the teams and colleagues as they develop the content. The planning should include the way in which the reader or visitor is to be guided through the information and the emphasis to be put on each element. The progress meetings are to discuss the page content and layouts and review the design and copy treatment.

> **TIP** It is important that someone other than the page make-up person checks the pages as they are being worked on. Feedback on the layout is always useful, and it is difficult for anyone who has been closely involved with developing a page or spread to judge whether it works and fulfils the predetermined criteria. Another pair of eyes can notice problems or errors and may see areas where the content or layout might be improved.

The amount of autonomy granted to the person making up the pages varies according to how a publication's production team operates, and with individual editors. Some editors are very 'hands on' and like to be involved with checking proofs or unpublished web pages during the page make-up process. Others are prepared to trust the expertise of their team and wait until the page is more or less finished before looking at it.

Editorial and production briefs/job sheets

There needs to be a system of recording the information and instructions for each page, either on paper or as a digital file, to be distributed to all those involved. These may be forms created using specialist page planning software or as Word documents or Excel spreadsheets that are stored on a central server. The forms can include the editorial briefs that describe what is required for each feature or story and the overall theme of the issue or website, and production job sheets that cover the technical processes and production specifications.

The information for any editorial or production work should include all the basic details, even if this means repeating facts such as the publication name or website address, and the print issue date or upload deadline, because, although some media staff work only on one title at a time, others may be working on a number of publications in different media at the same time. It is good practice to set up checklists for the main information. A picture wish list is also useful, as it gives the picture editor, design and production teams or person making up the pages a guide as to what needs to be sourced or commissioned. To avoid confusion, each page should be given a name – a key word or phrase that is used as an identifier and to label all folders, files, copy and pictures related to that page. The key word, sometimes called the catchline, should also be used on the briefing sheet and any other production documents.

It is good practice to organise your work using clearly labelled folders and subfolders.

The minimum requirements of an editorial brief should be an outline of background information, possible contacts and references and a synopsis of the way in which an article is to be treated – the story key – and whether it is to appear in print and/or online. It is a basic requirement that those working on a title read, or at least scan through, the copy, but it is also helpful if the mood and feel of the piece is summarised on the form. The information for print has to include the issue date, section or heading; the number of pages and their order (lefts, rights or double page spreads); for the web it should also list the section and any hyperlinks to other pages, blogs and sites. The submission and production deadlines must also be included.

Freelance contributors should be provided with a separate brief on what they are required to write or produce. This may need to include an explanation of your title and its editorial stance, design style and audience. The written and visual material commissioned for a feature or page must be checked against the briefing form to make sure it has been supplied as requested, is suitable for the context and that the quality is acceptable. Occasionally, problems arise such as images that

communicate a different message to the copy, with the result that they have to be retaken, re-sourced, photoedited or heavily cropped.

The production manager, art or picture editor needs to keep track of who has been commissioned and what they have been asked to do, and record when it is submitted in a log or diary. Copy chasing involves pursuing text and pictures that have not been submitted by the requested date. It is a good idea for those involved in page make-up to keep checking with the other departments, as there can be last-minute editorial or technical changes, such as new or revised copy and additional pictures or other assets. Ideally, all the material should be ready for inclusion on the website or page before the production process begins. Unfortunately, due to scheduling demands, it is not uncommon for print issue pages to be started with a gap left for late copy or pictures.

The editorial briefing form

The editorial briefing form should cover all the information needed to develop a visual treatment for a section, article or individual story:

- Title
- Key word
- Editorial copy and production deadline/publishing date
- Page running order: issued by editor or production manager
- Subject: synopsis and mood of piece
- Page flag: may change to follow article subject
- Word count per page/number of pages, article or news item
- Imagery: number and subject of images
- Additional layout information
- Advertisement details: position, size and client
- Cross-media links: websites, tweets, blogs
- Contact details

TIP While briefing and other forms are very useful in preventing confusion and keeping a formal record of what has been commissioned, it is good practice to discuss your ideas with colleagues and contacts before proceeding to ensure everyone is clear on what should be done.

Contact lists

The media company may maintain a central list of contacts such as freelance writers, photographers or other contributors, web management and printing companies. However, many individuals build up their own lists of trusted contacts that they continue to work with throughout their career. These should include the details of the in-house staff involved in the production process and other departments within a company such as IT, finance and HR. It is also good to build up a record of contact details for people such as scientific advisers, specialist organisations, potential interviewees and PR staff that provide tickets for events or shows. Contact details should be available on the central server for all those involved in producing pages that might need such information.

TIP When building a contact list, you should record as many different methods of contacting people as possible. You may also need their website addresses to view examples of their work. You should also note any other relevant information, such as whether they have an agent and any particular areas of expertise.

See Chapter 9 action sheet: Desks, jobs and teams
www.pearsoned.com/hand

Editorial production schedules for print publications

The page production schedules help everyone involved in page production to organise their workload. The timetable starts when contributors need to supply their material and ties in with advertisers' deadlines and printing company's or web producers' production schedules.

The main factor in deciding a print publication's schedule is the date and time on which the printing company has requested that the pages be supplied. This is called the **press deadline**, and the timetable followed by all those involved in the editorial stages and production is worked backwards from that point (see Chapter 10, page 310). The actual publication date may be a day or even weeks after the press deadline, as the final production processes, including printing and distribution, can take anything from less than a few hours for

Yearly print magazine schedule

Editorial and advertising copy deadline	Press deadline	Cover date
15 December	12 January	February
12 January	9 February	March
5 February	9 March	April
5 March	13 April	May
3 April	11 May	June
5 May	8 June	July
2 June	6 July	August
9 July	10 August	September
3 August	7 September	October
3 September	12 October	November
1 October	7 December	December

This example shows key deadlines for a monthly print magazine.

a daily newspaper to several weeks for a multi-page glossy magazine.

Another consideration in establishing a production schedule is the time sensitivity of the information. News pages and front covers that feature up-to-the-moment events go to press last, while regular columns or pages and features may be assembled and laid out earlier in the process. Marketing and promotional material may need to include images of a front cover, which would then have to be prepared months in advance of the issue. It is not unknown for the Christmas cover of a magazine to be photographed in August.

Web and blog schedules

Although much of the Web seems to be instantaneous and infinitely flexible, most media websites consist of a mixture of spontaneous reaction to events and pre-planned content. Media companies' websites have an editorial production schedule based around a submission date that allows adequate time to compile, prepare and test material to meet any regular update deadlines. This can be the same date that the publication goes live on the Web, or a day or more before. Web-ready advertising has to follow a separate deadline – ranging from 72 hours to 10 days – that allows enough time to test any animation and video to ensure the files work on the site as intended.

The nature of online media dictates the pace of the production process. News websites are often updated

Online magazine schedule – rolling deadlines apart from special focus features and promotions

	Special focus	Copy/ advertising submission deadline	Online
Jan/Feb	Ski/ snowboarding	1 December	3–5 December
Mar/Apr	Valentines/ romance	1 February	3–5 February
May/Jun	Health & Nutrition	1 April	3–5 April
July/Aug	Summer festivals	1 June	3–5 June
Sept/Oct	Exhibition tie-in	1 August	3–5 August
Nov/Dec	Christmas/ winter sun	1 October	3–5 October

This example shows how an online magazine might work to rolling deadlines, but the schedules can include date-specific events and special features.

on a rolling basis with the result that the pressure to provide and publish new content is constant. It is in this kind of fast-moving environment that journalists and other non-web designers are most likely to be asked to handle production tasks. For other sites, such as webzines, the updates may not be as frequent. The pace of content change would ideally be based on what the website's users want, but more often it is dictated by what the publishers or media company can achieve or afford (see page 68).

Website visitors may expect major events to be covered if a hot story breaks. Regular events such as national holidays and topics to the site or blog, such as a ski show or sporting events, will be scheduled to appear on certain dates. This helps the advertising and marketing departments and sets a timetable for in-house and external contributors. For example, a women's lifestyle webzine will always need its Valentine's Day editorial and advertising material to be commissioned, submitted, checked and made ready for uploading by 14 February.

See Chapter 7 action sheet: Editorial schedules
www.pearsoned.com/hand

'Content is king.'

Anonymous

'It is fresh news and content is still king... when there is new content, people come back to read.'

Jason Goldberg, chief product officer, XING

Page handling

When planning the layout of the content, you have to bear in mind the target audience and what will engage them, and not allow your own personal preferences to colour your judgement. The structure of many online and printed publications will already have been set, and it is important that the subjects and images chosen stimulate your reader's or visitor's interest and make them want to stay on the site or look further into the title. A page layout should encapsulate the nature of the contents, with clean, strong typography and imagery to make readers want to look inside or click through and see more. Pictures communicate more immediately to a reader or website user than just a type-based page. However, typography alone can be successfully used to describe the contents, although it also has to be positioned so that it is functional, readable and attractive.

As the reader or visitor reads on or clicks through a publication, the layout of the pages should not appear repetitive, but be varied to keep the reader's attention. Websites are designed around a plan that allows the visitor to move through a scheme of pages that vary in usage, but the treatment of the pages will vary from decorative splash screens with little copy through to complex home pages and on to simpler pages containing long articles. There may be more than one template for each type of web page, and some choice where items can be placed, so it is good practice to alternate the templates and positioning between pages.

The design structure that works best for most printed titles is to counterbalance page layouts by contrasting calmer, simpler layouts with busy, complex pages to keep the reader's interest. In a celebrity or gossip magazine, the overall pattern is for short bursts of quick-to-read information with a large number of pictures. There may be some slightly longer articles, but these are often broken down into bite-sized chunks. In more serious and high-end magazine features, the first page often begins with a single, very large full bleed picture combined with the headline and standfirst, followed by pages with smaller images and the copy. The overall effect places the greatest impact at the start and draws the reader in, while the text-heavy pages provide a slower paced reading experience.

Copy handling

The material for a page will come from a range of sources. The contributors will all have their own way of working and may not be familiar with your editorial production system. When the copy comes in from writers, it is assessed by the editor and passed on to the copy or subeditors who check the text for errors and factual accuracy and put it into house style. This includes how the publication prefers to write such things as proper names, abbreviations and quantities. The copy or subeditor will check the copy for spelling and punctuation as well as reading to make sure it makes sense. They will also carry out a fact check: are the names spelled correctly and consistently through-out the piece; are the dates, events and any facts and figures verifiable?

However careful the writer may have been, it is always useful to have another person's point of view on the writing and to make sure the copy can be easily understood. There also needs to be a judgement on whether the material can be presented in the visual style of the publication. Once the copy has been sub-edited, the text file should be renamed using a key word relating to the page and the issue/date/page number, and stored in a folder ready for page make-up.

Fact checking for the Web has to be done quickly to keep up with the information flow, and there is a time pressure on web production teams that might encour-age some people to skim through or even skip the checking stage. This is inadvisable. Many mainstream media brands rely on their professional standard of copy to maintain their reputation against myriad competing sources, and recent cases of misreporting, plagiarism or downright fiction by journalists have led to those responsible losing their jobs and have damaged the industry.

Subediting

Subbing copy includes checking the copy for spelling, grammar and word usage, house style and that any facts included are accurate.

Common grammatical and word usage errors

When he arrived at court, the judge was told that Hopkins had been driven from his home by his wife.

Later, the accused asked Mrs Reddington if she could fill her hot water bottle from the geezer in the kitchen.

But Emma is as determined as ever and is pouring over all the books she can find.

The Huns' enemies were overwhelmed by Ghengis Khan's vast hoard.

Cigarettes may effect your health.

Commonly misspelled words

seperate = separate
recieved = received
acheived = achieved
independant = independent
their = belonging to them
there = a location
they're = contraction of they are
it's = it is
its = belonging to it

Warning It is important to make sure freelance contributors' copy conforms to the editorial standard of the publication or website, even though most media products cover themselves by including a legal disclaimer stating that the views expressed in the publication are not necessarily those of the publishing company.

See Chapter 9 action sheet: Copy handling
www.pearsoned.com/hand

Editorialising the image

Images can add to the value of the textual content by emphasising certain points in a story, make a statement or highlight a political issue. Pictures can show what the person being interviewed looks like or, in the case of fashion and products, the clothes and items. Images can also be used to establish the mood and tone of the piece. Whatever pictures are chosen for a story or article, they must comply with the design ethos, and the handling, cropping and placing of the imagery should be as consistent as possible. Some titles always put their pictures in coloured or tinted boxes or patterned borders to make the page busy and eye-catching, while others keep the photographs upright and use them in combination with blocks of type to build clean, geometric modernist pages. One thing all publications have in common is the need to source distinctive, strong pictures.

It is important that a lead picture captures the mood as well as the subject of the copy.

TIP A headline and lead picture should have a clear visual link and reinforce each other, as well as attract attention to the story or feature. It is good practice to balance the main image against the type elements, and use any directionality in the image to direct the eye toward the headline, standfirst etc. (see, pages 132–3). The letterforms in the headline can be made to echo shapes in the picture, to draw the eye back to the image. The larger type elements and the main visual should create interest, to convince a reader or visitor that the item or article is worth reading.

Evaluating pictures is not just a matter of selecting a suitable subject. You need to consider the colour and the tonal value – whether the image is light or dark. The tonal value has a strong influence on the overall balance of a page; for example, a pale image used as a lead picture may not be strong enough to hold the eye, while a vividly coloured or overly dramatic shot may distract from the rest of the page. The colours in the images need to be balanced against the other items on a page. The colour of a picture can be used as the basis for selecting the colours for headlines and tinted boxes. Alternatively, a contrasting colour can be chosen, for example a cool text colour to counterbalance a vibrant image. Some titles restrict the choice of colour to only those in the house style palette; others may permit the creation of additional colours that are more sympathetic to the content.

Websites do not usually have a free colour choice, and pictures should be selected that work with or provide a pleasant, non-clashing contrast to the set colour palette. If you are working on a CMS, you will be restricted to house style colours. This is also true of websites based on CSS. However, a media company may employ a web designer who works in a web design package that offers more control over a wide range of colours, type and picture positions for the pages.

Warning A bad or irrelevant picture should never be included just for the sake of placing an image on the page. Rather than risk using a poor image that may reduce the impact of the page, a more suitable solution might be to break up the text by using a pull quote, boxed item or to balance the headlines and copy with white space (a content-free, open area).

Web images, whether photographs or video thumbnails, should have as much visual impact as possible at the size they first appear on-screen and be of sufficient quality that the viewer can zoom in. Pictures should complement each other and provide a visual connection between the current page and any related pages, with galleries and slideshows to feature good photography. Images can be used to develop a story in sequence as the website user moves from page to page. You need to take into account all the type and graphic elements on a page, as well as the subject matter of the copy when choosing an image, and how well the image works with other pictures on the page. The images should be selected to stimulate interest in both the connected story and the website's other content. It is a good idea to make pictures clickable as this encourages visitors to follow a story or item and to access other facilities.

Compare the tone, scale and crop of pictures to make sure they work with each other. Try to avoid faces looking out of the page as this directs attention away from the content.

In the blink of an eye

Research has found that a website has just 50 milliseconds (1/20th of a second) – the time it takes to blink – to attract attention, so it is very important that the pictures have an immediate impact to prevent the viewer clicking away. Pictures intended for home page thumbnails should be kept simple and direct and not allowed to become over-complex. It is important to brief a photographer on how, where and at what size an image is to be used, so they can compose their images accordingly.

Try to avoid cut-offs – a section of a story or article isolated by the positioning of the pictures – as in this example where the third column of copy has been isolated by the positioning of the picture.

Take care on a double page spread to ensure that the fold or spine, shown by the grey panel, does not obscure faces.

Picture research, sourcing and commissioning

Imagery is an integral part of media communication, and most of the stories used in both print and online are illustrated. Some media companies have their own library of images, picture editors and researchers, so pictures for an article can be sourced in-house. When a feature is commissioned from a freelance writer, they may be asked supply the images, or a photographer will be briefed to work with them and set up a photo shoot. Most titles rely on sourcing their images from outside companies and contributors and this will require you to research a subject and source suitable images. There are various websites you can go to to obtain imagery on a wide variety of subjects, and specialists who can be asked to take or create pictures (see Chapter 7, and page 345). The major stock image websites have a search engine or you can ask their picture researchers to research a subject for you. These sites allow you to build up a lightbox of selected images before making your final choice. Image sharing websites such as Flickr, are a mixture of professional and personal photographs and a search may not produce usable pictures.

Most titles have a picture budget that dictates the number and type of images. You may be in the position of commissioning photographs and illustrations from professionals, or if there is a more limited budget you may need to obtain free images. High-end fashion magazines often commission famous photographers to go to exotic locations for their shoots. At the other end of the scale, titles that do not have a picture budget can use free publicity shots supplied by PR and marketing companies, or photos or videos supplied by their readers and visitors.

Photographs are not always the best way of illustrating an article. A technical feature might be explained more clearly by using graphs and charts, while a lifestyle or very conceptual piece might work

TIP It is a good idea to build up and store a collection of images that may be useful in the future. These can be images that have already been published, such as portrait shots of people that may be used on a regular basis. Images can also be collected from giveaway DVDs, free samples from stock image banks and the results of image searches. If you have the skill and resources, you may also take the photographs.

better with illustrations. An exclusive portrait shot adds creditability to an interview, while standard PR pictures can be bland and may have already been used by other titles. Commissioning images may involve briefing a photographer or film-maker to shoot in a publication's house style, for example using a certain lighting or lens effect. It may also mean matching the theme or personality of the subject to the publication, for example posing an airline executive inside or in front of an aeroplane for a business publication, or pictures of luggage set against a studio jungle backdrop.

News images are supplied by agencies such as Associated Press (AP) and Thomson Reuters that provide photographs, podcasts, mobile alerts and RSS feeds

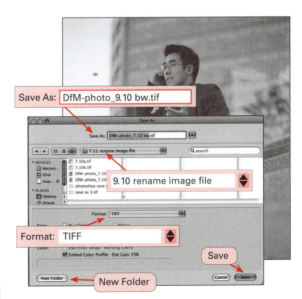

All image files should be clearly named to indicate their use and subject. Once the picture has been prepared for its target media in Photoshop, use Save As from the File menu to change the image file name and save it to a page or issue location on the server.

Warning Remember that all images must be checked for copyright restrictions and that permission to use 'free' images may be restricted. The fact that an image has already appeared on the Web is no guarantee to its legal usage.

Source: Sam Todd

Good-quality commercial stock, still and moving images and PR shots are available for a wide range of subjects. However, the subject matter and photographic styles can be clichéd.

as well as video and films on global events. Reuters alone supplies worldwide news media with 7,500 videos and news footage each month, and its team of more than 600 photojournalists and editors submit approximately 1,500 stills each day. The company has an archive of news material that increases by over half a million images and 90,000 videos each year.

Major image banks such as Getty Images and Corbis charge a fee for picture and film usage (see page 345). There are a number of free or low-cost images websites such as Dreamstime.com, Freefoto and Fotololia.co.uk, among others, though these images tend to be more suitable for web than print. There are free videos available, but some are not suitable for commercial use and they may be illegally posted on the Web.

High-end publications such as interiors or fashion magazines and websites generally use professional photographers and film-makers because the quality of imagery is a major feature of the title. On other

mainstream titles, there is a trend towards people who have traditionally been expected to provide just the written content also being asked to create visual material. As a result, it is now necessary for many of those working in the media to be proficient in taking pictures or making videos and audio reports, as they may be expected to go out to an event or interview with an audio recorder and camera (see page 233).

Originals and copies

A copy should be made of the original (master) image to be used as a working picture file for the page. It is inadvisable to use the original sourced or commissioned image file without making a copy, as it is easy to misfile, accidentally delete a file, or the file may become corrupted. Damage to or loss of the original file can result in the embarrassment of having to ask for it to be sent again, and this could delay an entire production schedule.

Working with imagery

It is important that all images and videos are sourced or commissioned prior to the start of page make-up. The editorial team should have considered the visual treatment of the content from the very start of a print or online title's planning process; however, exactly what imagery will be needed may only become apparent as a page progresses. A feature can evolve and the emphasis change, and news images are only available at short notice. The time pressures of the page production system can lead to a situation where images have to be provided quickly. In order to be in a position to handle such a situation, it helps to know where you can obtain pictures that match the title's visual style and technical criteria and how much they are likely to cost.

Video

Moving images are an important part of a website's content, and a video should add informational value to a story or item and enhance a visitor's experience of the site. Videos can be commissioned from specialist film-makers, filmed by reporters or in-house staff, or purchased from image libraries such as Getty Images and Fotosearch offer editorial and creative stock footage and video clips. Whatever the source, the material selected for the site must fit the editorial and visual ethos of the title and play in a variety of media players and browsers. The moving imagery has to be representative of the subject of a website and integrate with the other content – it should not be gratuitous or gimmicky.

Generally, people prefer to watch a video rather than read through a long piece of copy, and a filmed report or interview is likely to take precedence over written content, so it is vital that all the main story points are made in the voiceover. However, a transcript or associated piece of writing is still important for hearing-impaired users, as is including picture alt tags. The text, heading and summary that accompany the video must contain searchable key words. Videos can be uploaded on to hosting sites such as YouTube and, if they prove popular, can boost visitor numbers to your website.

The thumbnail still from the video is used on the page to encourage people to click on the play button. You should choose a strong image that reflects the best of the content, rather than relying on the first frame or an auto-generated thumbnail. There should be a very obvious play button, clearly labelled 'play' or 'watch' to differentiate videos from still images. The headline and summary of the related story can also be play buttons.

The length of the package or clip has to be edited for the target audience and the nature of the website. A news clip should be brief and concise, while a video report can require a longer time span. In general, several short clips on a number of pages provide more interest for a website visitor than one longer film on a single page, but this depends on the target audience. News websites' home page video clips can be 15–20 seconds long, while news media and webzine features and interviews may run for 2–3 minutes. If the story or item has a longer lifespan, it may be worth offering a video download.

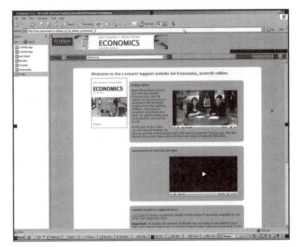

Interactive media are often the best way to present complex information or instructions.

Video players

Videos have to be viewed using a player and should conform to a standard aspect ratio of 400 × 300 pixels or 400 × 224 pixels. CMS and web authoring programs enable you to position a video on the page and apply dynamic features that expand the video to full screen view. Most media websites have specific technical requirements so the videos play smoothly. These include the speed (bit rate in kbs), file format (MP3/4), compression and encoding/decoding. The aim is to achieve the best possible video quality at the lowest bit rate.

The media industry has taken full advantage of the content sharing websites that have led to an expansion in the availability of information and visual material from a wide variety of people and organisations. News media in particular have benefitted from on-the-spot images and film reports provided by onlookers and even participants in events.

User-generated content

Mainstream news media do sometimes obtain videos and photographs from public video hosting sites such as YouTube and accept visual information from 'citizen journalists'. News media have always been prepared to show amateur film when it provided the best or only reportage of an event; the famous film of President John F. Kennedy's assassination in Dallas, Texas, in 1963 was captured on an ordinary hand-held movie camera by Abraham Zapruder, a Dallas businessman. When internationally significant events such as the 9/11 terrorist attacks or the Indonesian Boxing Day tsunami occur, any pictures, films or CCTV footage taken at the time can be used to convey the impact of the events. However, some news sites have been deliberately hoaxed by people sending in faked stories and films, and the BBC has a department that just deals with checking the validity and technical suitability of the user-generated content submitted to it. The widespread use of Photoshop and video-editing software means that both photographs and moving images should be checked for misleading editing and image falsification.

Warning All websites must comply with national copyright laws covering the use of moving imagery, and you should check the legal status of a UGC video before embedding or creating a link to it. The legal status of a video should be indicated on the host site, but be aware that people upload videos illegally. It is a good idea to contact the video uploader directly to ensure they are the copyright holder.

Copyright

Many people have the false impression that everything on the Internet is free for anybody to download and use, but, in fact, much of the visual material on the Web, both photographic and moving imagery, is subject to copyright. If you intend to source an image or video from the Internet, you should expect it to be copyright protected unless there is a clear statement that the copyright has been waived, and many images and videos on photo sharing or video hosting sites are only made available for non-commercial use. Permission to include copyright-protected images can be obtained in exchange for a credit or positive mention in the text, or the owner may request payment of a fee.

There are copyright-free images available under a **Creative Commons licence**, from websites such as Wikimedia Commons and Flickr, but care has to be taken as this often does not apply to commercial use and not all photographs and videos can be used without restriction. Under Creative Commons, some people

Stock image copyright

Stock image libraries hold the copyright for images and issue licences, governing the terms and conditions for their use. These include the media a photograph, illustration or video may be published in, which countries the agreement covers, and for how long you may display them. You should always retain a secure master file of your original image and keep a record of the original image bank's file name, should the licence need extending or if you wish to use the picture in another medium or country. The master file should be stored with care as some image banks may restrict further downloads.

waive all their rights in return for an acknowledgement (picture credit), and a green copyright symbol or a diagonal bar across the symbol can indicate images that are free for anyone to use. However, a number of people withhold some of the Creative Commons rights, especially in regard to professional media usage. The terms may also only apply for one region or country, or permit web usage but not reproduction in print.

You should not use a photograph if there is any question at all over its copyright status. Professional digital cameras record additional information about a photograph, such as information about copyright and author, as metadata that can be accessed via photo viewing software. Some modern cameras and camera phones can insert global positioning system (GPS) information to record the place and time that the image was taken, and cameras can also employ retinal image capture as the photograph is taken to identify the photographer and prevent the illegal use of copyrighted images.

TIP

- If you have negotiated an informal contract to use an image, you should also obtain written permission in an email or ask the owner to sign a release form, and ensure the image is only used as agreed.
- It is good practice to include a legal disclaimer to the effect that every effort has been made to comply with relevant laws and statutes. This should be included either with the image caption or credit, in the terms and conditions of the website, or on a panel in a print publication.

Copyright: playing it safe

- Be aware that search engines do not automatically filter for copyright.
- Make sure you use the search engine's advanced images search criteria to search for images labelled for commercial reuse.
- Be aware that YouTube and other video hosting sites do not monitor content for copyright or legal permissions.
- Do not reuse visual material from a blog without checking its source and copyright status.
- Check whether the requirement to credit the copyright holder forms part of the licence to show an image or video.
- Note if the licence restricts how the image may be used; for example, it is common for there to be a stipulation that it is not altered in any way.

Working with advertising

Advertisements are sold in advance of publication, and an advertiser will be asked to supply digital artwork to the advertising department by a set date as press-ready pdf or JPEG files for print, or as gifs, JPEGS or for a website. The arrival of each is logged in by the advertising department and checked against the pre-bookings recorded. These are listed on a schedule for the publication or website, to make sure that all the bookings have been submitted and allocated a space. The advertisements must conform to legal standards and may not contain any inappropriate content. The production department checks the digital files are in the correct format as there can be technical problems with material supplied by clients. Advertisements may need to be adjusted; for example, a fast-looped animated advertisement for a website might need to be returned to the client company or agency to be amended to comply with technical guidelines and health and safety criteria.

> **TIP** Check all advertisements as they are received, because amending them may involve an agency and its client, and it may take a considerable length of time for any revisions to be agreed by all parties.

Clashing content

The agency often conceives its advertisements as part of a campaign, rather than an element of any particular media product. This can mean that the advertisements may not blend in well when placed in a print publication or on a website. Print magazine bleed advertisements can cause problems, such as when they clash with each other and with editorial pages, as coloured backgrounds that go right to the edge of the page may make the reader's eye jump between them. You should leave the inner margin clear on editorial pages that face advertisements, especially if there are similar colours or images on both pages.

If there are quarter- or half-page advertisements that fall within the type area of a print publication, there should be one or two lines left free between the advertisements and the editorial, or a fine horizontal line drawn though the space, or a vertical line drawn down the centre of the gutter to provide a visual divide between the advertisements and editorial content. The

same rule applies to the Web, and space (padding), a line or box can be used to divide advertisements from other content, especially in the case of busy animated advertisements. Most websites have stringent rules covering these types of advertisements that limit the rate of image repeats and loops. Advertisements featuring sound can also be contentious, as some visitors prefer to listen to their own music while on the Internet and others dislike being forced to listen to audio advertisements. A solution may be to ask the clients to supply advertisements that operate on rollover or have to be clicked on, so that users have the option to view the animated version or listen to an audio file.

Right: page layouts often have to accommodate both editorial and advertising content.

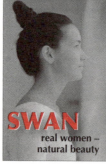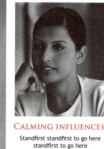

Left: try to avoid images that mirror each other, as in the example shown here.

> **TIP** It is a good idea to liaise with the advertisement department to obtain examples of the advertisements and find out where they are to be sited in advance, just in case there are any problems that need to be resolved. It is also important to view or look at the advertisements *in situ*, to make sure they are compatible with the rest of the page(s).

Page creation design rules

The layout of a printed or web page is subject to a number of design rules. Some are specific to the publication or site, while others relate to more general factors such as making pictures a certain size in a specific section, keeping stories in rectangular shapes or short chunks, and where bylines, email, buttons and links are to be placed. These rules are useful for journalists and other media professionals to follow if they do not have specific design training and are required to work on print page make-up and/or web production. Standard practice also helps whenever it is necessary to work quickly to meet a deadline. Experienced design professionals with extensive technical knowledge may break these rules, but will only do so to overcome a specific problem or to create a special effect. Employing these rules will help you because they are known to work. On the whole, it is easier to try to work within the rules rather than circumvent them.

The house style establishes the design rules that maintain the publication's identity and structure. The production process is usually carried out by a team of people, and the pages of a printed publication or website may be worked on by more than just one person. Following the house style design should ensure that all the pages, no matter how many people are involved in their production, work as part of a 'whole', and that the pages are visually consistent throughout the publication or site. It is also very important to maintain good communications with the other people in a production team and discuss preliminary versions of the pages. At some stage, the print pages should be viewed in running order and the web pages clicked through to make sure they work together. It is good practice to have some system whereby the content and design is seen as a whole. Generally, the production manager or web editor will look at all the pages, but each production team member should check their own contributions and that their pages work with those produced by other people.

The role of the grid

A well-considered underlying grid acts as a guide to how pages are to be constructed and serves to

Non-printing guides

- Print layout templates represent the grid using non-printing guides in different colours that mark out the margins, columns and the baseline grid (see *How to work with layout*, page 103). These guides can be made visible or hidden to see a preview of the design.
- Most page make-up, design and imaging programs allow the user to place non-printing guides that can be dragged from the rulers – measurement strips to the top and left of the program window – to mark out alignments and assist with positioning in a design.

create continuity of visual expression from one issue or update to the next. Web grids provide a structure that makes it simple to communicate complex issues. Working with a grid can speed up the page production rate and improve a title's usability and helps to maintain the look and feel of a design. Page grids provide the foundation for print layouts and underlie most website pages. The grid operates as a guide to alignment and proportion.

Programming languages such as HTML use the pixel grid to define where items are placed on the page. Web grids provide the background structure for each page template, and these are not normally altered unless there is a major change such as a redesign. Web grids are used to hold the vertical alignment of the design, set regular spacing and provide a consistent look and feel to the pages. The average browser window's shape dictates the horizontal proportions of the grid (see page 92). Web pages are built from a complex regular grid of pixels and have to be geometric.

The web grid has to be followed; clever use of visual material can prevent a site appearing constrained. While all copy and images created in HTML or another programming language are restricted to rectangular or square forms, Photoshop can be used to create bitmapped artwork such as rounded edge boxes, or to run type and images at any angle or in irregular shapes. The Photoshop artwork is then positioned in geometric placeholders on the grid (see pages 140–1).

Layout skills

The primary aim of any layout is to create interest in the contents. Both print and online imagery and graphics should work to enhance the aesthetic value of a page. The placement of the contents should not only convey information but also create balance and directionality to draw the eye through the material. All the elements help to communicate the message. All the semiotic implications of the informational and visual components, both individually and as a page, should be considered. A happy, sunny picture contrasted to a gloomy or upsetting headline might be seen as ironic, or could just appear insensitive, thoughtless or confusing. A well-organised page that is eye-catching and thought provoking will convey the information clearly to the audience and help you to control how the latter follows the page content. The selection of type for a layout can ensure that the copy and any other text-based graphics are legible and comprehensible, and that the relative importance of the copy elements is unequivocal.

There are a number of page layout skills and techniques that can be used to create attractive, well-balanced pages that work within a house design style. These can help you to ensure that pages have clear read paths and are well signposted with a logical information hierarchy. The aim is to create good-looking pages with attractive imagery and pleasing colours that work together in a manner appropriate for the title, section and subject. The pages also have

to convey the mood and be visually appropriate for the profile of the media product. However, while beauty is often assumed to be synonymous with the ideal, some designs may just need to be functional, as a special interest group readership will buy the publication for reasons other than visual attractiveness. But for most titles, and particularly those in a competitive market-place, appearance is important and good page layouts are needed to enhance their marketability.

The visual character and perceived identity of a title will have been considered when the design style was developed. To lay out pages successfully within any

A successful layout will have a clear information hierarchy and a good balance between all the graphic items.

The overall look of web pages may be standardised but it is possible to control the pattern of the copy and decide on the position and nature of the images.

Source: Rudy VanderLans

1980s cutting-edge titles such as Émigré spearheaded the move from modernist design to deconstructionism.

Source: Rudy VanderLans

Graphic designer Rudy VanderLans pioneered layering information and breaking the grid.

design, type and pictures have to be carefully chosen and combined on the grid in a way that achieves a sense of balance and has a strong visual impact. Should a title or page not contain images, good layouts can be created by introducing contrasting type sizes from very large to small and employing background areas of coloured tints balanced by open white space.

Standardisation versus originality

For most media companies, it is more time and cost effective for page layouts to follow a predefined format. Websites tend to have a fixed page design: there may be a choice of template for a page and a range of type heading sizes, and, on some sites, it is possible to choose the position for a picture, button or link on a feature page. But mostly the page layout is pre-defined, which has the advantage of making it quick and easy to place and upload content (see page 142).

Production teams work under pressure to finish pages quickly, and one common solution is to use standardised layouts. The two main advantages to having a pre-set page layout is that the writers know in advance how much copy to submit, and those making up the pages know exactly where the content has to fit. This eliminates both the time and the stress of devising original layouts. This solution is more suited to formal or technical publications where the content does not rely on a creative visual treatment of the material. However, standardised pages can lack personality and make a title appear repetitive. Titles with design- or fashion-conscious readers or visitors often require more creative pages that reflect their audience's tastes and aspirations.

'Good looking designs work better'.

Don Norman, author, academic and usability expert

The aesthetic–usability effect

The **aesthetic–usability effect** is a design theory that states that aesthetically pleasing designs are not simply preferred to less attractive ones, but are seen as more functional. Research has also shown that people are more tolerant of errors in a design that is visually pleasing. Attractive designs can inspire affection and loyalty towards the publication or website. If a reader or viewer likes the look of the title and it fits in with their personal or career aspirations, they are more likely to identify with it, trust the information and continue to buy or view the product.

Many current newspapers have modernised their look but still base their design on established conventions of layout and type styles. The *Financial Times* has retained it signature pink paper, a key element of its identity, with pages laid out in a clean modular format.

There are financial reasons behind whether a title uses a standardised or original layout. The budget for producing a title takes into account the complexity and content of pages and the length of time they will take to set up, as this adds to the cost per page. For example, a feature spread would be assigned more money than an editor's opinion page. Pages are designed either to follow similar layouts and be quick to set up, or may have more creative layouts that are more time consuming to produce. However, even on standardised pages, layouts should be varied to avoid repetition for each issue or update.

Working on web pages

Web page production combines editorial and technical skills such as creating content for a specific website or page, and preparing graphic material that best uses the possibilities of the technology and media. Understanding the structure of your website will help you to create pages that make the most of the templates and to integrate the pages with the rest of the Internet. You should try to develop a thorough knowledge of how content handling software such as a CMS is used to produce pages and meet the demands of day-to-day production.

The templates will have been created when the look and interactivity of the site were designed. Templates provide a look for the page structure, type styles and colours to be used, and can have a selection of formats for the content areas that allow you to vary the position of the editorial, advertising and any other interactive elements. The copy needs to be written in a text-editing program so that any word processing formatting is removed. It is useful to know enough about HTML to recognise certain symbols such as arrows (< >). These would have to be replaced or deleted as HTML coding uses them to define instructions. A CMS allows you either to type directly into a copy window, or to paste in copy from a text-editing program. Web assets such as image, audio and video files should be prepared following the technical specifications of the site and uploaded through the CMS into a database.

The basis of most commercial websites is HTML/XML coding. This dictates where the menus, tabs, content areas and images fall and works with other programming languages to add functionality to a website. The CMS or page handling program is an interface between the content and the coding that translates the entered material into web-ready pages. CMSs vary in how they operate as the software is normally written

Web code

Web design programs generate code that contains reference points for where each element needs to be positioned on a page. This includes the position, shape, colour and size of content areas, menus, tabs and other graphics such as widgets.

either for a media company to handle a number of sites, or for an individual title. CMSs are constantly evolving to take in the latest web media trends and technological developments. It is not unusual to encounter a different CMS program each time you move from company to company, but the skills you acquire on one system are usually transferable to another. Good page handling techniques are applicable no matter what software is being used.

File naming

Browsers and CMSs require files to be named in a very specific way that relates to how they operate. Those managing, originating and editing content files for websites need to follow a clear naming protocol. The files should be saved in a folder system on the media company's main server before being entered into the CMS or program used to edit the website, and if the copy and pictures are to be shared between print and online titles, a dual folder and file naming system should be created.

Searchability

A website and its pages have to be findable when published on the Internet. You can increase the likelihood of your pages being visited by including as many identifying factors such as key word meta tags – the deep information attached to a file. These will help search engines locate your pages when somebody initiates a search. Search criteria need to be taken into account when writing headings and sells, throughout the copy and for picture captions, as search engines look for not only the word itself, but also how it has been used.

There are a number of rules to follow: every page should have relevant title and description tags in the page file name and any headings, sells and copy used on the page so that they can be found by all types of search engine. The title and description tags should be clear and accurate and must contain key words to

'The essential principles of web production consist not only of techniques for placing text, images, links and interactive components on a page, but also planning what the purpose of such a site should be.'

Jason Whittaker, educator and author

enable search engines to identify the website, page and its contents. The description tag supplies the summary for search engine listings, and it is very important to make sure it contains a selection of words that someone might think to use when searching for information on a specific subject. Title tags are also used by some browsers to index bookmarks and favourites.

Identifiers or key words should be mentioned in the headline, sell and crossheads, as well as throughout longer sections of body copy and in picture captions. This is because most search engines' **robots** (**bots**) that search for information look for positioning, proximity, repetition and frequency of words on a page.

However, Google has stated that title tags and repeated key words in headings will not improve a website's ranking for its search engine, as it takes over 200 factors into consideration. Boolean search engines, such as Google, are intuitive and can find the answer to quite complex questions. The bots look for identifying words within the page, then for the relevancy of the word to the search request as well as for connections and longer links between words. Google also sells higher positions on its search list so companies and organisations can ensure they come within the top five or ten.

Warning Do not use copyrighted phrases or other company's logos, trading or product names in a URL or title tags. Websites have been sued for doing so. There have been cases of websites using the name of a well-known title or media company 'with a twist' as their name. This is regarded as 'passing off' – trying to exploit another's reputation – and is illegal.

Understanding and managing the site plan

It is, of course, necessary to have visited the website you will be working on and become familiar with how it looks and operates. But when you come to plan the content and source the material needed for production, using the site plan, which is often depicted as a graph that shows how the pages connect to each other, will help you to visualise the linear and non-linear connections between pages. The site plan enables you to identify where it would be useful to include additional hyperlinks so that visitors can find their way between related content and sections.

Media websites divide their content into sections that are directly accessed from the home page, and many stories may be covered on a number of sections and pages, since there may be stories in other sections that relate to the topic. As well as directing visitors using the primary navigation system, it is good practice to set up a **web cluster** – a set of sub-pages on one subject that link a story on the home page to its category section and related pages. Page clusters should be planned to work as a series of connected items of information. The headings and sells on the home and other pages within a cluster can be exactly the same, or the secondary headline and sell may differ slightly, as the visitor has already shown some interest. A cluster should contain plenty of opportunities for a visitor to find associated stories, archived information or related websites.

Once you are confident you understand the site plan, the next stage is to source and edit material that matches the style for each page. This can include providing sufficient copy for the number of stories on a page, writing headings and sells that comply with the word count limit, as well as selecting images, videos and other media and deciding how they will be used. It is important when sourcing or assessing material for the pages to make sure that all content fits with the editorial style and that the assets are in the correct format. The online help pages and any other instructions should cover the technical requirements for the web assets, such as the file formats and the dimensions of images and video.

Usability: diggers and skimmers

Research carried out in 2006-2007 by the Poynter Institute, a US school of journalism, used eye-tracking technology to find out how much of a news story people read in different media. The researchers compared broadsheet and tabloid newspapers with news websites and found that their participants read more of a story they had chosen online than in a broadsheet and tabloid newspaper. The average amount read was 77% online, 62% in a broadsheet and tabloid readers averaged 57%. However, Jakob Nielsen, a well-known website usability expert, has found that the average website visitor reads less of the words on a feature page than a reader of a print title would for the same subject, and that the percentage drops in proportion to the length of an article.

The currently accepted view in the media industry is that many website users scan through before reading in detail, watching videos or downloading podcasts (diggers), while some people prefer pages they can scan through quickly (skimmers), although the amount and speed of reading vary according to the target audience and subject matter.

Sources: The Poynter Institute: *http://eyetrack.poynter.org/about.html* and Neilsen Norman Group: *www.useit.com*

Content on a page

The writing style for a website should be covered in the journalism house style and will vary according to the website's editorial stance. As well as the quality of the text, there are a number of technical factors you need to consider to make the copy on your website more effective. Online headlines have to contain the most relevant searchable key words, so may become quite long and detailed. However, many CMSs have a character limit for the main and other headings in a specified type style and size, and you should try to write headings that correspond to the character count. It is inadvisable to force a long main story heading to fit by choosing a smaller typesize, as this will disrupt the visual hierarchy of the page.

Sells also should be written to fit a particular word count as they need to work in conjunction with the headings and images. To make pages with longer features and news reports quicker and easier to read on-screen, the running copy should be presented in short paragraphs with an additional white space between the text blocks. The general advice, when commissioning or editing writing for the Web, is that features should ideally be kept under 400 words and subdivided with crossheads. Search engines are more likely to find your article if you include key words in the first paragraph, and it is a good idea for there to be other potential search words throughout the feature or report.

The open spaces between paragraphs break the **eye flow** down a page and create a frame around the text blocks. The side margins and vertical spaces guide the eye downwards and help to separate the other page elements, such as animated advertisements that might distract the visitor and make it hard to concentrate on the editorial content. Clear space around objects can help website visitors to assimilate information, and open areas prevent the graphic elements visually merging with one another or the text.

Crossheads may be employed to highlight the content of paragraphs, to provide extra navigation and **eye stops** for visitors scanning the page. You can also use highlighted hyperlinks in the text. Where images or videos are placed in a feature, the picture, its captions and any hyperlinks should have a reasonable amount of space around them. Because the items on the page may shift position in different browsers, there should always be a few pixels of padding (space) between separate items such as pictures and copy to prevent the text running into or on to the image.

'On the average web page, users have time to read at most 28% of the words during an average visit; 20% is more likely.'

Jakob Nielsen, PhD, Nielsen Norman Group

Padding

The CSS box model includes padding – the space inserted to ensure the copy and images do not clash. A CMS can include the option of pre-set text boxes, or space between text and images may need to be inserted manually.

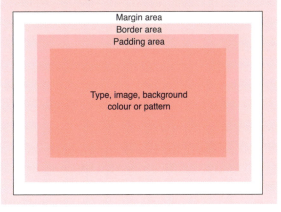

It is a good idea to offset adjacent images that relate to different stories as an alignment can cause them to be perceived as linked items.

In order to achieve a good visual balance, it is good practice to alternate the position of pictures from left to right on feature pages.

Web assets

When you come to handle web assets, you will need to confirm that supplied files are in the correct file formats. If there are problems with any files, you can either request that they be resupplied or make the adjustments yourself. This means opening the files and amending them in the relevant software, such as Photoshop for photography or Final Cut Pro for video. FLV (Flash video files) and QT (QuickTime) movies are the most commonly used formats for film, and most audio players use MP files. Video windows vary between the square-ish, old TV dimensions and wide screen, and the width and height of video files will be specified for your website. If a video is the wrong size for your site, you can adjust this in a video-editing program. Photographs can be resampled to the correct size for thumbnails and any other fixed picture position. Hyperlinks can be embedded on a feature page to video hosting sites, or a pop-up window used to open the file in a sound or movie player (see page 233).

Some journalists and marketing teams produce their own film reports and packages for a website. They may submit web-ready work in the correct format, or you may have to select and edit the material. Video reports usually include sound, and any audio files may also have to be encoded following the guidelines. The memory size of video and audio files has to be considered when they are edited, as not only are very large files difficult to work with and upload. They can make the website slow to download and may not play well on less powerful computers. It is possible to reduce the memory size of a video, but this will result in a loss of quality.

Photographs and other graphics for the Web should be selected or commissioned with their target size in mind. More than one image should be sourced for each item as major stories and features need a thumbnail for the home page, as well as a selection of different images for interstitial and feature pages. Photographs and graphics have to be JPEGS, PNG or gifs, and most website pictures must conform to a fixed ratio, such as 4×3 or 16×9 (the same proportions as standard and widescreen TV).

The dimensions of thumbnails and images on home pages are normally fixed and should not be changed. Pictures should be sympathetically scaled and cropped to fit their designated (target) space. Images need to convey visual information clearly and make sense within the proportions of the target space. For example, if a very tall person has been photographed next to a short person, and the target space is a wide, shallow picture box, the image can be hard to crop. It is a good idea to select a

Warning Pictures should never be distorted to fit the image areas and should completely fill the specific dimension of the picture box.

Try to make sure that pictures used for a slideshow or gallery are cropped to the same aspect ratio, and that elements are cropped to a consistent scale within the icture frame.

Design for Media

Tea picker, China   boy and girl on beach

All images should be given an alt tag caption that can be read by screen readers as this is required by disability legislation.

key area of a photograph for a thumbnail, because if the whole image is over-reduced, the subject may become so small that it is hard to make out any details.

Although the choice of type you can use in a CMS may be restricted, it is possible to save type as an image (graphic text – see page 187). For example, a headline in a decorative typeface can be created in Photoshop as a JPEG and uploaded in the same way as a photograph. However, bitmap type is not searchable, so any key words would have to be in the image file name or caption. Websites with a large number of images can be slow to download, and some sites recommend that graphic text be used only for brand names and when included on maps and charts.

ALT tag captions should be written for all imagery. Text recognition software reads the alt tags as spoken words for visually impaired people. Including alt tags is one step that can be easily made towards meeting the legal requirements for accessibility under British and US disability rights legislation. Visit *http://www. disabilityartsonline.org* for more information.

Access and publishing rights

The web editor or senior web manager is expected to assume responsibility for ensuring that all the material published on a company website is accurate and complies with the law. Intellectual property and copyright laws apply to everything published in the public domain, including on the Web. The advertising standards code of conduct also covers online advertisements. You or the media company could be sued if you allow something to be published online that is libellous or defamatory. It is important that the page production system is secure, and that it is not possible for an unauthorised person to enter unchecked material or publish a page.

There can be differing levels of access to a website: for example, a journalist working on a news section may only have the right to upload and edit news content and images. The editorial web team should be able to preview its pages offline, but usually the team is not allowed to publish the pages on the Web. The functional side of the website is normally only accessed by the IT/web company or person who manages the server side of the operation, as they handle the background functionality and are responsible for setting up the access rights to the website and CMS. It is a good idea to build up a relationship with the technical team as you may need its help from time to time.

Source: Charles Fox

Some stories are better told through images and using a slideshow can have a more dramatic impact than simply including pictures on a contents page.

Web advertisements

Uploading advertisements may be handled by the same people who update the editorial content, or by a separate production department or web company. You will need to check the advertisements are the right size and shape – skyscraper, banner, MPU ad – and that the advertisement appears in the space that has been booked and that it remains on the site for the agreed length of time. There are production criteria you will need to check, such as the file size limits; for example, the technical requirements may be for a 20k gif, 35k JPEG or 40k Flash file. Video advertisement files need to be checked to ensure they are compatible with the media company software. A gif or JPEG for the thumbnail should also be supplied. You should run any animated advertisements to make sure the advertiser has complied with any restrictions. This should be done on a test page with the other content to see how it will appear *in situ*. You should also check that the IT team/company is monitoring the click-on and click-through rates, and that any specific coding or scripts have been embedded.

All those involved in the web production process should run their own checks before their pages are submitted to the web editor or manager. They should ensure that assets such as pictures, audio and video files upload correctly and play, and that the page is as consistent as possible from browser to browser. Any new hyperlinks should be clicked on to make sure they work and load the right page, and existing hyperlinks should be tested to make sure the URLs are correct and current. Other interactive features such as menus, tabs, radio buttons, rollovers and any widgets should be activated to ensure the embedded app, script or action works. Once all the final tests have been completed, the draft page has to be saved before it is published. You should then notify the senior manager or editor, so they can give the page a final check before it is published.

> **TIP** Links to external websites should be checked regularly to ensure that they are working and that external pages and images are still online and have not been either deleted or changed.

Print page production

The print production process will vary from company to company and depends upon the software used, but the practices involved in working on page make-up are generally similar. Page make-up on most publications involves working in a team, and any individual page may be reviewed by a number of people during the page production process. The page production role requires the ability to work well with people, combined with good layout skills and familiarity with a page make-up program.

The template: applying house design style

Templates are the base on which each page is built. They hold the basic elements of the design – the page size, margins, columns, gutters and baseline grid, together with all the title's typography. Page make-up programs use 'floating windows' such as the style sheet that stores typographic style. These can be customised to hold the style for each page or template and are saved as part of a document. A set of templates will be created to hold the look of a title. There may be individual templates for general subjects such as features or news, or there can be one template for each section or page. Templates can contain a number of master pages for regular items such as the cover or contents list. They will also normally include printer's requirements such as the registration marks and bleed.

Templates are used to store repeated graphic items such as page furniture.

Try to avoid breaking the house style as this can lead to untidy pages that do not match the brand standard.

A publication's templates are normally stored in a folder on the media company's main server to be accessible to everyone working on page make-up, such as an art editor and the chief sub, and are used to set up the new pages for each issue. In order to begin work on a page, the relevant template is selected and saved with a new name to create a separate page file in the issue folder. The issue folder normally contains a number of page folders used to hold the material for each page. Templates cannot be overwritten without being saved under a different name, unlike ordinary documents.

Templates are used in conjunction with the house design style guide to format the page layouts. Each template holds the page design structure and any standing artwork, such as the section or page flags, headers or footers and folios; the house design rules describe how to update, style and position the type and images. The design rules are used to ensure that the pages remain consistent, and are often very detailed. It is not uncommon for type and images to have the distance between each item specified. The vertical distance is expressed in units of the baseline grid: for example, there may be a precise number of lines between the headline and a standfirst, and between the standfirst and the start of the lead picture (see page 137). The guidelines will include directions and practical advice on where and how to use boxed copy, captions, bylines, etc., as well as exactly what typographic styles from the paragraph style window to use. There are normally detailed instructions on how to apply the house colour palette, for example how strong a tint to run under black type, and the percentage of colour to use as a background behind white type (see page 170).

The house design guide will describe the general design principles and style to be followed, such as whether the pages should be cool, geometric and modernist or bright, busy and lively. For some publications, such as newspapers, the house design style directions and the template are tightly defined and strictly adhered to. The design criteria of magazines are also closely followed: business, news and financial titles, as well as those on practical subjects such as gardening or cookery, tend to maintain a consistent look. The mainstream glossies mostly keep to their visual brand style, but will allow more creative freedom. Some titles have templates and a house style that permit them to play around with the typography and layout, while staying within the design ethos of the publication. Contemporary, youth-oriented magazines often encourage their production team or person to react to the content and come up with page layouts that are more interpretive; however, they still use templates to provide a consistent underlying structure.

TIP It is necessary to become completely familiar with the house design style, but equally important to study the publication and/or website and analyse the look and treatment of already published material (see page 118). There may well be discrepancies in style from the house style guide and it is a good idea to discuss any differences with the editorial team. It may be that design changes have been made but not recorded, but it might be that the pages are not correctly laid out. It is better to check than repeat a mistake.

Master pages

Master pages are a secondary level of page template within the document. When a new template is set up, all the specifications enter into the document, such as the page size, number of columns, margins, etc., and become master page A. Templates can contain several master pages at the basic page size of the publication, and each one could hold a separate page style. Master pages can be set up for each of the editorial sections and for regular pages or spreads within the sections. The advantage of working with templates and master pages is that they store the house design, typographic styling and colour palette, making it easy to maintain visual consistency. This also saves the page production team or person from having to do repetitive tasks such as type styling.

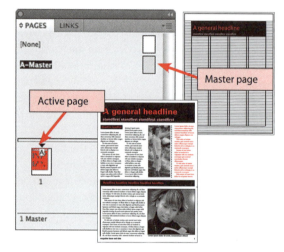

Layouts should be done on an active document page. The master page is for storing page furniture only.

Permanent items and page furniture

Master pages contain the permanent graphic elements of a publication and maintain the underlying positioning and structure of the master design, including the margins and columns (grid), page numbers (folios), running feet and heads (page furniture). They can also be used to hold regular pages with the standing artwork, for example a Comment page with the editor's mugshot and signature in position.

Standing artwork

You may have to use some artwork and photographs that appear in every issue or are a fixed part of the design. The standing artwork normally consists of photographs, graphic elements or icons that fall in fixed positions on the page in every issue, or which are used as permanent features. The page make-up program allows you to set up a library – a customisable window where graphic items can be stored for reuse. Standing artwork will also include items such as picture bylines or stock art for a letters page that may be used from time to time, but not always in the same position. The image files for these graphics must be kept on the server system, as the software does not embed graphics or photographs, unless instructed to do so through a specific menu command.

Setting up a document

When starting a new page make up it is important to select the template and master page for the subject that holds the design style you need to apply. This means that, when a new document is set up for an issue, those elements of the pages that have to be changed or updated – headers or footers, folios, page flags or section heads – need only be edited on the master page. A document can contain both master pages and active working pages that are accessed via the Pages window. This allows you to set up as many working pages as you want within the document, and to control the page order. It also allows you to apply the master page to a working page; for example, a contents master page could be applied to a left hand working page and the editor's Comment master page to the facing right hand page. A complete issue can be based on one template with a number of separate master pages. Any master page can be applied to a

Warning Master pages should not be used for page make-up. Changes to master page items affect all the related working pages in a document.

working page. The three main ways of working with templates and master pages are:

1 An individual template document with a left and right master page is used for every page or spread, such as Pg12-13 main feature or P3 news. On such publications, the same master page is used for each issue and only the date needs to be changed.

2 Templates with standard master pages are used for titles that do not always follow the same page running order. This type of publication may have three, four or five master pages with one for each individual section such as regulars, features and news. Where there are a number of different master pages, updates to datelines, headers, page numbers, etc., have to be made on each master page.

3 A single main template document is used with a number of master pages, each containing a page's or section's design style. This works by resaving the single template document as a series of separate working documents for each issue, updating the dateline and page number, and applying the appropriate master page to the working pages within that file.

How many pages should there be in a document file?

A publication with a large number of pages is usually set up as a series of separate documents. Most page make programs work more efficiently when the number of pages in each document is carefully managed. Publications are split into page groupings for production reasons as pages or sections may go to press at different times. Doing so also mitigates against the risk of a file corrupting, being accidently deleted or lost.

The Pages palette

Page make-up software uses an alphabetical system to label the master pages in the upper pane of the Pages window. The initial document set-up, entered via File > New, becomes master page A. The Pages window allows for the creation of other master pages with different grids. Each will be automatically assigned the next letter in the alphabet, but should be given specific names (e.g. A: News 4 Column Grid).

Pagination: true and untrue spreads

Those working on a title use the pagination (page and content running order) to keep track of what goes where and what pages have been completed. This also identifies how the publication will be broken down into groups of pages known as sections that correlate to the order in which the pages will be printed. The sections are used to plan the production work flow so that the pages are produced in order, with the most time-sensitive subject being worked on last. You will need to plan your workload to make sure the correct pages are worked on first. This can mean chasing people for copy and pictures that have not been supplied on time. There can be instances where it is not possible to start a page on schedule, but generally you should try to work in the order in which the pages need to be finished.

There are some technical and practical parameters that have to be considered when creating a page. You will be working on a computer screen, so the pages appear flat. However, printed publications are tactile objects that bend and flex depending on the number of pages and how they are held. You should study the title to see how any binding or curvature of the pages affects how the type and image are seen. One of the

TIP The page numbers (folios) should be set up on the master pages using the **auto page numbering function**. Page make-up programs open a new document as a right hand page with an odd number (right hand pages = **recto**; left hand pages = **verso**). When a template is set up for a publication, the Facing Pages option should be checked to create a document with left and right hand **facing pages**. If the section numbers in the document are reset to start with an even number, the pages will start with a left hand page; making this change allows the document to start with a spread.

most frequent dilemmas is whether it is practical to run the copy or images across two facing pages as the printing process has some restrictions that affect what can be achieved.

Working pages are set up, following the pagination, in various permutations such as a **double page spread** (dps) – an article set across a left and right page. Spreads come in two types. A **true spread** only occurs in the centre of a printing section or publication and is made up of one, wide sheet of paper with a fold or staple in the middle. A true spread may be treated as one page with type and graphics crossing the centre fold. However, true spreads in publications that are perfect bound – glued into a square back – can have a deep fold in the centre, depending on the number of pages in the issue. Because this fold can obscure some of the centre of the page, it may not be advisable to place copy and pictures across a spread. Most double page spreads are **untrue spreads** – facing pages that may be run on separate printing sections. As a general rule, type and images on untrue spreads in folded or stapled publications should not be placed across the centre margins of the publication, as separate printing sections do not always align perfectly (see page 326).

There may be colour matching problems with untrue spreads, as inking variations can happen on the press when separate sections are printed. This can cause a visible colour variation in the images and type on the left and right hand sides of a spread. Colours can also differ within a section, depending on the density of the ink on other pages, as this may spread (track) from one page to other pages. The sections of a publication may be printed at different times on different presses, and this can also increase the risk of colour variance between the pages.

Bleed

When a template is set up, the printing companies requirements have to be included. One of these is the **bleed area** – an extra 3–4mm space around the outside of the page. Any picture or graphic artwork that runs to the edge of the page requires an extra 3–4mm of image area to fill the 3–4mm of bleed area around the

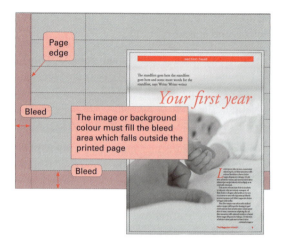

The 3-4mm bleed area outside the printed page provides a safety zone when the page is guillotined to ensure none of the image or background colour is lost.

page. The purpose of bleed is to ensure that the images and background colours are flush to the edge once the page has been guillotined. Printing presses can be enormous, operate at high speed, and may vibrate. Printing plates (see page 320) or the paper can occasionally be misaligned or slip. Printing companies' guillotines are large and cut through many sheets of paper at the same time, making it difficult to cut with exact precision. The additional area of image or colour is used to ensure that, if the page shifts or is mis-cut, there is not a white stripe of paper between the image or background colour and the edge of the publication.

Images and type should not be positioned at the outer edges of a page, because if the guillotine is out of alignment, some of the letters or image could be cut off. On a typical A4 publication, at least 4mm of space should be left between the page edge and type elements. Critical content in pictures such as faces should not be allowed to fall too close to the page edge, in case they are sliced off.

> **TIP** Bleed pictures and background colour boxes should be 3-4mm wider and deeper on their outer edges than the area to be printed, and that extra amount of image or colour should extend into the 3-4mm space around the edges of the document.

Assessing the material

It is a good idea to start a layout by bringing all the copy and pictures on to the page in order to assess the material you have to work with. This is sometimes called a **cast-off** – an initial rough layout. Viewing all the material on a page helps to judge just how copy much there is and how much space the copy will take up in the correct type style. It is also important to look at all the page-ready positional images, since there may be a choice of visual material that has to be judged for editorial and house design suitability (see page 202). Seeing the pictures on the page should give an indication of how large they can be used in print; however, looking at pictures in a page make-up program can only provide a general guide to their printable quality, as the software uses the file preview and does not embed the actual image (see page 103).

Page make-up programs are expensive specialist design software that is not intended for copy creation, and normally the text for a page will be typed in Word. Word is the most commonly used text-editing package, which makes it convenient to use for circulating copy for checking. It also has a better dictionary and grammar checker than page make-up software, although it should not be totally relied on (see page 276). Copy imported from Word should be kept in plain text, as any formatting such as using the software's headline styles, or words in italics or bold, will be cancelled out when the style sheets are applied.

Before starting on a page, the Word document should be read through to gain an understanding of the copy and to decide what visual treatment the page may

need. It is also necessary to check that you have all the copy, as writers sometimes divide up their work into sections within one document, or send several files, and there can be more than one story in a single document as well as embedded images, graphs or text in boxes that have to be extracted separately. Alternatively, copy may be supplied as one long piece over many pages that includes suggestions for the headline and standfirst, as well as captions and other information, including notes on images.

It is often necessary to cut copy to fit a layout. This can be done either by using an editorial collaboration program or by linking any overmatter (extra copy) to a box on a separate page to be edited on-screen or on paper.

TIP It is a good idea to start by creating a rough layout (cast-off) to work out the position of text and picture boxes, and to see whether any other graphic elements need to be commissioned or sourced for the next stage of the page make-up process. A rough layout can show whether there is too much or too little content and provide a guide to how the material will look in context. Bringing all the material together should also assist with the selection of suitable colours that match or complement the images.

Building the page

The contents of a publication will change within the parameters of the design day by day, week by week or month by month. While the design house style establishes how the actual material will look on the page, you should not allow the rules to become a straitjacket that constricts good ideas or creative thinking. You should also work with contributors from the beginning of the process to help to develop their ideas.

Journalists sometimes fail to consider how their copy might be communicated using type and pictures on a page, and some ideas that work well in writing can prove less than straightforward to convey in visual terms. Publications work best where a pictorial concept for the content presentation has been agreed between the editorial and production teams before beginning the digital page make-up. Discussing the article or story in advance should help to clarify the underlying theme and resolve any inherent visualisation problems so that a layout can be planned that best suits the material while maintaining the design ethos (see page 272).

Warning The number of boxed items on a page should be limited to maintain visual cohesion as too many individual graphic units can break up the read path and make the content hard to follow.

The page layout process

Print pages are put together by placing text and pictures in boxes – self-drawn content fields – on a template using industry-standard software. The aim is to construct a balanced, easy-to-follow arrangement of information that is aesthetically pleasing and, crucially, employs content that has been well planned and successfully realised on the page (see *How to work with layout*, pages 108–11). The pages should work as individual designs within the context of the whole publication and have a distinct look that relates to the specific message of the section, article or story. However, they must not become so different that the identity or information flow of the title may be lost. A page should be a component rather than a standalone item, although consistency does not mean uniformity, and juxtaposing contrasting layouts works to keep the reader's interest.

TIP The visual framing of the content on a page arises from the structure, order, pacing and overall patterning and is created by a sequence of strong or softer emphases. Drawing up an overview of the subject before the page make-up process is begun should ensure that the layout leads the reader logically through the content and helps in working out the visual balance. Page layouts that have been pre-planned should come together on-screen with ease, as most of the key decisions will have been made, and this should speed up the production process.

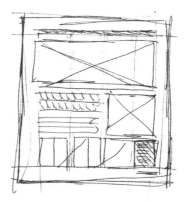

Even the quickest of sketches can show a variety of design solutions and help you to decide how best to lay out a page.

Lead pictures and headlines

The lead picture can be the key to the entire layout, because once the lead picture's position has been decided the other elements should fall more easily into place. The proportions, size, visual emphasis and implied direction of the main image may also be used to determine where the headline and standfirst should go. Headlines are usually placed at the top left of a page or item; however, altering the standard layout can work to provide a visual 'hook' into a feature as breaking conventions can jolt the reader into paying greater attention.

There is a number of design techniques that can help with creating more varied pages (see pages 121–4, and the resource list on page 347 for further information): for example, the Rule of Thirds – a grid system made up of three equal vertical and horizontal divisions. This could be applied to a feature on a three-column grid. A large landscape picture could be used to fill across the top third, with a two- or three-line headline below, placed in the two left hand columns of the centre section. The heading could form a vertical type block to provide a contrast to the horizontal image. The bottom third of the page could contain the standfirst and some of the running copy.

The Rule of Thirds is a classic design principle which divides a space into three horizontal and three vertical sections as shown above.

Source: Photos courtesy Alain Carpentier

While most web headlines tend to follow a traditional format, some websites do use a different approach, often in conjunction with interactivity.

Visual direction

How a picture is placed on a page and its visual emphasis and lines of direction can be used to guide the reader's eye. For example, if a full face or semi-profile portrait is placed on the right hand side of the layout with the eyes looking to the left, the reader's gaze will be led back to the start of the article. Once the position of the most important elements – the lead picture, headline and standfirst – has been established, the structure of the rest of the layout – secondary images, running text, captions, boxed copy, etc. – should be easier to resolve (see *How to work with pictures*, page 218).

Page hierarchy

Most pages have a hierarchical visual and informational structure which is created through controlling the juxtaposition and relative size of the text and pictures. It is important that a page layout establishes the **running order** – the pre-determined degree of editorial emphasis – and that the position, scale, tone and colour of the elements that make up a page (copy, images, graphics and page furniture) create a logical **read path** – a sequence of information that allows the reader or viewer to follow and assimilate the content.

A layout needs to draw the reader's or viewer's eye on through the page or sequence of pages. However, this does not mean that a layout has to read from the top left downwards. It is perfectly possible to create a layout with the headline and lead picture lower down the page or to one side providing the headline's typography and the main image are visually stronger than any other items on the page.

You need to be very aware of the effect of your placement decisions and image selections – a smaller but brightly coloured picture positioned against the lead picture, or a secondary headline directly alongside the main headline can distract the reader's or viewer's eye away from the main read path (this is referred to as clashing pictures and headlines). Placing some news stories and feature sidebars in tinted background or outline boxes can help to separate the content and indicate the relative importance of the information.

Varying the type size helps to set up the visual informational hierarchy. People will normally assume that the largest headline is most important, and therefore they will look at it first. And 'the small type' means just that – details that someone does not want to attract attention to set in a very small typeface that indicates the copy is of less importance. The type in a layout

should move the reader through from the main headline to an introduction, standfirst or strapline and on to the main text. The size and weight of any other type styles, such as those used for sidebars, boxed copy and captions, should be balanced against the headlines and main copy to make the reading order evident. Colour can also be used for emphasis: bright red or dark blue type can stand out and grab attention, while soft green or pale blue lettering may recede into the page (see the *How to work with type* and *How to work with colour* pages for more information).

The diagram shows the tonal relationships between the elements of a page. In order to guide a reader or users through the layout, each item of editorial and visual content should be assigned a specific informational value which can be conveyed on the page by creating a hierarchical structure using scale, colour, tone and position.

> **TIP** It is a good idea to look at the page at a very reduced screen percentage view so that you see it as a pattern of shapes and colours. This makes it easier to judge whether the content running order and visual balance are correct.

See Chapter 9 action sheet: Page make-up
www.pearsoned.com/hand

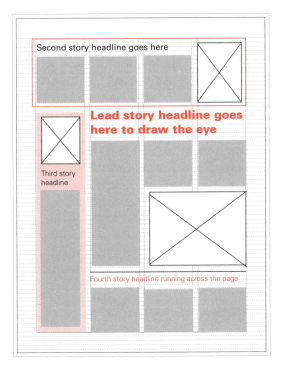

The lead story on a news page should be given the greatest visual weight.

The main headline can be positioned down page providing it has the greatest visual strength.

Text to picture balance

The **text to picture ratio** needs to be connected to the section or page topic, and the overall ratio is dependent on the editorial identity of the publication and whether it is text or picture led. Even if you have been supplied with really good photography and would like to use several large images, you should keep in mind that it is usually the written content that dictates the design considerations. Very few publications survive on their visual look alone, as most readers buy publications for information rather than visual stimulation.

There have been some famous exceptions to this rule, such as Benetton's 1990s picture-based *Colors* magazine, produced by Tibor Kalman, that provoked controversy and moral outrage in its day by publishing images of childbirth, war and a dying AIDS patient to promote a fashion store.

The graphic designer David Carson is famous for creating visual layouts that evoke a mood rather than relying on (or indeed making it possible for) someone reading the copy to understand what the feature is about. Carson is notorious for setting an article in a 1994 issue of *Ray Gun* magazine on the singer Brian Ferry in Zapf Dingbats – a font of symbols only. His explanation was that the article was so boring he thought no one would want to read it. Perhaps he was right, as countless celebrity interviews have been forgotten about, while his is still discussed many years later.

Link to Benetton Colors Magazine:
www.colorsmagazine.com/archive/

Print page flow control and proofing

The page make-up process may become totally engrossing and pressured, making it easy to become absorbed by the details of the process and to end up constantly tweaking the contents to try to achieve the perfect page. Magazines and newspapers need to have in place a system that ensures you remain in control of what is happening with the pages so that a work flow rate can be maintained, and that only the current version of the page make up document is being worked on.

It is good basic practice to ensure that all the production material for your publication is clearly labelled and kept together on the server. Making sure your copy and images are easy to find will assist with managing the content for pre-press production and archiving. Most media companies have an automatic overnight backup for their servers, and they may also have a disaster recovery backup in a remote location to ensure that the intellectual property of the company is safe.

Traditionally, the progress of layouts was monitored by printing out the pages at key stages and keeping a series of updated proofs in a folder, or pinned on a board, to keep track of the overall work flow and appearance of the issue. Proofs also gave the production and editorial teams an opportunity to check they are on schedule and to make sure all the pages follow house style, with layouts that are neither too similar, nor wildly different. Proofs provided an overview of what colours had been used and how well they worked with each other.

Print publications are normally created on in-house servers, and many publications now use server-based editorial collaboration software that allows the production and editorial teams to work jointly and at the same time on a page or series of pages. These are prepared on-screen and may not be seen together before production. Proofs should be printed out at various stages to get an idea of what the publication will look like on paper, and a final printed proof should always be run to make sure that all the pages work well together and that the issue's look has been maintained.

> **TIP** All old versions of the page files should be saved into a legacy folder. Keeping older versions on a server or backup system allows pages to be recovered should the current version be corrupted or lost–disastrous close to a production deadline.

Editorial collaboration software work flow

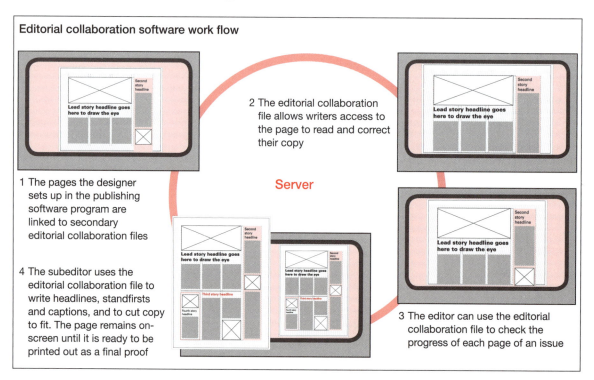

1 The pages the designer sets up in the publishing software program are linked to secondary editorial collaboration files

2 The editorial collaboration file allows writers access to the page to read and correct their copy

Server

3 The editor can use the editorial collaboration file to check the progress of each page of an issue

4 The subeditor uses the editorial collaboration file to write headlines, standfirsts and captions, and to cut copy to fit. The page remains on-screen until it is ready to be printed out as a final proof

The page production process for online and print involves a range of editorial and advertising planning skills. The abilities needed to create successful pages include layout and technical skills such as text and image handling for both media. Those working on production need to have some knowledge of how the print and web page work flow system operates, and the software employed by the media industry, in order to understand why they may be asked to carry out tasks in a particular way and to a timetable.

- The goal of media production is to get the final product into the marketplace and to the target audience, and the actions taken by all those involved should be focused on achieving this.

- All websites are server based; the World Wide Web itself consists of multiple linked servers. A website and its pages have to be searchable so they can be found on the Internet.

- The media company sets the editorial and advertising deadlines. Print deadlines are calculated in reverse from the time when the material has to be supplied to the printing company in order to be available to readers on a certain date. Websites may require files to be submitted by any time from 10 days to 24 hours before they are to be uploaded, to allow for checking and testing.

- Publications work best where a pictorial concept for the content presentation has been agreed between the editorial and production teams before beginning the digital page make-up.

- Subediting checks must include information such as names, places and times, and to confirm any facts and figures quoted in a news story or feature, as well as basic spelling and grammar.

- Images can be employed to cover information not mentioned in the copy and add to the value of the textual content by illustrating certain points, making a statement or highlighting a political issue such as famine, terrorism, etc.

- The brand or house style dictates the consistent appearance of an online or print title's design and should include rules for how the pages are to be set up. The content has to change within the parameters of the design day by day, week by week or month by month.

- Page creation design rules are useful for journalists and other media professionals without specific design training to follow if they are required to work on print page make-up and/or web production, and whenever it is necessary to work quickly to meet a deadline.

- The primary aim of any layout is to create interest in the contents, and all the page elements must help to communicate the message. A well-considered underlying grid acts as a guide to how pages are to be constructed and serves to create continuity of visual expression from one issue or update to the next.

- Desktop publishing design templates are the base on which each page is built. They hold the publication's page size and production requirements, such as bleed, and the basic elements of the design – the margins, columns, gutters and baseline grid, together with all the title's typography.

Activities and development

The questions and action points below will help you expand your knowledge of print and web page production. As well as reading this chapter and the *How to work with* sections in this book, you should study other production titles/websites from the list on page 358. Visit the *Design for Media* website for more fact and action sheets, sample templates, type schemes and colour palettes at **www.pearsoned.com/hand**

Questions

Question 1
Describe five steps you should take before beginning to lay out pages for print.

Question 2
What is the function of templates and master pages in print layout?

Question 3
What is the function of a web content management system?

Question 4
How many fields are commonly used to set up a news item on a website?

Question 5
What are the two colour modes that can be used on the Web?

Question 6
What is the relationship between advertising and editorial design, and should there be a visual resemblance?

Action points

Action point 1
Draw a diagram of a printed page from a magazine or newspaper showing the position of the main informational items by using coloured blocks to represent the headlines, standfirsts, main text (see page 103). Note the geometric underlying structure of the page and how the elements are balanced.

Action point 2
Create a mind map demonstrating the pacing and position of informational units through an issue of a current publication and/related website.

Action point 3
Study the major news sites and note what type styles, size and colour combinations they use.

(a) Choose a current news story and make up a chart of the word count, number of still images, video, audio, multimedia and hyperlinks employed by each company to the item.

(b) Consider how the website design and how much information provided in each medium vary according to editorial stance.

Answers to questions

Question 1
Study house design style, set up page folder, check/read copy and pix, open template, change issue/date.

Question 4
Four.

10 GOING TO PRESS – PUBLISHING ON THE WEB

This chapter discusses:

- Media production
- In-house proofs
- Print production from pdfs
- Lithographic printing
- Digital printing
- Communication industries
- Page production
- Web servers
- Financial transaction web forms
- Customer services
- Working with web experts
- Web programs
- Internet service providers (ISPs)
- Regional specific advertising

This chapter follows on from the description of editorial production in Chapter 9 and explains why having a reasonable understanding of the underlying technologies for print and web will enable you to prepare work successfully for cross-platform media projects. The chapter covers information that will allow you to liaise with production professionals and achieve the best possible results for print and web.

'The comparative advantage of mainstream media is not the ownership of presses, but the collaboration of professionals.'

Jason Pontin, publisher, *Technology Review*

'Performance load is the degree of mental and physical effort required to achieve a goal. If the performance load is high, the probability of successfully accomplishing the goal decreases. If the performance load is low, the probability of successfully accomplishing the task increases'.

W. Lidwell, K. Holden and J. Butler,
Universal Principles of Design

An understanding of print and web technology is vital to planning publications and websites, and writers, journalists, PR and marketing executives can all benefit from knowledge of the technical processes employed in cross-platform media production. Mastering production principles can help a writer tailor their copy to a particular platform, or a picture editor source media-specific imagery. If you work in the media, you should have some grasp of how the processes that technical specialists undertake as part of their job are translated into either printed or online products, because without a clear overview of the practices involved it would be difficult to operate in today's highly digitised media working environment. A good knowledge of production technologies and processes has been an element in the successful careers of many people in the media.

While print production can appear to be a more complex process than publishing on the Web, there is not very much difference in the amount of knowledge and skills needed to work successfully in either print or online. However, what can be achieved in either medium is controlled by the mechanical capacities and technological functions of particular forms of hardware and software. Every item used on a page has to be right for its purpose and each stage of the production process undertaken in the correct sequence and on time.

Visit the Pearson Education website for more titles on this subject

Media production

Today's media are constantly evolving. Not only are standard page make up and CMS programs upgraded at frequent intervals, but also the hardware and software employed by the industry are becoming increasingly powerful and compact and able to handle more of the production process. Media companies are taking advantage of these developments, and their employees are now expected to handle much of the production that formerly would have been done by specialists, while more content is being generated by outside individuals. The result of these changes is that people are under pressure to refresh their skills and knowledge in order to understand new concepts and processes.

One of the founders of Intel, Gordon Moore, observed as early as 1965 that the number of transistors that can be placed on an integrated circuit doubles approximately every two years. This has proved to be true and has become known as Moore's law. The computer industry has gone on to create smaller and more powerful machines and to introduce faster and more complex programs and apps with frequent updates. This presents a problem for those companies working in a digital environment, as every change has to be accommodated by all those involved. It affects production and page creation for both print and web, and means that everyone who works in publishing, advertising and related areas – in-house staff, employees of partner companies, freelancers and short-term contractors – has to keep their software and equipment up to date and constantly adapt to new developments.

Whatever the product, the final mode of delivery dictates the preparation of material, as described in the previous chapters, and greatly affects the production process. Print projects require high-resolution imagery and generally use the CMYK system of colour reproduction. Screen-based media employ lower-resolution imagery in RGB colour format. All the material selected for page creation on either platform should have been sourced and prepared using the correct specifications for the target platform. If the production criteria are not taken into account from the start of a project, there can be problems with poor-quality output and costly delays.

Print production has a linear structure, since it follows a schedule that progresses pages through a series of checks and controls prior to going on the press. The Web, on the other hand, can be more fluid and immediate, with content that may be frequently changed and updated. While a printed product cannot be altered in the same way, it is normally an ephemeral item that will soon be replaced by another. Regardless of which media, controls and checks should be in place to prevent embarrassing mistakes in the content, technical errors and missed press deadlines.

Print: controls and processes

A print title's content should be complete and free of errors before the pages are released to a printing company to enter the pre-press process (see page 320). All editorial and advertising material should go through a proofing system using editorial collaboration software or pdfs on-screen, and it is also advisable to check pages as printed proofs. It is good practice to keep a set of digital or paper sequential editorial and advertising proofs – a **running dummy** of the publication. This gives an overview of how well the design and colour balance is working and can highlight any visual conflicts between the pages and content.

The pages are produced to a set schedule that ensures a title runs smoothly from pre-press through to print and dispatch. In order to achieve this, there are controls and checks applied following page creation such as **preflight** – the industry's term for running software that checks the pages are technically correct for the printing process. Once the pages have been cleared by preflight, the title is sent to the printing company where a control proof is run to confirm the pages will print accurately on the company's system. The editorial team ensures that the content is correct and that there are no technical issues before the printing company starts the final preparations for press and checks the control proof. However, this sort of proof may not be a good indication of colour (see page 314).

In order to check colour accuracy, many media companies use colour-calibrated digital print production systems that produce a reasonable standard of proof on- or off-screen. However, publications such as high-end fashion or interiors magazines that require a precise representation of colour often ask printing companies to produce **colour-balanced proofs** that give a precise representation of the result that will be achieved on the press. Once the media company has approved a final proof, the printing company takes responsibility for the rest of the process.

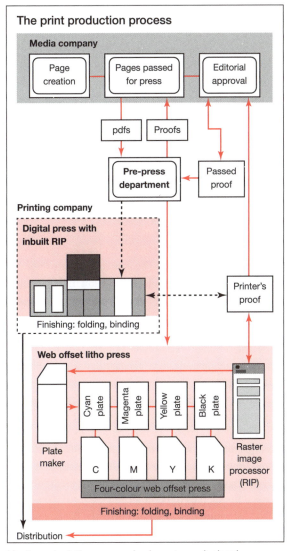

The print production process

Media and printing companies have to work closely together on the production of print titles.

> **TIP** The first **printer's proof** can be a pdf or a printout. It should be double checked by the title's production team, paying close attention to make sure that it matches the editorial and advertising proofs and that other errors, such as incorrect page numbers, have not been overlooked.

Liaising with printing companies

There can be a large number of people involved in producing a print title and, to prevent multiple and possibly contradictory instructions being given, it is advisable to limit the number of people who have actual contact with the printing company. Publishers may have a print buyer who handles all the costing and ordering of print, or it may be the province of the managing director or a senior office administrator. Whoever deals with the business side has to liaise between the in-house production team and the printing company to ensure that the publication is booked in and that they both know the number of pages, colour specification and how many copies are required. The printing company may also handle dispatch and delivery using databases of subscribers' names, addresses and details.

Large printing companies have customer service departments and often appoint a customer service representative (CSR) to look after a media company's account. It is good practice for the person who sends the pdfs or files to the printing company to email a list of what has been sent, and to confirm the print order. When using email or another system that does not confirm receipt, it is a good idea to ask the printing company to confirm that they have received the files and that they have been checked for any problems.

> **TIP** It helps to arrange frequent meetings to build a relationship by talking face to face rather than just on the telephone, or only exchanging emails. Printing companies are usually happy to give advice on how best to prepare material for their press and can be a good source of knowledge of printing and experience of the media in general. Most printers will encourage you to visit their printing plants to gain an understanding of what happens during the printing process

Schedules and deadlines

Printing companies allocate time on their presses to tie in with a title's production schedule. They set the printing schedule by calculating when they need to receive all the pages of a publication, as they have to leave sufficient time to complete the final production stages in advance of the final printing date. The timing of a

Print production deadlines

- Repro deadline
- Pass proof deadline
- Pass for press deadline
- Sign off running sheet (if the media company's representative is at printers)
- Sign off advance copy (a fully finished copy of the publication which may have been finished by hand)
- Dispatch deadline (bulk copies to wholesale distributors)
- Copies into retailers
- Cover date
- Display date
- Individual subscription copies to Royal Mail or other postal service

print job is based on the complexity of the printing, the number of pages in the newspaper or magazine, and the number of copies – the **print run**. Print production schedules have to allow for all the technical processes that have to be completed before a publication can be printed (see page 312).

A printed publication's editorial deadlines follow a timetable that is calculated back from the printer's deadline, which is based on the date when the title needs to be on sale to the public. All publishers work to a production work flow schedule for their issues or editions, and everyone involved, such as logistics and printing companies, has to be able to complete their work to an agreed timescale. Production managers use the schedule to book pre-press and printing time slots, plan distribution and transport, and notify mailing companies and retail sales outlets when to expect deliveries. The production timetable is also used to set the advertising copy and editorial deadlines (see Chapter 4, and page 274).

Websites have deadlines that are usually imposed by the media company in response to the market and target audience. There are no technical reasons for having a deadline as information can be uploaded at any time. What is important is that the content is in the right format, editorially accurate and that any actions such as hyperlinks and media players or embedded sound files function correctly. Every component to be used on the Web must match the site or CMS technical criteria. This requires carefully checking all supplied material such as stock photographs and video/audio files, processing the copy through a suitable text editor and adding any extra HTML or other coding, as well as preparing other images to match the specified pixel width and height. The most commonly used **aspect ratio** is 6×4, which matches the average proportions of a computer monitor. For example, the default image size for most home page thumbnails is 600 pixels wide by 400 pixels high.

Newspapers

The final date by which the approved pages have to be submitted to the printing company is known as the publication's **repro (reproduction) deadline**. All editorial and advertising deadlines are calculated back from when the final digital files have to be supplied to the printers. As national newspapers are now Web-led they no longer have a single editorial deadline, but print editions still work to fixed repro deadlines as papers may print anything from 200,000 to 3 million copies per day, which can take several hours, and the first copies need to come off the presses in the early hours of the morning in time to catch the night train, be taken by road to distant regions of the country or dispatched by air.

The average national newspaper will have a number of daily and weekly editorial print deadlines for the main paper, supplements and magazines. All written and pictorial material should be supplied to the production team on time as it will have a strict schedule to follow, including a repro deadline by which page production has to be completed and all the pages proofed and passed for press. The finalised page make up pages are converted into pdf files and the digital files are sent either to an external repro house – a company that handles the pre-press process – or straight to the printing company as most have their own preflight, proofing and plate making facilities. Large media companies, such as News International, have their own printing works and also print newspapers and magazines for other publishers.

Magazines

Monthly magazines with a large number of pages often have a series of progressive deadlines for sections and pages. These allow time for content to be generated and subedited, pages made up, and the cycle of amendments and revisions completed. The order of page production depends on the subject of the page or section. Any topical items such as fashion, sports or events will be given later deadlines, while non-time-sensitive stories, supplements and features will be started two or more weeks in advance of the final deadline. The production manager or whoever handles the editorial page flow will set up a chart of copy and page deadlines. Every section, spread and page has to be ready by the date and time specified for the proofing and pre-press process. Weekly magazines follow a similar schedule over a shorter time frame.

A publication's print advertising deadlines are closely linked to the editorial schedule, and third-party inserts and client advertisements must be supplied to comply with an agreed set of production dates. Advertising material may have to be appear in a particular issue if it is seasonal or linked to a promotion, for example for a retail sale or product launch, or if it is linked to the date of an exhibition or event. Most publications follow an advertising timetable, as they have to be booked in advance with a printing company, and content has to be generated and pages made up, advertising space sold, advertisements supplied and collated, and the launch or publication date promoted, even if only one edition is printed a year.

Making the deadline

Whatever date is set for the final pages to pass for press, it has to allow time for last-minute changes and to complete the editorial production process. The advertising team needs the copy deadline to be as close as possible to the publishing date so it can maximise sales and ensure the digital artwork files are supplied by clients and their advertising agencies. The deadline also needs to leave enough time for any minor unforeseen issues to be overcome, and for the printing company to deliver the finished print run for distribution.

There are many partner businesses involved in the publishing process that have a financial interest in the success of a publication, such as the media companies, printers, advertisers, distributors and retailers. All of those involved in the production of a print product need to cooperate to make sure the schedule and deadlines are achieved, as additional costs or financial penalties can be incurred if a title runs late at any time during the production processes.

Major media groups prefer to own their presses as this gives them complete control over their deadlines as well as potential cost savings, while others have a financial interest in a printing company. The News International media group that publishes *The Times* and the *Sun* owns the largest newspaper printing operation in Britain and prints publications for other media companies, as well as running its own titles. In 2008, the group began printing the *Daily Telegraph*, which had moved to full colour for the first time in its long history. The paper had formerly shared a press with the *Daily Express*. Smaller media companies may hire press time or organise a rolling contract with a printing company.

> To see a slideshow tour of the News International printing plant at Broxbourne, visit: *www.guardian. co.uk/media/gallery/2008/mar/17/newsinternational. pressandpublishing? picture=332986925*

> **Warning** Printers will generally try to do everything they can to get a publication out, even if it has been supplied later than arranged. Printing companies are used to dealing with the problems that occur when putting together as complex a product as a magazine or newspaper, and know to build some 'air' into their schedules to allow for inevitable delays. However, if you miss your press deadline by as little as an hour, the printing company may charge for overtime and weekend working to get your publication out on time. Presses are often fully booked by publications that all have time-sensitive distribution. If you do miss a deadline, despite 24-hour-a-day printing there may not be time available for many hours or even days.

Preparing for print

Once all the editorial pages have been completed and the advertising collated, the next stage is to ensure that all the digital artwork and any other material are checked and put into a suitable format to be supplied to the printing company. The process also involves double checking to make sure that only the final **passed for press** version of the page is used, and that the latest image files are ready to be sent to the printers. A copy of all the digital artwork should be collected in a folder, and a proof run of each page as a final check and record of what is being sent to the printer.

Preflight checks

Preflighting software examines all the component parts of a page make up or pdf file and warns if anything is not in the correct format for final output to plate and, ultimately, the press. Digital artwork for production should be preflighted prior to dispatch to the printers. It checks that the type software used in the document is installed or embedded and that all the image files in the page make up program are present on the system. Preflighting identifies and lists colour modes and can give a breakdown of CMYK and spot colour inks. Preflighting also checks whether there are print settings, such as bleed, and warns of problems such as missing pictures or low-resolution RGB images used in a print document. Adobe InDesign, Acrobat Professional and QuarkXPress can all run preflight checks.

Even though printing companies run their own preflight programs when they receive digital artwork or a pdf, it is good practice for those working on the publication to ensure the pages they supply have been correctly prepared to avoid having to resupply material. The production manager or team should always run a preflight check on the finished pages to make sure everything is present and in the right format.

Package/collect for output

The final, preflighted pages are generally supplied to the printing company as **press-quality pdfs** that are transferred via the Web. Printing companies often have specific press requirements and may supply page submission guidelines on how they require pdfs to be generated (see page 315). An alternative method to supplying digital artwork is to supply all the component

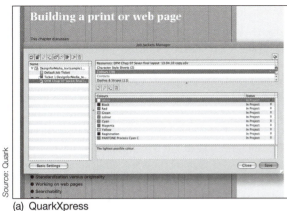

Source: Quark

(a) QuarkXpress

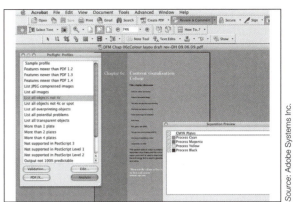

Source: Adobe Systems Inc.

(b) Adobe Acrobat

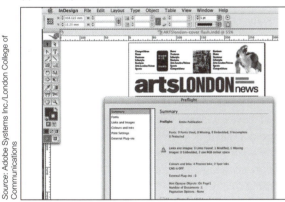

Source: Adobe Systems Inc./London College of Communications

(c) Adobe InDesign

A preflight check should be run before each page or document is dispatched to the printing company. QuarkXPress, Adobe Acrobat and InDesign all include preflight checking that reviews all the component elements and displays alerts if there are any problems.

> **TIP** It is a good idea to use the Collect for Output/ Package command to create a final folder of page make up, bitmap image and vector graphic files for archiving.

parts of the finalised page to the printer as an open dtp document in a folder containing all the related image files and font software. Some page make up programs have a facility – Collect for Output in Quark and Package in InDesign – that automatically collates copies of the document and image files into a new folder. It may be necessary to zip (compress) the folder before it is sent to the printing company via the Web or email.

> **Warning** It is important to check that the media and printing companies have compatible versions of the software. Some media companies work with heritage software as changing program versions can be costly. Software upgrades can involve having to install new computer systems and the files that control external devices such as printer driver software. A major upgrade could even mean replacing older computers with more powerful, faster ones with larger memory capacities and buying new typefaces.

Final approval

Digital files need to be processed and checked on a printing company's system. Some media companies have print production work flows that are fully integrated with their printers. These automatically check compatibility at each stage, and separate proofs may not be necessary. The pages will be either passed on-screen, or a digital proof run in-house for final checking. Where companies do not have integrated systems, the printing company will need the final page proof as a guide to show what the pages should look like in print. The printers will run a control proof from the supplied files on their system to ensure that no problems have occurred when they processed the page. The control proof is returned to the media company to be passed for press. This proof is then used by the printing company to check the accuracy of the press run.

If the product is a glossy magazine, corporate brochure or advertisement, it is not unusual for a printing company to be asked to retouch images and adjust the colour of image files, to ensure the best possible print reproduction quality is achieved. Where extra colour management work is undertaken, high-end colour proofs may be run for approval and used to match the colour output of the press (see page 319). There are several options for proofing that have costs and quality implications that have to be taken into account.

In-house proofs

There are a number of high-end inkjet proofing systems intended for use in-house by media companies. The prints produced by these proofers are called **contract quality** and are accurate enough to get a good idea of how the final page will reproduce. The advantages of an in-house proofing system are accessibility and speed, and the cost of each page is generally lower than a printing company will charge. Printing and media companies can both have identical colour-calibrated proofers that provide consistently matched results, which removes the need to send a paper proof from one location to another.

The main reason why a print title should be proofed on paper is that it is easier to get a true idea of the finished printed result. Looking at a page on-screen does not give an accurate impression of reading the title on paper. Much of the value of printed products lies in their weight, smell and tactile nature, and the proportion of the graphic elements within the dimensional frame of a page is an important factor in their aesthetic appeal.

Advertising proofs and retouching

Advertisements that are sent to media companies as digital files, either directly from advertisers or from agencies, should be supplied with press-specific calibrated colour digital or paper proofs. Colour-balanced proofs are necessary because advertisers and agencies often invest a great deal of money in an advertising campaign and are very particular about ensuring the colour accuracy of the images and logos. It is important that all advertising digital files and proofs match a publication's colour specifications and the printing company's press colour profile. An advertising proof may look right, but if it has not been correctly calibrated or profiled, the final printed version may not match the client's expectations. This may be costly, leading to complaints and disputes.

Advertising images, such as model shots for cosmetics and photographs of cars, are often extensively retouched and manipulated. Advertising agencies employ Photoshop experts whose job it is to alter and retouch images to please demanding clients that want their products to appear perfect. Agencies often produce several colour proofs to show the finished digital work to its best advantage. These proofs may not be accurate in printing colour terms and can be at a high photographic quality that cannot be reproduced on a press.

The print proofing process

- The approved editorial proof is sent from the media company to the printing company as formal notification that the latter can begin the pre-press and printing process.

- The printing company returns confirmation proofs prepared on its digital production system to the media company to ensure that no technical problems have occurred or mistakes been missed.

- Colour proofs may be run if the media company has asked the printing company to handle the colour reproduction.

- Printing companies may produce digital **virtual matchprints**, colour-balanced pdfs or hard proofs that are sent to the media company for final approval.

- The signed-off printer's proofs become **contract proofs** that show an agreed reproduction standard. These are used to ensure the printed colours match the colour proof with reasonable accuracy on the printing company's press.

- High-end titles may send a representative from the media company to be present at the printing company to monitor the last stages of the printing process and give approval for the final press run.

Adobe Acrobat portable document format (pdf)

Most media companies track the development of print publications using pdf proofs that can be accessed from shared servers and digitally distributed. These pdfs (**soft proofs**) allow for quicker turnarounds and cost less than printed (hard) proofs. The industry uses pdf proofing as normal practice. Many titles handle page production entirely on-screen and use pdf proofing and pdf-based automated printing systems. Improvements in monitor colour accuracy mean that the pdf proofs viewed on the screen closely match the press output.

Adobe Acrobat Professional and Distiller are pdf programs that embed and compress all the separate digital files used in a document, including typefaces and colour profiles, into a single file. It is also possible to save documents as pdfs from most of the main programs used in the publishing industry, such as Word, Adobe's Photoshop, Illustrator and InDesign, and QuarkXPress.

Adobe Acrobat Professional is used for soft proofing and to automate pre-production through to press. It has proof correction commenting tools. such as high-lighters and notes, that can be used to indicate changes that need to be made on the page make up document. Although corrections can be made to a pdf, it is good practice to make any significant changes to the page make up document, and in imaging software, and then remake the proof or press pdf.

While a production team works with Acrobat Professional and Distiller, the editorial team and anyone else who simply needs to read through the pages would normally use Adobe Acrobat Reader, a free program. Acrobat soft proofs can be checked on any computer or other digital device without the need for specialist page make up software and fonts to be installed. The advantages of using pdfs are that there is only one relatively small file for each page or group of pages, and as long as the pdfs are produced after the pages have been signed off, there should be little or no chance of anything going wrong further down the line.

There are three types of pdfs. Standard or print pdfs are used for editorial and general checking and can be printed from any desktop printer. Press pdfs are high

Remote proofing

Remote proofing systems allow pages to be corrected on a shared server using web-based software or FTP transfer, which removes the need for media and printing companies to keep re-emailing or up- and downloading page updates. The documents can be password protected so only certain people have permission to make changes. Smart phones, such as Apple's IPhone, offer remote proofing software that can handle high-resolution graphics. Remote proofing saves a great deal of time and changes can be seen instantly and in context.

The print page layouts are checked during the page production process either by using editorial collaboration software or by sending out a pdf soft proof. The pdf soft proof can be marked up in Adobe Acrobat using the highlighter tool and the notes tool that allow comments to be added. The corrections are then made on the layouts.

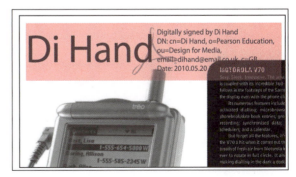

A high-resolution press pdf is made once the page make up documents have been finalised, passed for press and digitally or manually signed off.

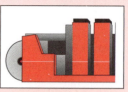

Standard pdfs: the most commonly used format for soft and hard proofing. The type software is embedded and the image quality is good, so the pages closely resemble the finished print result. Standard pdfs are used as a soft proof to be emailed and can be used for printing on some digital printing presses for short-run publications, but they are not suitable for most lithographic or high-resolution digital printing presses

Screen pdfs: the format used for viewing pages and e-publications on-screen and for the Internet. Screen pdfs do not embed the typeface software and the images are highly compressed to keep the file memory size as small as possible. This reduces the view quality and pictures may appear blurred. In general, screen pdfs are not suitable for printing out as hard proofs

Press-quality pdfs: the format used for outputting to film or plates for high-end printing. There is a range of ISO press-quality pdfs that are used by the print industry. Some printing companies will issue custom settings to match their presses. Press pdfs embed the typeface software and all of the digital information from the image files. This produces high-resolution pdfs that are suitable for printing presses

TIP: Standard pdfs are used for printed (hard) proofs and for emailing. You should check whether there is a limit on the size of file that the company or individual can receive. Screen pdfs should be used to distribute pages (soft proofs) by email or the Web for checking.

resolution and are produced once the page is ready to be sent to press. Screen pdfs are low resolution and intended for online use, but the page may not print out as it appears on-screen. How accurately colours in any of the pdf types are displayed on-screen depends on whether all the devices being used for editorial, production, proofing and printing have been colour profiled to match each other and regularly recalibrated to check that the colour settings remain stable.

TIP Brightly coloured walls may influence the perception of colour on-screen. It is best to paint the walls in a production area in a light, neutral shade to prevent any colour cast being reflected on to the screen or proofs. A screen saver or main desktop background should be a neutral, static colour, and not be set to show animated swirls, a favourite celebrity's photo or family holiday snaps.

Proofing on-screen

There are a number of factors that can affect how screen colour is perceived. The lighting in a room may throw a colour cast on a screen, and the level of natural light and weather conditions may cause on-screen colours to vary. To overcome this, daylight-corrected light bulbs should be used that produce a more naturalistic light than normal fluorescent or tungsten bulbs, which will also cause a colour cast.

Acrobat Distiller

Acrobat Distiller is the program used to produce pdfs for individual printing presses. The software controls how much or how little digital information is embedded and other detailed factors such as the choice of paper size, printing specifications and image compression. Distiller can create pdfs that are larger than the size of the publication to allow space for the bleed, registration and crop marks that fall outside the page trim area. Distiller acts as the background pdf processing software for many programs.

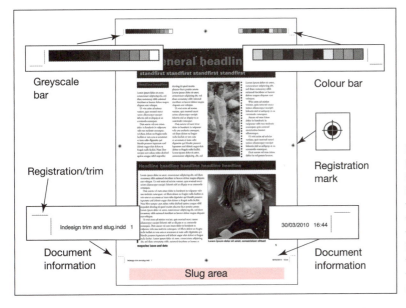

Greyscale
bar

Colour bar

Registration/trim

Registration
mark

Indesign trim and slug.indd 1

30/03/2010 16:44

Document
information

Document
information

Slug area

Press pdf page dimensions have to
be larger than the printed page size to
include printer's marks. Printer's marks
include **crop marks** that indicate the
trim, **registration marks** that show
where to align pages, **colour bars**
to aid colour reproduction, **page
information** for the title, date and
time of creation of the page file, and
the **slug area** for printer's notes and
information.

Print production from pdfs

Pages that have been passed for press and are ready to
be supplied to the printing company can be exported
directly from page make up programs, or saved as
PostScript (or EPS) **files** that are converted into pdfs
using Adobe Distiller. Acrobat is used for print production management and Distiller for automated page
production, often in conjunction with a printing company's pdf-based press management systems (see
page 316). Distiller is a highly technical program and
those handling the production of the final page files
may need extra training.

    All press pdfs and any other files should be placed
in named folders for each issue, section, batch of pages
and/or publishing date before being sent to the printing company. If any pages have to be sent after the
agreed deadline, it is good practice to place the page
file or pdf in a named folder rather than send it on its
own. This should prevent pdfs/files being missed when
they arrive at their destination or used for the wrong
issue. Larger server-based publishing management
systems automate the exchange of files between media
and printing companies. Most printing companies have
their own websites or FTP addresses and may accept
emailed material. Large amounts of data can be compressed using Zip or Stuffit into self-extracting folders.
Although it is possible to email press pdfs, it is not recommended, as they can be large in memory terms and
take a long time to send and receive.

The main types of digital transfer

- **File Transfer Protocol (FTP)**: production files are
  uploaded to a file server on a peer-to-peer basis (one
  computer at the hosting company has direct access
  to the Internet service provider's computer that
  sends the information to the customer's computer).
  FTP software, works in a similar manner to accessing
  a web page using an ftp address (e.g. FTP://address.
  com). FTP sites are normally password restricted to
  protect the ISP's servers and ensure users' security.

- ISDN (Integrated Services Digital Network): a fast,
  large-capacity telephonic transfer system that can
  run as broadband.

- Email is useful for sending soft proofs because the
  file memory size tends to be small, but it can prove
  unreliable for larger files.

- Webmail can be used to send files with a large
  memory size.

TIP Every make of press has slightly different output
parameters, and printing companies should be asked to
supply the specific Distiller preferences for their press.

Printer's and contract proofs

The automated print production systems used by major media companies enable them to go straight to press without in-house colour proofs, as editorial and production equipment is colour calibrated through the integrated work flow. Some media and printing companies will not accept hard proofs as their automated production systems require a specific form of pdf with industry-standard colour profiles that are matched to a press. Increasingly, budgeting constraints and new technological developments are reducing the use of hard contract proofs.

Those publications that require an extra level of accuracy may still choose to request printer's colour proofs. Smaller companies that do not have automated print production use printer's proofs to check the overall balance of the pages, and to carry out a final check for errors before they go on to the expensive stages of plate making and printing. Advertisers or advertising agencies that manage large campaigns, and companies producing high-end marketing material may have several versions of printer's proofs run until the colour and print quality matches their creative requirements. Advertising agencies use high-quality colour proofs to obtain client approval before the work is prepared for printing in individual publications.

Printer's proofs can be made at various stages of the print production process. They can be made from the pdf or page files, from printing films or the printing plates. Digital ink proofs use special toners or printer's wet ink and are printed on either a special proofing paper or the paper stock that will be used for the finished print run. While a digital colour proof will give a reasonable idea of how the page will look, there are other proofing systems available that give a closer representation of the final printed result.

Proofing systems

■ **Progressive colour proofs** are a set of pages that show the progression of adding CMYK colours in sequence on paper; that is, page 1, yellow; page 2, yellow overprinted with magenta, showing a red–orange effect; page 3, yellow–blue with red overprinted showing the oranges, greens, purples, etc.; and finally all four colours printed showing the completed CMYK

Typical print advertising specifications

Page trim 285 × 220mm
Page bleed 291 × 226mm (incl. 4mm bleed)
Half page 125 × 200mm   Half page 255 × 97mm
Quarter page 125 × 97mm   Eighth page 60 × 97mm
dps trim 285 × 440mm
dps bleed 291 × 446mm (incl. 4mm bleed)
Printing: four-colour process
Binding: perfect bound
All images: CMYK at 300dpi tiff (no LZW compression)
All white text set at 0%C, 0%M, 0%Y, 0%K.
Supply: press-quality pdf or page make up files with
    linked images and fonts
Press pdfs: press-quality Acrobat Distiller files incl.
    crop and registration marks
Images CMYK at 300dpi
Embed all fonts
Please supply on CD, DVD or email/FTP in pdf
Chromalin proof to be supplied with each advertisement
Screen 175lpi (lines per inch)
*No responsibility will be accepted for reproduction
colour quality without a colour proof*

image. All four individual colours are also produced as separate proofs. A press operator can use the progressive pages at each stage of the printing process to ensure correct ink densities as the sheets go through the individual colour blankets (see page 325).

■ **Digital colour proofs** are produced from computer files and printed on digital printers.

■ **Traditional colour proofs** are produced using film and photographic techniques.

■ **Wet ink colour proofs** are produced using the printing plates and printer's inks.

Warning Some digital proofing systems produce photographic-quality colour prints that cannot be reproduced on a press, and these should not be used as a definitive guide to the final press output.

TIP Proofs that use CMYK inks on the same paper as the publication will provide the best representation of how the final printed product will look.

Iris inkjet colour proofs

Iris inkjet proofs are photographic-quality prints created on a high-end inkjet printer straight from the digital information and are more than 95% colour accurate. The proofs are produced by spraying fine ink droplets at a resolution of 1200dpi and use CMYK plus two spot colours. There is a range of inkjet papers in gloss, silk and matt finishes that can give a similar effect to printing on the paper to be used for the actual print run. Iris prints are less expensive than wet ink colour proofs and quicker to produce as there are no intermediary stages (see 318). However, the process can be relatively expensive if multiple copies of each individual proof are needed.

Chromalin and Matchprint

Chromalin and Matchprint are proofing system brand names which are used generically in the publishing industry to describe a laminated proof. The proofs are created using the four-colour separated films or halftone screened pdfs (CMYK). The screens are photographically transferred on to four transparent plastic sheets, with one for each process colour. The sheets are fused together on a paper backing and then laminated. Chromalins and Matchprints take less time to create than wet ink proofs.

Wet ink proofs

Traditional **wet ink proofs** are created using printing plates that are put on to a special proofing press which inks the plates and prints the four-colour inks. The advantage of this type of proof is that it is printed using process inks, and special spot colours if relevant. The proof can also be run on the same paper stock as the finished product. Once the first proof has been made, it is relatively cheap to run multiple copies of each page. Wet ink is the most accurate of the colour proofing systems, but it is also the most expensive and time consuming.

TIP Always keep in mind the final printed product when assessing pages on-screen. Use full screen view to hide menu bars and screen savers, and view at 100% of the actual printed size when previewing pages.

Why print a proof if the page has been looked at on-screen?

While colour monitors have greatly improved over the last few years, the accuracy of the colour display still depends on whether, how well and how often the monitors have been colour calibrated (see *How to work with colour*, page 247). The digital presses used by large printing companies have pre-press facilities that include high-end colour-calibrated monitors. These can produce extremely accurate on-screen representations of CMYK colours in RGB. However, most screens used for production do not have this level of calibration, and individual preference settings such as brightness and contrast can produce further variations.

- Monitor screens are a different shape from most printed pages, and elements such as top menus, windows and option bars create a significantly different viewing environment

- The sides of a monitor form an external frame around the page that can alter a person's perception of the balance of a layout

- The percentage enlargement or reduction of the page view (zoom) can also change the perceived appearance of a layout

Warning All print material has to be separated into CMYK – a four-channel colour space. Even when an RGB image has been converted to CMYK and the monitor colour calibrated, the image is still viewed on-screen in RGB so the colours may not be exactly the same as the printed result.

319

Imposition

When printing companies receive the individual page files from a client, they will run them through a series of tests using their preflight software (see page 312), and all material submitted is scanned for viruses. The pages are given a final visual check against any colour proofs supplied by the media company or client, and to make sure they comply with any other printer's requirements.

Editorial production is usually carried out in **designer's view** – consecutive pages and spreads as they appear in the publication. Printing companies use a system called **imposition** to arrange the pages for printing and folding and that ensures they run in the correct order. Imposition can be done as part of an overall print production management system, or using specialist software.

Printers use imposition to plan the best way for a multi-page publication to be set up on the press. Imposition ensures the pages run in numerical order when a publication is printed and folded. This is necessary because publications are printed in sections on large sheets or rolls of paper that flip or circulate and rotate as they run through the press to print on both sides. It takes into consideration the way in which a press holds the papers with an allowance made for folding. The page order also has to be matched to the binding method – whether the publication is to be **stapled** or perfect bound (cut and glued).

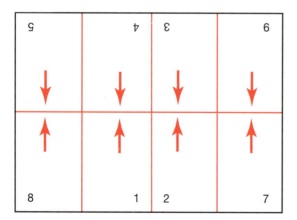

An eight-page imposition section places pages so that they will run consecutively when cut and folded.

Computer to plate (CTP)

CTP has largely replaced the previous process that transferred the image first to film and then to plate. Most publications prefer to use film-less processing as it saves time and money by eliminating one technical stage, and the introduction of direct imaging lithographic presses that do not use metal plates also allows for further savings in time and money. If film is generated, an image of the made-up page is ripped (see page 321) first on to photographically sensitised sheets, with one for every colour and varnish. The film is then photomechanically exposed and the image transferred on to photosensitive printing plates which are chemically treated to fix the page image on the plate.

Separations and printing plates

All litho-printed pages that contain images or shades of colours have to be separated into halftone screens, with one for each CMYK or spot colour being used. Separations can be produced by a page make up or imaging program, but are normally generated by the printing company during the pre-press process. The halftone screen colour separations are output onto a corresponding number of printing plates – thin sheets that can be made of plastic, paper or flexible metals, such as aluminium or zinc alloys. The page image is ripped (transferred) from a computer on to the plate's surface using a laser (**computer to plate, CTP**). The plates may also be photomechanically or photochemically processed. These methods are used to burn the type and halftone images on to the plate. There are different plate technical requirements for each make of press that include instructions such as whether the page image on the plate should be positive (right reading) or negative (wrong reading-in reverse).

Some modern automated litho presses are fully digitised with raster processing that lasers the page image directly on to a plate media roll. This type of computerised press works through the CTP process and allows for faster printing than metal plates that have to be changed for each print run. Files are sent from the pre-press computer to the press, and the images are either burned onto a special silicon dry plate or, for smaller digital presses, lasered directly on to the central drum of the press (see page 328).

Typically, printing plates are attached to a cylinder in the press, although some presses have a separately loaded roll of plate media. Ink is applied to the plate's image area and transferred directly to the paper or to an intermediary cylinder and then to the paper. On traditional litho presses, the plates are wrapped around a roller called a plate cylinder (see page 325). For digital litho presses, the page digital file can be sent directly to a plate through ripping.

The halftone screen: lines per inch and dots per inch

The halftone screens used by printing companies are made up of a series of dots or diamonds that are arranged in lines per inch. Unlike pixels, which at a given resolution would all be exactly the same size, the shapes that make up a line halftone screen vary in size depending on the density of the colour. The distance between the centres of each shape in a line sets the screen size. The screen size required is determined by the press type and paper: a newspaper printed on absorbent paper might use a screen size of 80 lines per inch (lpi), while a glossy colour magazine on coated stock might use 150lpi.

Litho presses use screens that vary between 80 and 200lpi, according to the quality of the printing required and the weight, surface and texture of the paper to be used. A printing company will check the pages at the pre-press stage to make sure all pictures and graphics are suitable for the intended screen output.

The pixels that make up an image file need to be smaller than the output screen density, because if the screen dots are too large the jagged edges of the pixels may become visible. The proportional density of

Raster image processing

A raster image processor (RIP) reads the computer code instructions for a page and translates them into bitmap raster imagery made up of dots that form the halftone screens (see page 248). Some pre-press tasks can be handled during the ripping process, such as colour management, trapping and imposition.

RIPs come in three forms:

1 Firmware: an in-built program that runs the microprocessor within a desktop printer, digital or computerised press
2 Software: programs that process pages for print and can be used with proofing printers and presses
3 Hardware: printing companies use powerful standalone RIP computer processors that handle many of the pre-press functions

CMYK colours should also be checked, as images that are made up of high percentages of each colour may become dark and flat on some more absorbent papers.

Colour printing, inks and varnishes

The four-colour process is the most economic way to print colour and is used for most printed material; however, some media companies and advertisers may demand absolute accuracy for their corporate or brand colours and require a special ink to be mixed. Most commonly Pantone and other ink manufacturers' systems are used to specify and formulate coloured inks for a logo, masthead or brand colour. CMYK inks cannot reproduce fluorescent, pastel or metallic colours and if a gold, silver or other special colour is required, non-process inks have to be used.

How to match media, paper and image resolutions

Paper stock	Halftone screen	Lines screen	Image resolution and dimensions
Newsprint – high absorbency	150dpi	75 lpi	Resolution: 150dpi, size: target printed dimensions
Newsprint – lower absorbency	200dpi	100 lpi	Resolution: 200dpi, size: target printed dimensions
Magazine stock – low absorbency	300dpi	150 lpi	Resolution: 300dpi, size: target printed dimensions

The chart shows how to match the absorbent qualities of the type of paper to average halftone and line screen resolutions, and the related resolution at which images have to be prepared for printing.

Spot varnishing is where a coating is printed on to all or some of the page. It can be accommodated on a CMYK press, although varnish normally requires a press with an ultraviolet dryer.

Every application of ink or varnish incurs a cost. The cheapest way to print is in black only, and every additional colour used increases the price of a print run. Two-colour printing is the least costly way to add a colour; the process normally uses black plus one colour and can employ percentages of the two inks to create other tones (see *How to work with colour*, page 260).

There are standard colours created by mixing percentages of transparent process inks, such as Warm Red (100% magenta, 100% yellow) or Reflex Blue (100% cyan, 70% magenta), which are used by many designers and printers. Single colour Pantone inks can also be used on their own and for two-colour printing with black.

Some short run publications may print sections in black only, or use two-colour printing in order to save on the cost of separations, plates and inks (see page 320), or use two-colour printing and restrict full colour CMYK to specific sections, as in this book. Running some or all of a publication in two colours means sections can be printed on more cost-effective presses. It is possible to run a publication with sections containing pages 1-64 in two-colour black and red inks, pages 65-81 in full colour CMYK using four inks, and complete the publication with pages 82-146 in the two colours. However, in two-colour printing, photographs can only be in black, the second colour or a **duotone**. Full colour images have to be printed in a CMYK section.

Standard inks

Most publications are printed using standard CMYK colours. Many larger presses have automated storage tanks that pump standard CMYK ink continuously, while others use four-colour ink cartridges (similar to a toner refill). If a special or spot colour, metallic ink or varnish is required, the ink rollers may have to be cleaned as well between jobs and this can substantially add to the cost of a print run.

TIP Make sure you are using the appropriate colour matching system specification for your title's stock as inks look different on various types of paper.

Matching colour inks to paper type

Companies such as Pantone produce a range of colour matching systems linked to the type of paper to be used. For example, colours for a glossy magazine should be specified using coated ink, while 'newsprint', the paper used by newspapers, would need uncoated ink.

Pantone solid coated mixed ink: coated paper
Pantone solid uncoated: uncoated paper
Pantone solid to process Pantone to CMYK: coated and uncoated paper
Pantone Process coated: coated paper
Pantone pastel coated: coated paper
Pre mixed pastel colours: all paper types

US-based Pantone is the most commonly used colour matching system in Britain, but there are other international companies such as Focoltone, Toyo and Truematch that produce similar colour ranges.

The paper or stock (substrate)

Paper has a semiotic message that can provoke a reader to make a judgement based on whether they think the stock feels expensive or not. A balance has to be achieved between what the press can handle, the cost to the media company and the values that the publication wishes to convey. A serious newspaper or glossy magazine that makes a feature of design and photography will use a whiter, better finished stock than a mid-market weekly magazine or tabloid newspaper whose audience is more interested in the topicality of the content than the quality of the reproduction. A magazine publisher may also vary the stock it uses between its full-sized and pocket editions, as the weight and feel of paper has a relationship to page size and can affect the usability and handling of the product.

Paper is produced in standard sizes. The **ISO A paper sizes** are used by many countries around the world, but not by the USA which has its own paper sizes. This would not be a problem except for the fact that many computers, desktop printers and computer programs originate in the USA and feature American default paper and document sizes. It is possible to buy European or British versions of most programs, but those working on international co-editions do need to be aware of the differences in paper sheet proportions and web roll width as well as size.

International A paper sizes

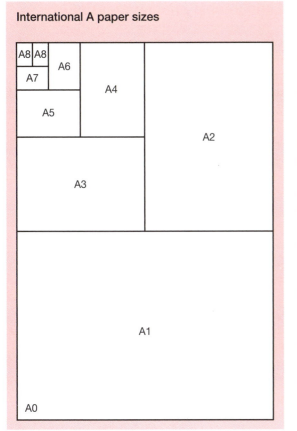

width	height		width		height
A0 841mm	× 1199mm		A5 148mm	×	210mm
A1 594mm	× 841mm		A6 105mm	×	148mm
A2 420mm	× 594mm		A7 74mm	×	105mm
A3 297mm	× 420mm		A8 52mm	×	74mm
A4 210mm	× 297mm				

TIP Make sure all your software's printing instructions are set to international standards if you are working in Britain or Europe. The paper size in a program's page setup for print must be A4 or another ISO paper size, because leaving the paper size setting on US Letter (say) may jam an A-size printer. ·

The most economical way to specify paper is to stay with the standard sizes for the region or country, as printing companies will be able to cut the greatest number of pages out of the proportionally sized large paper rolls or sheets they use. A publication may also need to fit a standard envelope for a particular postage category. The most commonly used paper size in Britain, A4, is a narrow rectangle, however many publication designers prefer to use a wider shape (see page 81). If a designer knows the size of the large roll or sheets of paper to be used on a press, it is possible for them to work with the printing company to calculate how to get the greatest number of pages in another size or shape out of a standard roll or sheet of paper. Paper manufacturers will produce custom sizes to order.

Printing time and costs

The three main types of printing used for media products are **web** and **sheet-fed offset lithography (litho)**, which are wet ink processes, and **digital printing**. Traditional printing presses may cost millions and digital presses many thousands of pounds. As all printing businesses want to maximise their investment, printing companies often run several shifts on a 24-hour system to get the most from their expensive machinery. Each printing press may be booked out in advance to ensure the press is fully utilised. Printer's charges are based on the time it takes to produce a given quantity of issues of

Software programs are used to calculate the cost of producing titles to very tight margins.

a publication – the press time. This depends upon the number of copies, pages and inks to be used, as well as how the publication is bound and finished (see page 326). A media company's print buyer will take into account the fact that printing press speeds and run capacities vary and will look for a printing company that has the most efficient and economic press for the title.

Lithographic (litho) printing is the most commonly used method for printing newspapers and consumer magazines. The cost of litho printing includes the preparation that has to be done prior to printing; press **make ready** – filling ink heads, mounting printing plates and loading paper; and cleaning the press after the print run with special ink dissolving solutions (wash up). A media company will try to agree a schedule with a printing company that is economical in terms of printing costs and gives the longest possible lead-in time. However, if a printing company is asked to turn work around more rapidly than agreed, it may need to charge more.

On many modern litho presses, the main functions are managed digitally with computer-controlled plate loading, ink coverage, colour quality and remotely managed loading of paper sheets or web rolls on to the press. Make-ready time has reduced from as long as several hours to less than an hour and, together with the introduction of faster litho presses that can print more than 85,000 copies per hour, this has reduced some of the printing costs for newspapers and magazines.

The principles of lithographic printing

Lithographic printing relies on the fact that grease and water do not mix. Printing plates are coated with a greasy chemical that is applied to the areas to be printed. Once the plates are on the press, a thin film of water is applied that adheres to the non-greasy areas of the plate. When the ink is rolled on to the plate, it sticks to the greasy print image and is repelled by the damp areas of the plate, so that only the inked type and images are printed. The dampening and inking process is repeated every time a page is transferred on to paper.

Lithographic printing presses

Litho presses have a number of ink heads or units. Inside each one there is an ink reservoir and a series of rollers. One roller sits in the ink and rackets round, while another makes contact to pick up some of the ink and transfers it to other rollers. The system is designed to control the level of inking, and only a small number of the rollers actually touch the plate cylinder. Another smaller roller unit damps the plate so that the ink is repelled from non-imaged areas. The page image does not pass directly from the plate on to the paper, but is offset in reverse from the **plate cylinder** to a **blanket cylinder** – a large rubber covered roller. The rubber is backed with canvas so it will not damage or mark the paper. The paper runs between the blanket cylinder and the **impression cylinder**, and the page image is transferred the right way round. The impression cylinder holds the paper firmly against the blanket cylinder to prevent the page moving out of position and becoming smudged or blurred.

Web and sheet offset litho

Offset litho is the most commonly used form of printing. Sheet-fed litho is a process whereby single large sheets of paper are run flat through the press, making contact with the blanket cylinders. Web offset litho uses large rolls or webs of paper that run through the press on a series of conveyor belts. Web offset presses print much faster than sheet-fed presses and can handle more copies at once. Modern presses can be huge – two or more storeys high – and run at enormous speeds. Computerised presses are almost completely automated and can produce copies more quickly than manually controlled machines. News International has a number of large-scale computerised printing plants in Britain with presses that run up to 86,000 copies per hour. The presses at its previous printing plant in Wapping could only run up to 30,000 copies per hour.

Presses print the pages of a publication in **sections (signatures)** made up of multiples of four pages. A press may be able to print 4, 8, 16 or 32 pages in each section. The way printed sections run through a press can result in left and right hand pages that face each other in designer's view being printed in a different section. For example, if a 64-page publication is divided into

Komori System 35S 16-page web offset press with inline bundler/stacker.

Source: Komori UK Ltd.

The Komori Lithrone 20L-420 sheet offset printing press.

Source: Komori UK Ltd.

Source: Tom Taylor

Visit Tom Taylor's photostream to see and hear a video of a large press in motion: www.flickr.com/photos/scraplab/4037258256/in/photostream/

four 16-page sections, page 16 would be in section A and page 17, which faces it, would be in section B.

A printing company will calculate the best possible combination of page sections to minimise the press time and costs. A media company will ensure that the number of pages in a publication corresponds to the printer's section plan. Running a 'bastard' (uneven) number of pages will result in having to print the pages individually, and the extra work involved will cause extra costs and may cause problems when binding the issue.

The stages of printing on an offset litho press

1. Make ready: testing the press, checking the ink levels and loading the paper
2. Installing the plates on the press and aligning the plate roller to the printing **blanket rollers** that transfer the page image to the paper as it runs through the press
3. Damping and inking the plates: a **dampening roller** applies a film of water to each printing plate and inking rollers apply the required number of inks to the greasy areas of the plate
4. Running test pages to check all the plates are in register (aligned)
5. Printing a number of pages that display the press standard colour bars used to check the ink density and coverage. A visual check is also made to ensure the colours match the media company's contract proofs as accurately as possible
6. Initiating the final print run with the press at full speed. The printing is automatically monitored during the run to ensure the inking and colour remain consistent. The printer will take a running sheet (a printed page) at frequent intervals to ensure that the colours match any proofs supplied by the publisher within an agreed tolerance (percentage of variation)
7. Cleaning the press (wash down) after a job is printed. The used plates are removed and the printing blanket rollers cleaned to remove the ink impressions to prepare the press for the next job.

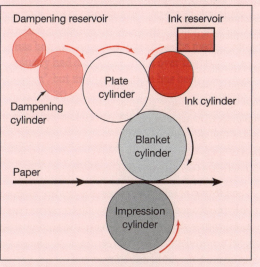

The offset litho process uses a series of metal and rubber rollers to transfer the linked image from the printing plate to the page.

Folding, binding and finishing

Once the pages have been printed, the large sheets containing the sections are folded to the final size and the pages collated in the correct running order. The front and back covers are added and all the pages are bound together and guillotined. The process of handling the pages once they come off the printing press is known as finishing. For more complicated projects, other processes may be required that involve sending the printed page sections to a specialist finishing company (see page 327).

Sheet-fed presses either print on one or both sides of a sheet of paper that are then stacked as flat sheets by the press and allowed to dry. The stacks of printed sheets are transferred to a finishing line where machines crease and fold the sections. These are placed on a collator that combines all the sections. The final stage is for the cover to be wrapped around the other sections and either stitched or glued prior to guillotining.

Large web offset printing presses normally have an in-built oven that instantly dries the ink and an internal **finishing line** that folds, collates and bundles the pages in one continuous process.

Binding

The method of binding depends on the number of pages, type and thickness of paper. Stapling – **saddle stitching** – is most commonly used for magazines and brochures, but if a magazine has more than a certain number of pages, the staples may not hold or even go through all the folded pages. **Perfect binding** – gluing the pages into a square backed cover – is normally used for a title with a large number of pages. The back or spine has to be wide enough for the pages to attach, perfect binding may not be suitable for issues with less than 32 pages.

There are two main methods of binding:

1 *Stapled or wire bound*: the page sections are dropped in order on to a collator, starting with the centre spread section, with the covers wrapped around the outside. Staples are driven through the central fold. The process is also known as saddle stitching.

2 *Perfect binding*: the page sections are folded and collated alongside each other. The inner margin edges are cut, dipped in glue, then ground and formed into

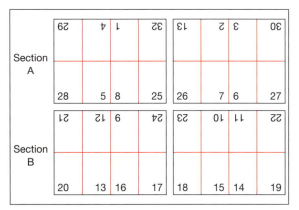

A 32-page saddle-stitched section.

A 32-page perfect-bound section.

a flat, squared-off back edge. The cover section has to be designed to match the depth of the squared-off back in order for the cover to wrap perfectly around all the page sections.

Once the cover has been wrapped around the text pages, and the publication has been stapled or perfect bound, the three remaining outer edges are guillotined to remove the excess paper containing the bleed area and gripper edge strip. This gives a clean, flat edge to the trimmed pages.

TIP There are programs available that you can use to calculate the width for a perfect-bound magazine's spine based on the number of pages in an issue and the paper being used. However, it is always advisable to confirm the spine width with your printing company.

Promotional items and hand finishing

Publications often use free gifts to increase sales. The printing industry's terms for free gifts are tip-ons and add-ons. The size and shape of the promotional item affects how it can be attached to, or distributed with, the title. Some printing companies can handle mounting straightforward, flat items on a cover or page as part of the finishing line. However, more complex or delicate items may require hand insertion. The time needed to include promotional items or hand finishing has to be allocated within an existing schedule, to ensure the company can meet the publishing deadline.

Printing companies will normally have a list of freelance finishing workers, or they will send the magazines for outworking by a specialist company. Not all printers may have the expertise or equipment on site to cope with the more complex finishing processes, and there are finishing companies that carry out tasks such as shape cutting or more elaborate folding and binding, as this can require specialist equipment. The printing company that holds the contract with the publishers will add in the cost of these processes and of any additional transportation to their charges.

Special effects printing

There is a range of specialist printing technologies that may need to be outsourced. These include printed holographic panels, created using **lenticular** technology, that can be used for special effects covers. This type of 3D or motion effects image is generated by a special lens and printed on a substrate of ridged material that, depending on the angle it is viewed from, appears to move or have depth. Special effects printing is often commissioned from expert companies.

Insertions

A printing company other than the one producing the magazine often supplies advertising and marketing insertions that are not printed as part of the publication, such as brochures, leaflets and subscription flyers. These can be inserted on the finishing line – known as loose insertion – or bound in to the spine of the magazine. Publications with inserts are often sold in polybags to prevent the insertion becoming lost. Plastic wraps are also used to keep insertions, cover mounts and free gifts safe from damage or theft.

Logistics

Some media companies that publish national and international editions send their page files to be printed in other countries or regional centres, as printing overseas or local editions can reduce transport costs and delivery times. Publishers of less time-sensitive titles may choose to print in countries where prices are not as high as in the UK, as this can prove to be cheaper, even taking into consideration the cost of shipping the issues back to this country. It is sometimes cost effective to transport print runs to international delivery companies in Europe for posting back to the UK, as they offer cheaper postal rates than the Royal Mail.

Print production finishing line process

Die cutting	Using tailor-made dies to cut unusual shapes Cutting can be computerised (CNC cutter)
	Places additional creases in paper for gate-folds etc.
Creasing	Free gifts glued to cover
Tip-ons	Clear plastic pouches used to contain inserts or magazines
Polybags	Effects used to suggest movement or depth
3D/lenticular	Adding tamper-proof seals
Security binding	Applying a plastic film to an area or whole page
Laminating	Pushing the image out from the paper to create a raised shape
Embossing	Pushing the image into the paper to create an impressed shape
Stamping/debossing	An image pushed into or out from the paper without ink
Blind em(de)bossing	Applying metal coating to letterforms, stamped or em(de)bossed shapes
Foil blocking	

Digital printing

Digital printing is the term used to describe a range of printing presses that transfer the page image from computer files such as pdfs directly on to the paper. Digital presses do not require plates or the complex system of rollers used by offset litho presses. They can be set up more quickly and handle short print runs more economically than conventional litho presses, and each individual page can be personalised.

Digital printing allows editorial and advertising deadlines to fall much closer to the publication date, which gives the media company the benefit of including last-minute editorial updates. Before the Internet, publications would be printed in one country and flown around the world. Now, media companies send their files to overseas printing companies for **remote digital printing** in any quantity, anywhere in the world. The *Daily Mail* and *Mail on Sunday* and the *Guardian* have all formed agreements with American print companies to print and issue their editions. A British media company, Stroma, part of Océ's Digital Newspaper Network (DNN), prints up to 60 to 70 international newspapers a day, and may run anything from 5 to 500 copies of a paper, depending on demand.

The print quality from digital presses can be very high, with almost photographic reproduction of images, depending on the paper used, and can have a better colour range and consistency than some litho presses. Digital presses enable very short print runs that would be prohibitively expensive to print on a litho press. It is an economical and convenient way to print medium-length runs of niche interest magazine or industry newsletters that may need a fast turnaround. It also gives media companies the ability to customise advertising and marketing campaigns.

The digital press manufacturers are working on increasing the operating speeds; however, at present, litho presses are still faster and more cost effective when printing longer runs. This is because most litho printing costs are incurred in setting up, and once the press is running the cost of printing each issue drops dramatically as more copies are printed. The standard method of charging for digital printing is a cost for each page impression and this puts it at a disadvantage on longer print runs. Although the new generation of digital presses are becoming faster, digital printing toners and inks remain expensive compared with litho ink. However, digital printing wastes less paper than a litho press and is more flexible as additional issues can be printed as and when needed.

Digital newspaper printing systems

There is an increasing number of digital printing systems such as the HP T300 Color Inkjet Web press and Kodak's digital newspaper system which can print full broadsheet newspaper formats, and Océ produces a digital press that can run up to 4,000 copies per hour for a 32-page tabloid newspaper.

HP Indigo 7000 digital press

1 Laser imager (writing head)
2 Photo imaging cyclinder (PIP drum)
3–7 Inking rollers (BIDs)
4 Proof tray exit
5 Touch screen/ILD colour adjustment
6 Output stacker
7 Large ink cans
8–9 Exit conveyor and perfector
10–11 Paper feed rollers
12 Vertical paper feed
13–17 Paper input trays
18 Paper feed unit
19 Impression cyclinder
20 Paper input feed roller
21 Imp. ventilation
22 ITM ventilation
23 ITM external heating
24 Attention light
25 Blanket cyclinder (ITM drum)
26 Cleaning station
27 Charger roller

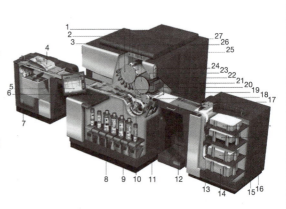

Source: Picture courtesy HP

How a digital press works

Large digital presses can print at very high resolutions (3600dpi – three times the resolution of a desktop printer). They work like a very advanced photocopier or laser printer.

- The pdf or digital file is ripped directly to the digital press and a bitmapped image of the page is transferred on to an electrostatically charged internal drum by laser beam.

- Pulses of laser light are fired to reverse the electric charge in the corresponding photoreceptors on a drum inside the press. The charge attracts the toner/ink to the photoreceptor, leaving a ghost image. Only negatively charged receptors pick up the toner/ink to form the image; the positive photoreceptors remain clear of colour.

- The spinning drum transfers the toner image to paper using static electricity. Once the page image has printed, the charge is released and the drum clears of toner or ink as it spins, removing the previous image and leaving it free to accept a new page.

- Every colour has to be printed separately, so a single page in CMYK would pass four times through a digital press.

- Once printed, the page is passed through heated rollers (400 °F) (205 °C) to seal the colour toner or ink on to the paper. The high temperature used to fix the toner/inks means that some types of paper are not suitable for digital printing.

Communication industries

Many printing companies use both litho and digital presses. They will consult with their clients on what production and printing systems will be best to achieve the most economical results for the quality they require, and to comply with any environmental concerns or targets they may have. Printing companies can handle all aspects of the product, for example managing a mixed media distribution of a special interest or business publication where some copies are posted directly to customers, while others are sent as a pdf via the Web or email with a number of issues being dispatched to retailers.

A number of companies have dropped 'print' from their name, as their main activity has changed and they now provide a range of communication industry services.

This change in business emphasis ties in with the fact that media companies are no longer just publishers, but now operate through a range of platforms and in a number of related sectors such as technology and database management, advertising and marketing.

Print on demand (POD) is seen as the next step as the media industry moves away from the sale and return model. Digitally printed publications have the potential to change how newspapers and magazines work as they open the door to **microzoning** – the term for replacing elements of a publication's content with new material relevant to a specific local audience. This can include incorporating four or eight pages targeted at a local or special interest audience and tailored advertising and promotions. It can also be applied to user-generated content, where a group or organisation could be invited to submit their copy and pictures directly to the editorial department for inclusion. The flexibility of the process also allows for publications to be printed whenever they are ordered, rather than to a set deadline. As digital presses improve in quality and reduce in size, it may become possible for newsagents to print out individual copies of newspapers and magazines in their shop for each customer.

Printing and the environment

Until recently, most of the litho printing inks and solutions used for press wash down contained pollutants. For many years the printing industry used inks that contained poisonous metals such as lead, cadmium and mercury, and the chemical solutions employed to clean them off the presses were alcohol based. The ink drying agents emitted volatile organic compounds (VOCs) that, as they evaporated, reacted with sunlight and

Visit *www.1stbyte.co.uk* for information on digital printing; it also has a good animated version of a small digital printing works.

British Printing Industries Federation: *www. britishprint.com*

PIRA International (consultancy): *www.pira.co.uk*

Print Week magazine: *www.printweek.com/*

Print Monthly magazine: *www.printmonthly.co.uk/*

this contributed to ozone damage and photochemical smog. The fumes also presented a health risk for printing plant workers, and printing plants had to comply with stringent health and safety rules. Today, the printing industry is moving away from these products in order to reduce the environmental impact of the printing process.

The printing industry has introduced eco-friendly inks and water-based solvents. Many chemical-based litho inks no longer contain poisonous heavy metals and are being replaced by ranges of new printing inks that are water based and contain vegetable oils such as soya that do not produce VOCs. New eco-solvent inks have been developed that do not produce toxic fumes and improve conditions for print workers.

Digital printing is generally considered to be greener than litho and it does score well in terms of less paper waste and energy consumption. There is an issue over the manufacture and disposal of plastic toner cartridges; however, the digital print industry has recycling and safe disposal systems in place. Digital printing inks can cause a problem when paper is cleaned for recycling that has been compared with putting a coloured sock in a whites wash. The Digital Print De-Inking Alliance (DPDA) is looking at the environmental issues raised by the de-inkability of digital print.

Economic pressures

The growing ecological awareness of the printing industry is good news for the environment, but it has placed financial pressures on the printing industry at a time of rising costs and squeezed margins. New presses need to comply with emissions control and environmental requirements, and it is expensive to adapt older presses to meet current legislation and agreements. This, together with higher prices for materials, has meant that some small printing companies have found it hard to remain competitive, or match the lower prices charged by printers in Eastern Europe and China. This has led to business failures, consolidation and staff redundancies in the US and Western Europe printing industry.

The high level of competition in the industry over the past few years has led to big media companies acquiring printing, production and advertising businesses.

Environmental improvements

The printing industry has made a commitment to comply with the ISO directive for environmental management that covers the actions a company or institution should take to limit both its own environmental impact and that of its customers and suppliers.

- Printing companies are undertaking to achieve zero carbon rating.
- New presses should obtain emissions certification related to the Kyoto Protocol.
- The printing industry has embraced the concept of corporate social responsibility.
- Printing companies are reducing previously high levels of noise and pollution.
- New press designs have been developed to reduce paper waste and save trees.
- Automated print management systems provide better maintenance information and can lead to increased press efficiency.
- The greater accuracy of modern presses reduces the amount of ink wasted.
- The use of vegetable inks and non-alcohol wash solutions reduces VOC emissions.
- Water-based plate dampening reduces VOCs.
- Printing plants are being built to include renewable energy systems and to recycle excess heat from presses.
- Printing companies are actively pursuing greener purchasing policies such as using tree-less paper.

A number of medium-sized design, printing, finishing and distribution companies have merged to form communication groups offering an integrated package of services. At the same time, emissions regulations coupled with increasing operating costs and expensive materials are making made it increasingly difficult for small printing businesses to compete against the larger groups. The overall effect has been to reduce the market choice for publishers that do not have their own printing and production companies, and to increase the cost of producing print titles in Britain.

Web media

Web culture is fast moving and immediate and there is constant pressure to have new material available and ready to be published online. This makes it extremely important that you apply controls and checks to maintain the quality and accuracy of the content and ensure that all the technical elements function correctly. In order to be able to do this, it helps to have a grasp of the basic principles of the Internet and its technologies.

The Web has an established set of production procedures and technical specifications for multimedia, web forms, interactive social media, etc. Many of the tasks, such as uploading files, will be familiar if you have used the Internet; however, it will be to your advantage to understand how web technology is used by the media industry. This can involve knowing how the hardware and software work but, with such a wide range of technologies, it is not expected that you have expertise in all areas. Most media companies will either have a team of people with a varied range of skills who work cooperatively on their online products, or outsource web development and management to specialist companies.

Web production is divided into three main areas. The first level is the program interfaces that the editorial team employs to upload content and that the public use to view the pages. Underpinning what we see on-screen is all the communications and computing technology, the second level, such as networks, servers and the programs that control the production and functionality of websites. This is referred to as the front end of the process. The global network that provides the standardised protocols and hardware that make the Internet work is called the back end, the third level. This infrastructure consists of database software and computer coding language programs that are run on large groups of interconnected servers (server farms).

TIP If you are working on an intranet website within a company, it is a good idea to ask the IT department or support company to ensure that the same browser and version is installed on all the computers to prevent compatibility problems

The browser

A browser converts the HTML code so that it can be read by any computer and displayed as the pages you see on-screen. When a web address is typed in, the browser software makes a connection to the web server and downloads the page as code. The browser follows the coding instructions that tell it how to display the page, locates and downloads all the media files that make up the page and places them in position.

There are several browser programs that handle and display pages in different ways. This inconsistency, and the fact that older versions of each browser may still be in use, mean that a decision has to be taken on what range of web browsers will be supported when a media website is set up. Unfortunately, it is not possible to control what browser a website may be viewed with, and an image that is in the right place on a web page in the current version of Internet Explorer may not even be visible on the screen in an older version of another browser. It is essential to test pages in a number of browsers before they go live to check that the pages display correctly. Alternatively, separate versions of the pages can be produced for each browser, and a process called 'sniffing the browser' used to identify the program that the visitor is using and send instructions to the web server to download a compatible page.

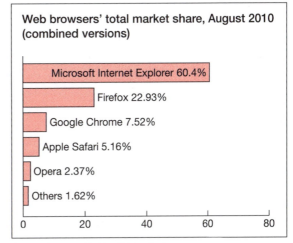

Web browsers' total market share, August 2010 (combined versions)

Microsoft Internet Explorer 60.4%
Firefox 22.93%
Google Chrome 7.52%
Apple Safari 5.16%
Opera 2.37%
Others 1.62%

Source: Data provided by NetApplications: *http://www.netmarketshare.com*

Page production

Pages are usually created on the media company's system using a CMS that has been tailored to the title's requirements, and the program will handle and process the content to web-ready level. Alternatively, each page can be prepared in a web design program, but this can require specialist knowledge or further training. CMSs are designed to be a quick and efficient way of entering and uploading the page content and of automatically archiving the material. The copy and other media files are stored in a database on a server. When a page is ready, the CMS program's instruction to publish uploads all the files to a web server that responds to requests from a visitor's browser to view the page.

While there can be considerable time pressure on the pre-publishing process, it is important that all editorial and technical controls and checks are completed before a page is published. Although you can remove a page containing mistakes from the Web, copy errors can be seen as unprofessional and technical problems that affect whether the page or website works can reflect badly on the title, and may discourage users from revisiting the site. Extra care should be taken when writing headings and sells for RSS feeds and news alerts, as many of these cannot be deleted once issued. The Internet relies on the interrelationship between millions of computers and other devices, and it only takes one incorrect thing to cause a problem. What might be seen to be only a minor technical defect on your site could cause problems for other sites that have hyperlinks to your pages. Spelling errors can affect whether the page can be found by a search engine, as well as how it is listed.

Web servers

Once the pages have been published and uploaded, the web server's software handles the various functions required to run a website. The main web server may run in conjunction with a database server that has software which accesses the interactive functions of a website, such as a system that moves older stories progressively down a menu or list and into an archive, or one that operates a retailing system which allows a visitor to choose and order from a catalogue. **Database**

Passwords and security

Database server systems can be used to set up and manage gateway password protection. Media companies that charge for access to their information use web database logons to restrict, monitor and control the availability of their titles. The home page is normally open to all Internet users, but only subscribers with a user name and password can access premium content, for example financial reports or market analysis. Other free services, such as the ft.com's share portfolio tracking, are password protected because they contain personal information.

management systems (DBMS) and database server systems, such as MySQL or Oracle, ensure that the files for any interactive elements on the website reach the visitor's browser. Software and files held on the database server are sent to the web server and then to the visitor's browser to enable form filling and interactive media, such as a video, to be played. Sites with many pages featuring animation, TV and video may require multiple host servers to produce the necessary capacity to deliver content to a large number of visitors at the same time.

Customer services

Media companies like to develop relationships with their website visitors, and people expect a website to have a response mechanism for their enquiries and feedback, especially if it features subscription offers, personalised retail and other services. Customer services can include email and mobile alerts that can be requested by a visitor to match their individual interests, and many titles have discussion forums to allow their visitors to comment on the topics covered by the websites, and to socialise with each other. Media websites will often include hyperlinks with a story or feature to discussion threads and writer's blogs, as well as opportunities for people to submit pictures or video of an event, or on any general topic. An online production job may well entail monitoring a discussion thread to ensure nothing inappropriate gets published.

Web forms should be fully trialled by a test panel to ensure they are clear and easy to use, and active forms should be regularly checked to make sure all the fields and buttons are active and any hyperlinks or actions

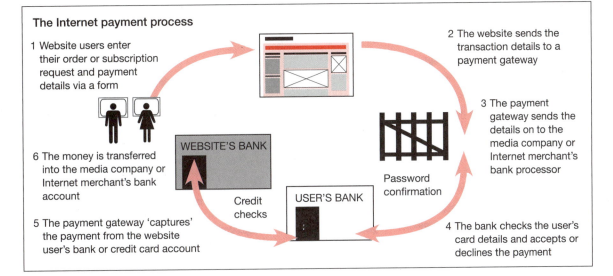

The Internet payment process

1 Website users enter their order or subscription request and payment details via a form

2 The website sends the transaction details to a payment gateway

3 The payment gateway sends the details on to the media company or Internet merchant's bank processor

Password confirmation

WEBSITE'S BANK

USER'S BANK

Credit checks

6 The money is transferred into the media company or Internet merchant's bank account

5 The payment gateway 'captures' the payment from the website user's bank or credit card account

4 The bank checks the user's card details and accepts or declines the payment

are functioning. Despite a temptation to use forms to find out everything you can about a website's visitors, they should not include too many obvious marketing questions, as this may annoy people. And the longer the form, the less likely it is that people will complete it.

Large media companies with IT and web departments can handle the set-up and running of their own web forms, but many smaller media companies often employ outside specialists who undertake the scripting, form design, maintenance and database management needed to create web forms and keep them functioning. The information received from forms is transferred into a database to be used by media companies for marketing and customer interaction, and it is important that web databases have any incorrect, out-of-date or malicious entries removed. Web forms can be password protected and made safe from spammers and identity thieves, and security should be regularly upgraded.

Financial transaction web forms

Many websites need to handle financial transactions for retail, subscriptions and other charges for content. Because all online payment schemes have to be extremely secure, most media companies work with established Internet merchants or employ a finance company such as PayPal to process the payments. When a visitor completes a payment form, the transaction is directed to the finance company or Internet merchant,

and it carries out a secure transaction from the customer's bank or credit card account. Media companies use banks, credit cards and person-to-person (P2P) payment schemes to reassure visitors that a trusted company is handling the actual payment, that their personal financial details will remain confidential and that the system confirms the payment has been made.

There are other ways of providing feedback and advice for visitors, such as an email link that launches either an email program with the recipient's address already in place, or a pop-up window for webmail or instant messaging help services and forums. What is important is that the media or other company sets up a response system or employs a partner specialist firm that will react quickly to the request for help or information. Visitors can find it annoying when their urgent message is left unanswered for several days, or they receive a curt emailed acknowledgement followed by a lengthy gap before anyone answers their question or plea for help.

TIP Any website that has a service which requires visitors to enter personal or financial details should comply with the international PCI data security standards. It is also a good idea to reassure visitors by including the logos of other supporting organisations that verify Internet shopping, such as VeriSign and PayPal.

Working with web experts

The rapid technological development of the Internet offers an enormous numbers of opportunities and innovations, and the media industry has to react quickly so that its products do not appear outdated. The knowledge required to understand and implement new technologies within a short timescale may mean a company does not have the in-house expertise or computer capacity, and may need to work with IT specialists and web technologists, programmers and coders as well as website designers, video and film editors and sound engineers. The people who specialise in these areas are often enthusiasts who have considerable knowledge and skills, and they are likely to be aware of the latest online developments. It is worthwhile keeping a constant dialogue going with them to ensure the company's websites remain cutting edge.

Media companies that employ outside IT specialists should have an agreement drawn up covering technical support for their websites. Ideally, once a site is launched, it should just keep working, but in the real world things do go wrong. A web management or hosting company may be responsible for advising the production team on the technical aspects of its work, and for overseeing maintenance of the server side, such as updating programming and software components. Journalists and others who produce content for websites are generally not expected to deal with technical malfunction in the CMS, or any server-side problems. However, it is a good idea to check the pages regularly and to draw attention to any functional problems that may occur.

Code validation

The best way to identify problems and test the coding that a page is built from is to use the World Wide Web Consortium's (W3C) Markup Validation Service (http://validator.w3.org). This is a free open source website that checks XHTML, HTML and other types of coding. The site address or URL is typed in and the service will run software to validate the mark-up language against the W3C standard. This test only examines code and is not a full check of an entire website.

Coders and programmers

There are a large number of specialists in online media such as experts in database development who can write tailored database programming, and programmers who can prepare computer coding that adds functionality and actions to a website. They can supply services such as HTML, XML, Flash and Ajax coding and CSS that can be used to design a website. There are also websites that offer free or customised coding and scripts. Web programmers have a vital job to do as they make a website function, and the coding has to be 100% accurate. As coding is the method by which online information is located and transferred, seemingly minor errors can cause serious problems. A simple error in page text coding such as a ' ; ' instead of a ' : ' can stop a page working. It could take all day for a non-expert to spot the error, but a programmer would probably see it straight away. If you post a letter 'snail mail' with some mistakes in the address, it will probably get to its destination, but if a hyperlink code is typed in with just one incorrect character, it will not connect to the target page.

Programming languages

There are a number of computing languages used to produce web pages. The basic language of the web, HTML, was invented by Tim Berners-Lee to enable scientists to share research and other information through a grid of computers connected by telephone lines. Berners-Lee designed HTML to be a universal language that could be read by any computer. Today, most websites employ a mix of programming techniques and software to create a range of functions. These may include forms that will alert someone if they miss a field, calculating how much people have to pay for the goods they have ordered, streaming TV/film/video and 3D online gaming.

There are several types of programming languages and each has a particular function:

■ HTML (Hypertext Markup Language) is the tag-based programming language used to describe the page structure and employed by web browsers to assemble the component files that make up a web page, and to format the type.

■ XML (Extensible Markup Language) was developed by W3C when HTML was reformulated in 2000 to increase its usability. XML is used in combination with HTML to form XHTML and is a background text-based programming language that identifies, transfers and stores data. Unlike HTML, it does not display information or visual content. It is used to create custom tags that expand the functions of a website and control how well it works with database servers. XML holds data in a separate file that works in conjunction with programming languages. It is more compatible across platforms and accessible to a wider range of software, and prevents data loss when an operating system is updated. It can also be used to create programming languages, such as the RSS feeds that are used on news websites.

■ JavaScript, Perl and Microsoft's VBScript are scripting languages that set up the instructions for an interactive page element, such as a drop-down menu or a form. JavaScript is the most commonly used of these languages, and web design programs like Adobe Dreamweaver include menus of the most common JavaScript actions such as button rollovers, mouseovers and drop-down menus. JavaScript can be customised and used to write advanced actions like a web survey, competition or simple game.

■ Dynamic HTML or DHTML combines JavaScript and other technologies and can be used to create moving or action linked graphics.

■ Ajax is a merging of JavaScript and XML. It improves on the performance of both and is compatible with the most commonly used browsers.

■ Xcode is Apple's free development software suite that allows independent developers to create iPhone and iPad apps. It is based on the ANSI C programming language but also supports a range of other languages including Java.

Form actions

The interactive forms used on websites for subscriptions and retailing are created using HTML. Forms can contain special controls such as tick boxes, fields to enter information and multiple choice drop-down menus, with instructions on how to use these items.

Content field	Rollover
File field	Scrolling area
Group field area	Submit–reset button
Hidden field	Push buttons (other
Image field	actions such as
Interactive list menu	calculate, search, etc.)
(includes hyperlinks)	Text label button
List menu (drop down)	File select
Mouseover	Tick box
Multiple-click buttons	Radio buttons
One-click button	

Web programs

While coding underlies all websites, most people work with WYSIWYG industry standard programs such as Dreamweaver that do not require you to be able to code, as they provide menus and automated scripts for most of the main components of a web page:

■ Adobe Dreamweaver organises the files that make up the pages for a website into a folder and uploads the files to a web server. Dreamweaver has coding capacity that can be used to write non-standard HTML and XML tags and to create CSS, as well as handle Flash and JavaScript.

■ The component parts of a Flash website load independently, so individual content items can be refreshed without affecting the entire page. Flash includes XML programming, which adds to its range of possible actions. However, because a Flash website is an image file, there can be downloading problems on some computers. The fact that the copy is no longer in a text language can limit its searchability and adaptability for disabled users, although Flash does work well with a screen reader.

There are other programs related to video and sound editing that fall outside the remit of this book. For more information on multimedia visit:
www.pearsoned.co.uk

Web hosting companies

The web is a 24/7/365 service and a website has to keep functioning and be updateable. Although some media companies manage their websites from their own web server, many prefer to upload their pages to a specialist web hosting company that has the infrastructure to handle a number of different company sites. The advantages of using a hosting service are that it is in a position to upgrade its equipment and technical knowledge continually. Web hosts usually have a large number of servers, often in more than one location. These groups of servers are known as server farms. It is normal practice for a website to be hosted on more than one individual server, so that if a single server is out of action the website is still accessible (mirror sites). Server farms have a large processing capacity to provide the maximum amount of accessibility to websites.

Web hosting companies employ expert technicians who are able to handle technical or hardware failures more easily than a site managed by an individual media company. Web hosting companies are often staffed around the clock and have the fastest T-speed fibre optic Internet broadband connections, allowing for rapid downloading of pages by users.

Website hosts charge for **bandwidth** – the volume in gigabytes of data uploaded to a server by the media company and downloaded by visitors. Web hosts also charge for the server space, that is how many giga/megabytes of storage space the site takes up on the hard drive, and extra for multiple mirror sites.

It is always useful to know how people are using your site, and web hosting companies can track usage through server logs generated by the browser. These show who has logged on to a site, which pages they visited and for how long. Many medium to large media businesses employ web service companies that specialise in Internet tracking and analysis, and register their sites with the Audit Bureau of Circulation to obtain independently verified figures.

Small to medium companies can buy sophisticated tracking programs, such as Spector Pro, to monitor their website traffic in detail, and there is also free website tracking software such as Google Analytics. Some web tracking programs can locate the visitor's source computer and view their Internet history – what other sites they have visited. Media companies use tracking data such as **click-through rates** (CTRs) – how many times an advertisement has been clicked on divided by the number of times the page containing it has been viewed – as well as unique user numbers to determine how much clients will be charged for an advertisement.

Estimated time taken to perform online activities

Connection speed	56kbs	512kbs	2Mbs	8Mbs	16Mbs	24Mbs
Download 250kB web page	36 seconds	4 seconds	1 seconds	0.3 seconds	0.9 seconds	0.1 seconds
Download 5MB music track	12 minutes	1 minute 22 seconds	21 seconds	5 seconds	3 seconds	2 seconds
Download 25MB video clip	1 hour	6 minutes 50 seconds	1 minute 45 seconds	26 seconds	13 seconds	9 seconds
Download low-quality film (750MB)	31+ hours	3 hours 20 minutes	52 minutes	13 minutes 6 seconds	6 minutes 30 seconds	4 minutes 22 seconds
Download DVD-quality film (4GB)	7+ days	19 hours	4 hours 38 minutes	1 hour 48 minutes	36 minutes 11 seconds	24 minutes

Source: Ofcom

A high-speed connection with a large bandwidth is ideal for web production systems.

The main types of web hosting services

- Shared web servers and Internet connections: using space rented on another company's server with a shared ISP.

- Co-location: a company owns a web server that is housed at a web hosting company or ISP which manages the day-to-day running and maintenance.

- Managed hosting services: the media company runs its own website with a hosting company managing the background technology and handling the maintenance.

- Dedicated hosting: a server and Internet line are reserved by a web host for one media company's exclusive use.

Internet service providers (ISPs)

ISPs are the companies that provide access to the Internet for businesses, organisations and individuals. There are several major players in this area such as 3, BT, O2, Orange, Tiscali, Virgin and Vodafone. They operate across a range of platforms and devices and offer connectivity for broadband DSL and ADSL, cable, dial-up, satellite, wireless, **IPTV** (Internet Protocol Television) and VoIP (Voice over Internet Protocol). The market is very competitive, and all ISPs are keen to obtain corporate clients with multiple websites so they can charge higher business rates based on large volumes of data traffic. A large media company will negotiate with an ISP to obtain the best charging schedule possible to set its web operating costs.

Regional specific advertising

The challenge for media companies is to find ways in which the obvious advantages of the Web can be translated into financial gains. One solution is to sell into the global market rather than only carry advertising from the country in which the website is based. Server databases can hold advertisements from any country and be set up so that a different advertisement is displayed to a regional website visitor in their own language. Newspaper websites such as Telegraph.com run country-specific advertising on their news pages, with approximately 33% of their advertisements coming from Britain, 33% from the USA and 33% from the rest of the world. If you are working on a site that is using regional content microzones (see page 24) or regional advertising, you will need to develop a system to manage content in more than one language and to track the replacement advertising files for each region.

New technologies and search engines have been developed which analyse web users' browser history, with the aim that people receive targeted advertising content based on their previous page viewing. It is possible that, before long, a program will be developed that will allow people to request the type of advertising as well as editorial content they want to see, based on their individual leisure, brand and product interests.

Source: Guardian News & Media

The Guardian was one of the first major newspapers to build a successful online presence. Their website has enabled them to develop a global liberal readership, and to market their own services as well as displaying section-specific advertising to their target audience.

Typical web advertising specifications

Advertisement	Website section	Dimensions	Maximum file size	File formats
Banner	All	468 × 60 px	30k	swf, gif, jpg
Skyscraper	All except homepage	120 × 600 px	30k	swf, gif, jpg
Double skyscraper	Homepage only	300 × 600 px	35k	swf, gif, jpg
Standard MPU	Homepage, News features	300 × 250 px	30k	swf, gif, jpg
Leaderboard	All	728 × 90 px	30k	swf, gif, jpg
Blog banner	Daily update	468 × 60 px or 728 × 90 px	20k	gif, jpg
Blog thumbnail	Daily update	75 × 113 px	5k	gif, jpg
Blog text link	Daily update	n/a	40 words	Text

Typical specifications for web advertisements will indicate the dimensions in pixels, file memory size and format for each location within the site.

The Web has developed from a series of pages using text and static images into a multimedia environment, and its potential to evolve further is currently only limited by the broadband speeds available to many users. People now use the Internet in a completely different way from when it was first launched. They want instant information, related to where they are and what they want to do next, and the media have to adapt to these lifestyle changes.

The websites of the future are likely to be more personalised and customer driven, and the media must be ready to operate in this one-to-one world. The technologies that will enable media companies to achieve this are already available. The introduction of fibre optic telephone lines will provide much faster download speeds to drive the move towards more video-based interactive pages, and smart phones and tablets mean that the audience can access the Internet from any location.

The media industry is constantly finding ways to work with these and future technologies. As websites become more fluid and intrinsic to how we live, media products will need to deliver information in a more pictorial, individualised way, and this will require an additional set of production skills.

Source: Courtesy of CNN

CNN was founded in 1980 by Ted Turner. It was the first 24-hour television cable news channel. Its traditional broadcast service is now argumented by its website which features live web video and audio reports from its global bureaus. The rolling news is enhanced by an extensive searchable archive of news features and background information.

Summary Going to press/publishing on the Web

The rapid changes in digital technology have made it necessary for everyone in the media industry to have sufficient knowledge of production practices and processes to be able to adapt to the impact of innovation. An understanding of traditional printing processes as well as current web production systems will help you to learn new methodologies and skills, as most production developments evolve from past and current media.

- Media products run to a fixed timetable for print; website content is updated on a rolling basis.
- Print and web advertising deadlines are linked to editorial schedules, and client advertisements must comply with all production and/or printing requirements.
- A publisher or senior editor must 'sign off' all pages before they are published on the Web or in print.

Print

- A signed-off proof is the formal notification from the media company to a printing company that it can proceed with the editiorial pages or advertisements.
- Adobe Acrobat standard pdfs are the format used for soft proofing and digital printing. An Adobe Acrobat press pdf is the high-resolution format used for outputting to printing plates or film for printing on lithographic and high-end digital presses.
- The two main types of printing process used for media products are digital press printing and wet ink litho presses – web offset and sheet fed.
- Litho-printed pages that contain images or shades of colours have to be separated into halftone screens, with one for each of the component CMYK colours. The halftone screen separations are transferred onto a corresponding set of printing plates.
- Paper has a semiotic message: a reader will make a judgement based on whether they think the stock feels expensive or not.
- Finishing is the printing industry's term for the stages that follow the printing process, such as folding, cutting and binding.

Web

- Every component to be used on the Web must match the website or CMS's technical criteria. A website should be checked prior to being published and regularly reviewed once it is online to ensure the content is correct and all elements are working.
- Media companies often work with IT specialists and web technologists, programmers and coders as well as website designers, video and film editors and sound engineers who have expert knowledge and skills, as well as awareness of the latest online developments.
- A main web server is the base where all the programming language files, HTML, CSS, JavaScript and images that make up each web page are stored. A second type of web server allows all other web servers to communicate with each other and run the Internet.
- Media companies may manage and host (publish) websites on their own web server, or upload their web pages to a specialist web hosting company that may also handle maintenance and supply technical support.
- ISPs are the companies that provide access to the Internet for businesses, organisations and individuals.
- Server databases can hold content and advertisements from any country and be set up so that different pages or advertisements are displayed to a regional website visitor in their own language.

Activities and development

The final sets of questions and action points are intended to encourage you to investigate further the technology and production techniques employed by the media and related industries, through monitoring media products, checking for new developments and gaining awareness of current practice. Visit the *Design for Media* website for more fact and action sheets, sample templates, type schemes and colour palettes at **www.pearsoned.com/hand**.

Questions

Question 1
Explain how the content of a website page is transferred and displayed in a browser window.

Question 2
Visit the corporate website of a major magazine publishing company and download the advertising information of a well-known magazine, for example, to obtain the rates for Wallpaper magazine, go to the IPC Media website: *http://specle.net/uk/ipc-media/wallpaper*. How would the specifications apply to an advertiser using a colour image on a full page bleed advertisement?

Question 3
What bandwidth requirements should be taken into account when choosing a web host company for a gadgets and games magazine website that has a tie-in to a TV show and will feature online gaming and sell merchandise?

Question 4
What production skills might be needed to prepare pages for a music magazine website that features video and audio content?

Question 5
Download the digital advertising information of a well-known magazine website, for example, IPC Digital Wallpaper Magazine's website: *http://www.ipcadvertising. com/resource/pir6ku8uaqhshodbktm1b3a9.pdf*. List the specifications for supplying a skyscraper advertisement. Are there any restrictions on the format, animation or video content? Consider what the reasons might be for any such restrictions?

Action points

Action point 1 – print
Examine a leading print magazine or newspaper.

(a) What type of paper has it selected (see page 321)?
(b) What percentage of the publication's content is made up of text, and how much of image? Calculate the percentage balance between the two?
(c) How might the nature of the content have influenced the choice of paper?
(d) Is the title perfect bound or saddle stitched? Why would the type of paper, number of pages and the layout of the contents affect the choice of binding format?
(e) Can you identify any text mistakes, colour reproduction faults or binding errors within the publication? What are the most likely causes of such problems (i.e. faulty printing, incorrect paper specification or human error)?
(f) Research how many copies of the publication are issued each day/week/month. In your consideration, would a litho or digital press best produce that number of copies?

Action point 2 – web
Examine a major news or magazine website. How many different media (audio, video, etc.) have been used, and are there interactive elements such as the following?

Advertising hyperlinks to allied websites
Animation
Date/time and weather reports
Embedded media players
Feedback forms
News RSS feeds or special interest aggregators
Online payment schemes
Online TV
Podcasts
Retail cost calculation
Social media links
Sponsored hyperlinks
Video and sound links to streaming media

Investigate the technology and software required to make these actions function.

CONCLUSION

Design helps you stand out from the crowd (source)

Adapt and adopt has become the mantra now that the traditional divisions between print publishing, TV and film have blurred as the Internet has taken over as the pre-eminent form of medium. Newspapers and magazines, once the dominant means of mass communication, have had to adapt to a world where people are exchanging their own information, photographs and films of events more quickly than many news media can cover the subjects. In broadcasting, TV channels are struggling to maintain their large audience numbers in a multi-channel, interactive world as people can download programmes to view whenever they wish. People now have the opportunity to

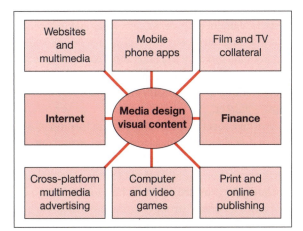

Design is essential to the creative industries as it often acts as a catalyst for change, since designers are often quick to adopt new technology, and contributes to the financial success of all media.

create their own media and share them with others, and YouTube's millions-strong audience has become a major platform for entertainment and knowledge. YouTube's dominant presence has led media companies, and the businesses which would have formerly advertised in their titles, to produce their own videos for the site to communicate with their audience and promote their products in a new way.

These shifts in audience behaviour and how people consume information have led to a change in the way that the media industry communicates and earns its income. The range of digital technology that people are expected to use and their understanding of the creative skills required to communicate their messages have become more complex and sophisticated. Design and production knowledge, once the domain of specialists, is now essential to all those working in media industries and multi-tasking has become the established way of working.

The digital revolution means we can now text and tweet and blog – with new communication ideas and technologies constantly being launched. The general visual standard of messages has improved, and there is increasing pressure to make them 'faster, smarter'. This has had an enormous impact on the media. Once, the industry had complete control over the 'means of production', but its dominant role has been challenged over the last 20 years through the spread of software that allows individuals to create their own magazines, websites, blogs and mobile apps. The erosion of the industry's monopoly on media has prompted the question: do they still have a function? There are pundits who claim that the new global Internet society is the first true mass media, as it allows everyone to contribute.

Traditional media companies still have an advantage over individuals who produce their own titles as they can draw on a pool of talented, well-trained people able to work within an established structure, who bring with them a comprehensive set of skills. One of the most valued of these is design, as it can clarify and describe events, portray people and elucidate facts as well as providing entertainment, humour, social

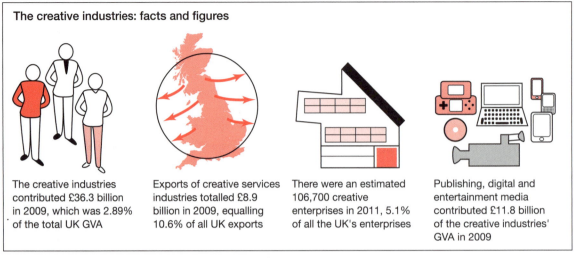

The creative industries: facts and figures

The creative industries contributed £36.3 billion in 2009, which was 2.89% of the total UK GVA

Exports of creative services industries totalled £8.9 billion in 2009, equalling 10.6% of all UK exports

There were an estimated 106,700 creative enterprises in 2011, 5.1% of all the UK's enterprises

Publishing, digital and entertainment media contributed £11.8 billion of the creative industries' GVA in 2009

GVA = gross value added   IDBR = Inter-Departmental Business Register

Source: DCMS, 2012

interaction and hard information. Design is the visual intermediary that connects readers and visitors to the writers, editors, photographers and all those who create, supply or provide content, whether they be artists, musicians or celebrities.

Design is communication

In this book we have emphasised how the industry is structured and funded, how design is employed by the sector and given practical advice on production techniques. These areas are completely interrelated: media products have to generate revenue, and the level of money they may make in a given market for a specific audience will fix the size, scope, frequency and media in which they can be produced – and all of these factors influence the design. Whether you are developing a title for yourself or a media company, every visual choice must have relevance to current political, social and cultural factors, come from shared experience and be rooted in the same world as its audience.

Design in the media is not just for decoration. Nor are content and design separate entities: both are intrinsic to the look of the title and should be considered together at all stages of producing material for print and online. To use design well, you need to see it as more than just a way of making something, anything, look

'Investment in design expertise is low risk and yields substantial returns'.

Margaret Bruce and John Bessant, *Design in Business*

good. At its best, design can be used to provide a practical solution to overcome problems such as constantly changing technology, rapid content renewal, economic instability and fragmenting audiences. By taking a more holistic view, design can produce a solution that acts as a revenue generator, adds value to a brand and reduces costs. Design not only allows companies and individuals to realise their ideas, but also makes their brands stand out from the thousands of other titles. Knowledge of design techniques and cross-media production can give those working in the industry an edge in a very competitive market.

We have covered the most important theories of design that should be considered before researching, selecting or sourcing material for a news story, feature, advertisement or any other item of media collateral. We have also provided advice on how to create pages that make a visually strong contribution to a media title. Our diagrams and instructions on page layout and use of type, pictures and colour illustrate these central tenets of design. They will help you with the main practices and techniques needed to create media titles and products such as pre-planning, information design, content visualisation, page presentation and production.

The book and its associated website contain pertinent and practical advice on content visualisation as they outline the four key elements of design: layout, imagery, typography and colour. The *How to work with* pages are valuable assets for anyone who needs to develop their technology and production knowledge and skills. Learning how to control a layout and all the visual elements on a page means being aware of the semiotic meaning of placement, type and pictorial content and colour. The chapters on typography, imagery, layout and colour will help you to work on content presentation and understand the complexities of design and how it can communicate on many levels.

Design for Media gives you a foundation of skills that can be extended to build further knowledge of technology and production. We have tried to cover all the most influential changes brought about by the digital revolution and the growth of the Internet. In truth, any technological information may well be out of date by the time the book is published. New digital devices and software products are being introduced all the time. One of the important skills you will need is the ability to accommodate change. Every device and computer program is designed to achieve a particular result, be it page handling templates, content uploading, generating images or preparing media-specific files. All the technology is aimed at a final outcome of disseminating information and making media communications work.

The digital era will continue to cause profound changes in the media and the world, and the speed with which technology moves can make it easy for you to be left behind. Being able to handle the technology and understand the underlying principles of design will help all of us adapt to whatever the future may hold.

CONTACTS AND RESOURCES

Brand agencies

Blue Marlin: brand design agency
www.bluemarlinbd.com

Coley Porter Bell: brand agency
www.cpb.co.uk

Design Bridge: international branding agency
www.designbridge.com

Elmwood: international brand design consultancy
www.elmwood.com

Impact IM: brand design company
www.impact-im.co.uk

Interbrand: international brand agency
www.interbrand.com

Johnson Banks: identity and brand design agency
www.johnsonbanks.co.uk

Lewis Moberly: brand design agency
www.lewismoberly.com

Navyblue Design: international brand communications agency
www.navybluedesign.com

Nucleus: brand design agency
www.nucleus.co.uk

Rufus Leonard: brand, digital and technology agency
www.rufusleonard.com

Venture Three: international branding agency
www.venturethree.com

Wolff Olins: international branding agency
www.wolffolins.com

Colour industry organisations and companies

CIE: international colour industry regulator
www.cie.co.at

CMG: international group for colour professionals
www.colormarketing.org

Focoltone: colour matching system
www.kikuze.com/focoltone

ICA: colour forecasting service
www.internationalcolourauthority.org

Pantone: colour matching system
www.pantone.com

Communications, marketing and advertising

Aegis: international marketing communications group
www.aegisplc.com

AMV BBDO: international advertising agency
www.amvbbdo.com

Bartle Bogle Hegarty: international advertising agency
www.bartleboglehegarty.com

Brilliant Independent Media Specialists: independent media agency
www.brilliantmedia.co.uk

CHI and Partners: advertising and communications company
www.chiandpartners.com

DCH: independent advertising agency
www.dch.co.uk

DDB: international advertising agency
www.ddblondon.com

Dentsu: international advertising agency
www.dentsulondon.com

Euro RSCG London: international advertising agency
www.eurorscg.com

Fallon London: international advertising agency
www.fallon.co.uk

Grey London: communications agency
www.grey.co.uk

Havas: international marketing communications group
www.havasmedia.com

Heath Wallace: international website services group
www.heathwallace.co.uk

Imagination: international communications company
www.imagination.com

Interpublic: international advertising and marketing company
www.interpublic.com

JWT London: international advertising agency
www.jwt.co.uk

Leo Burnett: international advertising agency
www.leoburnett.com

Love Creative: advertising, design and digital agency
www.lovecreative.com

M&C Saatchi: international advertising agency
www.mcsaatchi.com

McCann Erickson: international advertising agency
www.mccann.com

Mother London: international advertising agency
www.motherlondon.com

Ogilvy Group UK: international advertising agency
www.ogilvy.co.uk

Omnicom (BBDO, DDB and TBWA): leading global advertising and marketing communications services group
www.omnicomgroup.com

Publicis: international marketing communications network
www.publicis.co.uk

Red Bee Media: digital media agency
www.redbeemedia.com

RKCR/Y&R: advertising agency
www.rkcryr.com

TBWA: international advertising agency
www.tbwa-london.com

The Nielsen Company: media information group
http://uk.nielsen.com

WCRS: advertising agency
www.wcrs.com

Weiden + Kennedy: international advertising agency
www.wk.com

WPP: international marketing communications group
www.wpp.com

Creative and design agencies

AllofUs: interactive design consultancy
www.allofus.com

AQKA: international creative agency
www.akqa.com

Attik: creative communications company
www.attik.com

Bostock and Pollitt: creative agency
www.bostockandpollitt.com

Dare: creative agency
www.thisisdare.com

Emperor Design Consultants: design and communications company
www.emperordesign.co.uk

Gluelsobar: creative agency
www.gluelondon.com

Hat Trick Design: design agency
www.hat-trickdesign.co.uk

Karmarama: creative agency
www.karmarama.com

Libertine London: creative agency
www.libertinelondon.com

Pentagram: international design consultancy
www.pentagram.com

Rapier: creative agency
http://rapieruk.com

Stocks Taylor Benson: graphic design agency
www.stbdesign.co.uk

Studio 8: graphic design agency
www.studio8design.co.uk

The Chase: graphic design and branding consultancy
www.thechase.co.uk

Tomato: creative agency
www.tomato.co.uk

Image banks, online resources and photo libraries

British Association of Picture Libraries and Agencies: industry association for picture libraries and agencies
www.bapla.org.uk

Corbis: leading image bank
www.corbisimages.com

Flickr: photo sharing website
www.flickr.com

Fotolia: image bank
http://en.fotolia.com

Getty Images: leading image bank
www.GettyImages.co.uk

Hulton Picture Library: a library of historic photographs owned by Getty Images
www.hultongetty.com

iStock: leading image bank
www.iStockphoto.com

National Press Photographers Association: national association for visual journalists
www.nppa.org

Rex: entertainment events and celebrity portraits
www.rexfeatures.com

World Press Photo: international not-for-profit organisation for photojournalists
www.worldpressphoto.org

Journalism

Journalism.co.uk: leading website for journalists
www.journalism.co.uk

Journolist: offers writers, editors and journalists help on using the Internet.
www.journolist.com

Media and advertising industry organisations and forums

Advertising Standards Authority (ASA): advertising industry regulator
http://asa.org.uk

Association of Publishing Agencies: customer publishing industry association
www.apa.co.uk

Audit Bureau of Circulation: independent media industry auditors
www.abc.org.uk

BRAD Insight: information providers on British media industry
www1.bradinsight.com

British Association for Print and Communication: business association for the print and creative industries
www.bapc.co.uk/

Broadcasters Audience Research Board (BARB): broadcast industry research
www.barb.co.uk

D&AD (Design and Art Direction): industry association promoting training and excellence in advertising
www.dandad.org

Department of Culture, Media and Sport (DCMS): government

department with responsibility for the media and creative industries
www.culture.gov.uk

Design Business Association: industry association for design businesses
www.dba.org

Internet Advertising Bureau (IAB): online advertising industry association
www.iabuk.net

Media Standards Trust: not-for-profit organisation that encourages high standards in the media
www.mediastandardstrust.org/home.aspx

National Union of Journalists (NUJ): organisation representing journalists in Britian and Ireland
www.nuj.org.uk

Radio Joint Audience Research (RAJAR): radio industry research
www.rajar.co.uk

Technology, Entertainment, Design (TED): conferences and events featuring leading world figures
www.ted.com

The Periodical Publishers Association (PPA) (Magazine.net UK): magazine and business industry association
www.ppa.co.uk

UK Web Design and Industries Association: web design and industry regulator
www.ukwda.org

Media groups

Archant: regional newspaper media group
www.archant.co.uk

BBC Worldwide: news and general interest publishing media group
www.bbcworldwide.com

Cedar: contract publishing media group
www.cedarcom.co.uk

Centaur Media plc: B2B publishing media group
www.centaur.co.uk

Condé Nast: consumer and contract publishing media group
www.condenast.co.uk

Dennis Publishing: men's interest and computing publishing media group
www.dennis.co.uk

Emap B2B publishing media group
www.emap.com

Financial Times: financial news media group
www.ft.com

Future Publishing: special interest publishing media group
www.futureplc.com

H. Bauer: general interest publishing media group
www.bauer.co.uk

Hachette Filipacchi: women's interest publishing media group
www.hf-uk.com

Haymarket: consumer and contract publishing media group
www.haymarket.com

IDG: technology publishing media group
www.idg.com

Imagine: special interest publishing media group
www.imagine-publishing.co.uk

IPC Media: general interest publishing media group
www.ipcmedia.com

John Brown Publishing: contract publishing media group
www.johnbrownmedia.com

NatMag: general interest publishing media group
www.hearst.co.uk

Nature Publishing Group:
www.nature.com

News Corporation: news and general interest publishing media group
www.newscorp.com

Northern and Shell Media Publications: news and general interest publishing media group
www.northernandshell.co.uk

Peachpit Press: cross-media technology and software publisher
www.peachpit.com

Pearson: educational publishers
www.pearsoneducation.com

Redwood: contract publishing media group
www.redwoodgroup.net

Reed Business Information: consumer and B2B publishing media group
www.reedbusiness.co.uk

The Daily Mail and General Trust plc: news and general interest publishing media group
www.dmgt.co.uk

The Economist Group: financial news media group
www.economist.com

The Guardian Media Group: news and general interest publishing media group
www.guardian.co.uk

The Independent Media Group: news and general interest publishing media group
www.inmplc.com

The Telegraph Media Group Ltd: news and general interest publishing media group
www.telegraph.co.uk

Trinity Mirror: news and general interest media group
www.trinitymirror.com

View Publications: fashion and colour industry magazines and websites
www.view-publications.com

Wilmington: B2B publishing media group
www.wilmington.co.uk

Media, journalism, advertising and PR magazines and websites

.net magazine: the leading magazine for web designers and developers
www.netmag.co.uk

Campaign: leading magazine for the advertising industry
www.campaignlive.co.uk

ComputerArts magazine: web designers' magazine
www.computerarts.co.uk

Design Week: leading magazine for the design industry
www.designweek.co.uk

eye magazine: international graphic design magazine
www.eyemagazine.com/home.php

Media Week: leading title for the commercial media industry
www.mediaweek.co.uk

PR Week: leading magazine for the PR industry
www.prweek.com/uk/home/

UK Press Gazette: journalism news and jobs
www.pressgazette.co.uk

Media research, blogs and comment

Leatrice Eiseman's blog on colour:
www.eisemancolorblog.com

magCulture.com: the magCulture blog, written by John Leslie, celebrates editorial design
http://magculture.com/blog/

Magforum: blog on all aspects of magazines and magazine publishing by Tony Quinn
http://magforum.wordpress.com

Nielsen Norman Group: leading experts on usability
www.useit.com

Personalize Media: blog by Gary Hayes on social and networked media
www.personalizemedia.com

The Poynter Institute: US school of journalism undertaking eyetracking research into media usage
http://www.poynter.org/latest-news/media-lab/mobile-media/151844/poynter-tablet-research-tap-touch-pinch-swipe-eyetrack-stories-staffing-revenue-and-more/

Media software training

About.com: desktop publishing: graphic design and publishing training
http://desktoppub.about.com

Adobe: the Adobe websites offer help and advice on all Adobe programs
www.adobe.com
www.adobe.co.uk

AdobeTV.com: Adobe software programs' training videos:
www.tvadobe.com

Photoshopessential.com: Photoshop training
www.photoshopessentials.com

QuarkXPress: basic training for Quark 8
http://8.quark.com/learn_more.html

Museums and galleries

British Library Newspaper Collection: newspapers and comics archive
www.bl.uk

Design Museum: collection and special exhibitions on modern design
http://designmuseum.org

Museum of Brands, Packaging and Advertising: Robert Opie Collection and special exhibitions
www.museumofbrands.com

National Media Museum: collections and special exhibitions on photography, film and TV
www.nationalmediamuseum.org.uk

National Portrait Gallery: collections and special exhibitions on art and photographic portraits
www.npg.org.uk

The Photographer's Gallery: archive and special exhibitions on photography
www.photonet.org.uk

News agencies

Associated Press: global news network
www.ap.org

The Press Association – PA Newscentre: multimedia news content provider
www.pa.press.net

Thomson Reuters: news media group
www.thomsonreuters.com

Online news providers

BBC:
www.bbc.co.uk/news

CNN:
http://edition.cnn.com/EUROPE

Google News:
www.google.co.uk

Sky News:
http://news.sky.com/skynews/UK-News

Typography

Typetester: screen type visualiser
www.typetester.org

GLOSSARY

2D quick response (QR) barcodes: a barcode consisting of squares that can be read by QR-compatible scanners, smart phones, tablets with cameras and similar Internet-ready devices.

A and B paper sizes: international standard paper sizes. A sizes refer to trimmed paper sizes, B sizes refer to press paper sizes.

ABCs or ABCe: The Audit Bureau of Circulation provides certified figures for circulation, distribution, traffic and related data for a range of media including print, web, events and other Internet-based devices.

above the line: advertising aimed at building the brand identity using tv, print, web and outdoor.

absolute text sizing: absolute text sizing maintains the size set by the web designer so that it does not vary when displayed in a browser.

active colours: colours that appear to come forward on a page or screen.

ad spend: the budget an advertising client has designated for a campaign or advertisement.

ad views: the number of times a web page containing an advertisement is downloaded and the advertisement viewed.

additive colour: the three additive primary colours are red, green and blue.

additive primaries: colour elements that, added together, make up white light (red, green, blue).

advertising revenue: the income a media company derives from client advertising.

advertising space: a defined space on a print or web page reserved for advertisements.

Advertising Standards Authority (ASA): advertising industry business association.

advertorials: advertisements that resemble features.

adwords: searchable key words that cause an advertisement to be displayed on a search engine's results pages.

aesthetic–usability effect: a principle which states that people react more favourably to attractive designs.

alt tag caption: a label, activated by the mouse that displays or voice activates, the text or caption that accompanies a web page image.

analogous colours: colours that fall close to one another on a colour wheel.

analogue (*US: analog*): a telecommunications technology that employs the variations in strength of broadcast signals to transmit sound and vision.

animation time limit: a fixed length of time for an animated advertisement or promotion to run and repeat.

anti-aliasing: the technique employed by bitmap imaging programs of blending the colour of pixels into the background to give a smooth appearance to the edges of diagonal and curved lines. This may also be referred to as dithering.

aperture/f-stops: the aperture of a camera controls the amount of light allowed through a lens to reach a digital sensor or film while a camera's shutter is open. The diameter of an aperture is measured in f-stops. A lower f-stop number admits more light. Higher f-stop numbers make the aperture smaller so less light is admitted.

application program interfaces (API): the set of commands, functions and protocols computer programmers use to write software.

art director: the senior designer with responsibility for managing the visual aspects of a title or ad campaign from concept to production.

art editor: the designer responsible for page make-up and production on a print and/or online title.

aspect ratio: the width to height ratio of a digital device and therefore the proportions applied to computer program windows and still and moving images for the Web.

Audit Bureau of Circulation: a media industry auditing organisation (see ABCs or ABCe).

auto page numbering function: the master page facility in a page make-up program that automates the page numbering.

baby-face bias: the tendency to prefer small-featured individuals.

background: the visual plane that is perceived as being the furthest away from the viewer; the colour or pattern that fills a page, screen or boxed area.

bandwidth: the speed in bits per second at which information can be transmitted along a telecommunications channel.

banner: a wide rectangular advertisement that is normally placed at the top of a web page.

baseline: the notional line that runs along the base of upper and lower case letters used to measure the distance between lines of type.

baseline grid: consistent line spacing used throughout a print publication to fix the horizontal alignment of the main text and other page elements.

below the line: marketing communications that support a major advertising campaign.

Berliner: US paper size used by newspapers such as *The Guardian*.

Big Idea: an advertising agency term indicating a campaign concept that a client should find highly attractive and that can be realised across different media.

bit: binary information transfer. A bit is one binary digit: 0 or 1. This is the smallest unit of information used by a computer (8 bits = 1 byte).

bitmap: an image made up of pixels (bits). The colour of each pixel is indicated by a table of values – the map. Also called raster graphics.

blanket cylinder (blanket rollers): one of the rollers on an offset litho printing press. The blanket cylinder cushions the paper as it passes over the impression cylinder that holds the image.

bleed area: an extra 3-4mm space outside the trim area of a print page that has to be included where images and background colours extend to the edge of a page.

body copy: the term for the main running text of a print publication. The body copy type style, size and leading specification for a title are normally kept consistent throughout. A body copy typeface is one that has been designed to remain legible and readable at a smaller size.

body–face ratio bias theory: a design principle that suggests that the proportion shown of body to face in an image affects how intelligent the subject is perceived to be.

bots (robots) or spiders: computer programs used by search engines and other websites to perform automated functions.

boutique or hot shop advertising agency: a creative advertising agency that specialises in developing advertising concepts and design.

BRAD Insight: a company that provides media marketing and business information to the media industry.

brand (brand identity): the identity of a product, service or event that allows it to be recognised by its target audience and which establishes its value in the marketplace.

brand or marketing manager: a job which entails maintaining and increasing the value of a brand.

broadband: a system of telecommunication that employs a wide band of frequencies to transmit information.

broadsheet: the paper size used by newspapers such as the *Financial Times*.

buffering: Internet data is downloaded in a number of small packets rather than all at once. Buffering is the term for the first packet of data to be downloaded. In streaming media, buffering refers to the amount of data a media player has to receive before it can play an audio or video file.

bulks (bulk circulation): the number of copies distributed of a print publication, most often a newspaper. This is not the same as the number sold.

bullet: a round symbol used to indicate a paragraph or items in a list.

cap height: the distance between the baseline and the top of a capital letter of a typeface.

caption: a short piece of copy that provides information about a picture.

cascading style sheets (CSS): cascading style sheets maintain the basic appearance of a website. They are used by web developers to set the type styles, colour and structure of web pages.

cast-off: calculating the number of characters that will fit across a line, in a paragraph, down a column or on an entire page.

chief subeditor/subeditors: the manager in charge of the subeditors who ensure that the spelling, grammar and house style of the content is correct before the title is published in print or online.

chroma: the degree of colour saturation of a hue.

classified ad: a small advertisement, most often of type only, although some may feature images.

click-through rates: average percentage of the number of people that clicked on an advertisement (click-throughs) per hundred ad views.

cloud computing: the term for hosted web computing services such as webmail.

CMYK: cyan, magenta, yellow and black – the subtractive primary colours used in four-colour printing.

coated colour selector: a colour swatch book used for specifying and checking how colours will reproduce on coated paper.

cold colours: a descriptive term for colours that contain blue or green hues (may also be referred to as cool colours).

colour bars: a target strip of individual cyan, magenta, yellow and black tinted squares printed to the side of a page that is used by printing companies to adjust ink density on the printing press.

colour-balanced proof: a printed proof that has been colour adjusted to match the title or client's colour standard.

colour calibration: adjusting the colour of a computer monitor, camera or scanner to match a desired colour setting or output standard.

colour charts: charts used for naming or specifying colours; highly accurate colour swatches used for calibration.

colour luminosity: how light a colour is.

colour matching system: a system of formulated ink colours used to communicate colour specifications.

colour mode: the term used by imaging software for a colour system such as CMYK and RGB.

colour saturation: the intensity of a colour.

colour separation: the process of breaking down a page or image into coloured components that match the number of inks to be used on a press – normally the four-process CMYK inks. Each separation contains only the percentages of colour required to recreate the image in colour on press.

colour space: a means of identifying all the colours in a colour gamut, for example the natural spectrum visible to the human eye, or RGB and CMYK that can be displayed, reproduced or seen on a particular device such as a computer, smart phone or tablet.

colour spectrometer: a device that measures colours by analysing their light wavelengths and converts them to colour values for CMYK, RGB, hexadecimal colours, colour matching systems, etc.

colour target chart: a sequential diagram of standard colour samples used to establish the colour standard for calibration for a specific device.

colour temperature: a graphical representation of the range of colour temperatures in kelvins (cold, blue to warm, red).

colour wheel: a circular diagram or device showing the positional relationship between chroma (primary colours) and hues (the tints that fall between them).

column: a vertical panel of type.

complementary colours: hues that fall opposite each other on a colour wheel: red–green, blue–orange, yellow–violet.

composing stick: a small hand-held adjustable tray in which a typesetter sets lines of individual metal letters across the required width.

compression: reduces the size of computer files by discarding data.

computer to plate (CTP): a digital pre-press printing system that transfers digital data directly on to a printing plate.

content management system (CMS): a computer program and related applications that allow a media company to manage websites, upload content, create new pages and publish online.

contra deal: an agreement between two or more parties to exchange goods or services of equal value.

contract publishing: the production of media products by a specialist media company on behalf of a business or organisation.

contract quality proof (contract proof): a printed proof that is regarded as a contract establishing the required colour reproduction standard between the client and a printing company.

copy chasing: contacting writers, photographers and other contributors to ensure content is submitted on time.

cost per viewing: a method of charging for online advertising where the advertiser pays for each proven unique user view of an advertisement or website.

cover lines or sells: the copy on the front cover of a magazine used to attract readers.

Create Outlines: a vector graphic program facility that converts typefaces into vector-based artwork objects

Creative Commons licence: the legal agreement governing the use of Creative Commons photographs, videos and other graphic material.

creative or design director: the person in charge of the creative department at an advertising agency or the design department of a media company.

crop: to remove the unwanted parts of an image.

crop marks: horizontal and vertical lines that mark out the side edges of a page to be printed. These are set at each corner of the artwork to show the printing company where to cut a page out of a large printed sheet.

crosshead: a heading that falls in the run of text set in slightly larger or bolder type. Crossheads are used to 'chunk' – subdivide – text and to introduce a change of topic within the copy. In design terms, they help to break up long runs of text.

crowdsourcing: the term used by media organisations for sourcing information from the general public.

customer magazines: magazines produced by contract publishers for their clients.

cutout: creating an outline around the subject of a picture to separate it from the background of the image. Type is often wrapped around a cutout image to break up the geometric appearance of a page.

dailies: newspapers that are published from Monday to Friday/Saturday.

dampening roller: one of the rollers on an offset litho printing press. The dampening roller moistens the plate cylinder.

data capture: the term for generating and storing visual and sound data such as photographs and videos.

database management systems: software or applications that give access to information stored in a database.

deadline: the time/date by which a print or online title must be ready for publication.

deconstructionism: a philosophical movement that originated from the writings on literary criticism of Jacques Derrida which challenges traditional views and accepted norms.

default typesize: the input typesize automatically used by word processing and design programs, such as 12pt Times or Helvetica.

de-intermediarisation: the process of reducing the number of specialist intermediary companies employed by media companies to produce print and online titles that has resulted from the increasing functionality of digital technology.

depth of field: the distance that is in focus between the nearest and most distant elements in an image from the camera lens when an image is captured.

design brief: a document outlining the media company's design and business development requirements for a new title or design project.

designer's view: the consecutive sequence of pages in a page make-up program. The alternative is the printer's view, which shows the pages in press sections (see imposition).

desktop publishing: the term coined in the 1980s to describe producing print publications within an office or home environment.

development brief: outlines the strategic objectives, general development principles and production criteria for a title.

digital magazines: publications viewed on the Web.

digital printing: office printing using inkjet and laser printers; digital printing presses that can print computer files directly on to paper and other materials.

Dingbats: a typeface that may consist of symbols, icons, maps and other graphic devices.

display ads/advertising (print and web): advertisements that are placed throughout a print or online title. These may occupy a spread or page in a magazine or be positioned in a banner or box on a web page.

display type: display type refers to typefaces that have been designed to work well at larger sizes and that are used for headlines, posters, etc.

dither: see anti-aliasing.

domain name: the element of a website address that identifies a company or person.

double page spread: a magazine or newspaper feature or other linked content printed on facing left and right hand pages.

dots per inch (dpi): all printed images are made up of dots of varying sizes, and the number of dots per inch defines the print quality.

drop cap/raised cap: an enlarged capital letter at start of a feature or section of copy that either drops into or stands proud of the paragraph.

drum scanner: a laser scanner where the transparency or image is wrapped around a drum with a lens that can create extremely colour-accurate high-resolution digital files.

dummy: a mockup of a print title or design showing the proposed content in position at the printed dimensions.

duotone: an image created using two colours.

dynamic HTML (DHTML): a set of technologies and programs that add functionality such as rollovers and animation to websites.

editor: someone who edits a title (chief, managing or executive editor), a writer, broadcaster or journalist (news editor, sports editor) or works in production (art editor, picture editor).

editorial–advertising ratio or balance: the amount of space allocated to editorial content balanced against the space that needs to be allotted to advertisements in order to raise sufficient ad revenue to make a title profitable.

Egyptian or slab serif: a typeface with angular or block-ended terminals.

eink: a form of display used by ereaders that resembles the printed page.

em: the height of a capital M in a point size used as a horizontal measure: for example, 1 em in 12 point is 12 points wide.

entry points: visual pointers that lead the eye on to a page.

epaper: a digital, portable display technology that resembles a printed page and is used for ebooks and similar media.

epublications: electronic publications created and distributed digitally.

ereader: a portable Wi-Fi device that can display and store ebooks etc.

eye flow: the path a reader's or viewer's eye follows when viewing the content of a page.

eye stops: interruptions in the eye flow that focus the reader's or viewer's attention on a specific point.

f-stops: see aperture.

face-up: similar editorial and/or advertising content falling on facing left and right pages that may or may not work well when viewed together.

facing matter: advertisements for which the client has paid a premium to ensure the ad is placed opposite relevant editorial content.

facing pages: two separate editorial features or unconnected content on adjacent left and right hand pages.

File Transfer Protocol (FTP): a method of exchanging files between computers on the Internet

finished artwork: the digital files for a finished approved design ready for the printing company or uploading to the Web.

finishing line: a set of printing equipment/machines used to fold, cut, bind, insert loose inserts and place printed work in polybags once it comes off the press.

flatbed scanner: the most commonly used type of desktop scanner that can digitise original images, transparencies and printed material.

focal point: the point of sharpest focus/interest when an image is taken.

font: a typeface (originally, one style of type from a type family).

font-face: a form of CSS that allows one to specify a font-face typeface that will override a browser's automatic type selection.

foreground: the part of a photograph or illustration that appears nearest to the photographer or viewer.

freemiums: high-quality magazines that do not charge a cover price and are distributed free.

full resolution: all the pixel data captured when a camera takes an image.

full service agency: an advertising agency that provides creative services, research, media buying, marketing and public relations for clients covering a wide range of media.

geometric sans serif: typefaces with a rectangular appearance.

gif (graphic interchange format): a file format for recording bitmap images using a 24-bit RGB colour space.

gloss paper: coated paper that has a reflective, smooth surface.

glyphs: all the characters that make up a typeface, including all the numbers and symbols.

go to bed: pass a publication for print (also known as closing a print issue).

graphic design (graphics): a design discipline that communicates messages by combining typography, imagery and page layout to produce print publications, websites, advertisements, etc. (graphics can also refer to the design material).

greyscale: a greyscale file is displayed on-screen using pixels in shades of grey ranging from black to white.

grid: an underlying page structure that provides a geometric framework which is used to compose cohesive, well-balanced designs.

grotesque: a traditional term that describes a style of sans serif typeface.

gutters: the narrow vertical space between columns on a page.

halftone screens: grids of dots of varying sizes that are used in printing to reproduce photographic imagery. Almost all printed material will have been screened as this is the most common method of reproducing coloured pictures and tints of colour.

hexadecimal colour system: a base-16 numbering system for web colours. All hexadecimal colour codes begin with the square or hash symbol (#).

high resolution: the size and number of pixels per linear inch (ppi) used to create an image; generally, the higher the ppi, the sharper the image. The resolution of print images is normally given in dots per inch (dpi) even though a digital image file consists of pixels. The default high resolution for a printable image is 300dpi/ppi (see dots per inch).

hot shop agency: agencies that specialise in creative solutions.

house design style: a company or title's design style that should be applied when producing products for a media brand.

HTML (Hypertext Markup Language): a computer coding language consisting of tags and rules used to create pages for the Web.

hue: the defining characteristics of a colour that allow it to be identified, for example red, green and blue, and any shade or tint of a colour such as pale pink, grass green or sea blue.

humanist typefaces: typefaces with characters that resemble hand-written letters.

image bank/photo agency: a company that licenses and supplies photography and video imagery.

imposition: placing pages in a sequence so that when they are printed, cut and folded they fall in the correct running order.

impression cylinder: one of the rollers on an offset litho printing press. The impression cylinder pushes the paper on to the inked blanket roller that holds the page image.

indent: a small space that sets the first line of a paragraph typically 2-3mm in from the left hand margin or column edge

Internet Advertising Bureau (IABUK): the body for the online advertising industry in the UK.

Internet Corporation for Assigning Names and Numbers (ICANN): the organisation that regulates website names.

Internet Service Providers (ISPs): companies that provide individuals and companies with access to the Internet.

interpolation: an image-editing process used to alter the resolution of an image by increasing or decreasing the number of pixels in the image. The process also estimates mathematically the values of the colour space to simulate missing colour data.

IPTV (Internet Protocol Television): a technology that delivers audio and video services over the Internet.

ISO paper sizes: internationally recognised standard paper sizes (excluding the USA).

JPEG: a file type created using lossy compression.

keyline/frame: a fine line framing an image box.

lads' mag: a mass market magazine aimed at young men.

leading: the space between vertical lines of type measured in points from baseline to baseline (line spacing). The type size and leading of typographic elements such as headlines or body copy is written as a fraction, for example 9/10pt indicates a 9pt typesize set on 10pts of leading.

lenticular: a biconvex lens used to process images that creates the illusion of 3D in print.

letter spacing: the space between the characters of a typeface.

letterforms: typeface characters.

Live Web: real-time events on the Internet filmed by webcams.

lossy compression: the system used by JPEGs and some video and sound files that reduces the amount of data each time a file is compressed by deleting data.

low resolution: 72 pixels per inch or below.

lower case: the small (non-capital) letters of a typeface.

luminosity: the whiteness or intensity of a colour.

margins: the top and bottom horizontal and the left and right vertical spaces between the page edge and the text area.

mark-up: written instructions on how to lay out a print page or a web language containing the instructions for a web page.

master pages: a non-printable background template in a page make-up document that is used to hold the publication's grid structure and page furniture such as folios and footers.

masthead: the brand title, logo and related graphics that identify a print publication or website.

matt uncoated paper: paper with a soft, non-shiny surface.

media: the means of mass communication, such as newspapers, magazines, radio or television (may be used with a singular verb); the group of professional journalists who constitute the communications and media industry; external media: objects or devices for data storage. The term is also used to refer to a specific area of the creative industries, such as the Web or print publishing, and to image, word, audio and visual files.

media buying: purchasing media space and time for advertisements.

media collateral: the range of media that support a product or service.

media creep: the effect of design elements transferring from one medium to another.

media player: a computer program that plays video and audio files.

medium resolution: 100-200 pixels per inch, the resolution required to print on absorbent paper such as newsprint.

megapixels: the number of pixels used by a digital camera to capture images (mega = million).

microblogging: a service, such as Twitter, that allows users to transmit short messages.

microstock sites: online image banks that offer low-priced royalty-free stock photography and illustrations mostly sourced from the Internet. The images are often provided by amateur photographers and illustrators.

microzoning: the practice of placing geographically appropriate web advertisements.

microzone publishing: a specialist division of the publishing industry that produces hyperlocal and niche special interest titles.

mid ground: the middle portion of a photograph or illustration that lies behind the foreground and in front of the background.

mobile TV, mobisodes, mobizines: media products for mobile devices.

modern or didone typefaces: serif typefaces that feature an extreme contrast between thick and thin lines.

mood board: a design technique that employs a collage of material pasted on to a board to evoke a mood or illustrate a design concept

movable type: reusable individual letterforms of a typeface made out of wood or metal used to build up words and lines of type.

neo-grotesque: modern sans serif typefaces such as Helvetica and Arial.

news aggregators: news search engine that can be programmed to search for a specific subject.

niche titles: magazines or websites that cover an area of specialised interest aimed at a particular audience.

offset lithographic printing: the most commonly used form of lithographic printing, where a 'blanket' is used to transfer the inked images and type on to the paper from the printing plate.

Old Style or Venetian: a traditional serif typeface.

open rivers: large spaces between words on consecutive lines of type that give the appearance of a vertical split in a column of copy.

operating system: software that enables a computer to function.

optimise (an image): setting the optimal compression format for a web image file.

outdent: a line or character that hangs outside a column of type.

overmatter (overset text): copy that cannot be fitted on a page or into a column, box, etc.

padding: the space between a box and the content of a box on a web page.

page budget: the amount of money allocated to produce a page.

page flag: the heading, normally positioned at the top of a page, that indicates the subject of the section or feature.

page information: a line of copy printed on a proof giving the name of the file, the page number and the date and time the page was printed.

page layout: placing design elements on a page to achieve balance and contrast.

page make-up: combining the technical operation of the software with design and production requirements.

passed for press: the agreement that pages are ready to be published.

passive colours: subdued colours that appear to recede on a page or screen.

PDA: a personal digital assistant, for example a Blackberry.

perfect binding: a method of binding magazines where the pages are glued into a square spine.

photo agencies: companies that represent photographers and license still images and video.

photo-editing (software): a program used to alter, adjust or manipulate images.

photojournalism: a branch of journalism that uses photography as the primary means of reporting news stories.

photolithography: a photochemical, pre-digital image transfer process.

photomanipulation: the practice of amending photographs to change their content or meaning.

pictorial direction: the elements in a picture composition that direct the eye.

picture credit: the name of the photographer, illustrator or image source of a photograph or picture.

picture memory bias: the theory that people remember pictures more readily than words.

pixel: the basic unit in the composition of an image on a digital television screen, computer monitor, camera and other digital devices.

pixel dimension: the horizontal and vertical measurements of an image expressed in pixels.

pixellated: an image that has been enlarged so that the pixels become visible.

pixels per inch (ppi): the pixel dimension (resolution) of an image.

placestreaming: using streaming media to show a location.

plate cylinder: one of the rollers on an offset litho printing press. The plate cylinder holds the printing plate or medium that has the page image to be inked on its surface.

platform agnostic: using the media that best explain or communicate a story, as opposed to a pre determined platform.

points: units of measurement used to describe the height of type and leading (line spacing).

pop-up: a screen window that appears with but separately from a website, often used for advertisements.

PostScript: a programming language that is used to create printable pages.

preflight: software that checks whether all the files in a document are in the correct format for printing.

press deadline: the time/date by which the pages of a publication must be delivered to the printing company.

press-quality pdfs: high-resolution pdfs suitable for output from a printing press.

press-ready artwork (mechanicals): boards on which the typesetting and images were pasted for analogue print processing.

prime positions: the positions in a print publication or on a website that garner the most audience attention.

print on demand: printing copies of magazines, newspapers and books/brochures to order, as opposed to the practice of printing a given number of copies based on predicted or previous sales.

print run: the number of copies of a newspaper or magazine to be printed during one continuous operation of a printing press.

printed under licence: an agreement that allows a magazine brand belonging to one media company to be produced and marketed by a media company in another region or country.

printer's Greek: meaningless copy in Latin used to mock up dummy and prototype pages.

printer's proof: a newspaper or magazine page printout produced by a printing company.

printing plate: a thin sheet of metal or other material on to which the image to be printed is exposed. The plate is either inked and applied directly to paper or held by the impression cylinder.

printing press: a machine that prints pages on to paper using wet ink.

production director/manager or editor: the senior person responsible for managing the production of a media company's websites, newspaper and magazine.

production journalist: a writer who works on page production for print and online whose job may also include generating video and audio reports, creating and managing blogs, issuing podcasts, etc.

progressive colour proofs: a set of consecutive pages that show the progression of adding each CMYK colour in sequence on paper.

proof: a printout of a newspaper or magazine page, or of an advertisement.

proof correction marks: BSI recognised marks used on a proof to indicate corrections and changes.

proofreader: an expert who checks page proofs for accuracy.

pull quote: a quote extracted from the copy used to add interest and draw attention to an article or interview.

rate card: a document or web page displaying the cost of advertising in a print or online title.

read path: the instinctive order in which a reader or visitor is most likely to work their way through the information on a page.

ready artwork (mechanicals): a pre-digital term for finished hand- or machine-made editorial and advertisement pages where the typesetting and images were pasted on to boards ready for the printer (see also finished artwork).

real time: an event that is displayed as it happens.

recto: a right hand page.

reflective light: light that reflects into the eye, lens or scanning head from a surface such as paper.

registration marks: a set of lines and target icons used by printing companies to align the paper and each colour plate on the press for printing.

regular feature bias: the theory that people prefer faces with well-proportioned features.

relative text sizing: allows the typesize and line spacing to adjust proportionally and in relation to other screen elements in different browsers.

remote digital printing: the practice of supplying material to a printing company in another region or country to print and distribute a title.

remote proofing: employing a mobile digital device or laptop to view screen-based proofs.

repro (reproduction): the technical processes of preparing artwork and digital files to produce CMYK printing plates or files ready to go direct to press.

resolution: the number of pixels within a linear inch that make up an image.

retouching: adjusting a still or moving image to remove imperfections or enhance the look of the subject.

RGB: red, green, blue – the colour mode used to capture and display colour on digital devices.

running dummy: working proofs of the pages of a print issue assembled in order in a folder or pinned on a display board.

running order: the sequence of pages in a print publication.

saddle stitching (stapling): a method of binding magazines where the pages are stapled through the centre fold.

sans serif: typefaces without serifs.

saturation: the measure of a colour's purity.

screen pdfs: low-resolution pdfs suitable for display on-screen.

search engine: a website that searches other websites for information.

sections (signatures): a group of pages printed on one large sheet or roll of paper in multiples of four which, when folded, appear in the correct running order.

sell: a short introduction to a news story or feature on a website.

separation: the process of splitting a colour image into separate colour layers (normally cyan, magenta, yellow and black) for press print production.

serif: typefaces with serifs – the opening and closing cross-strokes on the ends of the letterforms (terminals).

sheet-fed offset litho: a type of lithographic printing press that prints on flat sheets of paper.

shout out: a cover line or a comment taken from an article and used to add interest and draw attention to an article or interview.

showthrough: heavy inking that is visible on the reverse side of a sheet of paper.

sidebar: a side column on a page containing another editorial item or copy associated with the feature.

silk-coated paper: paper treated with a special coating to give a smooth, low surface shine.

sitemap or spider: a plan of pages that make up a website showing their interconnectivity.

skyscraper: a tall, narrow, rectangular web ad space.

slug area: an area outside of the bleed page containing project information.

soft proofs: proofs of pages or advertisements, normally pdfs, that can be sent by FTP, web- or email to be viewed on-screen.

software browser: a program that displays web pages.

special positions: positions booked by an advertiser to guarantee its advertisement is placed in an exact position, usually facing or on a related editorial page.

spectrophotometer: an instrument that measures wavelength and intensity of colour.

sponsored links: a form of advertising where a client advertiser pays a host website to carry a hyperlink to its website.

spot varnishing: a printing process where varnish is used instead of ink. The varnish places a coating that reflects light over specified areas of a design.

standard pdfs: medium-resolution pdfs suitable for output from a desktop printer and for some commercial digital printing.

standfirst: a separate paragraph in large type that introduces a feature.

stapling (see saddle stitching): binding pages together by inserting wire through the fold of sheets of paper.

stickiness: the quality of a website that encourages an Internet user to remain on and revisit a site.

stock: the paper to be used for printing.

stock image: a photograph or video from an image bank or photo library.

storyboards: a series of sketches or diagrams that show the narrative development of a film or video, or the page-by-page structure of a print publication.

strapline: a one- or two-line introduction to a news story.

subhead: a secondary headline on a page.

substrate: any material onto which you can print.

subtractive primaries: colour elements that, when added together, produce black (cyan, magenta, yellow).

supplements: newspaper sections and magazines that are printed as separate publications and distributed with the main paper.

tabloid or compact: a small newspaper.

teaser or tantaliser campaign: an advertising campaign that is run to raise consumer interest prior to an event or product being launched onto the market.

teaser strip: a strip of content information across the top of the front cover of a newspaper or magazine.

template: a page make-up document or web page that contains the house design style.

text to picture ratio: the balance between copy and image on a page.

tint: a colour that has been lightened by adding white or a percentage of printed colour produced by reducing the size and increasing the spacing of dots on a halftone screen.

tone: a colour that has been darkened by adding black.

transmissive light: light that is transmitted into the eye, lens or scanning head.

triple play campaign: an advertising campaign run across print, online and TV.

true spread: a double page spread printed across one unfolded sheet of paper.

type family: all the style of a typeface.

type foundries: companies that design and produce typefaces.

type or text area: the area on a page within the margins.

typefaces: named styles of type.

typesetting: the process of setting copy in the type sizes and typefaces specified by a designer, media company or advertising agency.

typography: the design and techniques of using type.

ultra niching: targeting a title on a very small, very specialised market.

uncoated colour selector: a colour swatch book used for specifying and checking how colours will reproduce on uncoated paper.

under 40 fonts: small-set type that is hard for older people to read.

unique selling proposition (USP): an advertising concept that promotes a unique or special feature of a client's product or service.

unique user (UU): a method of establishing how many users visit a website based on a single visit by one individual, not on how many times they revisit the site.

untrue spread: a double page spread that is printed on separate sides or sections before the paper sheets are folded.

upper case: the capital letters of a typeface.

vector graphics: line-based graphics where mathematical vectors determine how straight and curved lines are shaped between specific points. Vector graphic programs include Illustrator, InDesign and QuarkXPress.

verso: a left hand page.

viral advertising: viral marketing refers to an advertising campaign that encourages everyday contact between people to spread information in order to promote a product or service.

virtual matchprints: colour-balanced pdfs or soft proofs that are sent to the media company for final approval.

visual weight: the perception of visual emphasis that leads the eye to one item before another.

W3C standard colour names: the W3C (World Wide Web Consortium) approved a list of 16 valid colour names for HTML and CSS: aqua, black, blue, fuchsia, grey, green, lime, maroon, navy, olive, purple, red, silver, teal, white and yellow.

warm colours: a descriptive term for colours that contain red, yellow or orange hues (may also be referred to as hot colours).

web cluster: a group of web pages on the same, or related, topic.

web designer: a designer who originates the visual concept for a website, develops the look of the page and creates the graphic elements.

web editor: a production journalist working on a website.

web offset litho: a form of lithographic printing press that prints on to large rolls of paper.

web production manager: the person responsible for managing a website, often concentrating on the IT.

wet ink proofs: colour proofs printed using the same paper stock as the finished publication on a special proofing press.

white space: open areas on a page used as part of the design to counterbalance other graphic elements.

x-height: the average height of the lower case characters in a typeface measured from the height of the letter x.

BIBLIOGRAPHY AND RECOMMENDED STUDY

Advertising

Advertising: its business, culture and careers
Andy Tibbs
Routledge, 2010

The Fundamentals of Creative Advertising
Ken Burtenshaw, Nik Mahon and Caroline Barfoot
Ava Publishing, 2006

Biography

Brodovitch
Andy Grundberg
Thames & Hudson, 1989

Rupert Murdoch: ringmaster of the information circus
William Shawcross
Pan Books, 1993

Colour usage and production

Color: Messages and Meanings, a Pantone® color resource
Leatrice Eiseman
Hand Books Press, 2006

Colour proof correction question and answer book
David Bann and John Gargan
Phaidon Press, 1990

Digital colour for the internet and other media
Carole Zwick and Burkhard Schmitz
Ava Publishing, 2003

The elements of color
Johannes Itten
Wiley, 1961

The Standard 1
Delphine Hirasuna
Sappi Fine Paper North America
(pdf download from www.sappi.com)

Understanding Colour: an introduction for designers
Linda Holtzschue
Wiley, 2006

Design theory

A primer of visual literacy
Donis A. Dondis
MIT Press, 1974

Colour: travels through the paint box
Victoria Finlay
Sceptre, 2002

Design in Business: strategic innovation through design
Margaret Bruce and John Bessant
Pearson Education, 2002

Prioritizing web usability
Jakob Nielsen and Hoa Loranger
New Riders, 2006

Don't make me think
Steve Krug
Que, 2000

Everything Reverberates: thoughts on design
Katherine McCoy
Chronicle Books, 1998

Milton Glaser: graphic design
Milton Glaser
Overlook TP, 1983

Pioneers of Modern Design: A complete history
Jeremy Aynsley
Mitchell Beazley, 2004

Designing web usability
Jakob Nielsen
New Riders, 1999

The design of everyday things
Donald A. Norman
MIT Press, 1998

The Gutenberg Galaxy: the Making of Typographic Man
Marshall McLuhan
University of Toronto Press, 1962

Thoughts on design
Paul Rand
Studio Vista and Van Nostrand Reinhold, 1970

Understanding Alternative Media
Olga Guedes Baily, Bart Cammaerts and Nico Carpenter
Open University Press and McGraw-Hill, 2008

Universal Principles of Design
William Lidwell, Kritina Holden and Jill Butler
Rockport Publishers, 2003

Visual Communication: from theory to practice
Jonathan Baldwin and Lucienne Roberts
Ava Publishing, 2006

Why we see what we do
Dale Purves and R. Beau Lotto
www.purveslab.net

Digital design

A Practical Guide to Digital Design: designing with your computer made easy
Pina Lewandowsky and Francis Zeischegg
Ava Publishing, 2003

Being digital
Nicholas Negroponte
Vintage, 1996

Digital layout for the Internet and other media
David Skopec
Ava Publishing, 2004

Getting it right in Print: digital pre press for graphic designers
Mark Gatter
Laurence King Publishing, 2005

Production for graphic designers
Alan Pipes
Laurence King Publishing, 2001

The complete guide to digital graphic design
Bob Gordon and Maggie Gordon
Thames & Hudson, 2004

Visual Design for the Modern Web
Penny McIntire
New Riders Press, 2007

Web production for writers and journalists
Jason Whittaker
Routledge, 2002

Interviews and articles
Content and Presentation (article)
Mark Boulton, 2007
www.markboulton.co.uk/journal/comments/content-and-presentation

How to Save Media (article)
Jason Pontin
MIT Technology Review, 2009

Pixel Fonts, Legibility and Screen Economy (article)
Craig Kroeger
Adobe, 2001

Sir Tim Berners-Lee (video interview)
BCS, the Chartered Institute for IT, 2009

Social Media Makes No Sense For My Company (article)
Jennifer Snyder
hubspot.com, 2009

The ESPN.com Redesign (interview)
Eric A. Meyer
Mike Industries/Netscape Communications, 2003

The Guts of a New Machine (article)
Rob Walker
nytimes.com, 2003

Unilever to double digital spend – Keith Weed, CMO and Sir Martin Sorrell in debate (article)
Marketing Week, 2010

Web Design is 95% Typography (article)
Oliver Reichenstein
Information Architects, 2006

Photography
Advertising Photography: a straightforward guide to a complex industry
Lou Lesko
Thomson Course Technology, 2008

Langford's basic photography: the guide for serious photographers
Michael Langford and Efthimina Bilissi
Focal Press, 2007

Light and Lens: photography in the digital age
Robert Hirsch
Focal Press, 2008

On Photography
Susan Sontag
Penguin, 1979

The Genius of Photography
Gerry Badger
Quadrille Publishing, 2007

Publication design
Contemporary Newspaper Design: shaping the news in the digital age
John D. Berry
Mark Batty, 2004

Designing for newspapers and magazines
Chris Frost
Routledge, 2003

Grids: the structure of graphic design
André Jute
Watson-Guptill Publications, 1996

How to Understand and Use Design and Layout
Alan Swann
North Light Books, 2003

Magazine Design
Chris Foges (ed.)
RotoVision, 1999

Modern magazine design
William Owen
William C. Brown, 1991

Publication design workbook
Timothy Samara
Rockport, 2005

Typography
20th Century Type
Lewis Blackwell
Laurence King Publishing, 2004

Better Type
Betty Binns
Watson-Guptill Publications, 1989

Stop Stealing Sheep & Find Out How Type Works
Erik Spiekermann and E. M. Ginger
Adobe Press, 2002

The Crystal Goblet: sixteen essays on typography
Beatrice Warde
World Publishing, 1956

Thinking with Type: a critical guide for designers, writers, editors, & students
Ellen Lupton
Princeton Architectural Press, 2004

Type and Typography
Phil Baines and Andrew Haslam
Laurence King Publishing, 2002

Typefaces for Books
James Sutton and Alan Bartram
New Amsterdam Books, 1991

Type for the internet and other media
Veruschka Gotz
Ava Publishing, 2003

Typographic Design: form and communication
Rob Carter, Ben Day and Philip B. Meggs
Wiley, 2002

RECOMMENDED READING AND VIEWING

Documentaries

9/11, 2002, film, directed by James Hanlon and Rob Klug, DVD

Annie Leibovitz: life through a lens, 2007, directed by Barbara Leibovitz, DVD

Annie Leibovitz, 1993, directed by Rebecca Frayn, DVD

Art & Copy, 2008, directed by Doug Pray (only available in US and Canadian DVD formats at time of printing)

A conversation about advertising, with David Ogilvy, 1997, interviewed by John Crichton:
www.youtube.com/watch?v=0kfsnjcUNiw

Helvetica, 2007, directed by Gary Hustwit, DVD

Inside Saatchi & Saatchi, 2005, available on BBC Active

Media Revolution: stop press? The Money Programme, 2009, BBC2 (clips available)

Milton Glaser: To inform and delight, 2008, directed by Wendy Keys, DVD, download

Objectified, 2009, film, directed by Gary Hustwit, DVD

Selling The Sixties, 2010, BBC4, download

The Genius of Design, 2010, BBC DVD

The Lady and the Revamp, 2010, Channel 4
Video interview, Rachel Johnson:
www.channel4.com/programmes/the-lady-and-the-revamp/articles/video-interview-rachel-johnson

Virtual Revolution: how 20 years of the Web have reshaped our lives, 2001, BBC2:
www.bbc.co.uk/virtualrevolution

The media in books

A Crooked Sixpence by Murray Sayle, 1960, Revel Barker

Amsterdam by Ian McEwan, 1999, Vintage

Angels and Demons by Dan Brown, 2001, Corgi

e: a novel by Matt Beaumont, 2007, HarperCollins

Murder Must Advertise by Dorothy L. Sayers, 1933, HarperTorch

My Turn to Make the Tea by Monica Dickens, 1951, Penguin

New Grub Street by George Gissing, 1891, Oxford paperbacks

Scoop by Evelyn Waugh, 1938, Back Bay Books

Seventy Two Virgins by Boris Johnson, 2004, HarperCollins

Spin by Martin Sixsmith, 2004, Macmillian

The book, the film, the T-shirt by Matt Beaumont, 2003, HarperCollins

Towards the End of the Morning by Michael Frayn, 1967, HarperCollins

The media in films

Absence of Malice, 1981, director Sydney Pollack

All the President's Men, 1976, director Alan Pakula

Broadcast News, 1988, director James Brooks

Citizen Kane, 1931, director Orson Wells

Crazy People, 1990, director Tony Bill

Fear and Loathing in Las Vegas, 1998, director Terry Gilliam

Frost/Nixon, 2008, director Ron Howard

His Girl Friday, 1940, comedy adapted from *The Front Page*, director Howard Hawks

How To Get Ahead In Advertising, 1989, director Bruce Robinson

Prêt-à-Porter, 1994, director Robert Altman

Roman Holiday, 1953, director William Wyler

Shattered Glass, 2003, director Billy Ray

State of Play, 2009, director Kevin Macdonald

State of Play, BBC TV Drama, 2003, director David Yates

Sweet Smell of Success, 1957, director Alexander Mackendrick

The China Syndrome, 1979, director James Bridges

The Devil wears Prada, 2006, director David Frankel

The Front Page, 1931, director Lewis Milestone

The Paper, 1994, director Ron Howard

The Parallax View, 1974, director Alan J Pakula

The September Issue: Anna Wintour and the making of Vogue, 2009, director R. J. Cutler

Under Fire, 1983, director Roger Spottiswoode

War Photographer, 2001, director Christian Frei

Zodiac, 2007, director David Fincher

The media in TV programmes

Absolutely Fabulous, TV comedy 1992-2004, BBC, DVD

Drop the Dead Donkey, TV comedy, 1990-1998, DVD

Lou Grant, TV drama series, 1977–1982, DVD

Mad Men, TV drama, 2007–, Matthew Weiner for AMC, shown in Britain on BBC, DVD and download

Murder Must Advertise, BBC TV programme, 1987, DVD

Nathan Barley, TV Comedy 2005, Channel 4, DVD

Ugly Betty, TV comedy, 2006, DVD and download

TED talks

Marian Bantjes: *Intricate beauty by design*
www.ted.com/talks/lang/en/marian_bantjes_intricate_beauty_by_design.html

David Carson on design + discovery
www.ted.com/talks/lang/en/david_carson_on_design.html

Milton Glaser on using design to make ideas new
www.ted.com/talks/lang/en/milton_glaser_on_using_design_to_make_ideas_new.html

David Griffin on how photography connects us
www.ted.com/talks/lang/en/david_griffin_on_how_photography_connects.html

Ryan Lobo: *Photographing the hidden story*
www.ted.com/talks/lang/en/ryan_lobo_through_the_lens_of_compassion.html

Clay Shirky on institutions vs. collaboration
www.ted.com/talks/lang/en/clay_shirky_on_institutions_versus_collaboration.html

James Surowiecki: *When social media became news*
www.ted.com/talks/james_surowiecki_on_the_turning_point_for_social_media.html

Rory Sutherland: *Sweat the small stuff, 2010*
www.ted.com/talks/lang/en/rory_sutherland_sweat_the_small_stuff.html

Jacek Utko: *designs to save newspapers*
www.ted.com/talks/lang/en/jacek_utko_asks_can_design_save_the_newspaper.html

Videos

Making the Cog, 2003, making the Honda Accord Cog TV commercial
http://www.tellyads.com/show_movie.php?filename=TA3711

Making the Audi-A8 TV commercial, 2010:
www.germancarblog.com/2010/03/audi-a8-making-of-tv-commercial

INDEX